Benjamin D. Gordon
Land and Temple

Studia Judaica

Forschungen zur Wissenschaft des Judentums

Begründet von
Ernst Ludwig Ehrlich

Herausgegeben von
Günter Stemberger, Charlotte Fonrobert,
Elisabeth Hollender, Alexander Samely
und Irene Zwiep

Band 87

Benjamin D. Gordon
Land and Temple

Field Sacralization and the Agrarian Priesthood
of Second Temple Judaism

DE GRUYTER

ISBN 978-3-11-077670-6
e-ISBN (PDF) 978-3-11-042102-6
e-ISBN (EPUB) 978-3-11-042116-3
ISSN 0585-5306

Library of Congress Control Number: 2019957136

Bibliografic information published by the Deutsche Nationalbibliothek
The Deutsche Nationalbibliothek lists this publication in the Deutsche Nationalbibliografie;
detailed bibliografic data are available on the Internet at http://dnb.dnb.de.

© 2021 Walter de Gruyter GmbH, Berlin/Boston
This volume is text- and page-identical with the hardback published in 2020.
Printing and binding: CPI books GmbH, Leck

www.degruyter.com

Acknowledgments

This book developed out of a doctoral dissertation I completed in 2013 in the Graduate Program in Religion at Duke University. Initially the project was to be about the settlement patterns of Judean priests—where and how they lived outside of Jerusalem, and how their presence impacted village life. I began by examining the question of the priests' role in land management and never got much further than that, deciding in the end to write the dissertation on field consecrations in ancient Judaism. My heartfelt thanks go to my doctoral advisor, Eric Meyers, for his mentorship, guidance, and friendship through the years. I was also privileged to have Stephen Chapman, Laura Lieber, Evyatar Marienberg, and Joshua Sosin on my doctoral committee. The Perilman endowment of the Jewish Studies Program at Duke provided generous funding when I was a doctoral student.

Joshua Sosin has continued to work with me in developing a new reading of Lev 27, a source that is very important to this project. Years ago, he suggested that the chapter could be about securities on debt. Initially I disagreed, holding fast to the idea, which is well established already in rabbinic exegesis, that it is about donations to God. Eventually I came to agree with Josh. My thanks go to him for the idea and for his willingness to continue to work with me in developing it.

For the past four years my institutional home has been the Department of Religious Studies at the University of Pittsburgh, where I have benefitted from conversations with colleagues and students about this book. I am particularly grateful to Adam Shear and the late Linda Penkower for their support as department chairs, and to the Dean's office in the Dietrich School of Arts & Sciences at Pitt for granting me a semester off from teaching to work on the book. Since 2017, the Rosenberg-Perlow endowment at Pitt has allowed me to spend more time on research. Thanks also go to my research assistants Natasha Mayer and Sydney O'Brien of the First Experiences in Research program for all their hard work.

I presented some of the material in this book at conferences over the years and have benefitted from the feedback I received at them. Particularly fruitful were discussions with Andrew Monson, Carolin Arlt, Marie-Pierre Chaufray, Ann Goddeeris, and Lidia Matassa at the Irish Society for the Study of the Ancient Near East's third annual conference on "Money and Cult: The Role of the Temple in the Ancient Economy." Also helpful were responses from participants in a conference at the Israel Institute for Advanced Studies of the Hebrew University of Jerusalem on "Expressions of Cult in the Southern Levant in the Greco-Roman Period." Some of the content of Chapters 5 and 6 below appears in my contribution to the conference volume: "Debt Fraud, Herem Entrapment, and Other Crimes Involving Cultic Property in Late Hellenistic and Early Roman Judea," pages 255–67 in *Expressions of Cult in the Southern Levant in the Greco-Roman Period. Manifestations in Text and Material Culture*, edited by Zeev Weiss and Oren Tal (Turnhout: Brepols, 2017).

I published my interpretation of Romans 11:16, which appears in Chapter 7 below, in the article "On the Sanctity of Mixtures and Branches: Two Halakhic Sayings in Romans 11:16," *Journal of Biblical Literature* 135, no. 2 (2016): 355–68. I would like to thank Rebecca Denova, Douglas Campbell, T.J. Lang, Joel Marcus, and the participants in the Duke-UNC New Testament and Judaic Studies Colloquium for their assistance as I worked on that material, the results of which are in Chapter 7.

I am grateful to my readers in the Studia Judaica series at de Gruyter, particularly Alexander Samely and Günter Stemberger, for the careful attention they gave the manuscript. Alice Meroz and Sophie Wagenhofer in the editorial department were patient and helpful along the way, Jana Fritsche proofread the manuscript and saw it through to publication, and Florian Ruppenstein managed the production process. Nelly Beyman of the Israel Antiquities Authority helped me secure permissions to use several images.

Finally, I would like to give thanks to my family for all their support over the years, as well as to my partner James Arjmand. He tolerates my occasional distractedness with good cheer, provides reassurance, and laughs with me after a hard day's work.

Benjamin D. Gordon
Pittsburgh, Pennsylvania

Contents

Abbreviations —— IX

Figures —— XI

Chapter 1: Introduction —— 1
1.1   Sacred Land in the Ancient World —— 11
1.2   History of Research and Summary of Contents —— 19

Chapter 2: Field Consecrations in Leviticus 27 —— 29
2.1   Introduction —— 29
2.2   Consecration of a Patrimonial Field —— 36
2.2.1   The 50-Shekel Valuation Benchmark —— 38
2.2.2   Field Redemption —— 44
2.2.3   The Consecrated Field as Hypothecary Pledge —— 57
2.2.4   Seizure of a Patrimonial Field —— 69
2.3   Consecration of a Non-Patrimonial Field —— 71
2.4   Voluntary Herem Dedication of a Patrimonial Field —— 73
2.5   Anathematization of Land by Decree —— 78
2.6   Summary —— 81

Chapter 3: The Sacred Reserve of Yahweh in Ezekiel's Temple Vision —— 84
3.1   Introduction —— 84
3.2   The Sacred Reserve and Its Local Prototypes —— 87
3.2.1   Levitical Settlements Reimagined —— 91
3.2.2   A Non-Urban Sacred Reserve —— 95
3.3   Priests, Farming, and Temple Dependency —— 98
3.4   The Temple Collective and Sacred Property —— 105
3.5   The "Plot of the House of Yeho" on a Land Survey from Idumea —— 112
3.6   Summary —— 115

Chapter 4: Hellenistic Rulers, Jewish Temples, and Sacred Land —— 117
4.1   Introduction —— 117
4.2   The Land Endowment for the Oniad Temple at Leontopolis —— 121
4.3   A Sacred Garden next to a Synagogue at Arsinoe —— 130
4.4   The Hasmoneans and Sacred Land in Judea —— 132
4.5   The Ptolemais Hinterland and the Jerusalem Temple —— 136
4.6   Summary —— 145

Chapter 5: Field Consecrations in the Late Second Temple Period —— 147
5.1 Introduction —— 147
5.2 Fields in the Freewill-Offering Laws of the Damascus Document —— 150
5.2.1 Consecration of Forcibly Seized Assets —— 153
5.2.2 Consecration of Assets Claimable by Household Dependents —— 157
5.2.3 Forced Redemption of Consecrated Assets —— 158
5.3 The Proceeds from Agricultural Consecrations —— 160
5.4 Land Donations among the Yahad and the Jesus Movement —— 169
5.5 Agricultural Consecrations and the Herodian Temple Economy —— 170
5.6 Summary —— 179

Chapter 6: Herem Property and Landholding by Priests in the Late Second Temple Period —— 181
6.1 Introduction —— 181
6.2 The Herem Field in a Halakhic Text from Qumran —— 184
6.2.1 Herem and the Priests' Entitlements —— 186
6.2.2 Sanctity Protections for Herem Property —— 190
6.3 Landholding by Priests —— 195
6.4 Summary —— 203

Chapter 7: An Allusion to a Sacred Tree in Paul's Letter to the Romans —— 205
7.1 Introduction —— 205
7.2 Sacred Admixtures —— 207
7.3 Protecting Derivatives of Agricultural Consecrations —— 210
7.4 Sacred Olive Trees and the Allegory of Romans 11 —— 219
7.5 Summary —— 224

Summary and Conclusions —— 225

Bibliography —— 232

Index of Ancient Sources —— 269

Index of Subjects —— 282

Abbreviations

Ant.	Josephus, *Jewish Antiquities*
b.	"son of" (*ben*)
b.	Babylonian Talmud
BHS	Biblia Hebraica Stuttgartensia
C. Ap.	Josephus, *Against Apion*
CD	Damascus Document (Cairo Geniza)
CPJ	*Corpus Papyrorum Judaicarum*
DSD	*Dead Sea Discoveries*
FAT	Forschungen zum Alten Testament
HTR	*The Harvard Theological Review*
HUCA	*Hebrew Union College Annual*
IEJ	*Israel Exploration Journal*
INJ	*Israel Numismatic Journal*
JBL	*Journal of Biblical Literature*
JESHO	*Journal of the Economic and Social History of the Orient*
JJS	*Journal of Jewish Studies*
JNES	*Journal of Near Eastern Studies*
JPS	Jewish Publication Society
JSJ	*Journal for the Study of Judaism*
JSNT	*Journal for the Study of the New Testament*
JSOT	*Journal for the Study of the Old Testament*
JSOT Supp.	Journal for the Study of the Old Testament Supplement Series
LAB	Pseudo-Philo, *Liber Antiquitatem Biblicarum*
LXX	Septuagint
m.	Mishnah
MT	Masoretic text of the Hebrew Bible
NRSV	New Revised Standard Version
PAM	Palestine Archaeological Museum
R.	Rabbi
Rahlfs	Alfred Rahlfs (ed.), *Septuaginta*
RB	*Revue Biblique*
t.	Tosefta
VT	*Vetus Testamentum*
War	Josephus, *Jewish War*
y.	Palestinian/Jerusalem Talmud

Figures

Figure 1. Jerusalem and surroundings in the first century CE. Illustration by Balage Balogh.
Figure 2. Franciscan Monks making hay in Ottoman Palestine, ca. 1903. Library of Congress Prints and Photographs Division. Stereograph by C.H. Graves.
Figure 3. Map of the Persian provinces of Judea and Samaria.
Figure 4. Judahite stone scale weights in various denominations. Courtesy of the Israel Antiquities Authority. Photo: Miki Koren.
Figure 5. The Paleo-Hebrew Leviticus Scroll from Qumran. 11QpaleoLev, Col. 6, Lev 27:11–19. Courtesy of The Leon Levy Dead Sea Scrolls Digital Library; Israel Antiquities Authority.
Figure 6. Farmers plowing their field in Ottoman Palestine, ca. 1900. Library of Congress Prints and Photographs Division. Photographic print from the Frank and Frances Carpenter Collection.
Figure 7. The sacred reserve (in grey) in Ezekiel's Temple Vision. It is situated within an extra-tribal territory with land allotted for the city and prince as well.
Figure 8. Laborers in the fields of Sanur in Ottoman Palestine, c. 1908. Library of Congress Prints and Photographs Division. Stereograph by Stereo-Travel Co.
Figure 9. Map of Ptolemaic Egypt showing the location of Leontopolis in the Nile Delta.
Figure 10. A halakhic section of the Damascus Document on freewill offerings and field consecrations. 4Q271, Col. 4ii (= CD 16). Courtesy of The Leon Levy Dead Sea Scrolls Digital Library; Israel Antiquities Authority. Photo: Shai Halevi.
Figure 11. A laborer on a threshing board drawn by a horse at Saffourieh (Sepphoris) near Nazareth, 1940. Library of Congress Prints and Photographs Division. G. Eric and Edith Matson Photograph Collection.
Figure 12. Map of King Herod's Judea at its peak in the late first century BCE.
Figure 13. A halakhic text from Qumran commenting on a herem field. 4Q251, Frag. 14. Courtesy of The Leon Levy Dead Sea Scrolls Digital Library; Israel Antiquities Authority. Photo: Shai Halevi.
Figure 14. Jerusalem with its enlarged temple complex in the first century CE. Illustration by Balage Balogh.
Figure 15. The desert oasis of Jericho in the Jordan River valley, ca. 1867–1885. Many Judean priests lived at Jericho in the Second Temple period. Museum für Kunst und Gewerbe Hamburg. Photograph by Félix Bonfils.
Figure 16. An olive tree is trimmed in Ottoman Palestine. G. Eric and Edith Matson Photograph Collection. Library of Congress Prints and Photographs Division.
Figure 17. The grafting process for an olive branch using the tongue (a–c) and cleft (d–f) techniques. *Journal of the Department of Agriculture, Victoria* 1912, 128, Fig. 8.

Chapter 1
Introduction

> The temple has for its revenues not only portions of land, but also other possessions of much greater extent and importance, which will never be destroyed or diminished.
> —Philo of Alexandria, *Spec. Laws* 1.76

> One should not engage in business dealings with consecrated property or the property of the poor.
> —Rabbi Akiva, m. *Šeqalim* 4:3

This book explores how the Judean priesthood was involved in land ownership and agricultural cultivation in the Second Temple period (516 BCE–70 CE). It is informed by studies of other temple organizations from the ancient Mediterranean and the Near East, and by references throughout early Jewish literature to consecrated plots of land. The primary source material suggests that in addition to consecrations meant as earmarked gifts for priests or the temple, Judeans were consecrating land to secure loans issued from the holy treasuries, for example, or as a means of inhibiting a rightful claimant from gaining access to property. This aspect of early Judaism's institutional reach far beyond the confines of its houses of worship underscores its similarity to the religious organizations of the ancient world. It also reveals yet another aspect of place-making in the ancient Judean experience—how generic, undifferentiated outdoor space could be sacralized, and how that sacralization can inform our understanding of Second Temple Judaism's primary religious organizations of priesthood and temple.

The Judean priesthood is said in Ezra-Nehemiah to have total 4,289 in number (Ezra 2:36–42; Neh 7:39–45, 11:10–22, 12:1–26), giving some indication of its size around the fifth century BCE. The Hasmonean destruction of the Yahwistic shrine at Mt. Gerizim in the final decades of the second century BCE left the Jerusalem temple as the sole locus for the worship of the deity in greater Judea and it anticipated the precipitous growth of the institution in the first centuries BCE and CE. Meanwhile, another Yahwistic temple was founded in the second century BCE at Leontopolis in Egypt by a breakaway group of Judean priests of the Oniad family. The massive physical expansion of the Jerusalem sacred precinct by King Herod beginning in 20 BCE, a project which included the total rebuilding of the temple itself, resulted in a precinct with a circumference of nearly 1 mile, dwarfing that of all others in the ancient world. According to Josephus, a staggering number of 2,700,000 male pilgrims came to Jerusalem in the Passover of 66 CE (*War* 6.425), surely an exaggeration but one that gives the sense of the magnitude of this eastern pilgrimage city nevertheless. The economy of Jerusalem benefitted tremendously from the influx of pilgrims to the city on Passover, Shavuot, and Sukkot.[1]

Josephus has the priesthood numbering 20,000 men in his day (*C. Ap.* 2.108). This was an esteemed class whose members enjoyed prominent roles in the civil and judicial spheres of life, serving not only as the officers of the cult but also as judges, scribes, taxmen, and bureaucrats.[2] The high priest of Jerusalem had become the de facto ruler of Judea in the late fourth century BCE, and would assume that role again in the reign of the Hasmonean priest-kings from the mid-second century to the rise of Herod in 37 BCE.[3] Archaeological inquiry at late Second Temple period sites has demonstrated the extent to which priestly purity requirements were widely practiced throughout Judean society.[4] Motifs emerging on Late Antique synagogue decoration and in liturgical poems have attested

---

[1] For further background on the Second Temple priesthood and temple, with references, see §§1.2, 2.1, 4.1, 4.4, 5.5, and 6.3 below. On the size and grandeur of the temple itself after Herod's reconstruction of it, see Netzer, *The Architecture of Herod, The Great Builder* (Tübingen: Mohr Siebeck, 2006), 136–78, 273–75; Meyers and Chancey, *Alexander to Constantine: Archaeology of the Land of the Bible*, vol. 3 (New Haven: Yale University Press, 2012), 53–61; and Rocca, *Herod's Judaea: A Mediterranean State in the Classical World* (Tübingen: Mohr Siebeck, 2008), 377. On the magnitude of its pilgrimage festivals, particularly in the Herodian period, see Goodman, "The Pilgrimage Economy of Jerusalem in the Second Temple Period," in *Jerusalem: Its Sanctity and Centrality to Judaism, Christianity, and Islam* (ed. Levine; New York: Continuum, 1999), 69–76. For a general study of the pilgrimage festivals in Jerusalem, see Safrai, *Pilgrimage to Jerusalem in the Second Temple Period* (Tel Aviv: Am Ha-Sefer, 1965) [Hebrew]. Melody Knowles has examined the centrality of Jerusalem in the rhetoric and ideology of Judea in the period of the restoration of the temple under Persian auspices; *Centrality Practiced: Jerusalem in the Religious Practice of Yehud and the Diaspora in the Persian Period* (Leiden; Boston: Brill, 2006); see also idem, "Pilgrimage to Jerusalem in the Persian Period," in *Approaching Yehud: New Approaches to the Study of the Persian Period* (ed. Berquist; Atlanta: Society of Biblical Literature, 2007), 7–24.

[2] On the priesthood of the early Second Temple period, see Schaper, *Priester und Leviten im achämenidischen Juda: Studien zur Kult- und Sozialgeschichte Israels in persischer Zeit* (Tübingen: Mohr Siebeck, 2000), 130–53; on the priesthood of the later centuries of the period, see Himmelfarb, *A Kingdom of Priests: Ancestry and Merit in Ancient Judaism* (Philadelphia: University of Pennsylvania Press, 2006), passim, esp. 1–10.

[3] On the question of the political power of the high priest in the late fourth century BCE, see VanderKam, *From Joshua to Caiaphas: High Priests after the Exile* (Minneapolis: Fortress Press, 2004), 125, 136–37, 167, 180–81, 190–91, 222–23; cf. Rooke, *Zadok's Heirs: The Role and Development of the High Priesthood in Ancient Israel* (Oxford; New York: Oxford University Press, 2000), 243–65, esp. 250–52.

[4] Meyers and Chancey, *Alexander to Constantine*, 135–38; Magness, *Stone and Dung, Oil and Spit: Jewish Daily Life in the Time of Jesus* (Grand Rapids, MI: William B. Eerdmans, 2011), 16–31.

to the position of honor enjoyed by priests in Jewish communities centuries after the destruction of the temple in 70 CE.[5]

The Judean priesthood was a hereditary, kinship-based organization, with altar service rotating among different clans of priests.[6] These clans, which according to the book of Chronicles were 24 in number (1 Chr 24:1–18), may have not always cooperated so peacefully with one another. Josephus remarks that certain chief priests sent slaves to the threshing floors to take tithes due to other priests, with the result being that some priests starved to death (*Ant.* 20.179–81). In another remark Josephus condemns the high priest Ananias for the misappropriation of tithes (*Ant.* 20.205–6), while Philo explains the impoverishment of certain priests as a result of the neglect of the populace to give the proper offerings (*Spec. Laws* 1.154). This suggests a loose or ineffectual system of central administration in Jerusalem for the collection of holy dues. In its fragmentation into clans, the priesthood may have resembled the multidivisional-type or M-form firm that Robert Ekelund et al. see as characteristic of the medieval church.[7] The church had a central office that controlled financial allocation and engaged in strategy and long-term planning; its divisions consisted of bishoprics and monasteries, themselves multitiered organizations, which

---

5 See §6.3.
6 The lists of returnees in Ezra and Nehemiah mention five clans of priests totaling 4,289 in number; and two clans of Levites, totaling a mere 341 individuals in Ezra and 360 in Nehemiah (Ezra 2:36–42; Neh 7:39–45, 11:10–22, 12:1–26); see also 1 Chr 23:1–26:32. In the early Second Temple period the clan as a social unit would continue to be a principle organizing feature of society and the economy, as Joel Weinberg has discussed in "Das *bēit ʾāḇōt* im 6.–4. Jh. v. u. Z," *VT* 23, no. 4 (1973): 400–14. For a general discussion of the clan in ancient Israel and its Near Eastern context, see Schloen, *The House of the Father as Fact and Symbol: Patrimonialism in Ugarit and the Ancient Near East* (Winona Lake, IN: Eisenbrauns, 2001); see also Hopkins, *The Highlands of Canaan: Agricultural Life in the Early Iron Age* (Sheffield: Almond, 1985), 251–61; and Adams, *Social and Economic Life in Second Temple Judea* (Louisville: Westminster John Knox Press, 2014), 10–12. For the relevance of the family unit to the priestly writings of Torah and their understanding of how territory is occupied, see Vanderhooft, "The Israelite *mišpāḥâ*, the Priestly Writings, and Changing Valences in Israel's Kinship Terminology," in *Exploring the Longue Durée: Essays in Honor of Lawrence E. Stager* (ed. Schloen; Winona Lake, IN: Eisenbrauns, 2009), 485–96. The close familial alliance of priesthoods in ancient Israel is reflected in the careful attention to lineage in regulating service at Jerusalem and in other anecdotal sources, such as the affirmation of familial affiliation of the priests at Nob in 1 Sam 22:11, who are all to be of the house of Ahimelech. On the importance of lineage in the Israelite priesthood, see Haran, *Temples and Temple-Service in Ancient Israel: An Inquiry into the Character of Cult Phenomena and the Historical Setting of the Priestly School* (Oxford: Clarendon Press, 1977), 58–111.
7 *Sacred Trust: The Medieval Church as an Economic Firm* (Oxford; New York: Oxford University Press, 1996), 8, 20–21.

Figure 1. Jerusalem and surroundings in the first century CE. Illustration by Balage Balogh.

controlled individual dioceses, while abbots headed monasteries. The general office received revenues from these quasi-firms and redirected them among its various divisions. In the case of the Judean priesthood of the Second Temple period, systemic flaws in the redistributive system may have plagued the organization.

It is assumed here that members of religious organizations like the Judean priesthood can be motivated by much more than spiritual interests, such as salvation, but rather had worldly interests like their counterparts outside the organization.[8] Substantivist or primitivist economic models can be particularly helpful here, in their emphasis on the failings of rational-actor approaches in the study of ancient (or modern) economies.[9] Cooperation, collective guilt, honor, and social solidarity were key ethical norms in ancient societies like Judea, as well as institutions that guided economic behavior. Also relevant are the insights of New Institutional Economics (NIE), with its focus on the patterns of social interaction

---

[8] Alles, "Religion and Economy," in *Religion, Theory, Critique: Classic and Contemporary Approaches and Methodologies* (ed. King; New York: Columbia University Press, 2017), 601–12.
[9] For a summary of theoretical approaches to the study of the ancient economy, see Manning, *The Open Sea*, 3–38.

—the "institutions"—that govern the relationships of individuals.[10] One study related to Jewish history and rooted in NIE is Avner Greif's book on the Maghribi traders, an informal organization of Jewish traders active in the Muslim Mediterranean and known from eleventh-century documents in the Cairo Geniza.[11] Greif demonstrated the extent to which these traders benefitted from a coalition grounded in a common identity, shared a purpose as an organization, and cultivated beliefs about the organization's norms. Daniel Master has applied the insights of NIE to Iron Age Levantine economies.[12] Peter Altmann has employed NIE in a comparison of market trade in Babylon with Judea in the Persian period.[13]

It is also a main contention of this book that the Judean priesthood and temple offer an example of how religious organizations could be entrenched in ancient agricultural societies. Another example from the region, which has been more thoroughly discussed, are the ecclesiastical estates of late antiquity.[14] Jacob Ashkenazi and Mordecai Aviam have discussed how monastic farms in western Galilee contributed to the economic growth of nearby villages; monks leased plots of land in rural areas from wealthy landowners, strengthening their social ties with the local aristocracy.[15] One late ancient ecclesiastical estate,

---

[10] North, Wallis, and Weingast, *Violence and Social Orders: A Conceptual Framework for Interpreting Recorded Human History* (Cambridge: Cambridge University Press, 2009), 15.

[11] *Institutions and the Path to the Modern Economy: Lessons from Medieval Trade* (Cambridge: Cambridge University Press, 2006), esp. 58–60.

[12] "Economy and Exchange in the Iron Age Kingdoms of the Southern Levant," *Bulletin of the American Schools of Oriental Research*, no. 372 (2014), 81–97.

[13] "Ancient Comparisons, Modern Models, and Ezra-Nehemiah: Triangulating the Sources for Insights on the Economy of Persian Period Yehud," in *The Economy of Ancient Judah in Its Historical Context* (ed. Miller et al.; Winona Lake, IN: Eisenbrauns, 2015), 103–20.

[14] On ecclesiastical estates more generally, see Decker, *Tilling the Hateful Earth: Agricultural Production and Trade in the Late Antique East* (Oxford; New York: Oxford University Press, 2009), 48–51; Brown, *Through the Eye of a Needle: Wealth, the Fall of Rome, and the Making of Christianity in the West, 350–550 AD* (Princeton, NJ: Princeton University Press, 2012), 237–40, 469–75; Jones, *The Later Roman Empire, 284–602: A Social Economic and Administrative Survey* (Norman: University of Oklahoma Press, 1964), 732–33; and Lemerle, *The Agrarian History of Byzantium: From the Origins to the Twelfth Century* (Galway: Officina Typographica, 1979), 108–14. Church land in the region of Tyre produced annual revenue of about 1,500 *solidi* and in Antioch of 572 solidi. Constantine presented the entire island of Cordionon near Tarsus, along with its revenue of 800 solidi, to the see of Peter. For the landed gifts of Constantine to the see of Peter, see Davis, *The Book of Pontiffs (Liber Pontificalis). The Ancient Biographies of the First Ninety Roman Bishops to AD 715* (Liverpool: Liverpool University Press, 1989), 19–21.

[15] "Monasteries and Villages: Rural Economy and Religious Interdependency in Late Antique Palestine," *Vigiliae Christianae* 71, no. 2 (2017), 117–33.

which was excavated at Shelomi in western Galilee, produced an array of Mediterranean crops including grain, olives, grapes, and apples.[16] Judean desert monasteries were endowed with gardens and orchards used to enhance the monks' diets but also for sale in local markets.[17] It is argued here that the role of the early Christian church in market exchange was anticipated by the involvement of Judean priests in the agricultural hinterland.

The book's focus on the relationship between land and temple in ancient Judaism can contribute to a growing body of scholarship attempting to recharacterize the Judean priesthood.[18] The organization was once seen as a detached, status-obsessed group of urban plutocrats that were given to corruption. Jonathan Klawans has maintained that generations of scholars who have studied the Jerusalem temple—its administration included—have been negatively predisposed to it either because of Christian supersessionism, whereby the death of Jesus is viewed as nullifying the inherently flawed institution of the temple, or because of a Jewish form of supersessionism holding that the synagogue and rabbinical academy were improvements upon the temple.[19] James Watts has argued that the academic field has long been plagued by distaste for theocracy and as a result has fallen short in its treatment of the priesthood and its literature.[20]

---

[16] Dauphin, "A Byzantine Ecclesiastical Farm at Shelomi," in *Ancient Churches Revealed* (ed. Tsafrir; Jerusalem: Israel Exploration Society, 1993), 43–48; Decker, *Tilling the Hateful Earth*, 49, n. 68.

[17] Hirschfeld, *The Judean Desert Monasteries in the Byzantine Period* (New Haven: Yale University Press, 1992), 200–4. The industrial-size olive press excavated at Khirbet ed-Deir, for example, suggests a use beyond consumption by the forty or fifty monks who lived at the site and could reflect production for market sale; see Decker, *Tilling the Hateful Earth*, 50.

[18] The newly formed program unit at the Society of Biblical Literature, "Priests and Levites in History and Tradition," is a locus of scholarship shedding light on the priesthood; see the compilation of essays emerging from it, Leuchter and Hutton, eds., *Levites and Priests in Biblical History and Tradition* (Atlanta: Society of Biblical Literature, 2011) and especially pp. 2–5 there for a summary of the history of research and references.

[19] *Purity, Sacrifice, and the Temple: Symbolism and Supersessionism in the Study of Ancient Judaism* (Oxford; New York: Oxford University Press, 2006), 247.

[20] The result, according to Watts, is a tendency among scholars to celebrate the prophets and kings of Israel's history and overlook its priests; Watts, "The Torah as the Rhetoric of Priesthood," in *The Pentateuch as Torah: New Models for Understanding Its Promulgation and Acceptance* (ed. Knoppers and Levinson; Winona Lake, IN: Eisenbrauns, 2007), 319, 325–28, nn. 13, 18, 19; idem, *Ritual and Rhetoric in Leviticus: From Sacrifice to Scripture* (Cambridge; New York: Cambridge University Press, 2007), 154–61; see also a similar argument, with blame placed on Protestant thought, in Nelson, *Raising Up a Faithful Priest: Community and Priesthood in Biblical Theology* (Louisville: Westminster/John Knox Press, 1993), 101–5. As Watts points out, attempts to rehabilitate the reputation of the priestly writings have included dating them to the monarchic period, "so that they are represented as part of the mainstream of Israel's history rather than

Both projects were preceded by E.P. Sanders, who put forward a forceful critique of scholars that have highlighted too eagerly the moral failings of the Jerusalem temple and its priesthood, and have presented its sources of revenue as an added burden on an overly taxed population in the time of Jesus.[21] There has also been an attempt in scholarship to reassess the priesthood in a post-70 CE environment, characterizing them as an esteemed class of individuals who continued to enjoy special honors in Jewish communities of the Galilee and elsewhere.[22] An analysis of source material envisioning, regulating, or commenting upon the role of land in the Second Temple cult of worship can further our understanding of the ideological disposition of ancient Judeans to that cult.

Moreover, the chapters below explore ways in which sacred place-making was a feature of the lives of ancient Judean farmers—an early episode in what would become a long history of Jewish approaches to land and place. Theoretical discourse has underscored the normative social structures inherent in the construction of place, as well as the way places link an individual to broader social institutions. In the case of sacred buildings, this process can be facilitated through encoded traits such as design features or display elements, which can

---

appearing as a supplement to it"; or transforming their message "into something more palatable, such as advice for religious leaders or spiritual allegories or theological analogies"; *Ritual and Rhetoric*, 160. In fact, the legitimization of the religious and political claims of the Aaronide priesthood in Judea and Samaria is, to Watts, the original function of the Torah.

21 E.P. Sanders writes that the "overwhelming impression from ancient literature is that most first-century Jews, who believed in the Bible, respected the temple and the priesthood and willingly made the required gifts and offerings"; *Judaism: Practice and Belief, 63 BCE–66 CE* (London: SCM Press, 1992), 52. The conviction of the Jews to defend their temple against desecration and their willingness to die for Jerusalem in the war with Rome is further evidence to Sanders of their overall favorable disposition toward the temple establishment (ibid., 153–54). Nor can we assume that the tax burden of supporting the temple cult and its officials was too great to be manageable or even possible. E.P. Sanders has devoted considerable effort in overturning earlier assumptions of an overly burdensome taxation liability for average Judeans in the late Second Temple period (ibid., 90, 157–67). His analysis of what a typical poor farmer would have to pay the local authorities suggests to him a tax burden in the Early Roman period of around 30% of total annual income, including all holy dues, local taxes, and Roman taxes (ibid., 167–69).

22 Grey, "Jewish Priests and the Social History of Post-70 Palestine" (Ph.D. Dissertation, University of North Carolina at Chapel Hill); see also Irshai, "The Priesthood in Jewish Society of Late Antiquity," in *Continuity and Renewal: Jews and Judaism in Byzantine-Christian Palestine* (ed. Levine; Jerusalem: Dinur Center, Yad Ben-Zvi, and Jewish Theological Seminary of America, 2004) [Hebrew], 67–106; and Fine, "Between Liturgy and Social History: Priestly Power in Late Antique Palestinian Synagogues?," *Journal of Jewish Studies* 56, no. 1 (2005), 1–9. Cf. Weiss, "Were Priests Communal Leaders in Late Antique Palestine? The Archaeological Evidence," in *Was 70 CE a Watershed in Jewish History? On Jews and Judaism before and after the Destruction of the Second Temple* (ed. Schwartz and Weiss; Leiden: Brill, 2012), 91–111.

transform what otherwise would be undifferentiated space into a meaningful communal place. This process can also be influenced by objects, people, activities, and social groupings.[23] Place-making in outdoor space is a similar process but with different social functions. Political borders and property lines are examples of how social institutions can profoundly impact our experience of outdoor space. Other outdoor spaces closely tied to institutions include national parks, historical battlefields, college campuses, and graveyards. Sacralization is a form of place-making too—of protecting a place as holy in some way, whether for its symbolic value, its importance to a society's sense of itself, or its value to religious organizations.[24]

The sacralization of outdoor space in the ancient Judean context is usually discussed in the context of ethnic territory. The normative conceptualization of Judean territory as sacred—the "holy land" of the God of Israel—is in keeping with an ancient pattern of marking state territory as under the purview of a patron deity.[25] The Hebrew phrase *'ereṣ Yhwh* ("the land of Yahweh"), for example, appears in Hosea 9:3 as a reference to the entire territory of Israel, and *'ereṣ 'ăḥuzzat Yhwh* ("the land of Yahweh's own holding") in Josh 22:19 as a name for the Israelite tribal lands of Cisjordan.[26] One of the ancient monikers of the

---

[23] Mircea Eliade saw the home of a religious person as a cosmic center, the boundaries of which mark the transition from ordered existence to chaos; *The Sacred and the Profane: The Nature of Religion* (trans. Trask; New York: Harcourt, Brace and World, 1959), 20–22, 43. Barbara Mann has explored the ramifications of the "spatial turn" in the study of Judaism in modernity; see *Space and Place in Jewish Studies* (New Brunswick; London: Rutgers University Press, 2012), particularly the discussion of spatiality in the humanities and social sciences on pp. 11–25. Steven Fine has studied the elements of the sacred built environments of Judaism in late antiquity; see *Art and Judaism in the Greco-Roman World: Toward a New Jewish Archaeology* (Cambridge; New York: Cambridge University Press, 2005), 165–209.
[24] The special impact of land and landscape on the human experience, including its connection to religion, has been a subject of discourse among phenomenologists. See Tilley, *A Phenomenology of Landscape* (Oxford; Providence, RI: Berg Publishers, 1994); and Bintliff, "The Implications of a Phenomenology of Landscape," in *Die Landschaft und die Religion: Stuttgarter Kolloquium zur Historischen Geographie des Altertums 9, 2005* (ed. Olshausen and Sauer; Stuttgart: Franz Steiner, 2009), 27–45. On topophilia, or the love of place, and its connection to the agricultural revolution, see the various contributions to the volume Käppel and Pothou, eds., *Human Development in Sacred Landscapes: Between Ritual Tradition, Creativity and Emotionality* (Göttingen: Vandenhoeck & Ruprecht, 2015).
[25] Smith, *Where the Gods Are: Spatial Dimensions of Anthropomorphism in the Biblical World* (New Haven; London: Yale University Press, 2016), 71–108; Parker, *Greek Gods Abroad: Names, Natures, and Transformations* (Oakland, CA: University of California Press, 2017), 77–112.
[26] The Hebrew phrase *naḥălat Yhwh* ("the possession of Yahweh") may have referred to these areas, such as the city of Abel Beth Maacah in 2 Sam 20:19; for more on the phrase, see Weinfeld, *Social Justice in Ancient Israel and in the Ancient Near East* (Minneapolis; Jerusalem: Fortress

God of Israel, El Shaddai, may relate to his association with the uncultivated terrain of pre-Israelite pastoral groups.²⁷ The attribution of land and its productive capabilities to a deity could help unify disparate populations. It could promote cooperative relations among neighboring tribes and shape the individual's relationship to community.²⁸ "Each region is defined by the totem of the clan to which it is assigned," wrote Émile Durkheim.²⁹ The same principle can be applied to deities—outgrowths of totemic thinking, according to Durkheim.

Barbara Mann has discussed the impact of the exilic and the diasporic condition on the conceptualization of sacred space in Judaism.³⁰ She has noted that Judaism evolved from viewing sacred space as immanent to something more symbolic, spiritual, and farther from the "source." The tendency is evident already in the land theology of Philo and Josephus, which tended toward Hellenistic universalism, though in different ways; and also in the writings of the early rabbis, who recognized that in a post-temple era the home of the Jews and their deity must be transportable.³¹ The Christian tendency, on the other hand, has been to substitute the holiness of the biblical land with the holiness of Jesus,

---

Press; Magnes, 1995), 239–40. On 'ereṣ Yhwh, see Kwakkel, "The Land in the Book of Hosea," in *The Land of Israel in Bible, History, and Theology. Studies in Honour of Ed Noort* (ed. Van Ruiten and de Vos; Leiden; Boston: Brill, 2009), 178–79. For places where the word 'ereṣ is used with reference to Yahweh, see 1 Kgs 8:36, Isa 14:25, Jer 2:7, Ezek 36:5, 38:16, Joel 2:18, Ps 85:2.

27 Römer, *The Invention of God* (trans. Guess; Cambridge, MA: Harvard University Press, 2015), 881.

28 On the productive and allocative attributes of ancient deities, see Boer, *The Sacred Economy of Ancient Israel* (Louisville; Westminster John Knox Press, 2015), 141–45.

29 *The Elementary Forms of Religious Life* (trans. Cosman; Oxford: Oxford University Press, 1912), 13.

30 *Space and Place*, 12–14.

31 Halpern-Amaru, "Land Theology in Philo and Josephus," in *The Land of Israel: Jewish Perspectives* (ed. Hoffman; Notre Dame, IN: University of Notre Dame Press, 1986), 65–93; for further discussion of land theology in Josephus and Philo and a charting of eschatological approaches to land in *Jubilees*, *Testament of Moses*, and Pseudo-Philo, see idem, *Rewriting the Bible: Land and Covenant in Post-Biblical Jewish Literature* (Valley Forge, PA: Trinity Press International, 1994). On rabbinic land theology, see Kraemer, *Rabbinic Judaism: Space and Place* (London; New York: Routledge, 2016); and Safrai, *Seeking Out the Land: Land of Israel Traditions in Ancient Jewish, Christian and Samaritan Literature (200 BCE–400 CE)* (Leiden; Boston: Brill, 2018), 76–224. The rabbinic authorities worked to delimit the clear boundaries for the biblical land of Israel in order to help in the performance of "commandments dependent on the land" and to forward claims in an ideological conflict with early Christianity and Rome; see Stemberger, "Die Bedeutung des 'Landes Israel' in der rabbinischen Tradition," *Kairos* 25 (1983), 176–99; and Safrai, *Seeking Out the Land*, 76–203.

whose life and works gave sanctity to the land.³² Meanwhile, the establishment of the State of Israel in 1948 prompted a new chapter in Jewish land theology. J.Z. Smith summarized it nicely when he wrote that with the establishment of the State of Israel, the earthly power and fruitfulness of holy land once again moved to the fore of Jewish life. "Increasingly Israel's return to the earth elicits a return to the archaic earth religion of Israel," he wrote.³³

Yet these conceptualizations of sacred national territory should not mask the sacralization of space in the private sphere. This brings us to one final way in which this book can contribute to our understanding of ancient Judaism. It can deepen our understanding of the ancient Judean farmer's attempt to forge a spiritual connection with the divine through the sacralization of land. The small farms that were so commonplace in Second Temple Judea were largely self-subsistent operations worked by a family. Occasional larger farming operations notwithstanding, the goal of these small holdings was typically the raising of grain and livestock and the production of other staples of the Levantine economy, such as olive oil and wine, for subsistence needs.³⁴ These farms were a basic component of the human experience and a microcosm for one's place in the world. The dedication of land to the deity could have been a pious attempt to bring the divine into the farm, as it were, and to embue undifferentiated agri-

---

32 Davies, *The Gospel and the Land. Early Christianity and Jewish Territorial Doctrine* (Berkeley: University of California Press, 1974); see also Paschke, "The Land in the New Testament," in *The Earth and the Land: Studies about the Value of the Land of Israel in the Old Testament and Afterwards* (ed. Koorevaar and Paul; Berlin: Peter Lang, 2018), 277–304, esp. 279–80. For a tempering of W.D. Davies's argument that Jesus rejected territorial Judaism, see Wenell, *Jesus and Land: Sacred and Social Space in Second Temple Judaism* (London: T&T Clark, 2007). Wenell forwards the position that Jesus did in fact draw on the biblical land promise but did so as part of a new structure where those of low social status and without significant property would join together as equals in a new Holy Land, the sanctity of the land free of the purity concerns of Sadducees and Pharisees and the land itself no longer owned by a select few.
33 *Map is Not Territory: Studies in the History of Religion* (Leiden: Brill, 1978), 106. Smith follows in the footsteps of Richard Rubenstein, who had claimed that the rebirth of Israel "marks the rebirth of the long forgotten gods of the earth within Jewish experience"; see *After Auschwitz: Radical Theology and Contemporary Judaism* (Indianapolis: The Bobbs-Merrill Company, 1966), 130–42. For other discussions of the role of the ancient Land of Israel in the modern Israeli ethos, see Sand, *The Invention of the Land of Israel: From Holy Land to Homeland* (London; New York: Verso, 2012), 67–118, 177–253; and Ben-Arieh, "Perceptions and Images of the Holy Land," in *The Land that Became Israel: Studies in Historical Geography* (ed. Kark; New Haven; Jerusalem: Yale University Press; Magnes Press, 1989), 37–53.
34 Adams, *Social and Economic Life*, 82–99; Pastor, *Land and Economy in Ancient Palestine* (London; New York: Routledge, 1997); see also Borowski, *Agriculture in Iron Age Israel* (Winona Lake, IN: Eisenbrauns, 1987), passim.

cultural space with deep personal meaning. In the rabbinic tradition, as in other religious traditions, the care of land was a sacred duty. Simplicity and integrity, rather than profit, were to motivate the land's cultivation and were to stand behind all human relations. Land held intrinsic value to the rabbis beyond all other forms of property, as a gift from the divine and as a source of value.[35] Yet the sacralization of land on small farms, as the evidence from the Second Temple sources shows, was a fact of life long before the codification of the Mishnah.[36]

1.1 Sacred Land in the Ancient World

The "temple economy" or the "sacred economy"—the flow of goods and resources through large temple organizations, and the impact of those organizations on the economies in which they were embedded—has been well developed in studies on ancient Egypt, Mesopotamia, and Greece.[37] The sacralization of cultivable land for the purposes of supporting temples was a major component of the temple economy. Priests and other high-ranking officials affiliated with temples could sustain their organizations through property ownership, including land, buildings, herds, and slaves. Since temples were permanent foundations, the real estate they owned could form a stable component in local holdings. They

---

35 Neusner, *The Economics of the Mishnah* (Atlanta: Scholars Press, 1998), 95–102; and see also Rosenfeld and Perlmutter, "Landowners in Roman Palestine 100–300 C.E.: A Distinct Social Group," *Journal of Ancient Judaism* 2, no. 3 (2011), 327–52.

36 Incidentally, the use of the term "field sacralization" in the title of the book is not to exclude orchards and groves; it simply follows the language of Lev 27:16, wĕim miśśĕdēh 'ăḥuzzātô..., which begins the Torah legislation on the matter and would also serve as the basis for the heading of a seminal chapter on the subject in the Mishnah, המקדיש את שדהו (*m. 'Arakin* 8:1). The "consecration of agricultural real estate" would be the more precise—albeit unwieldy—description of the practice.

37 Chankowski, "Divine Financiers: Cults as Consumers and Generators of Value," in *The Economies of Hellenistic Societies, Third to First Centuries BC* (ed. Archibald et al.; Oxford; New York: Oxford University Press, 2011), 142–65; Dignas, *Economy of the Sacred in Hellenistic and Roman Asia Minor* (Oxford; New York: Clarendon Press; Oxford University Press, 2002), 13–35; Linders, "Sacred Finances: Some Observations," in *Economics of Cult in the Ancient Greek World: Proceedings of the Uppsala Symposium 1990* (ed. Linders and Alroth; Uppsala; Stockholm: S. Academiae Ubsaliensis; Almqvist & Wiksell, 1992), 9–12; Kozuh, *The Sacrificial Economy. Assessors, Contractors, and Thieves in the Management of Sacrificial Sheep at the Eanna Temple of Uruk (ca. 625–520 B.C.)* (Winona Lake, IN: Eisenbrauns, 2014); and various studies in Lipiński, ed., *State and Temple Economy in the Ancient Near East: Proceedings of the International Conference Organized by the Katholieke Universiteit Leuven from the 10th to the 14th of April 1978* (Leuven: Departement Oriëntalistiek, 1979).

could receive land by donation or by forced seizure for indebtedness. They could charge rent on the land, supplementing revenue sources that fluctuated year to year, such as voluntary donations and agricultural tithes. They could also grant land to military veterans, priests, and other officials.[38]

The phenomenon of temple ownership of land is attested across the major cultures of the ancient Mediterranean and Near East. The temple of Ptah at Memphis, for example, profited from 2,538 hectares, or 9.4 sq. miles, of land, during the reign of Ramses III (1186–1155 BCE).[39] The Great Papyrus Harris indicates that Ramses III donated an area of roughly 300,000 hectares, or 1,150 sq. miles, to Egyptian temples during his reign. The estates of Amun at Karnak received most of the land; the mortuary temple of Ramses III himself too was a major recipient.[40] In the Hittite realm, priests worked plots in the possession of the local deity, with each cultic center conceived of as a city of the gods and each holding significant tracts of temple-owned land.[41] By the mid-first millennium BCE in Mesopotamia, the Eanna temple in Uruk and the Ebabbar temple in Sippar were in possession of sizeable and geographically scattered properties in their respective hinterlands, with the lands typically leased out to tenants in exchange for rent payments in kind.[42] In addition to endowments, the Eanna ap-

---

[38] Manning, *The Open Sea: The Economic Life of the Ancient Mediterranean World from the Iron Age to the Rise of Rome* (Princeton, NJ: Princeton, 2018), 124, 174; Horden and Purcell, *The Corrupting Sea: A Study of Mediterranean History* (Oxford; Malden, MA: Blackwell, 2000), 429–32; Trigger, *Understanding Early Civilizations: A Comparative Study* (Cambridge: Cambridge University Press, 2003), 326–28; Van de Mieroop, *The Ancient Mesopotamian City* (Oxford; New York: Clarendon Press; Oxford University Press, 1997), 146–58; Steinkeller, "The Renting of Fields in Early Mesopotamia and the Development of the Concept of 'Interest' in Sumerian," *JESHO* 24, no. 2 (1981).

[39] Thompson, *Memphis under the Ptolemies* (Princeton, NJ: Princeton University Press, 2012), 72.

[40] Janssen, "The Role of the Temple in the Egyptian Economy during the New Kingdom," in *State and Temple Economy* (op. cit.), 505–15, esp. 511.

[41] Weinfeld, *Social Justice*, 234–36; Taggar-Cohen, "Covenant Priesthood: Cross-cultural Legal and Religious Aspects of Biblical and Hittite Priesthood," in *Levites and Priests* (op. cit.), 20–21, n. 42.

[42] See the discussion on the temple estates of the Ebabbar in Jursa, *Aspects of the Economic History of Babylonia in the First Millennium BC: Economic Geography, Economic Mentalities, Agriculture, the Use of Money and the Problem of Economic Growth* (Münster: Ugarit-Verlag, 2010), 328–60; and on the Eanna, see Janković, "Uruk," in *Aspects of the Economic History of Babylonia in the First Millennium BC: Economic Geography, Economic Mentalities, Agriculture, the Use of Money and the Problem of Economic Growth* (ed. Jursa; Münster: Ugarit-Verlag, 2010), 419–28, 435–37.

pears to have actively purchased land and confiscated plots from its debtors.[43] Laborers were sometimes temple slaves.[44]

Temple land could be under the aegis of the palace or of local elites, with kings or influential officials giving instructions to the temple administrators on how to manage payments to personnel.[45] However, scholars have debated the extent to which temples enjoyed autonomy vis-à-vis royal administrations. B.J. Haring, for example, has questioned whether landed assets of mortuary temples in New Kingdom Egypt were indeed managed by the royal government. On the contrary, he writes that the "resources of Egyptian temples served mainly for their own maintenance, but their position as important landholders and producers also brought its public responsibilities."[46] By the Achaemenid period, imperial authorities strove to reduce the incomes of the temples without offending the local populace.[47]

The over-representation of temple archives on the Mesopotamian documentary record led earlier generations of scholars to exaggerate the prominence of temple lands in the ancient Near Eastern economy.[48] The "temple city" model

---

43 Ibid., 423.
44 On the institution of the *arua* ("given ex voto") in Mesopotamia (particularly of Ur III, 21st–20th centuries BCE), see Gelb, "The Arua Institution," *Revue d'assyriologie et d'archéologie orientale* 66, no. 1 (1972), 1–32, esp. 5–10; see also Renger, "Interaction of Temple, Palace, and 'Private Enterprise' in the Old Babylonian Economy," in *State and Temple Economy* (op. cit.), 254.
45 In Mesopotamia, Rachel Clay has argued for heightened administrative involvement in temple lands from as early as the Sumerian period; "The Tenure of Land in Babylonia and Assyria," *University of London Institute of Archaeology, Occasional Papers* 1 (1938), 13, 29. Maria Ellis notes instances of kings in the Old Akkadian period distributing temple land to their followers; *Agriculture and the State in Ancient Mesopotamia: An Introduction to Problems of Land Tenure* (Philadelphia: Babylonian Fund, University Museum, 1976), 3, n. 7. Muhammad Dandamayev brings evidence for the phenomenon in Babylonia of the first millennium BCE; "State and Temple in Babylonia in the First Millennium B.C.," in *State and Temple Economy* (op. cit.), 591–92. As Dandamayev notes, there were instances in which Nabonidus himself leased temple land to individuals. See also Horden and Purcell, *Corrupting Sea*, 429.
46 *Divine Households: Administrative and Economic Aspects of the New Kingdom Royal Memorial Temples in Western Thebes* (Leiden: Nederlands Instituut voor het Nabije Oosten, 1997), 396.
47 Dandamayev, "State and Temple in Babylonia," 596. See also Oelsner, "Krisenerscheinungen im Achaimenidenreich im 5. und 4. Jahrhundert v.u.Z.," in *Hellenische Poleis II: Krise—Wandlung —Wirkung* (ed. Welskopf; Berlin: Akademie-Verlag, 1973), 1059–60; Stolper, *Entrepreneurs and Empire: The Murašû Archive, the Murašû Firm, and Persian Rule in Babylonia* (Istanbul: Nederlands Historisch-Archaeologisch Instituut te Istanbul, 1985), 44, n. 30.
48 Ellis, *Agriculture and the State in Ancient Mesopotamia*, 3–4, nn. 6–7. Ian Morris and Joseph Manning have noted that overreliance on temple archives, along with a 20th-century fascination with big government, may have contributed to the tendency in scholarship to grant temples more economic influence than they actually had; "The Economic Sociology of the Ancient Med-

for ancient Mesopotamia, whereby all arable hinterland was thought to have been owned by the civic deity or deities and the city economy to have been a totalitarian redistributive system, has been challenged.[49] Now it is clear that private landholdings in Mesopotamia stood alongside those of palace and temple from as early as the third millennium BCE onward.[50] The holdings of Eanna in the mid-first millennium BCE, for example, were not overwhelmingly large and their yields were modest.[51] Less information is available on the landholdings of the other great temples of the region in that period, such as the Ezida in Borsippa, Ekur in Nippur, Esagila in Babylon, and Ekishnugal in Ur.

While in the ancient Near Eastern context scholars have diminished the significance of temple land in local economies, in the Greek context they have worked to demarcate the sacred as its own economic entity, landholdings included.[52] Moses Finley had claimed that "the so-called temple funds were deme funds, of course, and the administrative technique, common in Athens and elsewhere, of handling such moneys through the temple had no specific significance, legally or otherwise."[53] The statement has, according to Nikolaos Papazarkadas, "cast a long shadow" on scholarship, blurring the line between secular

---

iterranean World," in *The Handbook of Economic Sociology* (ed. Smelser and Swedberg; Princeton; New York: Princeton University Press; Russell Sage Foundation, 2005), 131–59, esp. 149–50.

49 For the classic articulations of the "temple city" concept in Sumer, see Schneider, *Die Anfänge der Kulturwirtschaft: Die sumerische Tempelstadt* (Baedeker: Essen, 1920); Falkenstein, *The Sumerian Temple City* (trans. Ellis; Los Angeles: Undena Publications, 1974).

50 For new formulations challenging this model, see "Private Land Ownership and its Relation to 'God' and the 'State' in Sumer and Akkad," in *Privatization in the Ancient Near East and Classical World* (ed. Hudson and Levine; Cambridge, MA: Peabody Museum of Archaeology and Ethnology, 1996), 109–17, esp. 112, 126, n. 20. Ur-Nammu's land register text (Ur III), for instance, refers to "the borders of God NN of city NN," implying fields adjacent were not owned by the god. See also Renger, "Interaction of Temple, Palace, and 'Private Enterprise'," 249–56; and Manning, *The Open Sea*, 175.

51 As Michael Jursa summarizes, "In short: the importance of the temples within the Neo-Babylonian economy in general and with respect to agriculture in particular is undeniable, but the sources clearly exclude ascribing paramount importance to this sector of the economy"; *Aspects of the Economic History of Babylonia*, 441–42.

52 Papazarkadas, *Sacred and Public Land in Ancient Athens* (Oxford; New York: Oxford University Press, 2011); Horster, *Landbesitz griechischer Heiligtümer in archaischer und klassischer Zeit* (Berlin; New York: De Gruyter, 2004). See also Isager, "Sacred and Profane Ownership of Land," in *Agriculture in Ancient Greece. Proceedings of the 7th International Symposium at the Swedish Institute at Athens, 16–17 May 1990* (ed. Wells; Stockholm: Svenska Institutet, 1992), 119–22; and Burford, *Land and Labor in the Greek World* (Baltimore; London: Johns Hopkins University Press, 1993), 21–26, 49–55, 180, 217.

53 *Studies in Land and Credit in Ancient Athens, 500–200 B.C. The Horos Inscriptions* (New Brunswick, NJ: Rutgers University Press, 1952), 95.

and sacred finances in the Greek polis.⁵⁴ Signe Isager had begun to question Finley's assumptions in the early 1990s.⁵⁵ While in certain cases the distinction between the sacred and secular sphere is difficult to maintain in the ancient Greek economy, generally public officials would have been aware of the special protections due to sacred assets and they would have worked to protect them for the welfare of the public.⁵⁶ Papazarkadas estimates that 4% of arable Greek land was considered sacred, which is to say divinely owned and managed by the polis as such.⁵⁷

In fourth-century BCE Athens, the ancestral sacrifices appear to have been entirely funded by the rent payments from sacred land, whose methods of collection and recording are detailed by Aristotle in *Athenaion Politeia* 47.4–5.⁵⁸ The best-documented case of sacred land is that owned by Apollo on the island of Delos, which was being leased out and cultivated intensively from the time of the earliest extant records there in the mid-fifth century BCE.⁵⁹ Rent payments on Apollo's land at Delos joined other sanctuary income, from taxes and interest payments on loans to cities, to help fund the *Delia* and cover the other routine expenses of the cult of Apollo on the island. When a tenant took over a piece of Apollo's land, the buildings, vines, fruit trees, and other features of the prop-

---

54 *Sacred and Public Land*, 4; and see 4–8 for a summary of views.
55 "Sacred and Profane Ownership of Land," 119–22.
56 The terminological difference in Greek documents involves things referred to as ἱερόν versus ὅσιον (ibid., 75–76, n. 256). For a discussion of the complicated case of deme landholdings and whether a distinction between sacred and secular is meaningful with respect to them, see Papazarkadas, *Sacred and Public Land*, 139–46. For orgeonic groups leasing land to fund cultic activity, see ibid., 191; and for other religious associations doing the same, see ibid., 209–10.
57 Ibid., 92–98, esp. 97. There were also lands associated with tribes, demes, phratries, gene, and orgeones. These were usually rented out and their revenues devoted to sacred purposes, though their status as sacred is hard to determine. Papazarkadas writes, "Produce from lands in the form of rentals appears to have subsidized the cultic activity of a series of public or semi-public groups throughout the Classical period—indeed in certain cases even in the early Hellenistic era—although the evidence comes mainly from the fourth century"; ibid., 240.
58 Rosivach, *The System of Public Sacrifice in Fourth-Century Athens* (Atlanta: Scholars Press, 1994), 121–27; Papazarkadas, *Sacred and Public Land*, 51–75. For a study of sacred land rented out in northern Attica, see Jameson, "The Leasing of Land in Rhamnous," *Hesperia Supplements* 19 (1982), 66–74.
59 Kent, "The Temple Estates of Delos, Rheneia, and Mykonos," *Hesperia* 17, no. 4 (1948), 243–338; Chankowski, *Athènes et Délos à l'époque classique: recherches sur l'administration du sanctuaire d'Apollon délien* (Athènes: Ecole française d'Athènes, 2008), 279–95; Horster, *Landbesitz griechischer Heiligtümer*, 167–72; Papazarkadas, *Sacred and Public Land*, 59–60, 294–95.

erty were inspected by officials representing the interests of the god. Details on the leasing of Apollo's land can be found on the *Hiera Syggraphe* of 300 BCE.[60]

Along with productive sacred properties in Greece, there were sacrosanct or explicitly uncultivable ones as well, which could have been used for the grazing of the deity's animals. The Sacred Orgas between Attica and Megarid is one example.[61] Another is Apollo's land on the plain of Krisa at Delphi, which was to be left uncultivated according to the Amphiktyonic Law of 380 BCE.[62] Apollo's holdings at Delphi included a considerable number of sacred animals. In 275 BCE, the god was gifted 50 oxen from a Lakedaimonian village, probably added to others in his possession at Delphi. In 117/6 BCE the Roman Senate requested that the Amphiktyonians, upon complaints of abuse and neglect, look into Apollo's income from his flocks.[63] Meanwhile, the imposition of sacrosanct status to land could have been carried out to assert rights to an area or to help settle land disputes.[64] Sanctification of land in secluded areas could have helped integrate the territory into the culture of the polis.[65]

The phenomenon of sanctuary ownership of land is evidenced as well in the Roman sphere, albeit less frequently than in classical Greece. The Vestal Virgins of Rome held land, for example.[66] So did one of Campania's most venerable sanctuaries, the temple of Diana Tifatina, which was endowed with a large tract of land in 83 BCE by Sulla as a show of gratitude for his victory over C. Nor-

---

[60] Kent, "The Temple Estates of Delos, Rheneia, and Mykonos," 267–85.
[61] Papazarkadas, *Sacred and Public Land*, 244–59; Horden and Purcell, *Corrupting Sea*, 428.
[62] Rousset, *Le territoire de Delphes et la terre d'Apollon* (Athènes: Ecole française d'Athènes, 2002), esp. 283–91. See also Papazarkadas, *Sacred and Public Land*, 11–13, 244–59; and Burkert, "Greek Temple-Builders: Who, Where and Why?," in *The Role of Religion in the Early Greek Polis: Proceedings of the Third International Seminar on Ancient Greek Cult, Organized by the Swedish Institute at Athens, 16–18 October 1992* (ed. Hägg; Stockholm: Paul Åströms, 1996), 28–29.
[63] Isager, "Sacred Animals in Classical and Hellenistic Greece," in *Economics of Cult in the Ancient Greek World: Proceedings of the Uppsala Symposium 1990* (ed. Linders and Alroth; Uppsala; Stockholm: S. Academiae Ubsaliensis; Almqvist & Wiksell, 1992), 15–19.
[64] Howe, *Pastoral Politics: Animals, Agriculture, and Society in Ancient Greece* (Claremont, CA: Regina Books, 2008), 88–92.
[65] McInerney, "On the Border: Sacred Land and the Margins of the Community," in *City, Countryside, and the Spatial Organization of Value in Classical Antiquity* (ed. Rosen and Sluiter; Leiden; Boston: Brill, 2006), 32–59, quote on 56.
[66] Wildfang, *Rome's Vestal Virgins: A Study of Rome's Vestal Priestesses in the Late Republic and Early Empire* (London; New York: Routledge, 2006), 72, n. 32; Campbell, *The Writings of the Roman Land Surveyors: Introduction, Text, Translation and Commentary* (London: Society for the Promotion of Roman Studies, 2000), 361.

banus.⁶⁷ Diana Tifatina's land was not leased out but worked by slaves managed by a bailiff, similar to the normal arrangement of *villae rusticae* with absentee landlords. In southern Italy private landowners slowly encroached on the sacred lands of Dionysus and Athena at Heraclea. The lands had also been badly neglected. The boundary lines were reaffirmed, and new markers were put into place; the land was also improved to be more productive for the cult.⁶⁸

These instances of sacred real estate are joined by the commonly found sanctuary groves in Italy and the provinces, whose functions were varied. Through a study of the sacred grove of the Augustan sanctuary on the Palatine Hill, Pierre Gros has argued that groves were more than an ornamental component in the sacred landscape; they were an integral part of the sanctuary experience, helping to regulate the worshipper's interaction with the deity.⁶⁹ The cult of Diana at Aricia managed a grove that provided a neutral site for meetings of political leagues, as was common in Latium.⁷⁰ The grove of the temple of an unnamed Gallic god at Massilia (Marseilles) assumes a prominent role in the description by Lucan of Julius Caesar's siege of the city; it is portrayed as a place of horror, with the remains of a cult of human sacrifice strewn about its trees.⁷¹ The grove known to have existed at the sanctuary of Leto at Xanthos in Asia Minor is reconstructed atop the hill commanding the site.⁷²

The widespread attestation of sacred land in the ancient world anticipates the landed properties of religious organizations in the Middle Ages and beyond. Mention has already been made of the ecclesiastical estates of late antiquity. Cistercian monasteries in medieval Europe offer another example, for they actively bought, leased, and exchanged lands in order to supplement their wealth. They enjoyed a low-cost internal supply of labor through the creation of a separate class of *conversi* monks who worked the land; this gave them a competitive ad-

---

67 Carlsen, "*CIL* X 8217 and the Question of Temple Land in Roman Italy," in *Landuse in the Roman Empire* (ed. Carlsen et al.; Rome: "L'Erma" di Bretschneider, 1994), 9–13.
68 Burford, *Land and Labor*, 24, n. 22.
69 "Le bois sacré du Palatin: une composante oubliée du sanctuaire augustéen d'Apollon," *Revue Archéologique*, no. 1 (2003), 51–66.
70 Green, *Roman Religion and the Cult of Diana at Aricia* (Cambridge; New York: Cambridge University Press, 2007), 89–90.
71 Fratantuono, *Madness Triumphant: A Reading of Lucan's Pharsalia* (Lanham, MD: Lexington Books, 2012), 111–16.
72 des Courtils, "From Elyanas to Leto: The Physical Evolution of the Sanctuary of Leto at Xanthos," in *Sacred Landscapes in Anatolia and Neighboring Regions* (ed. Gates et al.; Oxford: Archaeopress, 2009), 66.

Figure 2. Franciscan Monks making hay in Ottoman Palestine, ca. 1903. Library of Congress Prints and Photographs Division. Stereograph by C.H. Graves.

vantage in the production of wool.[73] In Paris in the mid-eighteenth century, monasteries held some 13.6% of residential dwellings in the city, with urban religious houses usually built in fringe belts in Paris and then rented out to tenants. To finance new construction, monks took out loans from the Parisian bourgeoisie.[74] Meanwhile, charitable land endowments in pre-modern Persia were set up for

---

73 Truax, "Building the Desert: Property Management According to the Early Cistercians," *Cistercian Studies Quarterly* 51, no. 1 (2016), 77–99; Ekelund et al., *Sacred Trust*, 51.
74 Perluss, "Monastic Landed Wealth in Late-Eighteenth-Century Paris. Principal Traits and Major Issues," in *The Economics of Providence: Management, Finances and Patrimony of Religious Orders and Congregations in Europe, 1773–c. 1930* (ed. Van Dijck et al.; Leuven: Leuven University Press, 2012), 51–74.

the upkeep of shrines and religious schools and for the financial support of religious figures.[75]

Nowadays the major world religions, particularly the Catholic church, are among the main landholders across the globe.[76] The Catholic church is currently the third largest individual landowner on earth, enjoying legal claim to 177 million acres at an estimated value of $1.7 trillion; in New York the church is the second largest individual property owner in the city. In India estimates put as much of 5%, or 15 million acres, in the form of Hindu endowments or land owned by Hindu temples.[77] Interestingly, of the major world religions, it is Judaism that is not marked by significant assets in land presently, its only real estate holdings consisting primarily of the modest urban and suburban acreage on which synagogues now stand.[78] The roots of Judaism's difference in this regard may stretch back into its earliest centuries on the world stage.

1.2 History of Research and Summary of Contents

The source material on which this book relies is a double-edged sword. On the one hand, the extant documentation of the Judean religious institutions of antiquity is extraordinarily rich in its narrative, legal, and philosophical texts. Artifacts and architectural remains from everyday life in the Second Temple Judea have also been extensively documented. But lacking among this corpus are good documentary and epigraphic sources that can speak to the temple economy, with the exception of two Persian-period documents recording what appear to be inventories of shekel donations to the temples of Jerusalem and of Elephan-

---

[75] Lambton, *Landlord and Peasant in Persia: A Study of Land Tenure and Land Revenue Administration* (London; New York: Oxford University Presss, 1953), 230–37, esp. 233. The land could be worked directly by the beneficiary or, more often, leased; in the latter case, the terms would be beneficial to the lessee. In certain cases, only part of one's estate would be constituted into charitable *ouqāf*.
[76] Cahill, *Who Owns the World: The Hidden Facts behind Landownership* (Edinburgh; London: Mainstream Publishing, 2006), 35, 38–40, 77–78, 117–18. As Cahill notes, the land is held now by the church not "to assert the core principle of monarchy" but merely for the support of the church and its priests, sisters, and brothers. On the "huge swathes of landed property" of the Greek Orthodox church, a matter of some controversy when Greek politicians have tried to expropriate them, see Papazarkadas, *Sacred and Public Land*, 8, n. 38.
[77] *Who Owns the World*, 123–32; see also Kent, *Sacred Groves and Local Gods: Religion and Environmentalism in South India* (Oxford; New York: Oxford, 2013).
[78] Cahill, *Who Owns the World*, 103, 500.

tine in Egypt, respectively.[79] We lack border stones for temple land, for example, or accounts of revenues and expenditures, debt notes, and other documentation recording the flow of goods and services through Yahwistic temples. Such documentary evidence has been essential for studies on the sacralization of land in Mesopotamia, Egypt, Asia Minor, and Greece. In the case of Judea, the lack of such evidence leaves us severely inhibited if not prevented altogether from reaching conclusions on the location of sacred plots, the utilization and productivity of such assets, their change over time, and their importance to the regional economy. Incidentally, this problem obtains for both the First and the Second Temple periods.

On the other hand, the primary source material does contain texts from the prophetic, legal, historical, and scholastic spheres that comment on and regulate the practice of field sacralization. These texts can provide a glimpse into the ideological predispositions among early Judeans toward sacred holdings as a feature of their life. They can shed light on different attitudes in antiquity toward the temple in Jerusalem as an honored institution. And they can point to efforts to uphold that honor by virtue of material gifts. The textual sources fall into three groups: (1) texts redacted in scriptural canon, specifically Lev 27 and Ezekiel's Temple Vision of 40–48; (2) various source material from the mid-second century BCE onward, including fragmentary legal texts from the Dead Sea Scrolls and miscellaneous sources in Philo, Josephus, and the New Testament; and (3) Tannaitic teachings, which are used here to enlighten the discussion and provide broader perspective for the sources from the Second Temple period proper.

A monograph-length study on how the Judean priesthood was involved in land cultivation has never been endeavored, and there are copious studies on

---

[79] The Elephantine document's superscript reads "This is (a list of) the names of the Judean garrison who gave money for YHW the God, each person 2 shekels." It bears some resemblance to an apparent donations list of the fourth century BCE from Ketef Jericho. On the Elephantine papyrus, see Cowley, *Aramaic Papyri of the Fifth Century B.C.* (Oxford: Clarendon Press, 1923), 65–76 (No. 22). The Ketef Jericho document could record the collection of the shekel tax or some other cash donation for holy purposes, based on its similarity to the shekel donation list from Elephantine; see Eshel and Misgav, "A Fourth Century B.C.E. Document from Ketef Yeriḥo," *IEJ* 38, no. 3 (1988), 142–57; and Eshel and Misgav, "Jericho papList of Loans ar," in *Miscellaneous Texts from the Judaean Desert* (ed. Charlesworth et al.; Oxford: Clarendon Press, 2000); Lemaire, "Administration of Fourth-Century B.C.E. Judah in Light of Epigraphy and Numismatics," in *Judah and the Judeans in the Fourth Century B.C.E.* (ed. Lipschits et al.; Winona Lake, IN: Eisenbrauns, 2007), 59. Eshel and Misgav, however, understand the document to be a loans list, with the recto possibly documenting a series of loans, and the verso payments on those loans; in certain cases, the same name appears on both sides, with the verso consistently giving a smaller sum.

the temple and priesthood that overlook the role of both organizations on the countryside.⁸⁰ The same is true for research into land-tenure practices of the region in antiquity.⁸¹ The relatively few published studies on the topic thus made an important contribution, even if they overlook much of the source material brought to bear in this book. For the Persian period, Joseph Blenkinsopp has considered the question of whether the Jerusalem temple held land.⁸² His article is based on Ezra 10, which tells of a national assembly of Judeans on the topic of intermarriage, presumably in the mid-fifth century BCE. Ezra is said to have declared that failure to attend the assembly would result in excommunication and confiscation of property. The property would be anathematized, which means it bore sacrosanct or herem status (Ezra 10:8).⁸³ The herem is best known as a

---

80 E. g., Haran, *Temples and Temple-Service*; Dahm, *Opferkult und Priestertum in Alt-Israel: ein kultur- und religionswissenschaftlicher Beitrag* (Berlin: De Gruyter, 2003); Cody, *A History of Old Testament Priesthood* (Rome: Pontifical Biblical Institute, 1969); Anderson, *Sacrifices and Offerings in Ancient Israel: Studies in Their Social and Political Importance* (Atlanta: Scholars Press, 1987); Zevit, *The Religions of Ancient Israel: A Synthesis of Parallactic Approaches* (London; New York: Continuum, 2001), esp. 123–266; Busink, *Der Tempel von Jerusalem von Salomo bis Herodes. Band II. Von Ezechiel bis Middot* (Leiden: Brill, 1980); Safrai, "Religion in Everyday Life," in *The Jewish People in the First Century: Historical Geography, Political History, Social, Cultural and Religious Life and Institutions* (ed. Safrai and Stern; Assen: Van Gorcum, 1976), 817–28; Oppenheimer, *The 'Am Ha-Aretz: A Study in the Social History of the Jewish People in the Hellenistic-Roman Period* (trans. Levine; Leiden: Brill, 1977), 29–51; Schürer et al., *The History of the Jewish People in the Age of Jesus Christ (175 B.C.–A.D. 135), Volume II, Revised and Edited* (Edinburgh: T&T Clark, 1979), 257–74; Sanders, *Judaism, 63 BCE–66 CE*, 146–90; Schaper, *Priester und Leviten*, 149–50; Schmidt, *How the Temple Thinks: Identity and Social Cohesion in Ancient Judaism* (trans. Crowley; Sheffield: Sheffield Academic Press, 2001), 191–244; Wardle, *The Jerusalem Temple and Early Christian Identity* (Tübingen: Mohr Siebeck, 2010), 23–27.
81 Jack Pastor's *Land and Economy*, the definitive volume on land tenure practices of the region in classical antiquity, barely touches on the topic; see p. 32 there for a dismissal of it. The question of temple land is unaddressed in Guillaume, *Land, Credit, and Crisis: Agrarian Finance in the Hebrew Bible* (Sheffield; Oakville, CT: Equinox, 2012); and Borowski, *Agriculture in Iron Age Israel*, though in the latter (21–30) there is some discussion of landholding by priests (on which, see below). Morris Silver similarly overlooks the issue in his treatment of the temple's role and of agricultural practices in the Iron Age economy; see *Prophets and Markets: The Political Economy of Ancient Israel* (Boston: Kluwer-Nijhoff, 1983), 19–25, 67.
82 "Did the Second Jerusalemite Temple Possess Land?," *Transeuphratène* 21 (2001), 61–68.
83 The term herem etymologically is related to Semitic terms for "holy" but must have carried the sense of a more permanent or lasting form of sanctity than verb forms based on the root *q-d-š* did. On its etymology and range of meanings, see Benovitz, *Kol Nidre: Studies in the Development of Rabbinic Votive Institutions* (Atlanta: Scholars Press, 1998), 69–71; Greenberg, "Ḥerem," in *Encyclopaedia Judaica, Second Edition*, vol. 9 (ed. Skolnik and Berenbaum; Farmington Hills, MI: Thomson Gale, 2006), 10–13; and Lohfink, "חָרַם ḥāram; חֵרֶם ḥērem," in *Theological Diction-*

mechanism of Israelite warfare, particularly in the Deuteronomistic accounts of the conquest of the Land of Canaan; the marking of an enemy city or people as herem would, according to biblical law, result in the total annihilation of that population in the manner of a whole-burnt offering and the destruction of any remaining property.[84] But by the Persian period, argued Blenkinsopp, any property confiscated from an individual declared herem, as in Ezra 10:8, would have joined the holdings of the temple in Jerusalem. Blenkinsopp thus called into question Joel Weinberg's assertion that the "citizen-temple community" of Persian Yehud differed from similar arrangements in the Achaemenid sphere in its lack of temple land.[85]

Peter Bedford has responded to Blenkinsopp's thesis by claiming that the landholdings of the Jerusalem temple were likely very small in the Persian period because there was no precedent for such a category of land in the Iron Age, nor would there have been labor available to work it.[86] Bedford has argued that in the Persian period the temple in Jerusalem was funded by an informal taxation system and lacked the political authority to demand tithes and other biblically imposed agricultural offerings.[87] Priests in other words could not have relied fully on the temple to support themselves and their families.

---

ary of the Old Testament (ed. Botterweck and Ringgren; Grand Rapids, MI: William B. Eerdmans, 1986).

84 As a result, forms of the Hebrew root *ḥ-r-m* are often used in the Hebrew Bible to connote the thorough destruction of the enemies of Israel, apparently as a form of offering to God. The prophet Jeremiah, for example, speaks of Yahweh bringing defeat upon Judah through his "servant" Nebuchadnezzar and quotes him as saying, "I will devote them to destruction (*wĕhaḥăramtîm*) and make them a desolation, an object of hissing—ruins for all time" (25:9). Then later he encourages the demise of Nebuchadnezzar's kingdom using similar language: "Destroy her (*wĕhaḥărîmûhā*), let her have no remnant!" He uses other *hipîl* forms of the verb in parallel with the root *p-q-d* ("attend to") and *ḥ-r-b* ("destroy") in 50:21 and as an antonym for the root *ḥ-m-l* ("show pity for") in 51:3. For further discussion, see §§2.4–5 and Chapter 6.

85 *The Citizen-Temple Community* (Sheffield: JSOT Press, 1992), 103–4; Blenkinsopp, "Did the Second Jerusalemite Temple Possess Land?," 62.

86 "The Economic Role of the Jerusalem Temple in Achaemenid Judah: Comparative Perspectives," in *Shai le-Sara Japhet. Studies in the Bible, its Exegesis and its Language* (ed. Bar-Asher et al.; Jerusalem: The Bialik Institute, 2007), 12*–13*. For brief discussions of temple land in Iron Age Israel, see Stevens, *Temples, Tithes, and Taxes: The Temple and the Economic Life of Ancient Israel* (Peabody, MA: Hendrickson Publishers, 2006), 82–85; and Henrey, "Land Tenure in the Old Testament," *Palestine Exploration Quarterly* 86, no. 1 (1954), 13–15; the latter appears in the context of the Levitical settlements.

87 "Temple Funding and Priestly Authority in Achaemenid Judah," in *Exile and Return: The Babylonian Context* (ed. Stökl and Waerzeggers; Berlin/Boston: De Gruyter, 2015), 336–51; see also idem, "Economic Role of the Jerusalem Temple," 3*–20*.

1.2 History of Research and Summary of Contents — 23

While totalitarian regimes based in palace-temple complexes and functioning along the lines of the Asiatic Mode of Production may have been operative in certain historical moments in the great hydraulic civilizations of the Near East, the usefulness of the model for rainfed Levantine societies is questionable, even in the period of the Iron Age monarchies. The newest archaeological research shows Jerusalem to have been small, scarcely populated, and impoverished in the Persian period, with Ramat Rahel to the south functioning as the center for imperial taxation.[88] The physical separation of this center undermines somewhat earlier theories of a powerful imperial-temple complex in the period. One such theory was Joel Weinberg's model of a citizen-temple community, thought to consist of a privileged polity of priests in close association with the Persian authorities, and of a landholding citizenry with a high priest serving as its main administrative leader.[89] Along similar lines, Joachim Schaper argued that the Jerusalem temple in the Persian period was a center for imperial tax collection, with representatives of the temple and the empire working together there to collect revenues for both administrations.[90]

Zeev Safrai has gathered evidence for the landed properties of the Jerusalem temple in the late Second Temple period.[91] Though it is a short study, he has offered the most thorough attempt to address the question thus far. He anchors his discussion on references in rabbinic literature to hekdesh, or "consecrated property" (e.g., *m. ʿArakin* 6–8, *m. Meʿilah* 3). This term can refer to holdings within the proprietary domain of the temple, or in a metonymic sense to the temple as an economic agent.[92] Rabbinic texts describe the auctioning of hekdesh land and

---

[88] On Ramat Rahel and Jerusalem in the Persian period, see §3.2.2. On the separation of imperial and sacred taxes in the Persian period, see Bedford, "Temple Funding," 341–48; and idem, "Economic Role of the Jerusalem Temple," 14*–20*.
[89] *The Citizen-Temple Community*. For a critique of Weinberg's thesis, see Altmann, *Economics in Persian-Period Biblical Texts: Their Interactions with Economic Developments in the Persian Period and Earlier Biblical Traditions* (Tübingen: Mohr Siebeck, 2016), 180–81; and Ska, *Introduction to Reading the Pentateuch* (Winona Lake, IN: Eisenbrauns, 2006), 226–27.
[90] "The Jerusalem Temple as an Instrument of the Achaemenid Fiscal Administration," *VT* 45, no. 4 (1995), 528–39.
[91] "The Agrarian Structure in Palestine in the Time of the Second Temple, Mishnah and Talmud," in *The Rural Landscape of Ancient Israel* (ed. Maier et al.; Oxford, England: British Archaeological Reports, 2003), 115–26, esp. 115–17. An abridged Hebrew-language version of Safrai's discussion in "The Agrarian Structure" appears in Safrai and Safrai, *Tractate Skalim (sic) (Moed E) with Historical and Sociological Commentary* (Jerusalem: E.M. Liphshitz, 2009) [Hebrew], 12–16.
[92] This is most apparent when it appears as the subject of verbs denoting financial transactions, as in the phrase "hekdesh has the upper hand" (e.g., *m. Šeqalim* 4:9, 5:4; *t. ʿArakin*

the seizure of property by the temple in order to recover debt (*m. ʿArakin* 6:2–3, 8:2–3). They include discussions of the status of agricultural derivatives of consecrated trees and fields (*m. Meʿilah* 3:6–8), and of redemption rights for hekdesh land (*m. ʿArakin* 8:1). These rabbinic teachings suggest ad hoc sanctification of space for the purposes of supporting the temple, with individual farmers assuming responsibility for protecting hekdesh status. But they cannot prove the existence of land benefitting the temple when it still stood because they derive from a much later era.[93]

These brief studies do not relate in any thoroughgoing way to Lev 27, the most important source of evidence on the question of field sacralization in Second Temple Judea. Its laws on landed property are the subject of Chapter 2 of this book. Lev 27 is a discrete addendum to the Holiness Code that was likely authored by a school of priests active in Judea in the sixth or fifth centuries BCE. Exegetes have read Lev 27 as concerned with the monetization of in-kind offerings. As argued in Chapter 2, the text is best understood as regulating the lending of silver from Yahweh's priests. The consecration mechanism marked not a donation given to the deity but the need to secure a loan issued from his holy coffers. Consecration in Lev 27, in other words, equalled hypothecation. This supplements Philippe Guillaume's analysis of agrarian finance in the Hebrew Bible, which focused on its role within patronage circles and the extended family.[94] It is impossible to know whether the Holiness Code ever functioned as normative law.[95] But in the least we can assume that priestly texts and the Holiness Code in particular held rhetorical power in the Second Temple period, when Judea tended towards theocracy in its political administration.[96]

4:3), a catchphrase underscoring the rabbis' sense that the temple is to be given special financial privileges.

93 Shemuel Safrai, for example, was more skeptical than his son Zeev Safrai on the matter of temple land. He wrote: "The sources do not contain the slightest suggestion that the Temple owned either slaves, houses, fields or any property whose revenues went to the Temple, as was not unusual in other ancient civilizations; see "The Temple," in *The Jewish People in the First Century*, vol. 2 (op. cit.), 879. For further discussion on the use of rabbinic texts in the historiography of the Second Temple era, see §5.1.

94 *Land, Credit, and Crisis*, 111–49.

95 On the question of whether biblical legal material can be used to reconstruct facts on the ground, see Westbrook and Wells, *Everyday Law in Biblical Israel: An Introduction* (Louisville: Westminster John Knox Press, 2009), 3; and Greengus, *Laws in the Bible and in Early Rabbinic Collections. The Legacy of the Ancient Near East* (Eugene, OR: Cascade Books, 2011), 7. See also Borowski, *Agriculture in Iron Age Israel*, 21.

96 *Ritual and Rhetoric*, 148–50.

Interestingly, Lev 27:21 states that herem property becomes not temple property but a private priestly holding—the same is indicated by the priestly law at Num 18:14—while Lev 27:28 rules that such property is unsellable and irredeemable.[97] Norman Habel has picked up on the implications of the Holiness Code's stance on the point and argued that the land laws in the code helped establish a rural power base for the priesthood, rather than one centralized in an urban setting by the temple.[98] According to Lev 27, the conveyance of land title to Yahweh meant, for all practical purposes, the transfer of that property to a priest, presumably for the benefit of himself and his family. This represents a considerably different approach to the institution of herem than what is implied by Deut 13:17, where the destroyed heathen city becomes herem and its terrain uncultivable in perpetuity. Understanding the dynamics of the conveyances involving consecrated real estate, whether as a hypothecary pledge or a charitable gift, can be a fruitful avenue of inquiry into the role of the Judean priesthood in agricultural life in the Persian period. It also suggests that the image in the Hebrew Bible of priests holding no portion of land and subsisting entirely from the offerings of the people (Num 18:20, 24; Deut 18:1–2) was far from reality.

An early articulation of the biblical ideal of a landless priesthood appears in the Temple Vision of the book of Ezekiel (Ezek 40–48), which is the subject of Chapter 3. Among the laws and ordinances of the Vision are details on the temple's financial sustainability, including regulations on the priesthood's income and on a special tract of land set aside for the priests' living quarters and pasturage of its holy flocks (*qōdeš min hā'āreṣ*, "sacred tract of land"; 45:1). This is an elaborate picture of sacred temple land. However, the land in question is to be uncultivated, its value lying not in its productive capability but in its symbolic role as a protective barrier for the priesthood. The Vision contrasts significantly the realities on the ground suggested by Lev 27. Instead of a priesthood holding land privately, it imagines holy men disengaged from agricultural production and subsisting entirely on the offerings of the people. This nationalized support system imagined by the book of Ezekiel was likely little more than an ideal, though efforts by Persian governors like Nehemiah in the mid-fifth century

---

[97] Moshe Benovitz similarly assumed that the herem property mentioned in Lev 27:28 joined the incorporated holdings of the temple rather than the private holdings of individual priests; see *Kol Nidre*, 85. Benovitz connects the *tēl 'ôlām* ("eternal ruin") of the condemned city in Deut 13:17 with the herem field consecrated voluntarily in Lev 27:28, asserting that both join the holdings of the temple, though they remain uncultivable. He suggests scribal tampering with the latter text to harmonize it with Num 18:14's clear granting of all things herem to priests; ibid., 85–86. See further discussion on the topic in §2.4.

[98] *The Land is Mine: Six Biblical Land Ideologies* (Minneapolis: Fortress Press, 1995), 145.

BCE to restructure the Jerusalem temple economy may have improved the temple's support system and expanded its incorporated holdings somewhat. An Idumean geographic survey of the fourth century BCE includes a line that can be translated as "the plot of land of the house of Yahweh." The surveyor may have been concerned that a violation of some sort might occur with the sacred plot in question, whether in terms of wrongful taxation, encroachment, or outright theft.

Chapter 4 presents evidence for Yahwistic temple land in the Hellenistic period. The Oniad temple at Leontopolis in Egypt was endowed with a tract of land. This was a gift from the Ptolemaic house meant to help with the long-term sustainability of the Yahwistic cult, and it was likely granted the status of sacred land (ἱερὰ γῆ). Moreover, an account in 1 Maccabees has a Hellenistic monarch offering the entire agricultural hinterland of the city of Ptolemais to the Hasmoneans as a source of sustenance for the Jerusalem temple. In the account, the offer was forcefully rejected, likely to make a point about improper sources of revenue for the house of God. These texts offer models for understanding the relationship between temple, landed property, and communal support of the entire priesthood in a period in which rent capitalism and latifundia begin to appear in Palestine.[99] A careful consideration of these texts can supplement Doron Mendels' project on the biblical land of Israel as a theme in the royal propaganda of the Hasmonean regime.[100]

Chapters 5–7 focus on the late Second Temple period. The chapters use the scattered evidence at our disposal, including a few key texts from the Qumran library and Paul's letter to the Romans. A legal section of the Damascus Document, which is discussed in Chapter 5, appears to address a case where a debtor

---

[99] Kloppenborg, "The Growth and Impact of Agricultural Tenancy in Jewish Palestine (III BCE–I CE)," *JESHO* 51, no. 1 (2008), 31–66; idem, *The Tenants in the Vineyard: Ideology, Economics, and Agrarian Conflict in Jewish Palestine* (Tübingen: Mohr Siebeck, 2006), 284–313, esp. summary of research on 285–87. Among Kloppenborg's sources are the Zenon papyri, which suggest that Apollonius, the finance minister for Ptolemy II Philadelphus, leased land to local farmers; and which include evidence for the rise of a class of powerful Judean landowners, the Tobiads among them. A certain "Jeddous" was audacious enough to refuse to pay down a loan to someone in the Ptolemaic regime, perhaps Apollonius's minister Zenon; see Tcherikover and Fuks, *Corpus Papyrorum Judaicarum* (vol. 1; Cambridge, MA: The Magnes Press; Harvard University Press, 1957), 115–8, 129–30. The Hefzibah inscription implies a high level of management of local Galilean villages by a certain Seleucid *strategos* named Ptolemy son of Traseas during the period of the Fifth Syrian War (202–1 BCE); Landau, "A Greek Inscription Found Near Hefzibah," *IEJ* 16, no. 1 (1966), 54–70.
[100] *The Land of Israel as a Political Concept in Hasmonean Literature: Recourse to History in Second Century B.C. Claims to the Holy Land* (Tübingen: J.C.B. Mohr, 1987).

consecrates to God property that had been put up as security on a loan. Early rabbinic texts allude to such a case and attest that a similar kind of consecration fraud was committed against wives seeking property that had been legally encumbered by a marriage contract. If creditors or wives facing this situation showed disregard for the sacred status of the encumbered property, they may have found themselves liable for a sacrilege penalty. The issue could have resulted in litigation involving jurists expert on Judean sacral law. Another crime involving cultic property that emerges in the Judean source material is what is termed here "herem entrapment." This refers to a dedicant consecrating property to God in order to deprive his laborers or household dependents—even his own aging parents—from benefitting from it in any way.

The temple was likely not accumulating a significant amount of land through such illicit means, though it is interesting to consider Philo's comment, in his description of sacred taxes, that "the [Jerusalem] temple has for its revenues not only portions of land, but also other possessions of much greater extent and importance, which will never be destroyed or diminished" (*Spec. Laws* 1.76). Contemporaneous geographic descriptions of Judea and scattered sources on the temple's supply network for raw materials can help contextualize this intriguing comment by Philo. These are discussed in Chapter 5 too.

Chapter 6 concentrates on a halakhic text (4Q251) from Qumran that reasserts the priesthood's claim to herem property. As suggested centuries earlier by Lev 27, this source indicates that Judean priests would continue to amass landed assets within the framework of herem. The most common scenario may have been simple charitable gifts to priests. However, given the influence of priests in Judean society in the late Second Temple period, and the wealth many in their ranks appear to have accumulated, the social dynamics behind such gifts likely extended well beyond the alimentary. The relative autonomy of clans of priests in the holding of property could have led to great disparities of wealth among them, which could have been a contributing factor to the organizational dysfunction described in the historical sources. Moreover, the fact that Judean priests may have held much of the land that was consecrated to the deity can help explain the relative absence of references to Judean temple land on historical record.

Chapter 7, the final chapter of the volume before the Summary and Conclusions, considers a short parable by Paul in Romans 11. In the parable, Paul compares the house of Israel to an olive tree. It reads "if the root is holy, so too the branches." This is a message on the transferability of the sanctity of Israel to new gentile members of the church. As argued below, it is indebted to Judean sacrilege law on agricultural dedications to the deity. The Mishnaic tractate of *Meʿilah* (3:6–8) has sanctity protections applying to all outgrowths, derivatives, and products of an agricultural dedication. The concept would justify a sacrilege penalty in the case of the misappropriation of agricultural products that grew from the plant after the point of endowment. Paul's line in Romans is a much earlier attestation of the principle. A project with a broader scope would provide the proper cultural context in second- and third-century CE Galilee for the Mishnaic materials on hekdesh, in order to more effectively distinguish rabbinic invention from halakhic traditions reaching back into the days of the Second Temple.

Chapter 2
Field Consecrations in Leviticus 27

2.1 Introduction

Judea was in precipitous economic decline in the middle of the sixth century BCE. With the aristocracy of the old kingdom of Judah deported, the population that remained after the Babylonian wars endured hardships characteristic of a post-collapse society.[1] The center of religious life shifted from Jerusalem to the region of Benjamin, just to its north, where the town of Mizpah served as the active administrative city, and Bethel it would seem was the primary place for the sacrificial worship of Yahweh.[2] These places were vital to the survival of the cult prior to the rededication of the Jerusalem temple in 516 BCE. From that point forward the new Persian province of Yehud had Jerusalem once again as its religious center, with the imperial administration anchored at the nearby palatial complex of Ramat Rahel. Recent archaeological discoveries have shown that Ramat Rahel was a center for tax collection, while the city of Jerusalem was little more than a hamlet hugging the slopes of a modest sanctuary.[3]

In the context of the economically depleted Persian province of Yehud, the Holiness School of priests, which was active in the late sixth or fifth centuries BCE, put forward a new vision of how Judeans were to see themselves and their land.[4] The work they produced is codified in Lev 17–26 and referred to

---

[1] Faust, *The Archaeology of Israelite Society in Iron Age II* (Winona Lake, IN: Eisenbrauns, 2012), esp. 167–80, 243–54; see also Lipschitz, *The Fall and Rise of Jerusalem: Judah under Babylonian Rule* (Winona Lake, IN: Eisenbrauns, 2005), esp. 272–359; Meyers, "The Babylonian Exile Revisited: Demographics and the Emergence of the Canon of Scripture," in *Judaism and Crisis: Crisis as a Catalyst in Jewish Cultural History* (ed. Lange et al.; Göttingen; Oakville, CT: Vandenhoeck & Ruprecht, 2011), 61–74.
[2] Knauf, "Bethel: The Israelite Impact on Judean Language and Literature," in *Judah and the Judeans in the Persian Period* (ed. Lipschitz and Oeming; Winona Lake, IN: Eisenbrauns, 2006), 291–350.
[3] For further discussion and references on Ramat Rahel and Jerusalem in the Persian period, see §3.2.2.
[4] Schwartz, *The Holiness Legislation: Studies in the Priestly Code* (Jerusalem: Magnes Press, 1999) [Hebrew], esp. 11–34; Knohl, *The Sanctuary of Silence: The Priestly Torah and the Holiness School* (Minneapolis: Fortress Press, 1995), 6–7, 229. Scholars tend to date the literary activity of the school to the sixth or even fifth century BCE. For the former, see Milgrom, *Leviticus 17–22: A New Translation with Introduction and Commentary* (New York: Doubleday, 2000), 1347, 1439–43; Otto, "The Holiness Code in Diachrony and Synchrony in the Legal Hermeneutics of the Pentateuch," in *The Strata of the Priestly Writings: Contemporary Debate and Future Directions* (ed.

as the Holiness Code. It calls on the children of Israel to maintain a sense of sanctity in their everyday lives through dietary regulations, the Sabbath, and festival rituals. It also imagines them as mere tenants on Yahweh's territory, recalling the temple estates of the Near East, where tenancy on a deity's land was seen as a special honor.[5] Like the Deuteronomistic approach, this was a universalizing model, but it has the deity positioned as landowner rather than one who gifts land in the manner of a royal grant.[6] "The land is mine," God declares in Lev 25:23, "with me you are but aliens and tenants." Resources extracted from the economy for the purposes of sustaining the deity's cult of worship could thus be presented as debts owed in exchange for the privilege of tenancy.[7] The inspiration may have come from Babylonia, where documents of the mid-first millennium BCE show that tenants on land owned by a temple were required to pay a

---

Schectman and Baden; Zürich: Theologischer Verlag Zürich, 2009), 135–56; and Knohl, *Sanctuary of Silence*, 101–3. For a dating into the fifth century BCE, see Nihan, *From Priestly Torah to Pentateuch: A Study in the Composition of the Book of Leviticus* (Tübingen: Mohr Siebeck, 2007), 616–19. For arguments on why the Holiness Code must post-date the Priestly Source, see Ska, *Reading the Pentateuch*, 152–53. Jeffrey Stackert has argued that the Holiness School redacted Leviticus alone; "The Holiness Legislation and Its Pentateuchal Sources: Revision, Supplementation, and Replacement," in *The Strata of the Priestly Writings: Contemporary Debate and Future Directions* (ed. Sarah Schectman and Joel S. Baden; Zürich: Theologischer Verlag Zürich, 2009), 187–201; "Leviticus," in *The Oxford Encyclopedia of the Books of the Bible* (ed. Coogan; Oxford; New York: Oxford University Press, 2011), 575–78.

5 Weinfeld, *Social Justice*, 231–47; Weinberg, *The Citizen-Temple Community*, 92–104. See also another articulation of the concept, based on Weinfeld, in Joosten, *People and Land in the Holiness Code: An Exegetical Study of the Ideational Framework of the Law in Leviticus 17–26* (Leiden; New York: Brill, 1996), 190. Joosten writes there: "Central to this complex of notions is the conception of the land occupied by the Israelites as temple land. The entire territory settled by the Israelites—ideally the entire land of Canaan—stands under the influence of the divine presence in the earthly sanctuary."

6 As written in Deut 11:12, "It is a land which Yahweh your God looks after, on which Yahweh your God always keeps his eye, from year's beginning to year's end." See Joosten, *People and Land*, 170, 174–75, 201.

7 Bedford, "Economic Role of the Jerusalem Temple," 8*–10*; Boer, *Sacred Economy*, 141–45; Schwartz, "Israel's Holiness: The Torah Traditions," in *Purity and Holiness: The Heritage of Leviticus* (ed. Poorthuis and Schwartz; Leiden; Boston: Brill, 2000), 52–58. As a result of the framing of Israelite settlement as tenancy on Yahweh's land in the Holiness Code, patrimonial land is not referred to there as *naḥălâ* ("inheritance"), as it is elsewhere in the Hebrew Bible, but as *ʾăḥûzzâ* ("holding"). The difference involves one's perspective on the "true" owner of the land. See Milgrom, *Leviticus 23–27: A New Translation with Introduction and Commentary* (New York: Doubleday, 2001), 2171–73; Levine, "Farewell to the Ancient Near East: Evaluating Biblical References to Ownership of Land in Comparative Perspective," in *Privatization in the Ancient Near East* (op. cit.), 223–52.

tithe of their produce to it.⁸ For example, descendants of Judean deportees from Gezer lived on land of the Ebabbar temple in the region of Bir-ili and paid tithes to it.⁹ The framing of Israel's land as Yahweh's, in the manner of a temple estate, spread the message that those residing on the territory were to see themselves as servants of the deity rather than servants of empire.¹⁰ As Jan Joosten put it:

> The Israelites, each of whom has received a holding of landed property, are pictured as asylants having found refuge on temple lands. In consequence, they must honour the divine owner and Lord of the land, through their gifts and through observance of his laws. They must also, as must the resident alien sojourning among them, preserve the purity of the land for fear of polluting the earthly dwelling place of YHWH.¹¹

The responsibilities of tenancy on the deity's land would have continued resonance throughout Judean intellectual history, and the ideological framework has been much discussed by scholars interested in the role of land in biblical theology.¹²

Moshe Weinfeld has noted instances when servants were freed by virtue of transfer to a sanctuary or economic realm of a local deity, such as the liberation by the Babylonian king Bel-ibni (reigned 702–700 BCE) of the town of Sa-Usur-Adad, which had been conquered by the Assyrians. The king gifted the town and its population to the goddess Bakur. That liberation document refers to the town

---

8 Jursa, *Der Tempelzehnt in Babylonien: vom siebenten bis zum dritten Jahrhundert v. Chr* (Münster: Ugarit-Verlag, 1998), esp. 84–90; Driel, *Elusive Silver: In Search of a Role for a Market in an Agrarian Environment. Aspects of Mesopotamia's Society* (Leiden: Nederlands Instituut voor het Nabije Oosten, 2002), 283–85; Bedford, "Economic Role of the Jerusalem Temple," 11*–12*.
9 Jursa, *Aspects of the Economic History of Babylonia*, 329, 359.
10 As Lev 25:55 reads, "For it is to me that the Israelites are servants: they are my servants, whom I freed from the land of Egypt, I Yahweh your God." The comment comes after a series of laws meant to prevent indentured slavery and other forms of harsh labor (Lev 25:39–54).
11 *People and Land*, 198; and for further discussion, see 178–80, 182–85.
12 Davies, *Gospel and the Land*, 24–35; idem, *The Territorial Dimension of Judaism* (Berkeley: University of California Press, 1982), 17–18; Jacob, "Les trois racines d'une théologie de la "terre" dans l'Ancient Testament," *Revue d'histoire et de philosophie religieuses* 55 (1975), 469–80; Brueggemann, *The Land: Place as Gift, Promise, and Challenge in Biblical Faith* (Philadelphia: Fortress Press, 1977), 47–53; Habel, *The Land is Mine*, 36–53; Wright, *God's People in God's Land: Family, Land, and Property in the Old Testament* (Grand Rapids, MI; Exeter, England: W.B. Eerdmans; Paternoster Press, 1990), 10–13; Joosten, *People and Land*, 137–92; Guillaume, *Land and Calendar: The Priestly Document from Genesis 1 to Joshua 18* (New York: T&T Clark, 2009), 102–22; Davis, *Scripture, Culture, and Agriculture: An Agrarian Reading of the Bible* (New York: Cambridge University Press, 2009), 60; Frankel, *The Land of Canaan and the Destiny of Israel: Theologies of Territory in the Hebrew Bible* (Winona Lake, IN: Eisenbrauns, 2011), 10–12, 397.

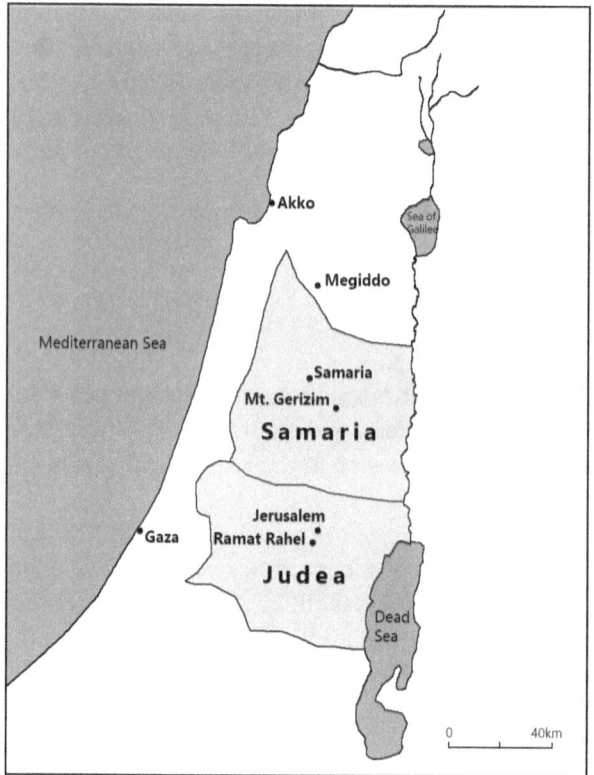

Figure 3. Map of the Persian provinces of Judea and Samaria.

as a holy city and stipulates that its inhabitants are to be exempt from forced labor. A similar pattern emerges in Herodotus' telling of the freedom from tyranny granted to the residents of Samos by Meandrios and their subsequent devotion to Zeus the Liberator (*Histories* 3.142).[13]

The liberation theme in the Holiness Code, with its vision of privileged tenancy on Yahweh's land, is bolstered by farming regulations working in favor of a rural landholding class. Most significant in this regard is the directive that pat-

---

13 *Social Justice*, 110, 233. Weinfeld writes: "Hence, the redemption of the people and its being planted in the holy mountain or the holy inheritance is based upon the model of liberation of the inhabitants from the yoke of kings and their transference to the holy inheritance, where they are subject to divine rule alone. Their land cannot be transferred to others, as they themselves dwell upon it as residents and strangers. It is also impossible to enslave them, as they are servants of God alone; see ibid., 241.

rimonial land should never be permanently alienated from the family. This is achieved through the protection of rights of redemption at any point for sold land (Lev 25:25–28) and through the institution of the Jubilee (25:8–17), which was an automatic release of all encumbrances on property every fifty years. These regulations would have promoted economic liberty while maintaining Judean ethnic ties to land.[14] The call for inalienability meant that land conveyances using the root *mkr* ("sell") in the Holiness Code transferred usufruct temporarily rather than title permanently and thus approximate leases.[15]

Often dismissed as utopian, the Jubilee becomes more practicable once we realize that individual harvests (rather than land title) were sold on this market.[16] A buyer of land would always have kept in mind proximity to the next Jubilee in negotiating the lease, as would a creditor offering a loan against some property, though clauses foregoing any future releases could have been written into loan contracts.[17] The widespread use of such Jubilee-exemption clauses could have quickly rendered the Jubilee irrelevant in Judean society, if it was ever practiced in a significant way. Indeed, in later Second Temple period literature the Jubilee is relegated to the status of a simple chronological unit and ap-

---

[14] On the Jubilee, see Bergsma, *The Jubilee from Leviticus to Qumran: A History of Interpretation* (Leiden; Boston: Brill, 2007); Fager, *Land Tenure and the Biblical Jubilee: Uncovering Hebrew Ethics through the Sociology of Knowledge* (Sheffield: JSOT Press, 1993), 52–63; Weinberg, "Das *bēit 'ābōt*," 400–14; Westbrook, "Redemption of Land," *Israel Law Review* 6 (1971), 367–75; and Rosenberg and Weiss, "Land Concentration, Efficiency, Slavery, and the Jubilee," in *The Oxford Handbook of Judaism and Economics* (ed. Levine; Oxford; New York: Oxford, 2010), 81–82.

[15] Clines, *The Dictionary of Classical Hebrew* (Sheffield: Sheffield Academic Press, 1993), vol. XX: 271 (*mkr*). Rabbinic Hebrew utilizes the roots ḥkr and śkr regularly to connote the renting of property, respecting the distinction between temporary and permanent conveyances in a manner that biblical Hebrew does not. Nevertheless, in ancient Israel and Second Temple Judea the renting of land was commonplace; see Kloppenborg, *Tenants in the Vineyard*, 290–95; Greengus, *Laws in the Bible*, 31–66; and Houston, *Contending for Justice: Ideologies and Theologies of Social Justice in the Old Testament* (London; New York: T&T Clark, 2006), 21–25; see also Borowski, *Agriculture in Iron Age Israel*, 21–26. Permanent sales described in the biblical text can require the notice that the money was paid at full price, as one finds with Abraham's purchase of the land at Machpelah (Gen 23:9), ruling out a temporary sale or gift that could expire for instance upon the death of the seller; see Westbrook and Wells, *Everyday Law*, 14.

[16] For a defense of the practicability of the Jubilee, see Guillaume, *Land, Credit and Crisis*, 247–49; but cf. Fager, *Land Tenure and the Biblical Jubilee*, 34–36. See also Russell, "Biblical Jubilee Laws in Light of Neo-Babylonian and Achaemenid Period Contracts," *Zeitschrift für die Alttestamentliche Wissenschaft* 130, no. 2 (2018), 198–203.

[17] Private contracts did this in anticipation of a possible universal debt-release declared by a newly crowned king, for instance; see Greengus, *Laws in the Bible*, 102. On the existence of such clauses in Neo-Assyrian documents, see Radner, "The Neo-Assyrian Period," in *Security for Debt in Ancient Near Eastern Law* (ed. Westbrook and Jasnow; Leiden: Brill, 2001), 285.

pears not as a functioning socio-economic institution.[18] Regardless of the Jubilee's impact, the Holiness Code's underlying interest in maintaining the bond between a landowning class and its patrimony has parallels throughout the ancient world.[19]

A second practice the Holiness Code adopted in favor of a rural landholding class was to price leases according to individual harvests, always keeping in mind usufruct and proximity to the next Jubilee. As it is put in Lev 25:15–17, "In buying [land] from your neighbor, you shall deduct only for the number of years since the Jubilee; and in selling to you, he shall charge you only for the remaining crop years: the more such years, the higher the price you pay; the fewer such years, the lower the price; for what he is selling you is a number of harvests." This worked to the benefit of an impoverished seller.[20] A landowner who had taken out a loan for seed may have been forced to sell their land in order to cover the loan in the wake of a poor crop year or due to some other reason such as illness, a shortage of labor or livestock, or the effects of war. Such sales under duress may have reduced the price significantly.[21] But the Holiness Code's pricing according to harvest years meant that sales under duress would not be below market value, so that the impoverished seller received more silver for the land than he would have otherwise.

A third practice promoted by the Holiness Code was the land sabbatical, which was a mandatory fallow period of arable land (Lev 25:3–7). It is usually

---

18 Bergsma, *Jubilee from Leviticus to Qumran*, esp. 297, 304.

19 A similar ethic of land-inalienability has been discussed in the Greek context. As Alison Burford has put it: "Land was never on sale enough to become simply a market commodity"; *Land and Labor*, 238, n. 68; Moses Finley has noted that while there were numerous terms for sellers of other things, there is no distinct terminology for the "seller" or the "broker" of land; *Land and Credit*, 270, n. 46. Among the Achaemenid-period priesthood of Borsippa in Babylonia, Caroline Waerzeggers has concluded that the "emotional value attached to the *bīt-abi* [clan] and its inherited property was strong. The patrimony belonging to the *bīt-abi* could consist of movables, real estate, as well as joint ventures, and the use of the term was therefore not restricted to priestly families as such"; see *The Ezida Temple of Borsippa: Priesthood, Cult, Archives* (Leiden: Nederlands Instituut voor het Nabije Oosten, 2010), 82, n. 375. Among the institutions of the priesthood meant to strengthen these ties and regulate economic affairs within the clan was the promotion of redeeming sold properties by members of the larger clan, in a manner reminiscent of Lev 25:23–24; see ibid., 83–97.

20 Wells, "The Quasi-Alien in Leviticus 25," in *The Foreigner and the Law: Perspectives from the Hebrew Bible and the Ancient Near East* (ed. Achenbach et al.; Wiesbaden: Harrassowitz, 2011), 137–38.

21 It is not clear whether family members who buy back ("redeem") the land would have been asked to pay the same reduced price in such a scenario; see Westbrook, *Property and the Family in Biblical law* (Sheffield: Sheffield Academic Press, 1991), 102–7.

understood as a practical response to the overexploitation of farmland, but it could also have been a means of facilitating land reclamation, as Phillippe Guillaume has argued.[22] According to Guillaume, the requirement that farmers cease working their land every seven years would have freed them to participate in major reclamation projects administered by the local authorities. In the period of the return from exile in the sixth century BCE, the considerable logistical challenge of absorbing new immigrants may have been mitigated by the land sabbatical, which freed up agricultural labor every seven years. The Holiness Code's sabbatical law, in other words, masked a kind of imperial corvée.[23]

After presenting these tenancy regulations for Yahweh's land, the Holiness Code ends in Lev 26 with a forceful speech by the deity on the blessings of observing the laws and the curses that will come about by spurning them. Living an unholy life, says the deity, will lead to famine, desolation, and exile. Yahweh will remove his people from the land that he bequeathed to them. He will force upon them dry cropless years as retribution for all the sabbatical years that went unobserved in generations prior, as if they accumulated in the form of a debt to him.[24] "Then the land shall repay its Sabbaths as long as it lays desolate," says the deity in Lev 26:34. If the Holiness Code was authored during the early Persian period, its threat of a future of hardship on the land can be read as ex eventu prophecy describing a reality known all too well to the priests who authored it.

Following the grave soaring rhetoric of Lev 26 is the addendum on valuations, Lev 27, which emphasizes the redeemability of persons, animals, real estate, and commodities devoted to the deity. It is a rather technical compendium of laws, recognized to be a discrete and cohesive document likely originating from the Holiness School too.[25] It offers a rare glimpse into the financial dealings of a priesthood devoted to the proper management of Yahweh's holy coffers and it reflects an economy that was trading widely in silver. It also demonstrates that the priests of Yahweh were involved in the commutation into cash of basic commodities of a Levantine farm and in the appraisal of land itself. While the authors of biblical texts emphasized elsewhere the importance of paying to Yah-

---

22 "פָּרוּ וּרְבוּ and the Seventh Year: Complementary Strategies for the Economic Recovery of Depopulated Yehud," in *Economy of Ancient Judah* (op. cit.), 123–49.
23 Guillaume, *Land, Credit and Crisis*, 234–39.
24 On this latter point, see Anderson, *Sin: A History* (New Haven: Yale University Press, 2009), esp. 75–77.
25 For a detailed discussion of the structure of the Holiness Code, see Milgrom, *Leviticus 17–22*, 1319–25. For an argument on how Lev 27 can be read as a cohesive part of Leviticus, see Douglas, *Leviticus as Literature* (Oxford: Oxford University Press, 1999), 243–44; but cf. Watts, *Ritual and Rhetoric*, 15–27, esp. 22.

weh's priests their due (e.g., Exod 23:16–19, Num 18:8–32, Deut 26:1–11), in Lev 27 the focus is on how things consecrated to Yahweh were valued and most importantly how they could be redeemed. As argued below, Lev 27's close attention to property valuation and redemption, along with the term of the consecration and the weight standard for payment, strongly suggest that the chapter regulated a secured lending operation run by Yahweh's priests, itself meant to bolster the economic standing of Judea's rural landholding class. The chapter also demonstrates that the priests were holding land themselves.

2.2 Consecration of a Patrimonial Field

First Lev 27 sets valuation amounts in the holy shekel for persons vowed to the deity (27:2–7) and establishes a few rules with respect to consecrated animals (27:9–12). Then it turns to real estate, and maintains that houses could be consecrated to the deity and redeemed at the valuation amount with an added fifth (27:14–15). Patrimonial fields could too, in which case the land's value was to be assessed by a priest according to a standard rate of 50 shekels per bushel (homer) of barley seed:

(16) If a person consecrates to Yahweh any of their patrimonial landholding, its valuation[26] shall be in accordance with its seed requirement: fifty shekels of silver to a homer of barley seed. (17) If the person consecrates his field as of the year of the Jubilee, it will transfer ["stand"] according to the valuation; (18) but if he consecrates it after the year of the Jubilee, the priest shall calculate the silver according to the years that are left until the year of the Jubilee and reduce the valuation.

וְאִם מִשְּׂדֵה אֲחֻזָּתוֹ יַקְדִּישׁ אִישׁ לַיהוָה וְהָיָה עֶרְכְּךָ לְפִי זַרְעוֹ זֶרַע חֹמֶר שְׂעֹרִים בַּחֲמִשִּׁים שֶׁקֶל כָּסֶף. אִם מִשְּׁנַת הַיֹּבֵל יַקְדִּישׁ שָׂדֵהוּ כְּעֶרְכְּךָ יָקוּם. וְאִם אַחַר הַיֹּבֵל יַקְדִּישׁ שָׂדֵהוּ וְחִשַּׁב לוֹ הַכֹּהֵן אֶת הַכֶּסֶף עַל פִּי הַשָּׁנִים הַנּוֹתָרֹת עַד שְׁנַת הַיֹּבֵל וְנִגְרַע מֵעֶרְכֶּךָ.

---

26 The second-person possessive pronoun on this word is out of place in a chapter otherwise devoid of second-person discourse. Furthermore, the pronoun does not make grammatical sense on the definite form *hāʿerkĕkā* in Lev 27:24. Speiser's solution, followed by Levine, is that the form with pronominal suffix became fossilized as the standard noun form; "Leviticus and the Critics," in *Yehezkel Kaufmann Jubilee Volume: Studies in Bible and Jewish Religion Dedicated to Yehezkel Kaufmann on the Occasion of His Seventieth Birthday* (ed. Haran; Jerusalem: Magnes Press, 1960), 30; Levine, *Leviticus: The Traditional Hebrew Text with the New JPS Translation* (Philadelphia: Jewish Publication Society, 1989), 30, 193. It is a compelling solution. Another view, put forward by Zorell and followed by Milgrom, is that the word should be vocalized *ʿerkāk*, a noun form that doubles the third radical and is similar to *šaʾănān* ("tranquil") and

According to the traditional understanding of these verses, a landowner with patrimonial title could gift some of his land to the deity. Sanctuary officials would assess the value of the gift, taking a land survey if necessary. They would then put the field up for sale at its valuation. The landowner who donated it could buy it back if he added the one-fifth to the valuation amount. This one-fifth is thought to have been a fine imposed on the dedicant, for desiring the property he had given to the deity. As with all land conveyances described in the Holiness Code, lands donated would automatically revert to the dedicant at the Jubilee. Thus, the value of the donation is a function of the number of harvests left until the next Jubilee. One interested in permanently alienating their land through consecration would need a special workaround. They would sell the field to another and then consecrate it—the consecration taking effect at the next Jubilee. At that point the landowner loses patrimonial title and the land joins the most holy holdings of Yahweh and is disbursed to a priest. Notwithstanding a few minor differences in the interpretation of the details, this is the common understanding of Lev 27:16–21.[27]

However, a close examination of the main concerns of the legislation—land valuation at the benchmark of 50 shekels for a plot requiring 1 homer of barley seed, and redemption rights with the addition of one-fifth in all cases but one—reveal a different set of incentives entirely. Before exploring those ramifications, let us first establish that the valuation process for a plot of land consecrated to the deity was a labor-intensive process for the priest commissioned with the task. It was also one potentially fraught with disputes between the priest and the dedicant.

---

ra'ănān ("fresh"). Zorell's notion is that the Masoretes mistakenly took the final kāp as a second-person masculine singular pronominal suffix, reflective of their tendency to replace older forms of that suffix āk with kā. See Zorell, "Zur Vokalisation des Wortes ערכך in Lev 27 und anderwärts," Biblica 26 (1945), 112–14. Zorell's reading was anticipated by Rashbam; see Milgrom, Leviticus 23–27, 2369–70. But this reading would require a radically different formulation for the final phrase of Lev 27:18, wěnigra' mē'erkekā, with a separable preposition and a noun with the prefixed hā-, giving wěnigra' min-hā'erkāk. Speiser's reading is preferable.

27 Milgrom's commentary is representative; Leviticus 23–27, 2365–436; see also Levine, Leviticus, 192–200; Haran, "'Ărākîm," in Encyclopaedia Biblica (Jerusalem: Bialik Institute, 1971) [Hebrew], 391–94; and Hieke, Levitikus, Zweiter Teilband: 16–27 (Freiburg: Herder, 2014), 1133–34.

2.2.1 The 50-Shekel Valuation Benchmark

According to Lev 27:16, the priest was to use a field's barley-seed requirement to establish its size. This was a common mensuration standard in the ancient Near East for relatively large plots of land; small plots were usually measured by reed or stick.[28] The seed-based system is attested, for example, in a deed of sale from Gezer (649 BCE) and in the Hebrew Bible.[29] It would have been used for fields where barley, wheat, millet, and legumes were cultivated, but likely not for orchards and vineyards.[30] Cultivated plots of that sort are not referenced at all in Lev 27, and it is not clear how an orchard or a vineyard would have been appraised had they been consecrated.

The valuation benchmark of 50 shekels is established in Lev 27:16 for a field requiring 1 homer of barley seed (= 1 kor, 180 – 220 liters). The homer is the largest unit of dry volume attested in biblical and rabbinic sources. The ephah (= bat, $1/10^{th}$ the homer), the seah (= $1/30^{th}$ the homer), the omer (= $1/100^{th}$ the homer), and the qab (= $1/180^{th}$ the homer) are the other known units of volume.[31]

---

[28] At Uruk, for example, any field less than 1,666 – 1,800 square cubits was to be surveyed with a measuring-stick (reed) system; when the field was large enough to justify the use of seed requirement measures, established equivalences of seed capacity and size were then consulted. See Powell, "Late Babylonian Surface Mensuration," *Archiv für Orientforschung* 31 (1984), 32 – 66; Sheldon, "Ancient Seed Mensuration and Leviticus 27:16," in *Leviticus 23 – 27*, 2434 – 36; Ben-David, *Talmudische Ökonomie: die Wirtschaft des jüdischen Palästina zur Zeit der Mischna und des Talmud* (Hildesheim; New York: Georg Olms, 1974), 73 – 80 (esp. 78); Gibson, "Agricultural Land-Management Methods and Implements in Ancient Ereẓ-Israel," in *Encyclopaedia Judaica, Second Edition*, vol. 1 (ed. Skolnik and Berenbaum; Farmington Hills, MI: Thomson Gale, 2006), 473; and Feliks, "Agriculture," ibid., 491. The reed as a means of measuring area is attested prominently in Ezekiel's "Temple Vision" (e.g., 40:3, 5; 41:8). In that Vision arable land is referred to according to cubit measurements rather than seed capacity.

[29] The cuneiform deed of land-sale from Gezer notes the size of the property according to the Neo-Babylonian volume measure of BÁN, though the measure itself is unknown for this particular tablet, as is the price; see Horowitz, Oshima, and Sanders, *Cuneiform in Canaan: Cuneiform Sources from the Land of Israel in Ancient Times* (Jerusalem: Israel Exploration Society and The Hebrew University of Jerusalem, 2006), 58 – 59. In 1 Kgs 18:32, the prophet Elijah's altar on Mt. Carmel is said to have been surrounded by a trench of a size "like a field requiring two seahs of seed."

[30] After the "song of the vineyard," the prophet Isaiah predicts a period of future hardship by noting that "ten acres of vineyard shall yield one bath, and the seed of a homer shall yield an ephah" (5:10). While the prophet gives the orchard an acreage, the size of the cereal field he indicates by its seed capacity.

[31] The rabbinic sages understand the smallest unit of legally significant arable land to require 9 qab, or $1/20^{th}$ of a homer, of seed (*m. Baba Batra* 7:2). See Kletter, "Weights and Measures," in

Of these, the homer, the ephah, and the omer are attested in the priestly sources, and the 50-shekel benchmark is more appropriate for them, given that they are based on a decimal system, than for the sexagecimal seah and the qab. Nevertheless, the seah and the qab may indeed have been utilized locally for land measurement, as Babylonian mathematicians, for instance, could easily move between the decimal and sexagecimal systems in their own calculations.[32]

A field requiring 1 homer of barley seed is called a "bet kor" in rabbinic parlance. It is estimated to have been 75,000 square cubits or 23,000 sq. m. (= 5.7 acres).[33] The more common rabbinic "bet seah" is thought to have been 30 times smaller, at 2,500 square cubits. Based on these estimations, a bet kor can be said to have been twice as large as the basic Mesopotamian land unit of 10,000 cubits, a measure roughly equivalent in size to the Egyptian aroura and the Roman iugerum.[34] It would have been slightly smaller than the average-sized plot in a group of Ebabbar texts of the Neo-Babylonian period used to establish rent payments.[35] And it is also just below what Arye Ben-David's calculates as the size of a typical farm in Roman Palestine.[36] It is not clear how the bet kor compared with the sūtu "of the land of Judah," which is a Judean measure for land area referenced in Assyrian sources.[37]

Priests commissioned with appraising land consecrated to the deity would have needed to reckon up and down according to field size and capacity. The relatively large size of the bet kor shows that the 50-shekel benchmark provided in Lev 27 required more top-down rather than bottom-up adjustments. The smaller equivalences of 5 shekels per ephah and 0.5 shekels per omer may have been the more commonly used as the priest adapted the benchmark to realities on the ground. We can get a sense of these challenges by examining much older cuneiform texts. A Neo-Sumerian field-plan text (Ur III, 21st–20th century BCE) is inscribed with a detailed sketch of a field on the obverse and a brief summary on the

---

The New Interpreter's Dictionary of the Bible (ed. Sakenfeld; Nashville: Abingdon Press, 2009), 835–37; and Gibson, "Agricultural Land-Management Methods," 472–74.
32 Powell, "Surface Mensuration," 38–40.
33 Ben-David, *Talmudische Ökonomie*, 73–80 (esp. 78); Gibson, "Agricultural Land-Management Methods," 473; Feliks, "Agriculture," 491.
34 Powell, "Surface Mensuration," 64.
35 I.e., the so-called imittu texts, where the plots average 27,500 sq. m (= 6.8 acres); see Jursa, *Aspects of the Economic History of Babylonia*, 348–50.
36 *Talmudische Ökonomie*, 135–41.
37 Postgate, *Fifty Neo-Assyrian Legal Documents* (Warminster: Aris & Phillips, 1976), 67–68.

reverse.³⁸ The surveyor in this instance utilized a standard field area in the shape of a trapezoid, subtracted from it that of a small triangular plot, and added to it that of a small rectangular plot and three other triangular ones in order to arrive at the closest approximation possible. Establishing the initial seed-requirement benchmarks was also complicated. Cuneiform texts with mathematical problems demonstrate the convoluted nature of the calculations.³⁹ Surveyors producing square-cubit measurements for quadrangular or triangular areas needed to take into account interval-width for furrows, the possibility of a faulty or broken measuring stick, and conversions of reed measurements into seed measurements, among other things. These mathematical exercises had real-world ramifications—affecting taxation or rent payments to temples, for instance. But they were often undertaken merely as a part of the temple-based scribal training process.

Perhaps similar exercises were introduced into the guild of the Yahwistic priesthood. In the very least we can point to the introduction of mathematical exercises into the region by the Late Bronze Age, as one tablet from Hazor attests.⁴⁰ One wonders if the land surveyors of the Yahwistic priesthood, who were schooled in the Holiness Code, would have in their assessment of land value taken into account that code's law of *pē'âh* (Lev 19:9, 23:22), which required the corners of fields to be left unharvested as an offering to the poor. This would have further complicated their efforts at assigning value to a field.

The priests' valuation may also have been disputed by the dedicant. To be sure, the use of fixed valuation standards for land would have reduced the number of such disputes.⁴¹ But as we have seen, establishing land area was not straightforward. One might also expect valuation standards to have been manipulated on an ad hoc basis for land of poor quality or for land exhibiting unusual characteristics. There are other cases in Lev 27 where the priest was expected to use their own judgment in property appraisal: the consecrated house (Lev 27:14) and the human consecration that is below market value (Lev 27:8).⁴² Dedicants

---

38 Friberg, *A Remarkable Collection of Babylonian Mathematical Texts. Manuscripts in the Schøyen Collection. Cuneiform Texts I* (New York; London: Springer, 2007), 137–140 (MS 1984); see also 140–46 (MS 1850 and others).
39 Nemet-Nejat, *Cuneiform Mathematical Texts as a Reflection of Everyday Life in Mesopotamia* (New Haven: American Oriental Society, 1993), 72–78.
40 Horowitz, "A Combined Multiplication Table on a Prism Fragment from Hazor," *IEJ* 47, no. 3/4 (1997), 190–97; Horowitz, Oshima, and Sanders, *Cuneiform in Canaan*, 78–80.
41 Sharfman, "Valuation in Jewish Law," in *The Oxford Handbook of Judaism and Economics* (ed. Levine; Oxford; New York: Oxford, 2010), 170.
42 Jacques Berlinerblau has noted that while the prices in Lev 27:2–7 are fixed, "this does not threaten the notion of autonomous regulation of content." He continues, "Insofar as this pas-

who disputed the validity of the priest's effort may have requested second or third appraisals. Thus, from the perspective of the priest, property appraisal for a consecration could have been a duty that required care and experience.

For a field requiring one homer of barley seed, which we estimate to have been the relatively large size of around 5.7 acres, the valuation would have resulted in a very large shekel value. After all, the official valuation thus sought to put a number on a half-century of cereal cultivation. As Lev 27:17–18 indicates, the sum quoted by the priest would have been for the total harvests in a Jubilee cycle. But does the standard of 50 shekels of silver mentioned in Lev 27:16 make sense as a value on that? Most assume that it does, perhaps because at first blush the verse would appear to be saying as much.[43] They would have the priest appraise a field that size at 50 shekels if consecrated at the Jubilee, 49 shekels if consecrated one year after the Jubilee, 48 shekels if two years after, and so on.

Yet this common view, whereby the 50 shekels are seen as a valuation of all the harvests in a Jubilee cycle, is problematic. Most significantly, such a weight in shekels would result in annual sums that are unmanageable in the local currency. This was a period before the introduction of coinage (a process that began only in the fifth century BCE), when money consisted of bullion or small pieces of hack-silver that were carried around and weighed out in bundles according to set standards and denominations.[44] The gerah, weighing about 0.55 gr (or less than a quarter of the weight of a single dime), appears to have been the smallest unit of local currency, and it would remain so for centuries.[45] The most common unit was the shekel. According to Lev 27:25, one "holy shekel" was equivalent to 20 gerahs. (Another shekel standard, which was 20% heavier, will be discussed below.) Given the 7 sabbatical cycles with 6 harvests each in a Jubilee, there would have been 42 cereal harvests in a Jubilee cycle. Divisibility into single harvests is called for explicitly by Lev 27:18. Yet the priest carrying out the valuation would not have been able to divide 50 shekels—or the 1,000 gerahs it comprised

---

sage knows of different items which are originally vowed and *later* (that is, at the time of payment) converted to the fixed equivalent, it still seems likely that when formulating their petitions supplicants were naming their own terms"; *The Vow and the 'Popular Religious Groups' of Ancient Israel* (Sheffield: Sheffield Academic Press, 1996), 116–17, n. 4 (quote).

43 Noth, *Leviticus: A Commentary* (Philadelphia: The Westminster Press, 1977), 206, though he does express reservations; Wenham, *The Book of Leviticus* (Grand Rapids, MI: William B. Eerdmans, 1979), 340; Milgrom, *Leviticus 23–27*, 2383.

44 For the bundling of silver pieces in the hand or in pouches in this period, see Deut 14:24–26.

45 The miniscule Yehud coins of the late Persian and early Hellenistic period carry a similar weight in bronze; see Barag, "The Coinage of Yehud and the Ptolemies," *INJ* 13 (1999), 27–38.

—into 42 harvests without having to round the resulting sum to the nearest integer. The redemption cost too would result in fractions of gerahs. Adding one-fifth to a 50-shekel valuation gives 60 shekels or 1,200 gerahs. Neither sum is divisible by 42. If the text's prototype does not work numerically, how would less clean-cut cases, for fields of variable sizes and consecration periods of variable lengths, have been appraised?

A preferable solution is to read the 50-shekel benchmark of Lev 27:16 as referencing not the value of the 42 harvests of the Jubilee but that of a single harvest. As explored below, this is a workable benchmark in the shekel weight metrologies, and it is serviceable for smaller land areas and for redemption payments including the one-fifth. It also makes sense with what we know of land value from texts in the Hebrew Bible.[46] One such text is the purchase by David of the threshing floor of Arauna in Jerusalem (2 Sam 24:18–23). Along with oxen for sacrifice, David buys the floor for a price of 50 shekels of silver. The exact same sum, according to the conventional understanding of Lev 27:16, would buy one the usufruct of a 5.7-acre field for 42 years![47] One is hard pressed to view this as in any way equivalent, in terms of economic value, to what David was purchasing. Yet if we view Lev 27:16 as referencing a single harvest, the equivalencies begin to make sense.

Another such text is Abraham's purchase from Ephron of the plot at Machpelah for the burial of Sarah (Gen 23:3–20). The purchase is carried out for a price of 400 shekels of silver and is meant to confer title, hence Abraham's insistence that the full price be paid. This would have prevented vindication by Ephron's heirs upon his death, cementing the permanence of the conveyance.[48] "A piece of land worth four hundred shekels of silver," Ephron says to Abraham in Gen 23:15, "what is that between you and me? Go and bury your dead." The statement makes sense if 400 shekels were perceived as a relatively low price for land title. Perhaps it was a small parcel or was of poor quality. To be sure, Abraham wanted it not for cultivation but because it included a cave suitable

---

46 For a discussion of land sales in the Hebrew Bible, see Altmann, *Economics in Persian-Period Biblical Texts*, 61–65.

47 It may have seemed a modest sum indeed in the eyes of the Chronicler, who quotes David's payment at the exorbitant amount of 600 shekels of gold (1 Chr 21:25), presumably to stress the cosmic significance of the threshing floor as the future site of the temple.

48 Many extant land-sale contracts contained a vindication or perpetuity clause to prevent just this scenario with regard to sales; see Van der Spek, "Land Ownership in Babylonian Cuneiform Documents," in *Legal Documents of the Hellenistic World. Papers from a Seminar arranged by the Institute of Classical Studies, the Institute of Jewish Studies and the Warburg Institute, University of London, February to May 1986* (ed. Geller and Maehler; London: The Warburg Institute, University of London, 1995), 176–77; and Westbrook and Wells, *Everyday Law*, 14, 110.

for burial. In this case we have the title of a non-productive plot valued at 400 shekels. In the case of Lev 27:16, if we assume the 50-shekel benchmark applies to a single harvest, we would have 42 harvests of a large field valued at 2,100 shekels.

A third relevant text is the most detailed description of a land sale in the Hebrew Bible—the story of the prophet Jeremiah being called upon to exercise his right of redemption for a field owned by his cousin Hanamel (Jer 32:6–15). Jeremiah follows through with the redemption for a price of 17 shekels of silver, writing the deed itself, sealing it with witnesses, and weighing out the silver on a scale. We are not told the size of the field or which crop was cultivated there. While one could understand this 17 shekels to have been for the title to the land, an interesting interpretation of the sale by Lisbeth Fried and David Noel Freedman posits that it took place in the middle of a Jubilee year—that is, 588/7 BCE—and that the 17 shekels were meant to cover the partial-year usufruct before the automatic redistribution of the land to the patrimonial titleholder at the termination of the Jubilee.[49] If such a reading holds, the price of 17 shekels for partial-year usufruct, which is to say no more than a single harvest, would be correspond well with a 50-shekel valuation for a single harvest of a relatively large field. If Hanamel's plot were a large tract of land, thus amplifying the righteousness of Jeremiah's deed, one would expect some mention to have been made of that in the text.[50]

---

49 "Was the Jubilee Year Observed in Preexilic Judah?," in *Leviticus 23–27: A New Translation with Introduction and Commentary* (ed. Milgrom; New York: Doubleday, 2001), 2257–71. The evidence in favor of the argument involves the notice in Jer 34:6–10 that Zedekiah carried out a mass manumission of slaves in this year, as well as the anecdote mentioned in 37:12 that Jeremiah took considerable risks to go to his hometown of Anatoth to participate in the distribution of landed property. But cf. Bergsma, *Jubilee from Leviticus to Qumran*, 158–60.
50 Implied in the account is the exceptionality of Jeremiah's act of redemption, as if under normal circumstances those with rights of redemption would have passed on the opportunity. It takes a special divine communication to convince Jeremiah to move forward with the transaction (32:6–7), and once it is completed, he treats it as an act with symbolic weight, portending the future redemption of the land after the people's punishment is carried out (32:15).

2.2.2 Field Redemption

(19) If the dedicant redeems the field, he shall add to it one-fifth of the silver of the valuation and it shall transfer to ["stand for"] him.

וְאִם־גָּאֹל יִגְאַל אֶת־הַשָּׂדֶה הַמַּקְדִּישׁ אֹתוֹ וְיָסַף חֲמִשִׁית כֶּסֶף־עֶרְכְּךָ עָלָיו וְקָם לוֹ׃

This is but one instance of several in the chapter (27:13, 15, 27, 31) where redemption rights are protected for the dedicant but come with the required payment of an additional one-fifth on top of the valuation amount. According to the early rabbis, the act of redemption occurred in the context of a sale run by the temple authorities, who were thought to have regularly put consecrated property, which they called hekdesh, up for auction. In one teaching, the rabbis have a bidding war taking place for consecrated fields (m. 'Arakin 8:1–3). The dedicant opens the bidding, helps drive up the price, and eventually wins the auction for an amount vastly exceeding the valuation. The original land consecration becomes in the rabbinic imagination an occasion for a sanctuary fundraiser.[51]

Milgrom follows the rabbis' assumption that the temple regularly sold properties consecrated to the deity. He writes:

> He who redeems his own property from the sanctuary pays a 20 percent fine, but if it is purchased by someone else no fine is involved. The distinction between redeemer and purchaser is perhaps based on the premise that the owner might be so attached to his property that he will have second thoughts about having dedicated it. Endless and fruitless bookkeeping would devolve on the temple staff, not to speak of the slight to Yahweh implied by such frivolity. The purchaser, though, has no emotional attachment to the property (it belonged to another); his purchase is a pure business transaction, which is precisely what the Temple intended when it put up the property for sale.[52]

He is describing endowment effect or divestiture aversion. According to this principle, persons tend to overvalue property once they have owned it. The priests of Yahweh were aware of this, his explanation assumes, and charged an added fee to take advantage of a dedicant's strong attachment to their property.[53] Related to

---

[51] The appraisal sets the price of the auction; for further discussion on these rabbinic texts and others similar to it, see §5.2.1.

[52] *Leviticus 23–27*, 2379 and see there for references in earlier Jewish commentary, working along similar lines.

[53] Sharfman, "Valuation in Jewish Law," 168–81, esp. 179. Note Sharfman's suggestion for the appearance of the redemption fee: as compensation for the underrepresentation of temple interests in the valuation process. The suggestion is based on the ordinance in *m. Sanhedrin* 1:3 that valuation panels for movables consist of three individuals with at least one priest present and that for land there be ten individuals on the valuation panel, one of whom will be a priest (in

this idea is the interpretation that the one-fifth supplement was meant to discourage anyone from grumbling against what they perceived to be a low valuation and reneging on the consecration as a result.[54]

Milgrom's mention of the "slight to God implied by such frivolity" alludes to Philo of Alexandria's understanding of the redemption surcharge. Philo called it a penalty for the dedicant's "lust of possession" in wishing to regain what he had given over to the priest (*Spec. Laws* 2.37). His understanding resurfaces in Rashi, John Calvin, and elsewhere.[55] It stems, one can assume, from the appearance of the same one-fifth that was charged for the misappropriation of sacred property in Lev 5:16 and for fraud with deposits and pledges in Lev 5:24. In these cases the one-fifth is added as part of the terms of restitution. In Lev 27 too one could be tempted to interpret the surcharge as a penalty imposed by Yahweh's priests.

With these explanations in mind, one must ask: If the one-fifth were waived for any buyer other than the dedicant, as both of these explanations have it, could a third party not buy the property at the valuation and sell it to the dedicant for an amount under the sum of the valuation plus one-fifth, keeping the difference? And for that matter, why should we assume that the priests were in fact opening the sale of consecrations up to persons other than the dedicant? According to biblical property law, purchase of a sold or otherwise encumbered patrimonial field was limited to the holder of patrimonial title or to some member of their kinship group who acted as redeemer on their behalf.[56] This is assumed by the Holiness Code's laws regarding sold patrimonial land (Lev 25:25–28).

In those laws, the purchaser must enable the seller or the seller's "nearest redeemer" to purchase the property at the sale cost. If the seller or his kinsman cannot come up with that sum, then the next Jubilee will bring about the redemption by default. Similarly, in the story where Jeremiah redeems the land that his cousin Hanamel had sold (mentioned above), other relatives had turned down the right of redemption and Jeremiah answers the call to act as redeemer

---

acknowledgment of the fact that Lev 27 has a "priest" making the valuation). However, this ordinance seems to be a clear-cut example of the rabbinic tendency to insert themselves anachronistically into temple operations that were managed by priests; see §5.1.

54 Gerstenberger, *Leviticus: A Commentary* (Louisville: Westminster John Knox Press, 1996), 443; Wenham, *Leviticus*, 337.
55 Rashi writes in his comment on Lev 27:13 that "scripture is stringent in requiring the fifth for owners," a view followed by Bula, *Sefer Vayikra* (Jerusalem: Mosad ha-Rav Kook, 1992) [Hebrew], 251; Levine, *Leviticus*, 194; and Milgrom, *Leviticus 23–27*, 2382. For a summary of Calvin's view, see Elliott, *Engaging Leviticus: Reading Leviticus Theologically with Its Past Interpreters* (Eugene, OR: Cascade Books, 2012), 306.
56 Milgrom, *Leviticus 23–27*, 2183–91; Fager, *Land Tenure and the Biblical Jubilee*, 93–94; Westbrook, "Redemption of Land," 369–70.

and to purchase the field (Jer 32:7). In other words, special measures were taken in this society to keep patrimonial land within the kinship group, and redemption rights were strictly protected. The wording of Lev 27:15 and 19 has the dedicant named explicitly as subject when the one-fifth supplement is described—not to exclude everyone else from having to pay that supplement, but to spell out the switch in subject from that of the previous verse, where the subject is the priest. It seems far more likely, given what we know of the ideology behind the Holiness Code and of Judean property law in general, that any transaction alienating a consecrated property from Yahweh's holdings could only be initiated by the dedicant or one acting as redeemer on his behalf; that it was and only could be an act of redemption, rather than a purchase; and that this act of redemption always cost the valuation amount plus one-fifth.

If the one-fifth was always charged, why did it exist? To answer this question, one must turn again to currency standards. The silver rarely survives on archaeological record, but the scale weights used to measure it and other commodities often do. In fact, a large corpus of scale weights in limestone, from sites within the kingdom of Judah in the late Iron Age, has survived and has been studied by Raz Kletter.[57] He demonstrates that the common shekel standard for the kingdom in that period weighed about 11.33 gr. The various denominations of the weights indicate a common unit of roughly 0.55 gr, which is identifiable as a single gerah and the smallest unit of currency in the system. As a result, Kletter could conclude that the common shekel equaled 24 gerahs.[58] This helps us appreciate the force behind the statement in Lev 27:25 that "every valuation shall be by the holy shekel: 20 gerahs shall make a shekel." It rules out the use of the common shekel standard for use in the valuation of consecrations.[59]

---

[57] *Economic Keystones: The Weight System of the Kingdom of Judah* (Sheffield: Sheffield Academic Press, 1998).
[58] Ibid., 70–84, 101–2; idem, "Weights and Measures," 835; Hendin, *Ancient Scale Weights and Pre-Coinage Currency of the Near East* (New York: Amphora, 2007), 80–86. For various biblical references to these shekel standards, see Exod 30:13–16; Num 3:47, 18:16; Ezek 45:12. In addition to the common shekel standard, we know of the *beqaʿ* (half of a common shekel), the *pym* (2/3rd of a common shekel), the *nsf* (5/6th of a common shekel), the *mina* (= *māneh*; 50 common shekels), and the *kikār* (3,000 common shekels). For archaeological evidence suggesting that the Judean mina was indeed 50 shekels rather than 60 (as was common in Mesopotamia), see Kletter and Beit-Arieh, "A Heavy Scale Weight from Tel Malhata and the Maneh (Mina) of Judah," in *Ugarit-Forschungen. Internationales Jahrbuch für die Altertumskunde Syrien-Palästinas, Band 33* (ed. Dietrich and Loretz; Münster: Ugarit-Verlag, 2001), 245–61.
[59] Scale weights on archaeological record bearing the inscription *nṣp* ("half") weigh roughly 5/6ths of the ordinary shekel and thus equal the 20-gerah holy standard; see Kletter, *Economic*

Figure 4. Judahite stone scale weights in various denominations. Courtesy of the Israel Antiquities Authority. Photo: Miki Koren.

The chronological disparity between the literary and archaeological sources of evidence for these two weight systems should not preclude contemporaneity.[60] The differential between the holy standard and the common probably continued well into the post-exilic era. Long-standing local market practices do not disappear with a single war, devastating as the Babylonian conquest may have been. Nor was the introduction of coinage into Judea a particularly rapid process, and once coins began circulating, they appear to have been based on the gerah rather than the obol.[61] What changed was that scale weights ceased to

---

Keystones, 140–41; see also Fox, *In the Service of the King: Officialdom in Ancient Israel and Judah* (Cincinnati: Hebrew Union College Press, 2000), 265.
60 After all, the Holiness Code of the sixth century BCE (with its 20-gerah holy shekel) and the assemblage of stone scale weights primarily of the seventh century BCE (with its 24-gerah standard) are not contemporaneous sources of evidence. On the dating of the Holiness Code, see §2.1; on the dating of the scale weights, see Kletter, *Economic Keystones*, 42–43. As Kletter explains, stone scale weights of the sixth century BCE are most likely heirlooms.
61 On the introduction of coinage into the region, see Mildenberg, "On the Money Circulation in Palestine from Artaxerxes II till Ptolemy I. Preliminary Studies of the Local Coinage in the Fifth Persian Satrapy," *Transeuphratène*, no. 7 (1994), 63–71; and Fantalkin and Tal, "The Canonization of the Pentateuch: When and Why?," *Zeitschrift für die Alttestamentliche Wissenschaft* 124,

be produced in stone. (Incidentally, stone would be utilized again in the Jerusalem markets in the first centuries BCE and CE, possibly in a nostalgic embrace of the Iron Age custom.[62]) From the sixth century BCE onward local weights would probably have been manufactured again in metal, the far more common material used for scale weights and one more easily recyclable, often significantly reducing preservation frequency. Unfortunately, archaeology offers us very little on the weight standards in use in the Judean markets between the stone scale weights of the late Iron Age and the cast-lead weights of the Hellenistic period.[63]

As I have argued elsewhere, the coexistence of two shekel standards at the time Lev 27 was written is the key to understanding the one-fifth surcharge.[64] It is the difference in weight between the lighter holy shekel and the heavier common shekel. The ramifications of this observation can be broken down into three main points:

(1) A valuation in holy shekels listed a silver weight that was one-fifth (20%) lighter than that same number of common shekels. The valuation or "list price" could be brought in line with market price only by the addition of one-fifth at redemption.

To illustrate this point, let us assume that a firstborn donkey (as would be relevant to Lev 27:27) carried a valuation of 10 holy shekels (= 200 gerahs). In such a case the donkey could be commuted to silver in two ways: one, through redemption at its valuation weight plus one-fifth, at a total cost of 240 gerahs; or two, through sale at market in the same shekel weight but using the market standard of 24 gerahs per shekel, also giving a total cost of 240 gerahs. In either case the animal carries the "same" price of 10 shekels. This can explain the rather odd formulation of Lev 27:27 on the redemption of the firstborn animal: "If it is an unclean animal, they can ransom [it] at its valuation, and they shall add one fifth to it; if it is not redeemed, it shall be sold at its valuation." That sale we assume happened at the local markets, which utilized the common shekel standard.

---

no. 1 (2012), 1–18, 15–16. On the continued use of the gerah rather than the obol as a standard, see Altmann, *Economics in Persian-Period Biblical Texts*, 168–73.

62 Reich, "Stone Scale Weights of the Late Second Temple Period from the Jewish Quarter," in *Jewish Quarter Excavations in the Old City of Jerusalem* (ed. Geva; Jerusalem: Israel Exploration Society, 2006), 329–89.

63 Hendin, *Ancient Scale Weights*, 91–93.

64 Gordon, "The Misunderstood Redemption Fee in the Holiness Legislation on Dedications (Lev 27)," *Zeitschrift für die alttestamentliche Wissenschaft* 126, no. 2 (2014), 180–92.

Table 1. Valuations of a field according to three standard sizes, as based on the 50-shekel benchmark given in Lev 27:16. These silver amounts assume a valuation standard for a single harvest, as well as redemption payments in the common shekel. The entire valuation system seems to be based on the standard of 1 gerah per omer per month.

Seed Capacity (Field Size)	Valuation		Redemption Cost		
	Holy Shekel, annual	Gerah, annual	Common shekel (holy shekel), annual	Gerah, annual	Gerah, monthly
1 homer (≈23000 sq. m.)	50	1000	50 (60)	1200	100
1 ephah (≈2300 sq. m.)	5	100	5 (6)	120	10
1 omer (≈230 sq. m.)	0.5	10	0.5 (0.6)	12	1

In addition to silver valuations for standard field sizes based on seed capacity, the priests must have kept running commodity lists of valuations for animals and other farm products, which could be consulted for the redemption of the firstborn and the tithes. Commodity lists of this sort have been documented elsewhere in the ancient Near East.[65] Restitution payments too may have been based on commodity lists. Wronged parties would have needed to be paid an additional fifth in order to be fully compensated at market value, which can explain why the one-fifth supplement appears in damages cases that were officiated by priests (Lev 5:16, 24).

(2) The 50-shekel benchmark of Lev 27:16 is serviceable for redemption payments in installments in the common shekel standard. It results in workable cash-in values on an annual or even a monthly basis, in both common shekels and gerahs, for the three main seed capacities (= units for land area) attested in the priestly sources, as shown on Table 1. This assumes that the 50-shekel benchmark applied to a single harvest, as argued in the above section. An amortization schedule kept by priests could have helped in the calculation of redemption cost

---

65 Oppenheim, "A Fiscal Practice of the Ancient Near East," *JNES* 6, no. 2 (1947), 116–20. On aspects of the accounting system in biblical Israel in Near Eastern perspective, see Levine, "Tracing the Biblical Accounting Register: Terminology and the Significance of Quantity," in *Commerce and Monetary Systems in the Ancient World: Means of Transmission and Cultural Interaction* (ed. Roillinger and Ulf; Stuttgart: Franz Steiner, 2004), 420–43.

in any month or year within the duration of the encumbrance, as hinted at by the wording of Lev 27:17–18. That cost approached zero as the Jubilee approached.[66]

The neatness of the system for both maximum and minimum land mensuration units is striking. It results in the tidy redemption rate of 1 mina (= 50 shekels) per homer per year on one end of the spectrum, and of 1 gerah per omer per month on the other. This latter feature is more significant because it suggests that this pricing benchmark was designed to be convenient and adaptable. The gerah was the smallest unit of money, while the omer was the smallest for land, at least based on the priestly source material. As a seed-based mensuration unit for land area, the omer is estimated to have resulted in a plot measuring 15 m per side.[67] The redemption cost of 12 gerahs pieces for a plot this size has the advantage of being divisible into monthly portions of one gerah each, allowing for small valuation adjustments to ensure that repayments in installments were workable in the local weight measurements. (Even still, we would expect partial redemption payments to have usually come in at harvest.[68]) A preference for nicely rounded numbers when silver equivalences were given for land and other commodities has been observed in other regions of the ancient world.[69] The advantages for simplifying transactions and bookkeeping may have outweighed any compulsion to arrive at absolute value.

---

66 On this technical aspect of the Jubilee as the date at which all Judean sales expired and all loans reached maturity; see Guillaume, *Land, Credit and Crisis*, 247–49.

67 Ben-David, *Talmudische Ökonomie*, 78. The Holiness Code stipulates that a measure of grain weighing an omer should be brought as a kind of "first sheaf" offering to Yahweh during the festival of Passover, the main barley-harvest festival (Lev 23:10–15). While the rabbinic qab is even smaller than the omer, the qab is mentioned in the Hebrew Bible only in 2 Kgs 6:25 and thus is absent from the priestly sources.

68 On harvest-time payments, see Greengus, *Laws in the Bible*, 105.

69 We find this tendency also in interest calculations, with the rate of 1 shekel per mina per month in Mesopotamia (where 1 mina=60 shekels) and of 1 drachma per mina per month in ancient Greece. Michael Hudson has argued that interest rates in the ancient world were set based on what the smallest unit fraction was in the society's fractional number systems; see "How Interest Rates Were Set, 2500 BC–1000 AD," *JESHO* 43, no. 2 (2000), 132–61. The preference for nicely rounded numbers is also evidenced for instance in date prices set by the Ebabbar temple at Sippar in Babylon, as Michael Jursa has discussed; *Aspects of the Economic History of Babylonia*, 449. On the creation of the 360-year day for record-keeping purposes in ancient Mesopotamia, see Goetzmann, *Money Changes Everything: How Finance Made Civilization Possible* (Princeton, NJ: Princeton University Press, 2016), 28–29. For standardized prices in land auctions at Athens, see *Rationes Centesimarum: Sales of Public Land in Lykourgan Athens* (Amsterdam: J.C. Gieben, 1997), 262–65; and Burford, *Land and Labor*, 80.

Table 2. Standard valuations for a field according to three units of area over a single sabbatical cycle, as based on the 50-shekel benchmark given in Lev 27:16.

Harvests to Jubilee	Seed Capacity	Valuation		Redemption Cost	
		Holy Shekel	Gerah	Common shekel (holy shekel)	Gerah
6	1 homer	300	6000	300 (360)	7200
	1 ephah	30	600	30 (36)	720
	1 omer	3	60	3 (3.6)	72
5	1 homer	250	5000	250 (300)	6000
	1 ephah	25	500	25 (30)	600
	1 omer	2.5	50	2.5 (3)	60
4	1 homer	200	4000	200 (240)	4800
	1 ephah	20	400	20 (24)	480
	1 omer	2.0	40	2 (2.4)	48
3	1 homer	150	3000	150 (180)	3600
	1 ephah	15	300	15 (18)	360
	1 omer	1.5	30	1.5 (1.8)	36
2	1 homer	100	2000	100 (120)	2400
	1 ephah	10	200	10 (12)	240
	1 omer	1.0	20	1 (1.2)	24
1	1 homer	50	1000	50 (60)	1200
	1 ephah	5	100	5 (6)	120
	1 omer	0.5	10	0.5 (0.6)	12

Tables 2 and 3 show standard valuations for fields in three standard sizes, according to the benchmark provided in Lev 27:16. The neatness of the resulting numbers is striking, whether for valuations or for redemption costs.

(3) The same 50-shekel benchmark happens to work very well with the shekel amounts given for the valuation of humans in Lev 27:3–7. According to the traditional interpretation of those verses, a person wishing to dedicate themselves or one of their dependents to Yahweh would make a vow declaring that intention and then be asked to pay the fixed valuation for the dedicated person's gender

Table 3. Standard valuations for a field according to three units of area over seven sabbatical cycles. The table continues the schedule of Table 2 in abbreviated form, giving only valuations and redemption costs for the sixth year of each sabbatical cycle.

Harvests to Jubilee	Sabbatical Cycle	Seed Capacity	Valuation		Redemption Cost	
			Holy Shekel	Gerah	Common shekel (holy shekel)	Gerah
42	1	1 homer	2100	42000	2100 (2520)	50400
		1 ephah	210	4200	210 (252)	5040
		1 omer	21	420	21 (25.2)	504
36	2	1 homer	1800	36000	1800 (2160)	43200
		1 ephah	180	3600	180 (216)	4320
		1 omer	18	360	18 (21.6)	432
30	3	1 homer	1500	30000	1500 (1800)	36000
		1 ephah	150	3000	150 (180)	3600
		1 omer	15	300	15 (18)	360
24	4	1 homer	1200	24000	1200 (1440)	28800
		1 ephah	120	2400	120 (144)	2880
		1 omer	12	240	12 (14.4)	288
18	5	1 homer	900	18000	900 (10805)	21600
		1 ephah	90	1800	90 (108)	2160
		1 omer	9	180	9 (10.8)	216
12	6	1 homer	600	12000	600 (720)	14400
		1 ephah	60	1200	60 (72)	1440
		1 omer	6	120	6 (7.2)	144
6	7	1 homer	300	6000	300 (360)	7200
		1 ephah	30	600	30 (36)	720
		1 omer	3	60	3 (3.6)	72

and age.⁷⁰ The verses give eight valuations for men and women in four age groups, the maximum value of 50 shekels applying to a male, 20–60 years old; the minimum value of 3 shekels, to a female, 1 month–5 years old. If one could not afford that sum, the priest would lower the amount, as stipulated in Lev 27:8. This type of "valuation of persons" dedication is known to have been practiced in Judea and elsewhere in the Near East.⁷¹ It probably developed out of the older custom of consecrating an individual to Yahweh for a lifetime of service at a shrine or sanctuary, or possibly for sacrifice on an altar.⁷² At some point the priests of Yahweh began calling for a sum of money to be gifted instead of the person. In some cases these consecrations were made as the result of a conditional vow made to the deity.⁷³

However, the common understanding that Lev 27:3–7 regulates "valuation of persons" dedications is based on what appears to be a corruption in the Masoretic Text, as shown by the Paleo-Hebrew Leviticus Scroll (11QpaleoLev) from Qumran. The corruption masks the fact that the dedicated persons in Lev 27:3–7

---

70 Commentators reaching back as far as Philo of Alexandria (*Spec. Laws* 2.34) and Flavius Josephus (*Ant.* 4.73) in the first century CE read the valuations schedule of Lev 27:3–8 as regulating just this type of monetary dedication, as do the rabbinic sages. The latter would devote an entire tractate of commentary in the Talmud to the topic (*ʿArakin*, "Valuations").

71 A historical account on the reform of sanctuary finances under King Jehoash of Judah mentions "the money for which each person is valued—the money from the valuation of persons" (2 Kgs 12:4). The Damascus Document refers to the "money of the valuation for the purposes of redeeming their soul" as one of the perquisites of priests (4Q270 2ii), in continuation of the tradition mentioned in 2 Kgs 12:4 and suggesting that at some point these "valuation of persons" dedications were conceived as necessary payments to save one's soul. The Mishnah notes that "Once the mother of Yurmatia said, 'I vow my daughter's weight,' and she went up to Jerusalem and weighed her and paid her weight in gold" (*m. ʿArakin* 5:1); and see Milgrom, *Leviticus 23–27*, 2411.

72 A late Iron Age bronze ringlet from Tel en-Nasbeh (12 km north of Jerusalem) commemorates a father's donation of his son to an unknown deity; see Horowitz, Oshima, and Sanders, *Cuneiform in Canaan*, 110. The prophet Samuel's rise to prominence resulted from his mother dedicating him to a life of service to God should she carry him through to term (1 Sam 1:11).

73 Haran, "ʿĀrākîm," 391–94; Cartledge, *Vows in the Hebrew Bible and the Ancient Near East* (Sheffield: JSOT Press, 1992), 52–53; Gudme, *Before the God in This Place for Good Remembrance: A Comparative Analysis of the Aramaic Votive Inscriptions from Mount Gerizim* (Berlin: De Gruyter, 2013), 42. In an earlier period, an individual could have been vowed to be sacrificed should the deity answer a petitioner's request. A well-known example from the Hebrew Bible is the vow of Jephthah in Judg 11:30–31 and apparent sacrifice of his daughter in 11:34–40. With the development of the Israelite taboo on human sacrifice, the former custom evolved into the payment of silver to the deity in lieu of the sacrifice itself. Thus, one could have appealed to Yahweh by vowing to offer the equivalent of himself, a member of his family, or a servant of his household and then paid the amount in silver once the petition was answered.

Figure 5. The Paleo-Hebrew Leviticus Scroll from Qumran. 11QpaleoLev, Col. 6, Lev 27:11–19. Courtesy of The Leon Levy Dead Sea Scrolls Digital Library; Israel Antiquities Authority.

were to be eligible for redemption, a proviso that would have been unnecessary if the verses dealt with a "valuation of persons" dedication. The verse in question is Lev 27:13, which based on the Masoretic Text must be read as allowing for the redemption with an added fifth of an unclean animal that was consecrated to the deity; the Masoretic Text gives the verb form *yig'ālennâh* ("If they redeem it (f.)") in the verse, clearly taking the unclean animal as its object. However, in 11QpaleoLev, dated ca. 100 BCE, the pronominal object on that form is masculine, "If they redeem it (m.)"[74] Certain Greek, Samaritan, and Aramaic versions of the Hebrew Bible continue the variant form.[75] Such a form works grammatically only if we assume an impersonal antecedent—i.e., something more inclusive than the animal just mentioned. Moreover, the placement of an inclusive redemption clause in 27:13 is better suited to the structuring principles of the chapter, where sub-sections end with a single generalizing clause applicable to the entirety of that sub-section.[76] Therefore, using these non-Masoretic manuscript traditions as our basis, one can render Lev 27:13 as follows: "If they redeem it [i.e., the human pledge or the animal pledge, whether fit for sacrifice or unfit for sac-

---

74 Freedman and Mathews, *The Paleo-Hebrew Leviticus Scroll (11QpaleoLev)* (Winona Lake, IN: American Schools of Oriental Research, 1985), 48–49; on the dating of the scroll, see Hanson, "Paleography," in *The Paleo-Hebrew Leviticus Scroll (11QpaleoLev)* (ed. Freedman and Mathews; Winona Lake, IN: American Schools of Oriental Research, 1985), 23.
75 These manuscripts include LXX Codex Vaticanus, Samaritan Pentateuch, and Targum (Sperber edition).
76 The exemption clause of 27:8 is another example, as is the currency clause of 27:25.

Table 4. Valuations of humans according to gender and age, as based on the standards given in Lev 27:3–7. These silver amounts assume a valuation standard for one year of labor, as well as redemption payments in the common shekel.

Human Pledge	Valuation		Redemption Cost		
	Holy Shekel, annual	Gerah, annual	Common shekel (holy shekel), annual	Gerah, annual	Gerah, monthly
Male, 20–60 yrs	50	1000	50 (60)	1200	100
Female, 20–60 yrs	30	600	30 (36)	720	60
Male, 5–20 yrs	20	400	20 (24)	480	40
Female, 5–20 yrs	10	200	10 (12)	240	20
Male, 1 m–5 yrs*	5	100	5 (6)	120	10
Female, 1 m–5 yrs	3	60	3 (3.6)	72	6
Male, 60 yrs–	15	300	15 (18)	360	30
Female, 60 yrs–	10	200	10 (12)	240	20

* Perhaps the schedule of valuations starts then because of the case of firstborn sons, who would not be eligible to be pledged up to that age because they were seen as God's property in any case and needed to be ransomed. According to Num 3:44–51, at one month the ransom price for the firstborn son is paid.

rifice], they shall add one-fifth to the valuation." In other words, a minor corruption of the Masoretic Text obscures the fact that redeemability is protected for consecrated persons too.

Furthermore, as with the consecrated field, the fixed valuations for consecrated persons result in serviceable numbers for redemption, whether on an annual or a monthly basis. Table 4 shows the full schedule. It assumes a single-year valuation standard. It also assumes that redemption payments were made in the common shekel standard.

It should also be noted that the valuations for humans given in Lev 27:3–7 are appropriate equivalencies for one year of labor, as based on the extra-biblical evidence at hand. A debt note from Tel Hadid in the Judean lowlands, dated 664/3 BCE, records a three-month loan of 1 mina of silver (50 common shekels) secured by a possessory pledge of the wife and sister of the debtor, who are to remain with the creditor, with interest charged only upon non-payment.[77] If the pledge's labor is in lieu of an interest payment, and we assume a 20% rate of interest, as was common with silver loans in this period,[78] then the wife and sister's labor would be valued at 10 or 12 shekels for three months, or 40–48 shekels per year. This results in an average market value of 20–24 shekels per year per woman. The value is remarkably close to the valuations for humans given in Lev 27, where a female 5–20 years old is valued at 10 shekels and a female 20–60 years old is valued at 30. Therefore, single-year usufruct makes sense as the basis for those valuations too.[79] One would expect Lev 27 to use the same temporal parameters for its pricing scheme across different kinds of properties.

Here too the 50-shekel benchmark is for a maximal unit of economic value with smaller units derivative of it. An examination of the lowest valued person listed—a female aged 1 month to five years, at 3 shekels—is telling in this regard. The redemption cost for such a person would break down into 6 gerahs per month for a year, allowing for partial-month payments if necessary and downward movement on the initial valuation should the priest lower it. For a male 20–60 years old, the redemption cost could be paid in installments of 100 gerahs per month over one year.

Therefore, redemption was secured for living properties and real estate consecrated to Yahweh. It was completed with the payment of the valuation amount with the addition of one-fifth. And it was based on a 50-shekel benchmark for persons and patrimonial land, which accommodates a workable redemption schedule in installments. Combine these redemption regulations with the chapter's overriding interest in the valuation of property, in the term of the consecration, and in the weight standard for payment, and the chapter begins to look far more like a code of laws on a secured lending operation rather than one on benevolent voluntary donations. In other words, the humans valued in Lev 27:3–7,

---

[77] Horowitz, Oshima, and Sanders, *Cuneiform in Canaan*, 63–64. See also Dandamaev, *Slavery in Babylonia: From Nabopolassar to Alexander the Great (626–331 B.C.)* (trans. Powell; DeKalb, IL: Northern Illinois University Press, 1984), 204–6; and Porten, *Archives from Elephantine: The Life of an Ancient Jewish Military Colony* (Berkeley: University of California Press, 1968), 72–80.

[78] See §2.2.3.

[79] Scholars have attempted to associate the 50-shekel price in Lev 27:3 with the cost of slaves on the Assyrian markets in the eighth and seventh centuries BCE, and some correspondence has been noted; see Kitchen, "The Patriarchal Age: Myth or History?," *Biblical Archaeology Review* 21 (1995), 52; and Milgrom, *Leviticus 23–27*, 2409. But for the Babylonian and Persian periods, these would be extraordinarily low rates for a 50-year period of service; see Dandamaev, *Slavery in Babylonia*, 204–6.

as well as the animals and real estate of 27:9–24, appear to have been hypothecary pledges to secure a loan.

2.2.3 The Consecrated Field as Hypothecary Pledge

The idea that Lev 27 regulates a secured lending operation is rooted in my ongoing collaborative study with Joshua Sosin of Duke University, who first proposed this reading of Lev 27 to me.[80] According to our argument, the priests of Yahweh were issuing silver loans to Judeans and securing those loans with hypothecary pledges—a security that stays with the debtor, who typically pays interest instead of forfeiting use of the pledge, as would happen with an antichretic loan. A vow of consecration was made to Yahweh by the debtor, signaling the charges that the deity now had on the pledged property. For a consecrated field, the priest may have erected an inscribed marker by the field to call attention to the claim.[81] Loan repayment could have come in a lump sum payment or in installments, likely at harvest time. Once the loan was repaid, the property was redeemed. To the best of our knowledge, no one has seriously considered the possibility that Judeans too appealed to their deity for credit. When scholars have discussed credit in ancient Judea, they tend to view it as having come from kinship groups and occasionally private entrepreneurs.[82]

The rate of interest was one-fifth of the valuation, or 20%, which was common for silver loans throughout the Near East; Michael Hudson has called it "one of the most stable rates in antiquity."[83] It derived from the simple fixed rate of

---

[80] The two of us are working on an article that explores it more fully. I have mentioned the idea in a few preliminary publications; see Gordon, "Debt Fraud, Herem Entrapment, and Other Crimes Involving Cultic Property in Late Hellenistic and Early Roman Judea," in *Expressions of Cult in the Southern Levant in the Greco-Roman Period. Manifestations in Text and Material Culture* (ed. Weiss and Tal; Turnhout: Brepols, 2017), 257, n. 10; idem, "Redemption Fee," 191, n. 35; see also Altmann, "Ancient Comparisons," 109, n. 14.
[81] On the use of boundary markers, see, e.g., Exod 22:24; Ezek 18:13, 17, 22:12; Prov 28:8; Hab 2:7; Ps 15:5; and Greengus, *Laws in the Bible*, 105, 286. Such stones are amply documented in the Greek world; see, e.g., Fine, *Horoi: Studies in Mortgage, Real Security and Land Tenure in Ancient Athens* (Baltimore: American School of Classical Studies at Athens, 1951), esp. 61–95.
[82] Seeligmann, *Gesammelte Studien zur Hebräischen Bibel* (Tübingen: Mohr Siebeck, 2004), 319–48; Westbrook and Wells, *Everyday Law*, 112–16; Boer, *Sacred Economy*, 156–63; Frymer-Kensky, "Israel," in *Security for Debt* (op. cit.), 111–224.
[83] "Reconstructing the Origins of Interest-Bearing Debt and the Logic of Clean Slates," in *Debt and Economic Renewal in the Ancient Near East* (ed. Hudson and Van de Mieroop; Bethesda, MD: CDL Press, 2002), 24. For further discussion on the 20% rate of interest for silver loans, see idem, "How Interest Rates Were Set," 133; Greengus, *Laws in the Bible*, 105; Oelsner, "The Neo-Baby-

one shekel per mina (= 60 shekels) per month, or 12/60ths per year (= 20%). An identical rate emerges from Lev 27, though the calculation is 10/50ths per year rather than 12/60ths, in keeping with the decimal system. It is important to note that the Holiness Code offers no blanket prohibition against charging interest, though other law codes in the Hebrew Bible appear to be quite disapproving of the practice, at least when it was applied to loans to fellow Israelites.[84] The Holiness Code merely forbids one to exact interest on money lent to an impoverished family member (Lev 25:36). That case involves an individual forced by circumstance to move onto the farm of a relative in hopes of saving enough money to redeem his own property from a buyer (Lev 25:25). It would be usurious and wrong, says the Code, to charge interest to such a kinsman, though the host was still benefitting from his labor.[85] By implication, interest is legal in the Code when exacted in any other scenario, as in a farmer seeking a subsistence loan from the deity.[86]

Nevertheless, the credit operation reconstructed here couches the loan as another kind of transaction between Yahweh and debtor—one that approximates a sale. The consecration transfers the property to Yahweh in exchange for cash; redemption transfers it back at an agreed upon 20% mark up. The arrangement recalls Murabaha financing by sharia-compliant banks in the Muslim world, which theoretically requires the bank to buy a commodity and sell it back to the borrower at a mark-up but in effect have morphed into simple cash-flows between parties.[87] It is also structurally similar to the purchase from Yahweh of the unclean firstborn animal (Lev 27:26–27) and the tithe (27:30–31), both of which were inherently the deity's but were being held by the buyer.[88] Only there the act

---

lonian Period," in *Security for Debt* (op. cit.), 291; Boer, *Sacred Economy*, 161, n. 38; and Wunsch, "Debt, Interest, Pledge and Forfeiture in the Neo-Babylonian and Early Achaemenid Period: The Evidence from Private Archives," in *Debt and Economic Renewal* (op. cit.), 234–36.

[84] Greengus, *Laws in the Bible*, 103; Seeligmann, *Gesammelte Studien zur Hebräischen Bibel*, 338–48; Neufeld, "The Prohibitions against Loans at Interest in Ancient Hebrew Laws," *HUCA* 26 (1955), 355–412; Williams, "Taking Interest in Interest," in *Mishneh Todah: Studies in Deuteronomy and Its Cultural Environment in Honor of Jeffrey H. Tigay* (ed. Fox et al.; Eisenbrauns: Winona Lake, IN, 2009), 113–32.

[85] Wells, "The Quasi-Alien," 147–51.

[86] Rasor, "Biblical Roots of Modern Consumer Credit Law," *Journal of Law and Religion* 10, no. 1 (1993), 167–70; Westbrook and Wells, *Everyday Law*, 115.

[87] El-Gamal, *Islamic Finance: Law, Economics, and Practice* (Cambridge: Cambridge University Press, 2008), 14–15, 64–67.

[88] When a firstborn animal is deemed unfit for sacrifice to God, perhaps by some defect or by its very nature as a non-offerable species—as would be the case with a donkey, for instance—the law allows it to be redeemed from God at its valuation plus the added fifth (Lev 27:27). The same standard applies for all tithes (Lev 27:31), the result of a 10% tax on herds, flocks, fields, and

of consecration is unnecessary, for the commodities belonged to Yahweh by their very nature.

Moreover, the use of the holy and common shekel standards concurrently allowed for the appearance of no mark-up at all. This is another upshot of those tidy redemption amounts in the common shekel standard. They mean that priests could have priced a consecration at a certain number of shekels and collected that same number of shekels for its redemption: 10 shekels out, 10 shekels in. The only difference is that the shekels lent out were in the holy standard, and thus weighed 200 gerahs; while those repaid were in the common standard, at 240 gerahs. The subterfuge avoids what could be perceived as an outright violation of the Hebrew Bible's interest prohibitions, such as the call to not "bite off" anything of the debtor's worth, as one common Biblical Hebrew word for interest suggests (e.g., Exod 22:24); or to not significantly increase the amount of the debt, as another does (e.g., Deut 23:20–21). It is possible that the holy shekel standard was manipulated at some point precisely to facilitate this subterfuge. In any case, by the time Lev 27 was put into writing, the "one-fifth" seems to have been recognized by all for what it was: a rate of interest. The text speaks freely about the need to pay it.

The regulations of Lev 27 traffic in the blurred territory between actual material indebtedness to Yahweh, as in owing him silver that was lent from his coffers, and spiritual indebtedness, as in sensing or declaring a debt to him due to the perception of a divine response to a prayer. The ancients may have not felt this distinction as clearly as we do. Instead of employing any of the basic Hebrew terms for collateral, pledges, loans, and debt, Lev 27 prefers to describe the encumbrance of pledged property in language connoting acts of devotion.[89] For living pledges, the pledged status is achieved simply by taking a vow; for real estate, it is by an act of consecration.[90] The vow and consecration safeguard the contractual promise.

---

orchards, which was levied in order to support the priesthood. Owners of these commodities may have decided to redeem them from God if they felt they could fetch a higher price than the valuation, if the replacement costs were significantly higher than that amount, or if it was seen as irreplaceable. On the flip side, priests disinterested in caring for firstborn animals, or unable to properly store tithed fruits and grains, may have lowered the valuation to encourage their redemption.

89 It should be noted that the terminology related to loan practices in the Hebrew Bible revolves around possessory (antichretic) pledges, as in Deut 24:11. See Frymer-Kensky, "Israel," 253; see also Premnath, "Loan Practices in the Hebrew Bible," in *To Break Every Yoke: Essays in Honor of Marvin L. Chaney* (ed. Coote and Gottwald; Sheffield: Sheffield Phoenix Press, 2007), 173–85.
90 The redactional principles of the laws of the chapter betray a certain economy of words by omitting parts of the apodosis in corollary laws (see, e.g., the law of the animal fit for sacrifice at

It is conceivable that persons responding to merely the perception of a state of indebtedness to the deity drew upon the same consecration mechanism to repay their "debt" to Yahweh. While the usual reason for indebtedness was loans, there are other situations that could give rise to the situation, such as penalties, taxes, or deferred payment for goods or services. The various obligations an individual had toward the deity, which could manifest as person-to-person relations between the individual and priest, may have been construed in the manner of a simple loan, as has been observed elsewhere in the ancient Near East.[91] These scenarios too are worthy of consideration. But the legislation of Lev 27 seems most likely to derive from an actual credit operation run by priests.

After all, if individuals felt they were in a state of spiritual indebtedness to the deity, they did have the option of making a herem dedication to him, as we shall see. According to Lev 27:28, such a dedication could be made on living or real property, offered the dedicant no chance of redemption or sale once a declaration is made, and conferred to Yahweh absolute and permanent ownership. Such a dedication also appears to have required no valuation. All of this bears the hallmarks of a simple gift. The mechanisms of Lev 27:2–25, with the restrictions they imposed and the risks they carried, suggest another set of motivating factors entirely. As noted above, the valuation process was time-consuming, expensive, and potentially fraught with pricing disputes. It could lead to fines, foreclosure, and permanent seizure of property (Lev 27:21, see below).[92] The annulment of the encumbrance required the payment of the substantial rate of 20%.

27:9, which is incomprehensible without relating it back to 27:2), implying that the conditional vow of Lev 27:2 could in fact lie at the heart of the laws of the entire chapter, field consecrations included. The sole difference would have been that real estate rather than a person was vowed to Yahweh and then dedicated to him should the prayer be answered, here too in response to a condition of indebtedness to him; see *The Vow*, 48–112. The separation and the switch in terminology is probably because Hebrew verb forms referring to consecration could carry a very specific sacrificial meaning with respect to movables, particularly animals, connoting eventual slaughter and consumption at the altar. There is no reason to assume that such a fate awaited the chattel pledges in the first half of the chapter. For further discussion on vows and consecrations, see Cartledge, *Vows in the Hebrew Bible*, 53; Wendel, *Das israelitisch-jüdische Gelübde* (Berlin: Philo-Verlag, 1931), 23; and Westbrook and Wells, *Everyday Law*, 23, 46–47.
91 Stol, "The Old Babylonian 'I Owe You'," in *Silver, Money and Credit: A Tribute to Robartus J. Van der Spek on the Occasion of His 65th birthday* (ed. Kleber and Pirngruber; Leiden: Nederlands Instituut voor het Nabije Oosten, 2016), 33; Wunsch, "Debt, Interest, Pledge and Forfeiture," 224–29; Westbrook, "Conclusions," in *Security for Debt* (op. cit.), 328. For a general discussion on debt and credit as metaphors for sin and moral redemption in ancient Israel, see Anderson, *Sin*, esp. 55–74.
92 For switching a consecrated animal with an unconsecrated one, for example, the dedicant is fined at a rate of 100%, as an additional animal is asked to be given to God (Lev 27:10).

One should not underestimate the potential of the religious impulse to compel individuals toward acts of sacrifice and devotion to a deity, but the formal characteristics of the fiscal mechanisms of Lev 27 suggest that its origins lay in a secured lending program.

While with antichresis the pledge moves into the domain of the creditor, who benefits from its use, the lending program Lev 27 regulated involved hypothecary pledges, which stayed with the debtor and were seized only upon default.[93] With hypothecary pledges, the creditor benefits from the interest payments rather than use of the pledge. The priests of Yahweh may also have preferred to secure loans in this way in order to avoid the expenses and potential complications of keeping antichretic pledges in their households. One verse in the Holiness Code (Lev 19:20) seems to refer to the thorny situation of a creditor sleeping with another man's unmarried daughter after that daughter had been pawned to him and brought into his home.[94]

The laws of Lev 27 likely facilitated agrarian loans to Judean farmers. Silver or in-kind equivalents would have been needed for tax payments, distress loans, or the purchase of food in between harvests. Money would have also have been necessary after an unexpected loss of stored foodstuffs, or for the procurement of seed, labor, and other supplies to cultivate fields and orchards.[95] Loans issued by Yahweh's priests would have given farmers the opportunity to use crops from future harvests to cover costs accruing in the present. For cereal fields, once the rains softened the soil, which had hardened during the long Levantine summer, a first plowing would have been necessary to make the ground porous; a second plowing would have prepared the soil for sowing. Work animals were required for both. Sowing would have been a relatively straightforward process, though

---

[93] Lev 27:9, for example, implies that milk and other products of a hypothecated animal can be seized along with the animal in a foreclosure process; if a pledged cow gave birth during the encumbrance period, its calf would be taken by the priest should the debtor fall into arrears. This all suggests that the animal remained in the domain of the debtor. Similarly, the law prohibiting substitutions of consecrated animals in 27:10 assumes the same. For a discussion of pros and cons of antichresis versus hypothecary pledges, see Ellickson, "Ancient Land Law: Mesopotamia, Egypt, Israel," *Chicago-Kent Law Review* 71 (1995–1996), 395–99; see also Westbrook, "Introduction," 1–3. In Neo-Assyrian Mesopotamia, hypothecary pledges were less common than antichretic pledges; see Radner, "The Neo-Assyrian Period," 270.
[94] Westbrook and Wells, *Everyday Law*, 19–20. For a general discussion of the use of antichretic pledges in the ancient Near East and in Israel, see Wells, "The Quasi-Alien," 143–47. See also Guillaume, *Land, Credit and Crisis*, 117, for a reading of Lev 25:23 to mean that land could never be put up as an antichretic pledge to secure a loan with a private creditor.
[95] On the uses of borrowed silver, see Altmann, *Economics in Persian-Period Biblical Texts*, 44–45.

Figure 6. Farmers plowing their field in Ottoman Palestine, ca. 1900. Library of Congress Prints and Photographs Division. Photographic print from the Frank and Frances Carpenter Collection.

precision was required. The cereal harvest was particularly labor intensive. Threshing required the use of sledges pulled by yoked animals to separate the ears from the stalks and of attendants to turn the pile and toss stalks toward the thresher. Attendants could be used for winnowing, sieving, and loading the straw and chaff into storage in their various sacks, bundles, or baskets. In the working of groves and orchards, there were tasks relating to the terracing, planting, vine-tending, and processing of fruits such as olives to prepare for consumption.[96] There would have been costs associated with each step of the process.

While simple subsistence loans would have normally have been short in duration, those regulated by Lev 27 could have been extraordinarily long term.[97] The use of valuation parameters with respect to the Jubilee (Lev 27:17–18) implies as much, as does the absence in the chapter of precious metals, textiles, rare goods, and other small movables, for such commodities were often put

---

[96] For a discussion of agricultural labor in the ancient Levant, see Hopkins, "'All Sorts of Field Work': Agricultural Labor in Ancient Palestine," in *To Break Every Yoke: Essays in Honor of Marvin L. Chaney* (ed. Coote and Gottwald; Sheffield: Sheffield Phoenix Press, 2007), 152–69.

[97] On long-term agricultural leases as a new feature in the Neo-Babylonian and Achaemenid periods, see Russell, "Biblical Jubilee Laws," 189–203.

up as pledges on short-term loans.[98] The automatic annulment of encumbrances at the Jubilee meant that securing a long-term loan from Yahweh, whether through landed or human property, would have been impossible late in the Jubilee cycle.

Table 5 gives a hypothetical amortization schedule for payments on a loan of 42 mina (= 2,100 holy shekels), which is secured by a field with a seed capacity of 1 homer. The duration is for 42 harvests—the full Jubilee cycle—and the rate is based on the 50-shekel benchmark given in Lev 27:16. In the "payment" and "balance" columns of the amortization schedule, the holy shekel values appear in parentheses, after the common shekel values, to demonstrate how the concurrent use of the two shekel standards could have masked the interest payment.[99] How these transactions worked in actual practice is a matter of speculation, as Lev 27 leaves out crucial details of the arrangement.

Table 5. Hypothetical amortization schedule for a loan of 42 mina (= 2,100 holy shekels) for a duration of 42 harvests, as based on the 50-shekel benchmark given in Lev 27:16. The loan is secured by a field with a seed capacity of 1 homer. The duration of the loan equals the full seven sabbatical cycles until the Jubilee. Payment in the common shekel would mask the 20% rate of interest, whose sum is 420 holy shekels or 10 holy shekels per mina. The schedule has the loan repaid in equal annual installments.

Loan Amount				Payment		Balance	
Holy Shekel	Gera	Harvests to Jubilee	Payment No.	Common shekel (holy shekel)	Gera	Common shekel (holy shekel)	Gera
2100	42000	42	1	50 (60)	1200	2050 (2460)	49200
2050	41000	41	2	50 (60)	1200	2000 (2400)	48000
2000	40000	40	3	50 (60)	1200	1950 (2340)	46800
1950	39000	39	4	50 (60)	1200	1900 (2280)	45600
1900	38000	38	5	50 (60)	1200	1850 (2220)	44400
1850	37000	37	6	50 (60)	1200	1800 (2160)	43200
1800	36000	36	7	50 (60)	1200	1750 (2100)	42000

---

98 See Gen 38:18, where a signet ring, bracelets, and a staff are pledged. On the biblical evidence suggesting very small, short-term loans for a relatively poor population, see Frymer-Kensky, "Israel," 251–63. On the tendency of farm loans to be short term, see Guillaume, *Land, Credit and Crisis*, 210–13.

99 Of course, it is possible that the holy shekel standard was used for both cash-out and cash-in payments, in which case the interest would have been plainly acknowledged in the records for all parties.

Table 5 *(continued)*

Loan Amount				Payment		Balance	
Holy Shekel	Gera	Harvests to Jubilee	Payment No.	Common shekel (holy shekel)	Gera	Common shekel (holy shekel)	Gera
1750	35000	35	8	50 (60)	1200	1700 (2040)	40800
1700	34000	34	9	50 (60)	1200	1650 (1980)	39600
1650	33000	33	10	50 (60)	1200	1600 (1920)	38400
1600	32000	32	11	50 (60)	1200	1550 (1860)	37200
1550	31000	31	12	50 (60)	1200	1500 (1800)	36000
1500	30000	30	13	50 (60)	1200	1450 (1740)	34800
1450	29000	29	14	50 (60)	1200	1400 (1680)	33600
1400	28000	28	15	50 (60)	1200	1350 (1620)	32400
1350	27000	27	16	50 (60)	1200	1300 (1560)	31200
1300	26000	26	17	50 (60)	1200	1250 (1500)	30000
1250	25000	25	18	50 (60)	1200	1200 (1440)	28800
1200	24000	24	19	50 (60)	1200	1150 (1380)	27600
1150	23000	23	20	50 (60)	1200	1100 (1320)	26400
1100	22000	22	21	50 (60)	1200	1050 (1260)	25200
1050	21000	21	22	50 (60)	1200	1000 (1200)	24000
1000	20000	20	23	50 (60)	1200	950 (1140)	22800
950	19000	19	24	50 (60)	1200	900 (1080)	21600
900	18000	18	25	50 (60)	1200	850 (1020)	20400
850	17000	17	26	50 (60)	1200	800 (960)	19200
800	16000	16	27	50 (60)	1200	750 (900)	18000
750	15000	15	28	50 (60)	1200	700 (840)	16800
700	14000	14	29	50 (60)	1200	650 (780)	15600
650	13000	13	30	50 (60)	1200	600 (720)	14400
600	12000	12	31	50 (60)	1200	550 (660)	13200
550	11000	11	32	50 (60)	1200	500 (600)	12000
500	10000	10	33	50 (60)	1200	450 (540)	10800
450	9000	9	34	50 (60)	1200	400 (480)	9600

Table 5 *(continued)*

Loan Amount				Payment		Balance	
Holy Shekel	Gera	Harvests to Jubilee	Payment No.	Common shekel (holy shekel)	Gera	Common shekel (holy shekel)	Gera
400	8000	8	35	50 (60)	1200	350 (420)	8400
350	7000	7	36	50 (60)	1200	300 (360)	7200
300	6000	6	37	50 (60)	1200	250 (300)	6000
250	5000	5	38	50 (60)	1200	200 (240)	4800
200	4000	4	39	50 (60)	1200	150 (180)	3600
150	3000	3	40	50 (60)	1200	100 (120)	2400
100	2000	2	41	50 (60)	1200	50 (60)	1200
50	1000	1	42	50 (60)	1200	0	0

It is important to keep in mind that silver often functioned as a virtual currency in the ancient Near Eastern economy. Amounts of silver could be recorded on accounts but never actually paid out in bullion. When payments were necessary for obligations, goods in kind may have simply traded hands and the silver accounts adjusted as a result. Payment by this means may have worked seamlessly among individuals familiar with one another in a village setting.[100] Regardless of what actually changed hands between priest and debtor, one can expect the parties to have worked out the nature of the obligation taken on, its duration, the manner of repayment, and provisions in the event that the debtor fell into arrears. A promissory note would likely have been written up too. Numerous such notes from the Neo-Babylonian period have been recovered in Iraq. They typically state the name of the debtor and creditor and include details on repayment, interest, pledge, sureties, witnesses, place, and date.[101]

The call to establish a lending program with unusually long-term loans involving landed securities may have been part of a concerted effort by Yahweh's priests to strengthen Judean ties to land as foreign credit became more common-

---

100 On the use of "virtual" silver currency in the ancient Near East, see Van de Mieroop, "Silver as a Financial Tool in Ancient Egypt and Mesopotamia," in *Explaining Monetary and Financial Innovation: A Historical Analysis* (ed. Bernholz and Vaubel; Cham, Switzerland: Springer International Publishing, 2016), 17–29; and Goetzmann, *Money Changes Everything*, 59, 100.
101 Oelsner, "The Neo-Babylonian Period," 290–91. See also Premnath, "Loan Practices," 174; Wunsch, "Debt, Interest, Pledge and Forfeiture," 229–34.

place.¹⁰² Priests may have sought to help farmers pay off debt to a foreign creditor, buy back their land for themselves, or redeem family land for someone in their kinship group. They could have drawn on what was likely a considerable collection of silver and other valuables in the holy coffers of the deity to prevent destitution of the sort described in Lev 25:25–46, where a farmer is forced to sell their land and even sell their dependents or themselves into debt slavery.¹⁰³ Another situation of economic distress is described in Neh 5:1–12. There farmers are having to take out subsistence loans to pay for food, or they are having to borrow money on their fields to pay royal taxes or possibly rents on royal land.¹⁰⁴ By helping Judean farmers keep their land, the laws of Lev 27 involving landed securities went hand in hand with the objectives of the Jubilee, with its themes of economic liberty. Yet it must be stressed that even if Jubilee observance were widespread for a period, creditors may easily have written Jubilee exemptions into their loan contracts, which as mentioned may have helped contribute to what appears to have been a very short life for the Jubilee as an institution, its demise hastening perhaps the conglomeration of wealth.¹⁰⁵

That priests could be suppliers of credit in Judea's ancient economy, approximating patrons, adds a new dimension to their relationship with the farming population. Typically, families in economic distress could turn to a patron to get what they needed; a generous patron would be flexible with the terms of repayment and merciful with respect to interest and pledge.¹⁰⁶ Here the priests take

---

102 Guillaume, *Land, Credit and Crisis*, 227–46; Naaman and Zadok have hypothesized that the Tel Hadid debt note, which is discussed above (§2.2.2), reflects a case of a local Judean taking a loan from a Mesopotamian creditor; "Assyrian Deportations to the Province of Samerina in the Light of Two Cuneiform Tablets from Tel Hadid," *Tel Aviv* 27 (2000), 176.
103 On the holy coffers, see Boer, *Sacred Economy*, 113–15, 202–3; on debt's utility in simple agrarian economies, see Goetzmann, *Money Changes Everything*, 41–42; for more on the cycle of indebtedness described in Lev 25, see Frymer-Kensky, "Israel," 261.
104 On the possibility that Neh 5:4 refers to rent payment rather than a tax, see Fried, "Exploitation of Depopulated Land in Achaemenid Judah," in *Economy of Ancient Judah* (op. cit.), 153–60.
105 The situation of great economic disparity addressed by Nehemiah's reform (Neh 5:1–12) in the mid-fifth century BCE responds to widespread debt-slavery that, at least theoretically, could have been prevented had the Jubilee laws been in place; in the least, one would expect some mention of it in the text. For more evidence showing that the Jubilee was hardly observed, see Fager, *Land Tenure and the Biblical Jubilee*, 34–36. On Jubilee exemption clauses in contracts, see §2.1.
106 On the patron-client relationship in ancient Israel, see Houston, *Contending for Justice*, 47–51; and Simkins, "Patronage and the Political Economy of Monarchic Israel," in *The Social World of the Hebrew Bible: Twenty-Five Years of the Social Sciences in the Academy* (ed. Brenner and Cook; Atlanta: Society of Biblical Literature, 1999), 123–44. On the system continuing to

on that role in some respects, guided presumably by the principles laid out in Lev 27—that valuation should be carried out according to universally recognized standards, that interest should not exceed 20%, and that title should return to the debtor upon repayment. As the beneficiaries of the tributary economy in Judea, through which offerings in kind were redistributed among the holy classes, the priests were akin to Near Eastern government functionaries who looked to support from countryside estates, which they themselves did not farm. Yet the picture suggested by Lev 27 shows that priests could also inject credit into the economy, whether they were acting as financial representatives of the temple or of their own clan, or whether they functioned with some independence from both. Their role as patron here is implied regardless of their institutional context, which cannot be ascertained, given the uncertainty of when Lev 27 was written.[107]

The wealth held by temple firms in antiquity was regularly drawn upon for loans, particularly in the great temples of Mesopotamia.[108] The banking practices of the temple of Apollo at Delos offer a well-documented example. In the earlier accounts surviving from that temple, of the 370s BCE, there is evidence of the lending of relatively large sums to mostly Attic cities, a practice that by the period of Delian independence would be replaced by smaller and more conservative loans, primarily to locals or to the city of Delos itself. Yet in this period at Delos one also sees the appearance of a class of businessmen referred to as *prodaneistai* ("lenders in advance"), who were entering into complicated fiscal deals with the polis and its temple of Apollo—taking short-term loans from Apollo, putting

---

function in the Persian period in Judea, see Altmann, *Economics in Persian-Period Biblical Texts*, 177–87, 196–200.
107 See §§1.2, 2.1.
108 For general discussions on temples and credit, see Linders, "Sacred Finances," 9–13, esp. 11; and Davies, "Temples, Credit, and the Circulation of Money," in *Money and Its Uses in the Ancient Greek World* (ed. Meadows and Shipton; Oxford; New York: Oxford University Press, 2001), 117–28. On Mesopotamia, see Johns, *Babylonian and Assyrian Laws, Contracts and Letters* (New York: Charles Scribner's Sons, 1904), 262–70; Charpin, *Gods, Kings, and Merchants in Old Babylonian Mesopotamia* (Paris; Leuven; Bristol: Peeters, 2015), 152–54; and Graeber, *Debt: The First 5,000 Years* (Brooklyn, NY: Melville House, 2011), 64–65. For a case of the Eanna at Uruk confiscating an orchard in lieu of cattle to settle an outstanding debt, see Janković, "Uruk," 423 n. 2418. On a property dispute involving the same temple where a house was pledged in exchange for a cash loan, but later proven to be owned by the temple, see Holtz, *Neo-Babylonian Trial Records* (Atlanta: Society of Biblical Literature, 2014), 102–6 (no. 26).

that money towards city expenditures, and being repaid slowly with funds from the city treasury.[109]

There are other examples. The Rhamnous temple in the Athenian deme publicized with some pride in the mid-fifth century BCE that it was lending out cash in packets of 200 and 300 drachmae to individuals and charging interest on the loans.[110] In the deme of Myrrhinous or possibly Hagnous, a decree on administration finances instructs the priests of the deme to lend out money by placing liens on plots of land or other forms of real estate.[111] The instructions read as follows: "If anyone needs money, the priests may lend money on satisfactory security of land or house or tenement house, and shall place a boundary stone on which they shall inscribe the name of the god to whom the money belongs."[112] The use of such boundary stones fits the common system of hypothecation in the Greek context.[113]

The debt regulated by Lev 27, along with the payment of one-fifth of the harvest to Yahweh, resembles a story from the Joseph cycle (Gen 47:13–26). In the story, famine has ravaged the land of Egypt and the farmers are beginning to starve. Joseph devises a plan to nationalize the entire territory. The farmers sell themselves and their land to the king, receiving from the sale the provisions they need to survive. The king, however, allows them to stay on their land as sharecroppers. The terms of the new arrangement call for them to give one-fifth of each harvest to the king as rent, keeping the rest. "So Joseph made it a statute concerning the land of Egypt, and it stands to this day, that Pharaoh should have the fifth. The land of priests alone did not become Pharaoh's" (Gen 47:26). The Egyptian priests could keep their land because, as it is written in Gen 47:22, they received a fixed allowance from the king, on top of the income they earned from their own holdings. In other words, the priests could survive the famine from that allowance and did not need to sell their land to the king.[114]

---

109 Gabrielsen, "Banking and Credit Operations in Hellenistic Times," in *Making, Moving and Managing: The New World of Ancient Economies, 323–31 BC* (ed. Archibald et al.; Oxford: Oxbow Books, 2005), 136–64, esp. 146–56.
110 Davies, "Temples, Credit, and the Circulation of Money," 117–19.
111 Rhodes and Osborne, *Greek Historical Inscriptions, 404–323 BC* (Oxford: Oxford University Press, 2007), 312–17 (no. 63); Fine, *Horoi*, 42; Papazarkadas, *Sacred and Public Land*, 131.
112 Translation follows Rhodes and Osborne, *Greek Historical Inscriptions*, 313, ll. 27–29.
113 Fine, *Horoi*, 94–95.
114 For discussions on the passage, see Hurowitz, "The Joseph Stories and Mesopotamian Writings: Enslaving the Egyptians (Gen 47:13–26)," *Beit Mikra*, no. 55/1 (2010), 94–106; and Fuller, "Debt-Slavery Passages in the Tanakh as a Lens for Reading Joseph's Enslavement of the Egyptians in Genesis 47:13–26: Explorations in Canonical Hermeneutics," *Biblical Theology Bulletin* 46, no. 4 (2016), 177–85.

The similarities between the Gen 47 story and the arrangement behind Lev 27:16–21 are striking. In both scenarios, farmers benefit from the vast resources of a ruling authority, whether Pharaoh or Yahweh. And in both the farmers continue to hold their land if they pay one-fifth of its produce to the authority who bailed them out. The key difference involves the nature of the initial transaction, whether sale or loan. In the sale of land in Gen 47, title transfers to the king and there is no possibility of redemption. In the loans thought here to lie behind Lev 27, the land is merely hypothecated, the title stays with the debtor, and redemption effects the land's full release. The terms of Lev 27, in other words, would have been much better for the farmer over the long run than those devised by Joseph for the Egyptian landowners in the story of Gen 47.

2.2.4 Seizure of a Patrimonial Field

(20) If he does not redeem the field and had sold the field to another, it shall no longer be redeemed; (21) when the field is released in the Jubilee, it shall be sacred to Yahweh, like the herem field; his patrimonial property becomes the priest's.

וְאִם לֹא יִגְאַל אֶת הַשָּׂדֶה וְאִם מָכַר אֶת הַשָּׂדֶה לְאִישׁ אַחֵר לֹא יִגָּאֵל עוֹד. וְהָיָה הַשָּׂדֶה בְּצֵאתוֹ בַיֹּבֵל קֹדֶשׁ לַיהוָה כִּשְׂדֵה הַחֵרֶם לַכֹּהֵן תִּהְיֶה אֲחֻזָּתוֹ.

Having laid out the terms of patrimonial field consecration and redemption, Lev 27:20–21 turns to a specific case for which the debtor loses patrimonial title. If he had sold the hypothecated field to another, he should have now had the means to settle the debt with Yahweh. But he does not. He hopes perhaps that the debt will be forgiven at the Jubilee, at which point he would have collected the field's value in silver twice over: from Yahweh at consecration and from buyer at time of sale. This is where the law of Lev 27:20–21 has teeth. It prevents the Jubilee from benefitting him in any way, while punishing him with the loss of his patrimonial title. His field now joins the permanent holdings of Yahweh and is disbursed to a priest. In other words, the law of 27:20–21 gives Yahweh rights of seizure over the hypothecary pledge if the debtor has sold the field but remains delinquent.

This is a more contextually sensible reading of Lev 27:20–21 than that put forward by commentators working on the assumption that the chapter regulates voluntary donations of land. Seeking to find some rational explanation for this law, they have exploited the fact that the verb *mākar* ("[he] had sold") has no explicit subject, and that its tense and sequential relationship to the antecedent *lo yigʾal* ("if he does not redeem") are open to interpretation too.¹¹⁵ According to one common reading, which surfaces in the NRSV translation and in copious commentaries, these verses indicate that consecration implies a forfeiture of patrimonial title and Jubilee rights.¹¹⁶ This is because the priests or the temple authorities could sell the property permanently once it was consecrated—a reading that follows in the footsteps of the rabbinic interpretation and necessitates a change in subject at Lev 27:20 from the dedicant (subject of *yigʾal*) to the sanctuary (subject of *mākar*).¹¹⁷ If the property is not sold, the dedicant retains his redemption rights. If he does not redeem, he still loses the field at the Jubilee. As Milgrom has pointed out, this is a problematic interpretation with regard to Hebrew syntax (among other things), for two parallel conditions linked in this way would call for two imperfect forms, *yigʾal* and *yimkōr* (i.e., "If he does not redeem...or if he/it sells..."), rather than an imperfect followed by a perfect.¹¹⁸

Others reconstruct a scenario where the dedicant has duped another into purchasing a field he has already consecrated; he collects payment and the buyer gets no field, for Yahweh already owns it.¹¹⁹ They read *yigʾal* and *mākar* consecutively and keep the dedicant as the subject of both. But this reading runs into a grammatical problem too because of how it treats the perfect form *mākar*, taking it as a simple past in a pericope that is otherwise marked by a string of imperfects. Here the lone perfect is best read as a pluperfect, with the sale having happened before non-redemption.¹²⁰ Furthermore, one would ex-

---

115 The latter question involves whether the two ʾ*im* ("if") clauses governing Lev 27:20 are to be read as consecutive or disjunctive (i.e., "If he does not redeem the field *and* [subsequently] has sold the field to another..." or "If he does not redeem the field, *or* [alternatively] if he has sold the field to another..."). The multiple readings emerging from any combination of these possibilities have been summarized in Milgrom, *Leviticus 23–27*, 2383–85; and Houston, "Contrast in Tense and Exegesis. The Case of the Field Vowed and Sold, Lev. XXVII 20," *VT* 49, no. 3 (1999), 416–17.
116 See, e.g., Noth, *Leviticus*, 206; Wenham, *Leviticus*, 340; Levine, *Leviticus*, 196; Westbrook, "Jubilee Laws," in *Property and the Family in Biblical Law* (ed. Westbrook; Sheffield: JSOT Press, 1991), 225; Brin, *Studies in Biblical Law: From the Hebrew Bible to the Dead Sea Scrolls* (Sheffield: JSOT Press, 1994), 45–46; and Houston, "Contrast in Tense and Exegesis," 416–17. The NRSV translation gives: "But if the field is not redeemed, or if it has been sold to someone else, it shall no longer be redeemable."
117 Sifra *Beḥuqotai* 10:12, Rashi, and Rashbam and the same set of assumptions guides the analysis of these regulations in Rosenberg and Weiss, "Land Concentration," 77–78.
118 *Leviticus 23–27*, 2385.
119 Porter, "Lev XXVII 20: Some Further Considerations," *VT* 50, no. 4 (2000), 569–71; Noth, *Leviticus*, 206; Westbrook, "Jubilee Laws," 225; Stern, *The Biblical Ḥerem: A Window on Israel's Religious Experience* (Atlanta: Scholars Press, 1991), 129.
120 Haran, "ʿĀrākîm," 393–94; Milgrom, *Leviticus 23–27*, 2385.

pect in such a case to find some mention of restitution to the defrauded buyer. Instead we have a priest benefitting from the crime.

Following Haran's identification of the pluperfect at *mākar*, Milgrom sees the situation as having been perfectly innocuous: the dedicant seeks to forfeit his Jubilee rights and does so by consecrating his previously sold field. Without the consecration the field would have gone back to him at the Jubilee. "Therefore, the owner's purpose in consecrating the land is that the sanctuary should take it over after the jubilee," writes Milgrom.[121] But this seems like an unnecessary workaround for a set of laws familiar with the herem mechanism, which also forfeits Jubilee rights, as Lev 27:21 makes clear. Why not simply declare the field herem at the Jubilee? Why not stipulate as part of the terms of consecration that the property is exempt from the Jubilee release? Even if we were inclined to read Lev 27 as regulations for voluntary donations, Milgrom's interpretation still leaves questions unanswered. A simpler and preferable reading of Lev 27:20 – 21, as stated, is that a debtor who sells the security and does not settle the loan with the proceeds of the sale risks losing title.

2.3 Consecration of a Non-Patrimonial Field

(22) If [it is] their purchased field, which is not a part of their patrimonial holding, (23) the priest shall compute for it the proportion of the valuation up to the Jubilee year and give the valuation over on that day, a holy thing to Yahweh. (24) In the Jubilee year the field shall return to the one from whom it was purchased, to whom the patrimonial landholding belongs.

וְאִם אֶת שְׂדֵה מִקְנָתוֹ אֲשֶׁר לֹא מִשְּׂדֵה אֲחֻזָּתוֹ יַקְדִּישׁ לַיהוָה. וְחִשַּׁב לוֹ הַכֹּהֵן אֵת מִכְסַת הָעֶרְכְּךָ עַד שְׁנַת הַיֹּבֵל וְנָתַן אֶת הָעֶרְכְּךָ בַּיּוֹם הַהוּא קֹדֶשׁ לַיהוָה. בִּשְׁנַת הַיּוֹבֵל יָשׁוּב הַשָּׂדֶה לַאֲשֶׁר קָנָהוּ מֵאִתּוֹ לַאֲשֶׁר לוֹ אֲחֻזַּת הָאָרֶץ.

The traditional reading of these verses is that a non-patrimonial field, when consecrated, should be monetized immediately and paid out in silver to Yahweh, in the manner of a "valuation of persons" dedication. The disagreement has been over how that silver is paid and who enjoys usufruct of the field until the coming of the Jubilee. Noth and Milgrom have the silver paid out in installments, with the field itself retained by the priests of Yahweh until the full valuation was covered.[122] Others have Yahweh receiving full payment as well as usufruct until the

---

[121] Ibid.
[122] Noth, *Leviticus*, 206 – 7; Milgrom, *Leviticus 23 – 27*, 2387. Milgrom argues that verb *nātan* can be read to mean payment in installments.

next Jubilee, in a kind of double offering.[123] Wenham has the silver paid immediately and the field remaining with the dedicant.[124] All of course assume that this was a type of voluntary donation to the deity rather than a manner of securing a loan from him.

Assuming the latter scenario, the debtor secures the loan with a pledge for which they do not hold title, for they have merely purchased usufruct for a set number of years. Therefore, the deity can have no claim on the field itself should the debtor fall into delinquency; in such a case, the priest could take possession of the harvest proceeds alone. It is for this reason that there is no mention in these verses of the redemption of the field. Also for this reason Lev 27:24 affirms that the patrimonial titleholder assumes no risk of losing the field permanently should a foreclosure process ensue. The priest's seizure of its harvest proceeds in that case would end automatically at the Jubilee and the deed of sale would be terminated too, as the Jubilee requires.

The priest's valuation is calculated according to the number of harvest years remaining until the Jubilee, as was the custom.[125] The priest then gives the loan amount over to the borrower immediately—this according to a straightforward reading of 27:23b. There is no reason to switch the subject of the two verbs in that verse from priest to dedicant, as commentators tend to do, presumably because they have not entertained the possibility that the priest would be giving over the valuation amount to the dedicant. Should one insist on the dedicant being the subject of the verb in 27:23b, an alternative (though less preferable) reading is that he is to pay the loan back on some future date, which is agreed upon by all parties and was likely at harvest time. The phrase *bayyôm hahû'* may be construed in this way.[126] Regardless of whether we interpret 27:23b as referring to cash-out or cash-in, the loaned sum is Yahweh's and as such is holy, as the text asserts.

---

[123] Levine, *Leviticus*, 197; Gerstenberger, *Leviticus: A Commentary*, 445.
[124] Wenham, *Leviticus*, 341.
[125] See Exod 12:4 for a clearer example of the word *miqsâh* having been used to connote proportionality.
[126] As in prophetic speech; see, e.g., Amos 8:3, Hos 2:18.

2.4 Voluntary Herem Dedication of a Patrimonial Field

(28) But as for anything herem that a person anathematizes for Yahweh from what is theirs, whether human, animal, or inherited landholding: it may not be sold or redeemed. Anything herem is most holy to Yahweh.

אַךְ כָּל חֵרֶם אֲשֶׁר יַחֲרִם אִישׁ לַיהוָה מִכָּל אֲשֶׁר לוֹ מֵאָדָם וּבְהֵמָה וּמִשְּׂדֵה אֲחֻזָּתוֹ לֹא יִמָּכֵר וְלֹא יִגָּאֵל כָּל חֵרֶם קֹדֶשׁ קָדָשִׁים הוּא לַיהוָה.

The herem dedication was a means of marking persons, animals, land, or objects as exclusively Yahweh's.[127] It alienated the property permanently from the dedicant, and thus meant that the property could no longer be sold or redeemed by him. It required no valuation. It conferred onto the property "most holy" status, to distinguish it not only from profane things but also from property consecrated to Yahweh temporarily, as in the case of a security on a loan. Here the deity holds exclusive ownership, as he does with firstborn animals and tithes, which are the two other kinds of property covered in the final section of Lev 27.[128]

That herem dedications were distributed to priests as a perquisite is clear from Lev 27:21, where a field seized from a debtor is marked as herem and becomes the priest's patrimonial landholding. It is also clear from Num 18:14 and Ezek 44:29, both of which assert that herem property is a priestly entitlement. Yet these sources mention nothing of whether such a property could be alienated by the priest once in his possession. Interestingly, as we will discuss in Chapter 6, the early rabbis claim that things declared herem lost their sanctity at the moment they were disbursed to a priest, becoming *ḥullîn* ("profane") in every respect.[129] As such they may have been freely sold and exchanged. But the passive formulation of "may not be sold or redeemed" in Lev 27:28 probably has the dedicant, rather than a priest, as its implied agent.[130] Had the sanctuary taken over the field from the priest, one would expect the priest to need to pur-

---

[127] For general discussions of the Israelite institution of herem, see Nelson, "Ḥerem and the Deuteronomic Social Conscience," in *Deuteronomy and Deuteronomic Literature: Festschrift C.H.W. Brekelmans* (ed. Vervenne and Lust; Leuven: Leuven University Press; Uitgeverij Peeters, 1997), 39–54; Stern, *Biblical Herem*, 89–187; and Greenberg, "Ḥerem," 10–13. See also §1.2 above.

[128] The restrictive adverb *'ak* ("but") begins both this case and the law of the firstborn preceding it, underscoring their exceptionality to the usual consecration process covered in Lev 27.

[129] See §6.2.2.

[130] When negated imperfects are used as imperatives in Lev 27 ("it shall not be exchanged" in 27:10; "it shall not be redeemed" in 27:20 and here in 27:28; "it shall not be ransomed" in 27:30) the implied agent is the dedicant. This reading follows Rashi; see also Bula, *Vayikra*, 259. Others read this as a prohibition directed toward the sanctuary; see Levine, *Leviticus*, 199; and Milgrom, *Leviticus 23–27*, 2394.

chase the field back from the sanctuary, precisely as the rabbis exegete in *m. ʿArakin* 7:4. So there is no reason to question that ḥerem property simply supplemented a priests' private holdings.[131]

Yet the tendency has long been to read Lev 27 as regulating incorporated sanctuary property. The tradition reaches back to the Damascus Document of the second or first centuries BCE, which invokes the chapter's regulations on field consecrations in halakhic rulings on freewill offerings to the altar of God —the "altar" used as a metonymy in the Damascus Document for the incorporated holdings of the sanctuary. (That text will be discussed in Chapter 5.) Rabbinic exegetical tradition follows suit in its understanding of the financial arm of the sanctuary as the primary economic agent behind the field consecrations of Lev 27, and thus the primary beneficiary of any gain that should be acquired from them. In that interpretive tradition, priests are acknowledged as an important and necessary part of the process—surely because of the repeated mention of the anonymous priest throughout the legislation of Lev 27—but in a diminished role. The valuation process for land, for example, is said by the rabbis to have been carried out by a committee of ten individuals, only one of whom needs to be a priest (*m. Sanhedrin* 1:3). Furthermore, the unnamed agent prevented from selling the consecrated field in Lev 27:28 is the temple treasurer according to an early midrash (Sifra, *Beḥuqotai* 12:4–5). Scholars like Levine and Milgrom among several others have accepted this aspect of the rabbinic interpretation of Lev 27.[132] Yet it is also possible that there was not a sprawling temple financial

---

131 On the tension between the fully sacrosanct and thus unexploitable status of ḥerem in earlier biblical sources, particularly the Deuteronomistic Sources, and that emerging from Lev 27:21, 28, which confer them to a priest, see Benovitz, *Kol Nidre*, 85–87; and Taggar-Cohen, "Between Ḥerem, Ownership, and Ritual: Biblical and Hittite Perspectives," in *Current Issues in Priestly and Related Literature: The Legacy of Jacob Milgrom and Beyond* (ed. Gane and Taggar-Cohen; Atlanta: SBL Press, 2015), 419–34; and see below, §§2.5, 6.2.2. On the specious claim that the Hebrew Bible prohibits priests from owning land altogether, see Milgrom, *Leviticus 23–27*, 2386; Zimmerli, *Ezekiel 2: A Commentary on the Book of the Prophet Ezekiel, Chapters 25–48* (Philadelphia: Fortress Press, 1983), 469; and Sanders, *Judaism, 63 BCE–66 CE*, 146–47. For more on private landholding by priests, see §§3.3, 6.3.
132 Baruch Levine titles this section of his commentary, "Funding the Sanctuary"; see *Leviticus*, 192. Jacob Milgrom writes that, in the priestly laws of the Hebrew Bible, "for all purposes, priesthood and sanctuary were one and the same," the implication being that if a priest stood to benefit, the sanctuary by extension stood to benefit. "Moreover," writes Milgrom, "how could any tenured field belong to a priest, when Scripture repeatedly forbids it (e.g., Num 18:20a; Ezek 44:28b)"? The answer, of course, is that the field belongs to the sanctuary, but the priest may benefit from its produce"; see *Leviticus 23–27*, 2386. For others who view the sanctuary as the beneficiary of this mechanism, see Stevens, *Temples, Tithes, and Taxes*, 83; Blenkinsopp, "Did

apparatus engaged in the agrarian finance of Lev 27, but rather individual priests holding God's wealth privately.

The incentives behind a herem dedication must have run the gamut from pious benefaction to coercion. In some cases, persons may have felt compelled to dedicate their property to the deity in fulfillment of a promise made to him as part of a conditional vow, such as one made before battle.[133] They may have felt indebted to Yahweh because of a sin committed.[134] Or they may have viewed the herem dedication more generally as a means of improving productivity on the farm—that giving a part of their land to a priest would summon the deity to bless the rest of it. This line of thought is found in Ezek 44:20, which encourages one to present a dough offering to a priest so that "a blessing may rest upon your home." Ownership by the divine of part of the family farm could have, from the perspective of the dedicant, imbued the property with life-giving sanctity or protected the property in some way.[135]

Judeans may have simply wished to help a priest in need by giving him and his family land. The priests of Yahweh were teachers of sacred law who lived throughout the villages of the Judean countryside, usually in clustered settle-

---

the Second Jerusalemite Temple Possess Land?," 66; Safrai, "The Agrarian Structure," 114; and Patrick, *Old Testament Law* (Atlanta: John Knox Press, 1985), 185–86.

133 The herem vow in a time of war is attested in Num 21:1–3. During the Israelites' wandering in Transjordan and the Negev, we are told of the capture of a few Israelites by the Canaanite king of Arad. The response to the capture is as follows: "Then Israel made a vow to Yahweh and said, 'If you deliver this people into our hand, we will devote their cities to herem destruction.' And Yahweh heeded Israel's plea and delivered up the Canaanites; and they and their cities were devoted to herem destruction. So that place was called Hormah." Medieval Jewish commentators, aware of the practice of sanctifying space by virtue of a herem vow, understand Hormah to have been given just this status. Rashi notes that Joshua proscribed the cities as ḥărmê gābôa ("the herem properties of the Most High"), and Ramban follows him. This aetiology on the origin of the name of the town Hormah includes within it the basic logic of a wartime vow by which divine support is petitioned through a promise that all booty will be offered up rather than taken for human benefit should a victory ensue. The similarity to Jephtha's personal vow in Judg 11:30–31, which resulted in the sacrifice of his daughter after his victory in battle, is clear; see Fishbane, *Biblical Interpretation in Ancient Israel* (Oxford; New York: Clarendon Press; Oxford University Press, 1985), 204; cf. Judg 1:1.

134 On offerings to the deity as a response to the "debt" incurred through sin, see Anderson, *Sin*, 50, 55–74. For examples of the common use in the Hebrew Bible of the verbal root š-l-m ("to pay") to convey the sense of fulfilling a vow, see, e.g., 2 Sam 15:7, Jon 2:10, and Isa 19:21, among many. For a special discussion of the root š-l-m in the contexts of vows, see Berlinerblau, *The Vow*, 179.

135 On the curing of ailment and illness through sacrifice or some other offering to God, see Douglas, *Leviticus as Literature*, 149.

ments among their own.[136] Though some approximated patrons as suppliers of subsistence loans, others appear to have relied upon their own networks of benefactors.[137] The well-connected priest would have enjoyed a more comfortable livelihood as compared to lesser known peers, and one can hardly reconstruct significant changes to this dynamic in the transition from Iron Age Israelite religion to Second Temple Judaism.[138] A good piece of land could have made for a particularly generous gift to such a person, and one bringing an expert in sacred law into the vicinity.[139]

Persons may also have declared their property *herem* as they approached death. Some may have hoped this would curry favor with the deity, so that they and their dependents and relatives surviving them would be remembered for good.[140] Others may have sought to cut off their heirs or other dependents.[141] Alison Burford suggests that in classical Greece less than pious motives for dedicating land to the gods could have included not only the desire to reduce the inheritance of an heir, but to reduce one's tax burden or visible wealth and thus one's expectations for civic benefaction.[142]

---

[136] On the priests' settlement patterns, see below, §§3.2.1, 6.3.

[137] See Deut 18:8 and 2 Kgs 12:6, both of which imply that priests were personally acquainted with individuals who offered them support.

[138] On priestly influence in Second Temple society and their use of scripture in propagating and maintaining this influence, see Watts, *Ritual and Rhetoric*, esp. 142–72. Women in priestly families, for example, appear to have been of a higher social status than other women; see Schectman, "The Social Status of Priestly and Levite Women," in *Levites and Priests* (op. cit.), 83–102.

[139] For a discussion on the expanded role of the priesthood into Torah-instruction in the Persian period, see Meyers and Meyers, *Haggai, Zechariah 1–8: A New Translation with Introduction and Commentary* (Garden City, NY: Doubleday, 1987), 194–96; on Levites and priests as leaders in Torah-reading ceremonies and Torah study in general, see Christian, "Middle-Tier Levites and the Plenary Reception of Revelation," in *Levites and Priests* (op. cit.), 173–98, esp. 195.

[140] The Mt. Gerizim temple lapidary inscriptions of the Hellenistic period—the fullest corpus of dedicatory inscriptions of the classical period in the region—invoke the language of divine remembrance of the dedicant. "To be remembered by the deity is desirable, equal to blessing," writes Anne Katrine de Hemmer Gudme in her study of the corpus, "and expected to be beneficient both for the person remembered and her or his dependents and relatives. Furthermore, the desired 'good remembrance' can be obtained by offering gifts and worship to the deity"; see *Before the God in This Place*, quote on 147.

[141] Such appears to be the concern behind Jesus's statement in Mark 7:9–13 condemning the Pharisees and scribes for allowing persons to renounce all support of their parents by declaring their property *qorban* (a "sacrifice" or offering to God), which presumably was another type of oath formula resulting in self-imposed dispossession; see §5.2.2.

[142] Burford, *Land and Labor*, 53.

Herem dedications may have been little more than inducements or bribes for priests, who enjoyed considerable influence in the judicial sphere. Their role in the courts stretches back into the Iron Age—Deut 17:8–13 has them as among the primary arbiters and protectors of law and order—and is affirmed by the latter prophets and the Chronicler.[143] The purveyors of biblical tradition characterize the tribe of Levi as sanctioned to use violence.[144] This is reflected in the character of their eponymous ancestor, who in the tribal poem of Gen 49 is said, together with his brother Simeon, to "slay men when angry, and maim oxen when pleased" (49:6). The very separation of the tribe of Levi as the clerical order of Yahweh is explained in biblical tradition as the result of their willingness to take arms against and execute the Israelites who have sinned against the divine by worshipping the golden calf (Exod 32). "And Moses said, 'Dedicate yourselves to Yahweh this day—for each of you has been against son and brother—that he may bestow a blessing upon you today'" (Exod 32:29).[145] The tradition of priests exacting violent punishment would continue through the Aaronide line of priests. The priest Pinehas, grandson of Aaron, would carry on the tradition of exacting violent punishment when he is said to have driven a spear through the bellies of an Israelite man and his Midianite mistress in Num 25:6–13.[146] In a society where priests could also be adjudicators and armed law enforcers, the potential exists for giving monetary inducements under the guise of dedication.

---

[143] Lohfink, "Distribution of the Functions of Power: The Laws Concerning Public Offices in Deuteronomy 16:18–18:22," in *A Song of Power and the Power of Song: Essays on the Book of Deuteronomy* (ed. Christensen; Winona Lake, IN: Eisenbrauns, 1993), 336–54; Meyers and Meyers, *Haggai, Zechariah 1–8*, 25–26, 194–96. Haggai serves as interpreter of priestly purity laws in Hag 2:10; the high priest Joshua is given prerogative over the courts in Zech 3:7. The Chronicler has King David dividing the Levites into various occupations related to their service in the Temple, among them six thousand "officers and magistrates" (1 Chr 23:4); and King Jehoshaphat appointing judges from the ranks of priests, Levites, and heads of clans (2 Chr 19:8). Regarding law enforcement, the Chronicler recounts the stationing of an army of priests and Levites from multiple divisions around the temple in the time of the coronation of King Jehoash, to protect him as he took shelter there (2 Chr 23). "The Levites shall surround the king on every side, every man with his weapons at the ready; and whoever enters the house shall be killed" (2 Chr 23:7). The priestly force eventually executed the deposed Queen Athaliah (2 Chr 23:12–15).
[144] Baden, "The Violent Origins of the Levites: Text and Tradition," in *Levites and Priests* (op. cit.), 103–16.
[145] Ibid., 109–12.
[146] Fishbane, *Biblical Interpretation in Ancient Israel*, 398; Collins, "The Zeal of Phinehas: The Bible and the Legitimation of Violence," *JBL* 122, no. 1 (2003), 3–21; Baden, "Violent Origins," 116.

The practice was vexing to many throughout the exilic and Second Temple period, as the source material indicates. Deuteronomy 16:18–19 condemns the bribing of judges and magistrates. Micah 3:11 includes instruction by a priest "for a price" among those wrongs that led to the fall of Jerusalem. Ben Sira 35:14 warns against offering Yahweh a bribe, "for he will not accept it." The Damascus Document (6:15) speaks of "the wicked defiling wealth through a vow and herem," a harsh condemnation of the accumulation of wealth by priests through seemingly pious dedications. The Rule of the Community (4Q258 1:12) lists herem declarations together with oaths and vows as things characteristic of those who scorn the God's word. The reasons for these condemnations may have been just as variegated as the motivations behind the herem dedications mentioned in Lev 27:28, but they reflect nonetheless long-standing concerns over the misuse of such offerings to priests. The topic as it relates to the late Second Temple period will be revisited in Chapter 6.

2.5 Anathematization of Land by Decree

(29) As for anyone that has been anathematized: they shall not be ransomed. They shall be put to death.

כָּל חֵרֶם אֲשֶׁר יָחֳרַם מִן הָאָדָם לֹא יִפָּדֶה מוֹת יוּמָת.

This regulation focuses not on property but on persons declared herem. Presumably the declaration was made as the result of judicial proceedings. The crucial difference in legal apparatus is signaled by the switch from the active verb *yaḥărim* in 27:28, where persons are dedicating others to Yahweh voluntarily, to the passive *yoḥŏrām* in 27:29, where they are anathematized and executed. Such a switch in apparatus is compulsory if the chapter is to make internal sense. Otherwise, if anyone declared herem were to be killed, why mention the human along with the animal and field in Lev 27:28 as properties that cannot be sold or redeemed? Furthermore, the repercussions of such a reading—that one could hand over somebody else as an eternal offering to Yahweh, at which point that person would be killed—approximate too closely human sacrifice to be plausible in this context, even if we assume that the priest had the right of refusal. Therefore, it seems that individuals dedicated to Yahweh in 27:28 were enlisted for service in a priest's household, but almost certainly not put to death in the manner of those anathematized by judicial decree in 27:29.[147]

---

[147] The Babylonians would employ the proscribed as slaves on their temple estates, compara-

What happened to the land of those condemned to death in this way? As a thing of lasting value, it may have been appropriated by priests. One recalls the notice in Lev 27:21 that a field foreclosed upon by Yahweh becomes "sacred to Yahweh, like the herem field; his patrimonial property becomes the priest's." Furthermore, both Num 18:14 and Ezek 44:29 protect the priestly right to enjoy the profits of anything declared herem in Israel. While this would seem to rule out things taken during a holy war against a foreign population, it does imply that priests were somehow profiting from herem when it was applied to an Israelite. That the deity could stand to benefit is central to the story of the fall of Jericho in Josh 6–7, where Achan is executed for misappropriating some of the herem valuables seized during the rout of the city and marked for the temple treasury (Josh 6:19, 7:21–26).[148]

The biblical sources are generally more concerned with conspicuous displays of death and destruction in cases where herem is imposed by decree, rather than with the fate of any landed assets that may have resulted from such a declaration. In Exod 22:18 of the Covenant Code, which is the earliest attestation of herem in the Hebrew Bible, one who offers sacrifice to other gods is anathematized by decree (*zōbēaḥ lāĕlōhîm yoḥŏrām*). The context of the law within the code suggests something other than simple execution.[149] Targum

---

ble to the proscription of the Gibeonites in Josh 9:27; see Stern, *Biblical Herem*, 133–34; and Milgrom, *Leviticus 23–27*, 2396.

148 On a reworking of the story in Pseudo-Philo, see §6.2.2. Mic 4:13 and Jud 16:19 offer examples of the voluntary dedication of herem valuables taken from battle. In 1 Sam 15:7–11, Saul is admonished for sacrificing to God some of the animals declared herem after his rout of the Amalekites. For general discussions of the practice of wartime herem, see Greenberg, "Ḥerem," 10–13; Weinfeld, "The Ban on the Canaanites in the Biblical Codes and Its Historical Development," in *History and Traditions of Early Israel: Studies Presented to Eduard Nielsen, May 8th 1993* (ed. Lemaire et al.; Leiden; New York: Brill, 1993); Fishbane, *Biblical Interpretation in Ancient Israel*, 199–209; Niditch, *War in the Hebrew Bible: A Study in the Ethics of Violence* (New York: Oxford University Press, 1993), 28–89; Rofé, "The Laws of Warfare in the Book of Deuteronomy: Their Origins, Intent and Positivity," *JSOT* 32 (1985), 25–37; and Nelson, "Ḥerem and the Deuteronomic Social Conscience," 39–54.

149 The law is part of a triplet of capital cases (Exod 22:17–19), though standard execution in the Covenant Code is conveyed by the expression *môt yûmāt* (e.g., Exod 21:15–17); see Propp, *Exodus 19–40: A New Translation with Introduction and Commentary* (New York: Doubleday, 2006), 204–5; and Houtman, *Exodus, Volume 3, Chapters 20–40* (Leuven: Peeters, 2000), 214. Thus, the application of herem status to the one who was proven to have committed the crime of illicit sacrifice must have implied something else. Enslavement to the priesthood along with the seizure of the proscribed person's properties (including any landed assets) by the sanctuary would have been an appropriate punishment for the wrongful sacrifice to a rival god, which would have been not only an affront to the covenant between Yahweh and Israel

Pseudo-Jonathan renders the word *yoḥŏrām* with the phrase "he will be killed with the sword and his possessions destroyed." Since the dispossession of one's heirs lies at the heart of anathematization, it would be fitting for landed property to be seized in such a case. This in turn could explain the juxtaposition in the Covenant Code of the punishment for illicit worship immediately before laws on various landless classes—the resident alien, poor, widow, and orphan (Exod 22:20–23)—because the fallout from a conviction for illicit worship would add to the landless as well, the heirs of the convicted now standing dispossessed of their patrimony.

In the book of Deuteronomy, a town found to be inhabited entirely of apostates is to be utterly destroyed, its inhabitants executed, and its structures and booty burnt, so that the place would remain an "eternal ruin" (*tēl ʿôlām*; Deut 13:16–18). The custom thus approximates a whole burnt offering—a *kālîl laYHWH* as it is called in Deut 13:17—which would have offered little appreciable benefit even to a priest. The fate of the town's fields and orchards in such a case is unclear, though one should keep in mind how the herem was used in the book of Joshua as a means of emptying the territory of Canaan of its inhabitants.[150] The implication there is that valuable land for cultivation could indeed result from acts of herem execution.

A case in Ezra is worth considering too. In Ezra 10:8, anyone who failed to come to Jerusalem for a national assembly concerning the issue of intermarriage is threatened with excommunication (*yibbādēl miqqĕhal haggôlâ*) and the anathematization of their property (*yoḥŏram kol-rĕkûšô*). The word *rĕkûš* ("property") in the verse could connote movables or real estate.[151] Yet again the question is

---

but also the denial of "nourishment" to which Yahweh alone, and his earthly representatives, had a rightful claim.

150 In the book of Joshua, the herem is applied to the cities of Jericho (6:21), Ai (8:26), Makkedah (10:28), Egon (10:35), Hebron (10:37), and Debir (10:39), and Hazor (11:11), as well as the whole land of Canaan (10:40) and the whole land of the Anakites (11:21). The legal apparatus is provided by Deut 7:1–5, which concerns itself with the need to stamp out idolatrous worship, as embodied by the Canaanites.

151 See particularly Ezra 8:21, where the word *rĕkûš* denotes livestock; see also Ezra 1:4, 6; 1 Chr 27:31, 28:1; 2 Chr 31:3, 32:29; and Dan 11:13. 1 Esdras 9:4 provides κτήνη ("livestock, cattle") here. Josephus (*Ant.* 11.148) writes that the property in question was οὐσία, a generic term for all real and movable assets (e.g., *Ant.* 11.103, 214, 269; but see *War* 2.122, 464; *Ant.* 18.194 and also Luke 15:12, where it clearly refers to land), and for *yoḥŏram* he uses a passive participle of the form ἀφιερόω, which elsewhere he applies to denote consecration for the benefit of the temple treasury (*Ant.* 3.201, 4.72, 15.364); see Rengstorf, *A Complete Concordance to Flavius Josephus* (Leiden: Brill, 1973), vol. I, 277. Unfortunately, quite little is known of excommunication practices in Second Temple Judea; see Horbury, "Extirpation and Excommunication," *VT* 35, no. 1 (1985), 13–38, esp. 21, 37–38; and Benovitz, *Kol Nidre*, 71–72, 106–7.

whether the land of the excommunicated individual would have been marked herem in the first place; and if so, if that meant it was to be left desolate or taken over by priests.[152] In Ezra 6:11, Darius declares that anyone who alters his decree to rebuild the Jerusalem temple will be impaled and his house made into a dung hill (*ûbaytēh nĕwālû yit'ăbēd*). It could be that Ezra's decree in 10:8 would have resulted in a similar display, with any landed property of the truant left to lie desolate. In the Greek sphere, citizens convicted of certain heinous crimes against the polis could have their land declared sacrosanct, which meant it could not be sold or cultivated.[153] In such a case the priest's prerogative would simply have been to enforce the taboo.

2.6 Summary

Since ancient times the regulations of Lev 27 have been thought to concern a special kind of monetized donation to Yahweh. Here it has been argued, based on an idea suggested by Joshua Sosin, that the chapter regulates a secured lending operation run by the priests of Yahweh. According to the laws of the chapter, persons in need of credit could have appealed to the deity and pledged to him a property—whether slave, animal, building, or field—to secure the loan. This pledge was hypothecary in nature, meaning that possessory rights remained with the debtor. The consecration signaled Yahweh's charges over the property. Shorter term loans would have been secured by movables and harvests from purchased fields; longer term loans by patrimonial fields, much like a mortgage. Repayment (= redemption) could have in all cases been settled in installments, assuming that the 50-shekel valuation provided at Lev 27:16 for patrimonial land (as well as the valuation schedule of Lev 27:3–7 for humans) relates to a single year rather than the entire Jubilee cycle. If it does, then the 50-shekel valuation for land allows for repayment at the rate of the silver weight of 1 mina per homer per year, which masks the even more workable redemption schedule of 1 gerah

---

[152] Joseph Blenkinsopp points to Ezra 10:8 to argue that the seizure of such assets was one way in which the temple could have accumulated land; "Did the Second Jerusalemite Temple Possess Land?," 61–68. Stevens too mentions the possibility; *Temples, Tithes, and Taxes*, 83. For more on the history of research into temple land in Judea, see §1.2.
[153] *Land and Labor*, 31, 49–50, 237, n. 40. Examples cited by Burford include the trial at Athens in 415 BCE of men accused of mutilating the Hermae (their properties were confiscated and put up for public sale); and the punishment by exile and by land confiscation of anyone at Mylasa in southwest Turkey for insulting the ruler Mausolus. In instances of land not sacrosanct, their purchase for the benefit of the state could have been viewed as a special civic duty; see ibid., 49.

per omer per month. In other words, the text provides a valuation benchmark that would have accommodated repayment in installments on an annual or even a monthly basis in tidy numbers in the local currency system.

These loans were at a fixed interest rate of 20%, as was common for silver loans in this period. The taboo on interest in Judean society is well known. Here the consecration masks the loan. Persons could "sell" (= consecrate) their property to Yahweh and agree to buy it back with a 20% mark-up. Even that mark-up could have been hidden, at least superficially. Raz Kletter's work on Judahite stone scale-weights has demonstrated that the holy shekel weight was 20% lighter than the common shekel in the late Iron Age. Therefore, one could buy 10 shekels in the holy standard, sell 10 shekels in the common standard, and come away with 20% more in silver.

This is not to imply that priests were engaging in an act of profiteering. With proper measures to mitigate against risk—such as the clause giving them recourse for delinquency in Lev 27:20–21—they were providing credit to a farming population in a period of economic decline in the wake of the Babylonian wars. The priests behind this document display a willingness to put Yahweh's reserves to work, to strengthen the local economy by promoting agricultural production, and to help distressed farmers stay on their land. The chapter lays out basic pricing standards while emphasizing redeemability. This can be related to the Holiness School's objective of strengthening Judean ethnic ties to the land.

Priests of the Holiness School may also have seen this as an effective way of keeping Judeans away from foreign creditors. In cases of foreclosure, fields mortgaged to Yahweh would have joined his holy properties, which for all intents and purposes became the priest's property (Lev 27:21). To the priests of the Holiness School, this may have been far better than foreclosure by a foreign creditor or a private Judean banker willing to sell to the highest bidder. In this way one can read the land-based regulations of Lev 27 as a close companion to the Holiness Code's Jubilee law, whose mandate for universal land release every 50 years was also meant to promote economic liberty.

For persons wishing to simply donate their land to Yahweh, or feeling compelled to do so for another reason, they had the option of a herem dedication (Lev 27:28). These dedications may have been in fulfillment of a vow, in repayment of a debt to the deity or to a priest, or in hopes of blessing the farm. Alternatively, since the material benefits of owning a herem property fell to the priests, individuals may have declared their property herem as a quid pro quo —in exchange for a favorable ruling in cases involving sacred law, for example; or as payment for overdue fines or for services provided by a priest. In certain cases, persons convicted of apostasy against Yahweh, or entire villages slaughtered as apostates, would have left behind possessions bearing herem status;

land also may have been similarly marked as taboo for regular human use. While the full implications of a herem designation remain unclear to us, it is obvious from Lev 27 that it gave ownership to Yahweh's priests.

Chapter 3
The Sacred Reserve of Yahweh in Ezekiel's Temple Vision

3.1 Introduction

As the priests of the Holiness School were developing regulations on how the land of Yahweh was to be properly cultivated, others in roughly the same period were laying out a blueprint for a new sanctuary of Yahweh in Jerusalem. Included in this blueprint were the parameters of a new relationship between the sanctuary and the land. They wrote their vision in the name of the prophet Ezekiel, whose life as a priest and whose experience of exile at the hands of the Babylonians provided a fitting voice for a message of reform. Their work, which was appended to the scroll of Ezekiel (chapters 40–48), is referred to as the Temple Vision.[1] It is a detailed description of how the temple is to appear, how it is to be managed, and how it is to be sustained after it has been rebuilt in an idyllic age. The message is said to have come to Ezekiel during the twenty-fifth year of his exile (i.e., 573 BCE; Ezek 40:1), some 13 years after Jerusalem was razed to the ground. However, it is thought to have emerged several generations later, in a period of regional transformation under the Persian imperial regime in the late sixth or early fifth century BCE. Its exact chronological relationship to Lev 27 cannot be ascertained. It could have been written as plans for a new temple in Jerusalem were being carried out or after they had been completed.[2]

---

[1] On the historical context and message of the hypothesized "Ezekiel school" in the exilic period, see Albertz, *A History of Israelite Religion in the Old Testament Period. Volume II: From the Exile to the Maccabees* (Louisville: Westminster John Knox Press, 1994), 427–36. For a summary of the history of research into the Temple Vision and an extensive bibliography, see Albertz, *Israel in Exile: The History and Literature of the Sixth Century B.C.E.* (Leiden; Boston: Brill, 2004), 345–52. For a presentation of textual strata and a proposed relative and absolute chronology for them, see Zimmerli, *Ezekiel 2*, 547–53.

[2] For a summary of views relating the Temple Vision to the Persian period, see Grabbe, *A History of the Jews and Judaism in the Second Temple Period. Volume 1, Yehud: A History of the Persian Province of Judah* (London: T&T Clark, 2004), 96–97. For further discussion on a Persian-period date for it, see Tuell, *The Law of the Temple in Ezekiel 40–48* (Atlanta: Scholars Press, 1992), esp. 78–102; on its dependence on the Holiness Code, see Lyons, *From Law to Prophecy: Ezekiel's Use of the Holiness Code* (New York; London: T&T Clark, 2009). For a dating to the Persian and Hellenistic periods, see Garscha, *Studien zum Ezechielbuch: eine redaktionskritische Untersuchung von Ez 1–39* (Bern: Herbert Lang, 1974). Walther Zimmerli suggests a date for the finalization of the Temple Vision just before the consecration of the temple in the 530s and 520s

The genre of prophetic book was popular in this period, with scrolls on the teachings of prophets like Isaiah, Jeremiah, and Ezekiel having circulated among a people in need of explanation for its recent travails. One feature of this genre is to present events that have already transpired as having been long-ago foreseen. These ex eventu prophecies would have been particularly resonant when they predicted the downfall of Jerusalem. Seeking a better understanding of how Yahweh's holy city could be forsaken, the authors of these prophecies were loath to revisit the errors of the past and were themselves probably part of a revitalization initiative for Jerusalem.³

Of primary concern to the authors of the Temple Vision is the sanctification of space. The authors have the sanctuary precinct divided into clearly demarcated areas, each characterized by its relative degree of holiness and proximity to the divine, each demarcated by walls and gates, and each accessed by specific individuals in a highly regulated fashion (Ezek 40:48 – 41:26).⁴ The authors organize space to negotiate social relationships among Yahweh's servants—priest above Levite, Levite above prince, and prince above the lay tribes—and to shield those individuals from foreigners (Ezek 44:9). The deeper social messages of this worldview have been explored in scholarship. Kalinda Rose Stevenson sees the Temple Vision's interest in space as having been fundamentally about access: the priests enjoy it with respect to the temple, the prince and the rest of Israel

---

BCE; see *Ezekiel 2*, 552–53. This *terminus ante quem* finds support in the fact that the Temple Vision includes no mention of a high priest, which is already presupposed in Zech 3:1, 8; see Albertz, *History of Israelite Religion II*, 612, n. 61. Albertz also notes that Ezek 40–48 avoids the term *melek* ("king"), while it is used in Ezek 1–39; ibid., 612 n. 70. He argues for a date somewhere between 545 and 515 BCE given the apparent nearness of temple reconstruction in the perspective of the author(s) of the Temple Vision; *Israel in Exile*, 352.

3 On the genre of the prophetic book from a form-critical perspective, see Ben Zvi, "The Concept of Prophetic Books and Its Historical Setting," in *The Production of Prophecy: Constructing Prophecy and Prophets in Yehud* (ed. Edelman and Ben Zvi; London; Oakville, CT: Equinox, 2009), 73–95; and idem, "Introduction: Writings, Speeches, and the Prophetic Books," in *Writings and Speech in Israelite and Ancient Near Eastern Prophecy* (ed. Ben Zvi and Floyd; Atlanta: Society of Biblical Literature, 2000), 1–30. On Judean awareness of their people's history in the land during the Persian period, and of their own hardship in the wake of the Babylonian wars, see Sara Japhet's "People and Land in the Restoration Period" in *From the Rivers of Babylon to the Highlands of Judah: Collected Studies in the Restoration Period* (Winona Lake, IN: Eisenbrauns, 2006), 96–116. For a discussion on Second and Third Isaiah, Haggai, Zech 1–8, and Malachi, see Ristau, *Reconstructing Jerusalem: Persian-Period Prophetic Perspectives* (Winona Lake, IN: Eisenbrauns, 2016), 188–95.

4 Philip Peter Jensen associates the concept of graded holiness with a specific strand of exilic and post-exilic Judaism; see *Graded Holiness: A Key to the Priestly Conception of the World* (Sheffield: Sheffield Academic Press, 1992), esp. 215 (quote), 218.

do not.[5] Jonathan Z. Smith reads the Temple Vision as a social map of an ideal cultic place, where power hierarchies (prince/priest, priest/Levite, priest/Israel) are maintained; he relates portions of the text to distinct social maps.[6] In a related vein, Susan Niditch understands it to be a microcosm where the drawing of boundaries between "us" and "them" is an overriding concern, as is the establishment of order among chaos.[7]

As argued in this chapter, the authors of the Temple Vision are also remodeling the priesthood's relationship to the land. They promote the removal of the priesthood from the countryside, with all the ramifications of such a move for the priests' role in land cultivation, credit, and stewardship. They envision a priesthood producing no wealth in the economy over which the temple presides, offering no economic stimulus and—much unlike the typical sacred plots of sanctuaries of the ancient world and of the realities behind Lev 27—managing no arable land. Furthermore, the reserve they have the priests inhabiting was to be situated at a significant distance from the city. This calls to mind the physical relationship between the actual temple in Jerusalem in the Persian period and the center of imperial administration at Ramat Rahel.

The Temple Vision's endorsement of a single residential quarter for priests revived old customs of communal living in the face of what appears to have been a fairly disperse priesthood in the Persian period, and one whose members included private landholders. An initiative by Nehemiah to incorporate sacred revenues addresses the challenges of a physically disperse priesthood too, and signals perhaps a major step forward in the collectivization process for Yahweh's wealth. A land-survey ostracon from Idumea possibly referencing a plot of the "House of Yeho" may reflect the outcome of this process. Dated to the late fourth century BCE, it is the earliest archaeological evidence for land sacred to the deity.

---

5 *Vision of Transformation: The Territorial Rhetoric of Ezekiel 40–48* (Atlanta: Scholars Press, 1996), esp. 11–95.
6 *To Take Place: Toward Theory in Ritual* (Chicago: University of Chicago Press, 1987), 58–60. For a similar reading of Ezekiel 40–48 as mapping social space, see Havrelock, "The Two Maps of Israel's Land," *JBL* 126, no. 4 (2007), 651–55.
7 "Ezekiel 40–48 in a Visionary Context," *Catholic Biblical Quarterly* 48 (1986), 208–24. The tribal locations of the Temple Vision required the transfer of the two and a half tribes east of the Jordan to new locations west of the river, perhaps because Transjordan was considered by the Temple Vision's authors to have been an unclean land; see Josh 22:10–34 and Nili Wazana's discussion of Ezekiel's borders for the land in *All the Boundaries of the Land: The Promised Land in Biblical Thought in Light of the Ancient Near East* (Winona Lake, IN: Eisenbrauns, 2013), 167–82.

3.2 The Sacred Reserve and Its Local Prototypes

The Temple Vision opens with Ezekiel flying from Babylon to Jerusalem and landing in the sanctuary precinct. He is guided through its spaces by a man with a bronze aura, who uses a cord and a rod to take measurements. Ezekiel records the measurements and describes the edifice he sees (Ezek 40:1–42:20). After his tour he witnesses the glory of Yahweh return to the place (43:1–12). The deity calls out to him and provides a series of ordinances on how this new temple was to operate and how the land was to be allocated to the tribes of Israel (43:13–48:35). Among these ordinances is a call to establish a sacred reserve surrounding the temple: a beautiful piece of land and a sizeable tract, equivalent to several kilometers square, with houses for priests and Levites and a pastureland for the holy flock (Ezek 45:1–6; 48:8–14). A river gushing forth from the temple is to flow through the sacred reserve and give water to Israel's territory (Ezek 47:1–12).

The first description of the sacred reserve is part of a section on temple operations and entitlements (44:1–46:24). It opens as follows:

(Ezek 45:1[8]) When you allot the land as an inheritance, you will contribute as an offering to Yahweh a sacred portion of land, an area 25,000 long and 20,000[9] wide. It will be sacred in its entire extent.	וּבְהַפִּילְכֶם אֶת־הָאָרֶץ בְּנַחֲלָה תָּרִימוּ תְרוּמָה לַיהוָה קֹדֶשׁ מִן־הָאָרֶץ אֹרֶךְ חֲמִשָּׁה וְעֶשְׂרִים אֶלֶף אֹרֶךְ וְרֹחַב עֲשָׂרָה אָלֶף קֹדֶשׁ הוּא בְּכָל־גְּבוּלָהּ סָבִיב׃

The description then elaborates on the size of its various components (45:2–5), which will include tracts of land for the priests and the lower-ranking Levites, and a space in the middle for the sanctuary itself. Dimensions are given throughout, as if the text were meant to be vocalized in conjunction with a visual aid such as a map.[10] The dimensions are regularly divisible by 50—a number that recalls the Jubilee in the Holiness Code (Lev 25:8–17).[11]

---

8 The text here and below follows BHS, while the translation is my adaptation of JPS. The MT of this and the second description of the sacred reserve is not without its problems and generally the Greek textual witnesses (LXX) have proven to be the more sensible and reliable, as is discussed further below in this section and in §3.3.
9 Translation of the width of the reserve follows LXX. On the problematic dimensions for the sacred reserve in MT Ezekiel, see §3.3.
10 Harold Brodsky, "Ezekiel's Map of Restoration," in *Land and Community: Geography in Jewish Studies* (ed. Brodsky; Bethesda, MD: University Press of Maryland, 1997), 17–29.
11 The 25,000 × 25,000 measurement for the people's offering including the city land, for instance, would be the length of the temple complex (500) multiplied by 50 for the Jubilee. Bennett Simon explores the symbolic value of these dimensions in the Temple Vision and argues

The second description of the sacred reserve is more elaborate than the first. It appears within the ordinances on the allotment of Yahweh's territory to the tribes of Israel (47:13–48:35). All tribes are to be located west of the Jordan River, perhaps because of purity concerns, and all are to be given a roughly equal territorial allotment spanning the entire breadth of land from the Jordan River to the Mediterranean Sea.[12] The sacred reserve comes below the tribe of Judah's holding and above Benjamin's—precisely where Jerusalem would fall on a map. It is joined by the prince's land (48:21) and the city and its farmland (48:18–19) in forming an extra-tribal parcel also spanning the entire width of Israel's territory:[13]

(Ezek 48:8) Adjoining the territory of Judah, from the eastern border to the western border, will be the offering you will contribute: 25,000 wide and equal in length to one of the portions from the eastern border to the western border. The sanctuary will be in the middle of it.

(9) For Yahweh, the offering you will contribute will be 25,000 long and 20,000 wide.[14] (10) And the sacred offering will be for the following:

וְעַל גְּבוּל יְהוּדָה מִפְּאַת קָדִים עַד פְּאַת יָמָּה תִּהְיֶה הַתְּרוּמָה אֲשֶׁר תָּרִימוּ חֲמִשָּׁה וְעֶשְׂרִים אֶלֶף רֹחַב וְאֹרֶךְ כְּאַחַד הַחֲלָקִים מִפְּאַת קָדִימָה עַד פְּאַת יָמָּה וְהָיָה הַמִּקְדָּשׁ בְּתוֹכוֹ.

הַתְּרוּמָה אֲשֶׁר תָּרִימוּ לַיהוָה אֹרֶךְ חֲמִשָּׁה וְעֶשְׂרִים אֶלֶף וְרֹחַב עֲשֶׂרֶת אֲלָפִים. וּלְאֵלֶּה תִּהְיֶה תְרוּמַת הַקֹּדֶשׁ:

---

that they are about "taming the wildness and extravagance" of both human transgression and divine wrath; "Ezekiel's Geometric Vision of the Restored Temple: From the Rod of His Wrath to the Reed of His Measuring," *HTR* 102, no. 4 (2009), 411–38, esp. 412–13. See also Bergsma, "The Restored Temple as 'Built Jubilee' in Ezekiel 40–48," *Proceedings, Eastern Great Lakes and Midwest Biblical Societies* 24 (2004), 75–85, esp. 78. Note also that the number 25 is regularly used for dimensions in the temple (e.g., Ezek 40:13, 15, 21).

12 See note on translation of Ezek 45:1 above.

13 Moshe Greenberg sees this second version as necessary (given the respective contexts of both descriptions) and not reflective of two versions; "The Design and Themes of Ezekiel's Program of Restoration," *Interpretation* 38, no. 2 (1984), 196–97, 202. The second account is, according to Greenberg, "logically subordinate to the complete scheme of chapter 48; but there is no way of knowing whether in fact the detail came to mind (and pen) first and the whole was spun out of it as a consequence, or vice versa (or another alternative)"; ibid., 197. For an argument on the dependence of this latter description on that of Ezek 45, see Block, *The Book of Ezekiel, Chapters 25–48* (Grand Rapids, MI: W.B. Eerdmans, 1997), 649–50; and Milgrom and Block, *Ezekiel's Hope: A Commentary on Ezekiel 38–48* (Eugene, OR: Cascade Books, 2012), 250–54.

14 See note on translation of Ezek 45:1 above.

3.2 The Sacred Reserve and Its Local Prototypes — 89

For the priests, [an area of] 25,000 on the north, 10,000 on the west, 10,000 on the east, and 25,000 on the south; the sanctuary of Yahweh will be in the middle of it. (11) The consecrated area will be for the priests from the line of Zadok, who kept my charge and did not go astray from among the people of Israel, as the Levites did. (12) And they will have a special allotment of the offering of land, a most holy place, adjoining the Levites. (13) The Levites will be alongside the priests, [in an area] 25,000 long and 10,000 wide. The total length will be 25,000 and the width 20,000.[15] (14) They will not sell any part of it. One will not exchange it or transfer it. It is prime land, for it is sacred to Yahweh.

לַכֹּהֲנִים צָפוֹנָה חֲמִשָּׁה וְעֶשְׂרִים אֶלֶף וְיָמָּה רֹחַב עֲשֶׂרֶת אֲלָפִים וְקָדִימָה רֹחַב עֲשֶׂרֶת אֲלָפִים וְנֶגְבָּה אֹרֶךְ חֲמִשָּׁה וְעֶשְׂרִים אָלֶף וְהָיָה מִקְדַּשׁ־יְהוָה בְּתוֹכוֹ. לַכֹּהֲנִים הַמְקֻדָּשׁ מִבְּנֵי צָדוֹק אֲשֶׁר שָׁמְרוּ מִשְׁמַרְתִּי אֲשֶׁר לֹא תָעוּ בִּתְעוֹת בְּנֵי יִשְׂרָאֵל כַּאֲשֶׁר תָּעוּ הַלְוִיִּם. וְהָיְתָה לָּהֶם תְּרוּמִיָּה מִתְּרוּמַת הָאָרֶץ קֹדֶשׁ קָדָשִׁים אֶל־גְּבוּל הַלְוִיִּם.

וְהַלְוִיִּם לְעֻמַּת גְּבוּל הַכֹּהֲנִים חֲמִשָּׁה וְעֶשְׂרִים אֶלֶף אֹרֶךְ וְרֹחַב עֲשֶׂרֶת אֲלָפִים כָּל־אֹרֶךְ חֲמִשָּׁה וְעֶשְׂרִים אֶלֶף וְרֹחַב עֲשֶׂרֶת אֲלָפִים. וְלֹא־יִמְכְּרוּ מִמֶּנּוּ וְלֹא יָמֵר וְלֹא יַעֲבוֹר [וְיַעֲבִיר] רֵאשִׁית הָאָרֶץ כִּי קֹדֶשׁ לַיהוָה.

The sacred reserve was to be an Eden-like paradise in mountainous terrain, the temple at its center towering over the landscape like a castle.[16] The reserve's gushing river, its verdant grove of trees, and its pastureland (Ezek 40:2, 45:4, 47:1–7) all conjure images of the pastoral. Dotted by dwellings of priests and Levites, the reserve is referred to in the Hebrew text as a most holy place (*qōdeš qādāšîm*; Ezek 48:12), suggesting that the glory of Yahweh was to be present in it;[17] and as an exemplary tract of dedicated land (*tĕrûmiyyâ mittĕrûmat hā'āreṣ*; 48:12), a phrase whose unique biblical form *tĕrûmiyyâ* signifies "the best of" something.[18]

---

15 As in previous note.
16 In Ezek 40:2, Ezekiel lands on the Temple Mount having flown in from exile by the power of God. "He set me down on a very high mountain," reads the verse, "on which there seemed to be the outline of a city on the south (*minnegeb*)." The "outline of a city" can be read to refer to the temple complex itself, with the LXX's ἀπέναντι ("opposite") suggesting that *negdî* was corrupted to *minnegeb*. Ezekiel is merely landing on the Temple Mount and being confronted by a huge edifice similar to a fortified city. On the sacred reserve's similarities to the Garden of Eden and its indebtedness to Near Eastern fertility mythology, see Tuell, *Law of the Temple*, 68–71.
17 Kasher, "Anthropomorphism, Holiness and Cult: A New Look at Ezekiel 40–48," *Zeitschrift für die alttestamentliche Wissenschaft* 110, no. 2 (1998), 201–2, 207; see also Joyce, "Temple and Worship in Ezekiel 40–48," in *Temple and Worship in Biblical Israel* (ed. Day; London; New York: T&T Clark, 2005), 156–57.
18 The form *tĕrûmiyyâ* is a feminine adjective of the class of nouns that add the suffix -*î* to convert a substantive into a modifier, as in *'ibriyyâ*, "Judean (f.)" and *mô'ăbiyyâ*, "Moabite (f.)"; see Cowley, *Gesenius' Hebrew Grammar as Edited and Enlarged by the Late E. Kautzsch* (Oxford: Clarendon Press, 1910), 240; and Joüon and Muraoka, *A Grammar of Biblical Hebrew*, vol. I (Roma: Editrice Pontificio Istituto Biblio, 1991), 264–65. Thus, Rashi uses the plural form of the word to

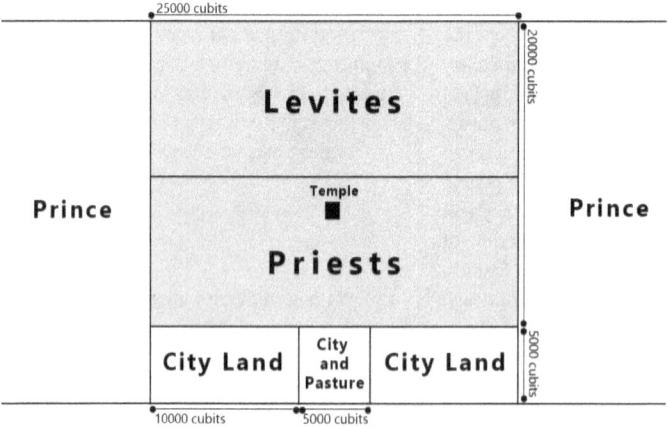

Figure 7. The sacred reserve (in grey) in Ezekiel's Temple Vision. It is situated within an extra-tribal territory with land allotted for the city and prince as well.

It was also to be a sizeable tract. Assuming that the book of Ezekiel uses the long cubit (52 cm=20.5 inches), the sanctuary and priestly quarter were to inhabit an area of roughly 130 sq km (=50 sq miles). The Levites' portion of land was to be identical in size, giving a total area of approximately 260 sq km for the sacred reserve.[19] The temple precinct, at 500 × 500 cubits (Ezek 45:2), was also to be rel-

---

mean "exemplary traits" in his Ecclesiastes commentary (11:3). The form would resurface in medieval and pre-modern Jewish writings; for a summary of its use in late ancient and medieval Jewish poetry and early modern Hebrew, see Eliezer Ben-Yehuda's particularly thorough entry in *Milon Ha-Lashon Ha-Ivrit* (Berlin: Langenscheidt, 1908–1959) [Hebrew], 7907–8. Yet the form *tĕrûmiyyâ* is taken as a synonym for *tĕrûmâ* in all the textual witnesses, leading many to posit that it is a corruption of that word. LXX reads ἡ ἀπαρχὴ δεδομένη ἐκ τῶν ἀπαρχῶν and Targum Jonathan ארעא מאפרשותא אפרשותא. BHS follows these traditions as do many commentaries and the King James in its rendering of it as simply "oblation"; see Zimmerli, *Ezekiel 2*, 522–23, who lists several. Zimmerli happens to accept the word as original and glosses it as "a particular consecrated area of land." Kasher also accepts its originality; *Ezekiel: Introduction and Commentary. Volume 2: Chapters 25–48* (Tel Aviv; Jerusalem: Am Oved Publishers; The Hebrew University Magnes Press, 2004) [Hebrew], 929. NRSV is also in line with this view by giving "a special portion," as is JPS with its gloss "a special reserve."

19 It is not clear whether the northernmost plot in the sacred reserve was of the priests or the Levites. Relying on the assumption that Ezekiel moves north to south, as he does in the allotment scheme of Ezek 47:13–48:35, Greenberg, Kasher, and Albertz have the priests occupying the northernmost section, which would place the Levites' land as a buffer between the priests and the city; Greenberg, "Design and Themes," 202, n. 37; Kasher, *Ezekiel 2*, 928; Albertz, *Israel in Exile*, 357. Others prefer having the sanctuary and the priests in the middle of the sacred reatively large. To put that in perspective, the Temple Vision calls for a sacred esplanade about twice the size of the Persian-period compound at Mt. Gerizim and half that of the Herodian-period precinct in Jerusalem.[20] This is an ambitious vision for territorial reform in a region whose sacralized land would have been scattered, small, and heterogenous.

3.2.1 Levitical Settlements Reimagined

Though many priests may have been living with other members of their clan in Jerusalem and in other villages across the countryside, the Temple Vision's placement of Yahweh's priests together in a single dwelling area within the sacred reserve—alongside pastureland for their animals—recalls the Levitical settlements of the Hebrew Bible.[21] These settlements are mentioned across biblical sources, their longest description coming in the Deuteronomistic History (Josh 21:1–40), where each of the 48 settlements of the tribe of Levi is said to have been fortified by a wall and each endowed with pasturelands called *migrāšîm*. The cities feature in legal material of the Hebrew Bible (Lev 25:34, Num 35:1–8), as well as in 1 Chr 6:39–66. The full list of 48 cities in Joshua 21 is almost certainly a literary fiction, many of the towns in that list having been located far beyond the realistic borders of Israelite settlement in the Iron Age.[22] But the Levitical settlement concept appears to have been rooted in reality. According to Nadav Naaman, the 13 cities given over to the Aaronide priests in the Josh 21 list do coincide with more realistic estimates regarding the borders of the Ju-

---

serve with the Levites to the north; see Eichrodt, *Ezekiel: A Commentary* (Philadelphia: The Westminster Press, 1970), 570; Zimmerli, *Ezekiel 2*, Fig. 7 on 535; and Stevenson, *Vision of Transformation*, Fig. 4 on 35.

20 For discussion and dimensions, see Magen, *Mount Gerizim Excavations, Volume II: A Temple City* (Jerusalem: Staff Officer for Archaeology—Civil Administration of Judea and Samaria, 2008), 143–45; on the Jerusalem precinct, see §§1.2, 5.1.

21 For more on the endogamous tendencies of the Judean priesthood and their communal settlement patterns, see §6.3.

22 Naaman, *Borders and Districts in Biblical Historiography: Seven Studies in Biblical Geographic Lists* (Jerusalem: Simor, 1986), 203–36; see also Haran, *Temples and Temple-Service*, 112–31; Jeremy Hutton, "The Levitical Diaspora (I): A Sociological Comparison with Morocco's Ahansal," in *Exploring the Longue Durée* (op. cit.), 223–34; and Leuchter, *The Levites and the Boundaries of Israelite Identity* (Oxford: Oxford University Press, 2017), 118–20. For a "minimalist" view of the cities list, understanding it to be a utopian creation, see Liverani, *Israel's History and the History of Israel* (London; Oakville, CT: Equinox, 2005), 337–41, Fig. 58; he follows Wellhausen, who saw the cities as entirely artificially constructed and associated with post-exilic Judaism; *Prolegomena to the History of Israel* (Charleston, SC: Bibliobazaar, 2007), 153–61.

dahite monarchy around the seventh century BCE and may reflect actual cities of priests established as part of the administrative reform of Josiah.[23] The other settlements, he claims, were added to the Joshua conquest narrative in order that each tribe and geographic region be similarly provided (in the literary imagination) with settlements of priests. Some may have been located at the sites of old Yahwistic shrines that were destroyed as part of Josiah's reform.[24] Others may simply have been residential quarters populated predominantly by priests and their families within towns with mixed populations.[25] The Holiness Code had sought to maintain the integrity of these priestly settlements by having deeds of sale expire at the Jubilee (Lev 25:32–33) in a manner similar to patrimonial land (25:28) and to rural houses integrally associated with that land (25:31), thereby preventing the priests from permanently selling their houses.

The sacred status of the Levitical settlements is suggested by the fact that some of them also served as cities of refuge or asylum towns (Deut 4:41–43, Josh 20:1–9). In the Israelite world, the institution of giving refuge to murderers, thieves, debtors, and other miscreants underwent its own development; typically this role was assumed by sanctuaries in the Mediterranean basin.[26] In biblical law the cities of refuge were meant for persons who had committed an unintentional homicide and were seeking haven from a blood avenger (Num 35:9–29, Deut 19:1–10). As Num 35:12 states, "These cities shall serve you as a refuge from the avenger, so that the manslayer may not die unless he has stood trial before the assembly." Their derivation from old shrine sites is possible.[27]

---

23 Naaman, *Borders and Districts*, 233–34. The town of Nob is described in 1 Sam 22:19, for example, as ʿîr hakkōhănîm ("the city of priests").
24 On the association in scholarship between defunct shrines and the Levitical settlements, see Mazar, "The Cities of the Priests and the Levites," *Supplements to Vetus Testamentum* 7 (1957), 193–205; Alt, "Festungen und Levitenorte im Lande Juda," in *Kleine Schriften zur Geschichte des Volkes Israel* (München: Beck'sche Verlagsbuchhandlung, 1953), 305–15; and Weinberg, *The Citizen-Temple Community*, 97. But cf. Haran, *Temples and Temple-Service*, 119–21. There Haran has demonstrated that many of the Levitical settlements were located at places for which there is no evidence of an earlier shrine; and that other early shrines made defunct with the centralization reforms were not associated with Levitical settlements.
25 Baruch Levine has argued for the more limited understanding of the term ʿîr; see "The Biblical 'Town' as Reality and Typology: Evaluating Biblical References to Towns and Their Functions," in *Urbanization and Land Ownership in the Ancient Near East* (ed. Hudson and Levine; Cambridge, MA: Peabody Museum of Archaeology and Ethnology, Harvard University, 1999), 421–53.
26 Auld, "Cities of Refuge in Israelite Tradition," in *Joshua Retold: Synoptic Perspectives* (Edinburgh: T&T Clark, 1998), 37–48.
27 See Exod 21:13, which appears to identify the altar at the local sanctuary as the site of refuge.

The authors of the Temple Vision appear to have associated the Levitical settlements in these sources with the Levites, who were second-class holy men without altar privileges. Their lower status is said to derive from the fact that they were not of proper Zadokite lineage (Ezek 44:9–16).[28] Their allotment in the sacred reserve is described in the MT (45:5) as *'eśrîm lĕšākōt* ("twenty chambers"), a reading that is contextually difficult and can be dismissed in favor of the LXX's πόλεις κατοικεῖν ("urban quarters for settlement"). This suggests an original Hebrew *'ārîm lāšebet*.[29] The same Hebrew phrase *'ārîm lāšebet* appears in relation to the Levitical settlements in Num 35:2 and in Josh 14:4, 21:2; in all these cases the Greek gives πόλεις κατοικεῖν. Assuming this to be the proper reading, the Temple Vision has the Levites' section of the sacred reserve factionalized into residential areas at a further distance from the temple than those of the Zadokite priests; and here we can render *'îr* as an urban quarter rather than an entire town.[30]

The pasturelands of the Levitical settlements, on the other hand, are referenced in the Temple Vision as part of the dwelling area of the priests. Pastureland would have been a necessary feature of a temple with an active cult of sacrifice. Animals designated for sacrifice would have needed to be fed and kept healthy. The same is true for animals consecrated by vow or act of dedication,

---

28 Leuchter, *The Levites*, 218–22. The Temple Vision appears to further restrict altar rights to a sub-group of Aaronides known as the "sons of Zadok" (48:11). Ezekiel himself was apparently a Zadokite, which was a priestly guild that the biblical narrative portrays as enjoying close ties with the local monarchy in Jerusalem from Davidic times onward, their eponymous patriarch Zadok officiating at the coronation of Solomon himself (1 Kgs 1:39). The non-Zadokite Aaronides may be referred to in Ezek 40:45 as those priests in charge of the "duties of the temple," which, as 40:46 makes clear, are to be distinguished from the "duties of the altar" reserved for the Zadokites. For a discussion on Ezekiel's terminology on this issue, see Haran, *Temples and Temple-Service*, 102–3. On the view that 40:44–46 predates the full division between altar priest and Levite, see Zimmerli, *Ezekiel 2*, 549–50; and Albertz, *A History of Israelite Religion in the Old Testament Period. Volume I: From the Beginnings to the End of the Monarchy* (Louisville: Westminster John Knox Press, 1994), 430.
29 Sic BHS; Eichrodt, *Ezekiel*, 567; Zimmerli, *Ezekiel 2*, 466; Kasher, *Ezekiel 2*, 875. See also O'Hare, *Have You Seen, Son of Man? A Study in the Translation and Vorlage of LXX Ezekiel 40–48* (Leiden; Boston: Brill, 2010), 89, n. 39 for references; and Albertz, *History of Israelite Religion I*, 614, n. 90. Cf. Stevenson, *Vision of Transformation*, 85, who again attempts to defend the MT; and Kasher, "Anthropomorphism, Holiness and Cult," 207, who assumes the MT to be original. If the MT were original, one might explain the chambers as gatehouses on the Levites' border with the city land, policing the border between the profane world and the outermost realm of the temple; see Konkel, *Architektonik des Heiligen: Studien zur zweiten Tempelvision Ezechiels (Ez 40–48)* (Berlin: Philo Verlagsgesellschaft, 2001), 134–35.
30 Levine, "The Biblical 'Town'," 421–53.

seized due to delinquency on a loan from Yahweh, acquired by priests as part of their own personal holdings, or gifted to them due to the animal's status as a firstborn or a tithe.[31] The pasturelands of the Levitical settlements, which according to Num 35:4 were to have an area of 1,000 cubits (or around 4,000 dunams) per settlement, may have been vestiges of lands associated with old Yahwistic shrines; as such they may have once enjoyed certain tax exemptions and freedom from confiscation.[32] They also may have come to be seen as sacred in their own right, which can explain why Lev 25:34 prohibits their sale. The inalienable status of Levitical pasturelands may also derive from the fact that they were held communally.[33]

The image in the Temple Vision is of holy men grazing their animals on pastureland in the shadow of the temple. Ezekiel 45:4 originally referred to the pastureland explicitly, though corruption in the Masoretic Text (MT) has obscured the reference. The MT's puzzling phrase *ûmiqdāš lammiqdāš* ("and a holy area [?] for the sanctuary") likely originally read *ûmigrāš lammiqdāš* ("and a pastureland for the sanctuary").[34] Textual witnesses support this reconstruction. Targum Jonathan translates the phrase as *kibś'ā lĕmaqdĕšâ* ("an ascent to the sanctuary"), suggesting a hillside, ramp, or via sacra of some sort leading up to the temple and offering good evidence for an original *migrāš* in the Hebrew.[35] The LXX understands the phrase as referring explicitly to the priestly dwellings, giving [τόπος εἰς οἴκους...] ἀφωρισμένους τῷ ἁγιασμῷ αὐτῶν ("[a place for dwellings...] set apart for their sacred office"), perhaps representing an attempt to read *mgrš* as a participle form.[36] That both witnesses refer in some way to the

---

31 Haran, *Temples and Temple-Service*, 116–17; on animals distrained due to delinquency on a debt to God, see §2.2.3.
32 Borowski, *Agriculture in Iron Age Israel*, 29. That they were vestiges of early pre-Deuteronomic temple land, see Henrey, "Land Tenure," 13–15; and Ahlström, *Royal Administration and National Religion in Ancient Palestine* (Leiden: Brill, 1982), 50–51.
33 Borowski, *Agriculture in Iron Age Israel*, 29–30.
34 The MT can be taken to refer to a space set apart for the temple and sanctified by the temple's very presence, but this requires the implausible scenario of conferring two different meanings to two words in a row. Dittography can be ruled out given the presence of the prefixed preposition on the second word. Furthermore, while the assumption that the word *migrāš* in the MT has been corrupted to *miqdāš* due to scribal error has some explanatory force, given that the letters *dālet* and *rêš* are easily confused, *gîmel* and *qôf* are not at all similar in appearance. The change seems intentional.
35 This is also very close to what Ezekiel describes in 45:2 with the term *migrāš*.
36 But note the appearance of the word ἀφωρισμένους in the nominative in P.967 (thus modifying τόπος, hardly a significant change in meaning), which is probably the earliest textual witness of LXX Ezekiel and perhaps reflective of an alternative literary edition; see Jahn, *Der griechische Text des Buches Ezechiel: nach dem Kölner Teil des Papyrus 967* (Bonn: Rudolf Habelt,

sanctuary, or to sanctity, buttresses the reconstruction of *lammiqdāš*. It also casts doubt on the preferred solution by most commentators—*ûmigrāš lāmmiqne*, "and a pastureland for livestock"—even if that solution hardly changes the picture.[37]

The phrase *ûmigrāš lammiqdāš* ("and a pastureland for the sanctuary") in Ezek 45:4—or even *ûmigrāš lāmmiqne* ("and a pastureland for livestock"), if that reading is to be preferred—may have been bothersome to scribal tradents of MT Ezekiel. Such an image may have called to mind the sacred pastures that were common next to pagan temples, particularly in Egypt.[38] Both Josephus and Philo polemicize against these pastures. Philo of Alexandria explains why it would be inappropriate for the Jerusalem temple to keep sacred animals or maintain a sacred grove on the premises of the complex (*Decalogue* 76–80, *Spec. Laws* 1.74–75). Josephus condemns Egyptian animal worship (*C. Ap.* 1.225; 2.66, 81, 86, 128, 140), and in the case of the Yahwistic temple at Leontopolis in Egypt, takes a dismissive tone in his retelling of Oniad's willingness to incorporate the local sacred animals into the Yahwistic cult there, a clear stab at the Oniads and their breakaway temple (*Ant.* 13.66–70).[39] In order to erase the trappings of a pagan sanctuary from the book of Ezekiel, the Masoretic tradents of the book may have sought an innocuous solution by reading here *ûmiqdāš lammiqdāš* ("and a holy area [?] for the sanctuary").[40]

3.2.2 A Non-Urban Sacred Reserve

The Temple Vision's program of unifying the priesthood together next to the temple would have shielded the priests from the potentially dangerous influences of the broader public. Their ministration would be unsullied by marketplace commerce or village-level interactions that could have been construed as a distrac-

---

1972), 94; and Lilly, *Two Books of Ezekiel: Papyrus 967 and the Masoretic Text as Variant Literary Editions* (Leiden; Boston: Brill, 2012), 301–17.
37 Eichrodt, *Ezekiel*, 569; Zimmerli, *Ezekiel 2*, 466; Albertz, *Israel in Exile*, 614, n. 89. But cf. Kasher, *Ezekiel 2*, 875, who accepts the MT.
38 Interestingly, Jacob Milgrom and Daniel Block have posited that the author of Ezekiel's Temple Vision was familiar with the Temple of Apollo at Delphi, a temple known for its sacred flocks; *Ezekiel's Hope*, 44–53; on Delphi, see §1.1.
39 See §4.2.
40 Assuming the reconstruction here is correct, the LXX would then be rendering *migrāš* into a participle modifying *bāttîm*, which is an unjustifiable but nevertheless clever gloss. Targum Jonathan reads *migrāš* into a ramp or ascent, even though in Ezekiel it usually gives for *migrāš* the Aramaic *rawaḥ*, "pasture area" (48:15, 17). A less potentially contentious option may have been preferred there as well.

tion from service or even a slippery slope into unethical behavior. While many priests who served at the Jerusalem sanctuary in the Persian period likely lived in the city, most were almost certainly dispersed throughout the region. The lists of returnees in Ezra and Nehemiah mention five clans of priests totaling 4,289 in number; and two clans of Levites, totaling a mere 341 individuals in Ezra and 360 in Nehemiah (Ezra 2:36–42; Neh 7:39–45, 11:10–22, 12:1–26). While we cannot know how reliable these numbers are, even a fraction of them would have been too much for a city thought to have been home to no more than about a thousand individuals in the Persian period (see below). Furthermore, there is evidence that priests held land in the region, as we shall discuss below.[41]

The reserve was to be at some distance from the city (Ezek 48:15), and as such was to be a distinctly non-urban place, free of the trappings of royal government and the commercial activity of city life. The full separation of the sacred reserve from the city is affirmed with the closing statement of the book of Ezekiel, where the city of Jerusalem is renamed *YHWH šāmmâ*, "Yahweh is there" (48:35). The name conjures an image of one standing in Jerusalem, pointing toward the temple and sacred reserve, noting that there is where the deity resides.[42] The Temple Vision's model of a reserve at a remove from the city breaks from Iron Age precedent. In royal Judahite Jerusalem of the Iron Age, the temple and palace were administratively integrated and physically adjacent to one another.[43] Here the intention may have been to protect the temple from contamination by the affairs of the royal court and the city markets. That the corruptibility of market activity was at the forefront of the minds of the authors of the Vision is evidenced by their call for justice among the princes of Israel and in the marketplace (45:9–12)—a call that immediately follows the first description of the sacred reserve. This concern is also evidenced by the requirement that the prince (*nāśî'*) have highly regulated access to the temple (46:2–10) and no further rights of seizure of private land (46:18). "My princes shall no more defraud my people but shall leave the rest of the land to the several tribes of the House of Israel," cries the prophet in 45:8.

Interestingly, the Temple Vision's extrication of the local ruling authority from the temple complex reflected realities on the ground in Jerusalem of the Persian period. The center of foreign administration and tax collection was not

---

41 See §3.3; and for later periods, see §6.3.
42 Joyce, "Temple and Worship," 159–60.
43 Lundquist, *The Temple of Jerusalem: Past, Present, and Future* (Westport, CT; London: Praeger, 2008), 38–43; Boyle, "The Figure of the Nāśî' in Ezekiel's Vision of the New Temple (Ezekiel 40–48)," *Australian Biblical Review* 58 (2010), 12–14; Greenberg, "Design and Themes," 199–200.

in Jerusalem in that period but at Ramat Rahel, some 4 km south of the city. Renewed excavations by an Israeli-German expedition in 2004–10 have shown that the palatial complex at Ramat Rahel was an uninterrupted center of foreign administration in Judea not only in the Persian period but in the preceding Neo-Assyrian and Neo-Babylonian periods as well.[44] The palace presided over a hinterland of arable land, olive groves, and orchards, and was a center for tax collection in kind. A staggering number of stamped jar handles bearing the provincial name Yehud were found at the site; they were part of vessels likely used for the transfer of taxed goods.[45] The palace, which would have been inhabited by the governor of the province, was adorned with aromatic plants and fruit trees, some of which were imported from Persia.[46]

Jerusalem on the other hand was little more than a hamlet of residences surrounding the temple site in this period. Scholars estimate that there were only about 1,000–1,200 inhabitants there at the end of the Persian period, all living in the relatively small area of the Southeastern Hill.[47] A even smaller population likely lived there in the early Persian period, before the era of steady growth in the fifth century and the fortification of Jerusalem during the governorship of Ne-

---

[44] Lipschits, Gadot, and Langgut, "The Riddle of Ramat Raḥel: The Archaeology of a Royal Persian Period Edifice," *Transeuphratène* 21 (2012), 57–79, esp. 69–73; and see also Lipschits et al., "Palace and Village, Paradise and Oblivion: Unraveling the Riddles of Ramat Rahel," *Near Eastern Archaeology* 74 (2011), 2–49, esp. 33–36.
[45] Lipschits and Vanderhooft, *The Yehud Stamp Impressions: A Corpus of Inscribed Impressions from the Persian and Hellenistic Periods in Judah* (Winona Lake, IN: Eisenbrauns, 2011), esp. 31–41. On the separate apparatuses for the collection of sacred and secular taxes in Persian Judea, see Altmann, "Tithes for the Clergy and Taxes for the King: State and Temple Contributions in Nehemiah," *The Catholic Biblical Quarterly* 76, no. 2 (2014), 215–29, esp. 228–29; and Lipschitz, "Achaemenid Imperial Policy, Settlement Processes in Palestine, and the Status of Jerusalem in the Middle of the Fifth Century B.C.E," in *Judah and the Judeans in the Persian Period* (op. cit.), 19–53 (passim).
[46] Langgut, Gadot, and Lipschits, "'Fruit of Goodly Trees': The Beginning of Citron Cultivation in Israel and Its Penetration into Jewish Tradition and Culture," *Beit Mikra* 59, no. 1 (2014) [Hebrew], 38–55, esp. 42–47.
[47] For an estimate as low as 400–500 individuals for the Persian-period city, see Finkelstein, "The Territorial Extent and Demography of Yehud/Judea in the Persian and Early Hellenistic Periods," *RB* 117, no. 1 (2010), 39–54. On the 1,000–1,200 estimate, see Lipschits, "Persian Period Finds from Jerusalem: Facts and Interpretations," *Journal of Hebrew Scriptures* 9 (2009), 2–30; and Geva, "Jerusalem's Population in Antiquity: A Minimalist View," *Tel Aviv* 41, no. 2 (2014), 131–60, esp. 141–43. For more discussion on these demographic estimates, see Meyers and Burt, "Exile and Return: From the Babylonian Destruction to the Beginnings of Hellenism," in *Ancient Israel: From Abraham to the Roman Destruction of the Temple* (ed. Shanks; Washington, D.C.: Biblical Archaeology Society, 2010), 220–24.

hemiah in the middle of that century.[48] When Ezekiel's Temple Vision is thought to have been written, Jerusalem's inhabitants may have consisted primarily of priests and Levites with their families—the rest of the priesthood dwelling in villages on the countryside. The authors of the Temple Vision may have sought to maintain this separation from the center of administration and commerce. Even the distances agree. The Old City of Jerusalem is some 4 km north of Ramat Rahel, and in the Temple Vision the sanctuary would also be a few kilometers from the city.[49]

3.3 Priests, Farming, and Temple Dependency

The placement of priests and Levites within the sacred reserve also absolves them of the responsibilities of land ownership. As Ezek 44:28 notes with respect to the priests, "no landholding shall be given them in Israel, for I am their landholding." This falls in line with the rhetorical position of Deuteronomy and the Priestly Source, which hold that the tribe of Levi is due the holy offerings of the people as compensation for the fact that they received no territory when Yahweh allocated Canaan to the tribes of Israel. As it is stated in Deut 18:1–2, the Levitical priests "shall live only off Yahweh's offerings by fire as their portion and shall have no portion among their brother tribes: Yahweh is their portion, as he promised them." (The listing of the priestly revenues follows in Deut 18:3–8.) A similar rationalization is given in Num 18:24 to explain why the Levites are to receive the tithe from the people.

In the Temple Vision, the support system for the priesthood is to be a combined effort of the people and the prince. The people are to make the initial land endowment for the sacred reserve, where the priests will live and graze the holy animals. The endowment is referred to as *tĕrûmâ* (Ezek 45:1; 48:9, 12), which in the priestly writings of the Hebrew Bible connotes a generic offering set aside for the priesthood (Num 5:9, 18:8; Lev 22:12, 15). The transfer of *tĕrûmâ* to a priest usually took place outside of the temple premises and without an accompanying

---

48 Mazar, "The Wall that Nehemiah Built," *Biblical Archaeology Review* 35, no. 2 (2009), 24–33, 66; cf. Ussishkin, "On Nehemiah's City Wall and the Size of Jerusalem during the Persian Period: An Archaeologist's View," in *New Perspectives on Ezra-Nehemiah: History and Historiography, Text, Literature, and Interpretation* (ed. Kalimi; Winona Lake, IN: Eisenbrauns, 2012), 101–30.
49 A sanctuary in the center would leave a little under 5 km on each side; the city is along one of those sides. This assumes a long (=52 cm) cubit in Ezekiel and a sacred reserve that is 10,000 cubits (ca. 10 km) wide; see above.

rite.⁵⁰ The people are also to contribute produce and other gifts in kind for the priests, including things bearing herem status, the first fruits, and the first of the dough, in addition to the meat from various sacrifices (Ezek 44:28–30, 45:13–17). The priests' entitled status would be established by genealogical line, which needed to be strictly protected (Ezek 44:9–16).

The prince is to fund the sacrifices for the festivals, new moons, and Sabbaths, as well as certain sacrifices for the expiation of the people (45:17). He is to be a *primus inter pares*, as Rainer Albertz has put it.⁵¹ The prince's large tract of land is envisioned as having extended from the sacred reserve westward to the sea and eastward to the Jordan (Ezek 45:7–10, 46:16–18, 48:21–22). If the prince is to be identified with the governor of Yehud, as some have claimed,⁵² the Temple Vision's portrayal of him as patron of the temple suits what we know of imperial support for sanctuaries in the Persian realm. While such support for Jerusalem did not, by all accounts, include a land endowment for the sanctuary and its priesthood, Cyrus's financial commitment to the rebuilding of the temple is said to have included 5,400 gold and silver vessels that were taken from the temple by Nebuchadnezzar and later seized by the Persians (Ezra 1:7–11; 5:14; 6:5). Another noteworthy instance of imperial patronage comes in Ezra 7:24, where the Persian emperor Artaxerxes I of the mid-fifth century BCE is said to have declared all servants of the House of Yahweh, altar priests included, exempt from imperial taxes.⁵³ The taxes mentioned in the remittance declaration are the *middā/mindā* ("tribute tax"), the *bĕlō* ("poll tax"), and the *hălāk* ("land tax"). This recalls a letter from Darius to a certain Gadatas, perhaps the satrap of Sardis around the early fifth century BCE, which asserts the special fiscal immunity to the "sacred gardeners" (*phytourgoi hieroi*) of the temple of Apollo at Aulai in southwest Turkey; Gadatas had subjected them to tribute and forced them to work non-sacred land.⁵⁴

---

50 In the scholarly literature it is often translated "heave-offering" based on the word's derivation and the supposition that the original rite involved the heaving or lifting of the offering during its transfer to the priest; see Milgrom, *Studies in Cultic Theology and Terminology* (Leiden: Brill, 1983), 159–70.
51 *Israel in Exile*, 372. On the special status of the prince here, see Boyle, "Figure of the Nāśî'," 1–16; Tuell, *Law of the Temple*, 109–10.
52 For a discussion and summary of opinions, see Tuell, *Law of the Temple*, 115–20.
53 Altmann, *Economics in Persian-Period Biblical Texts*, 221–243, esp. 242; and see also Grätz, *Das Edikt des Artaxerxes: Eine Untersuchung zum religionspolitischen und historischen Umfeld von Esra 7, 12–26* (Berlin; New York: De Gruyter, 2004).
54 Pierre Briant has pointed out the similarity; see *From Cyrus to Alexander: A History of the Persian Empire* (trans. Daniels; Winona Lake, IN: Eisenbrauns, 2002), 491–93, 584.

Figure 8. Laborers in the fields of Sanur in Ottoman Palestine, c. 1908. Library of Congress Prints and Photographs Division. Stereograph by Stereo-Travel Co.

The Temple Vision's endorsement of a landless priesthood entirely dependent on the support of the prince and the people came in the face of a reality that was more complex. While various sources of the Hebrew Bible promote the idea that the tribe of Levi was denied a portion of land when the deity allocated his territory to the tribes of Israel, it also includes a few mentions of priests holding land without censure. The banished high priest Abiathar is told by Solomon to return to his field at Anatoth (1 Kgs 2:26), which assumes of course that he owned one in the first place. Amaziah, a high priest at Bethel, is cursed by the prophet Amos and doomed to have his land "divided up with a measuring line" (Amos 7:17).

Moreover, as we have seen, the regulations of Lev 27 suggest an accumulation of agricultural property by a priestly class spread across the countryside in the Persian period. In addition to their role in land survey, appraisal, hypothecation, redemption, and foreclosure, priests in Lev 27 are the immediate beneficiaries of landed donations to the deity.⁵⁵ The tax exemptions that Artaxerxes I granted to priests in Ezra 7:24 included a remission of their land tax. Moreover, in Neh 11:20 a significant portion of the people of Israel and its priesthood are said to have resided in Jerusalem but others lived "each on his estate" ('îš běna-ḥălātô) throughout the towns of Judea, the priests and Levites included (Neh 11:20).⁵⁶ In Neh 12:10, insufficient tithing forced the Levites and singers to head back "each to his fields," leaving the temple inadequately staffed. In other words, the priests of Yahweh appear to have held land privately in the Persian period and to have used the fruits of their labor to supplement whatever prebendary income they received.

In Babylonia in the mid-first millennium BCE, the subsistence strategy of priests was based on land ownership combined with prebendary income from temple service. Priests there typically relied on the labor of others to work their land, leading Michael Jursa to characterize them as archetypical rentiers —an economic class that does not participate in the process of production.⁵⁷ Their typical portfolio consisted of gardens, houses, and prebends. As the market expanded in Babylonia in the mid-first millennium BCE, the traditional system of redistributing goods in kind through temple economies was replaced. Instead of receiving the necessities they needed to sustain themselves and their families from temples, priests began to receive wages instead, mostly in silver. The ramifications of this change were that priests were economically active in Babylonian markets, not only benefitting from their private holdings but also engaging in exchange to obtain the staples they needed to live.⁵⁸

---

55 For further discussion, see Habel, *The Land is Mine*, 112; and Fager, *Land Tenure and the Biblical Jubilee*, 98; and see above in Chapter 2.

56 See also a similar statement in Neh 11:3. On Josephus's embellishment of the account to include the notice that Nehemiah built for the priests and Levites houses and financed the construction himself, see *Ant.* 11.181–83 and further discussion below in §4.2.

57 Jursa, *Aspects of the Economic History of Babylonia*, 282–84; see also idem, "Silver and Other Forms of Elite Wealth in Seventh Century BC Babylonia," in *Silver, Money and Credit* (op. cit.), 67–68.

58 Jursa, "Money-Based Exchange and Redistribution: The Transformation of the Institutional Economy in First Millennium Babylonia," in *Autour de Polanyi: Vocabulaires, théories et modalités des échanges : [actes de la rencontre] Nanterre, 12–14 juin 2004* (ed. Clancier et al.; Paris: De Boccard, 2005), 171–86; see also Pirngruber, "Wages as Guides to the Standard of Living in First Millennium BC Babylonia," in *Silver, Money and Credit* (op. cit.), 107; Jursa, "The Remuneration of Institutional Labourers in an Urban Context in Babylonia in the First Millennium BC," in *L'archive des fortifications de Persépolis: état des questions et perspectives de recherches* (ed. Briant et al.; Paris: De Boccard, 2008), 387–427; and Altmann, *Economics in Persian-Period Biblical Texts*, 116.

The sacred dues in the Pentateuch were meant to provide some basic products to the priests of Yahweh, but subsistence farming must have been necessary for them in any case due to insufficient supply or to the rotation schedule of service at the altar. Scarcity of prebendary income for priests may have been particularly acute after 586 BCE.[59] The model of a priesthood supplementing their prebendary income with that of their own landholdings is assumed by the story of Gen 47, for example, where Joseph restructures the Egyptian economy in a time of famine. In the story, which is discussed in Chapter 2, most landholders sell their property and themselves to Pharaoh in order to have the means to survive, but the priests did not need to do so because they were able to live on the fixed allowance that Pharaoh gave them, despite the fact that their land was unproductive due to the famine (Gen 47:22). The geographic dispersal of priests in Judea, as well as their engagement in land cultivation and absence from full-time service at the altar, must have been seen by the authors of the Temple Vision as a far cry from what Yahweh had intended for his land.

The Temple Vision also sets the Jerusalem temple apart from the traditional paradigm in the Near East, where temples could achieve some measure of fiscal autonomy by holding property in land and collecting rent on it.[60] The Ebabbar temple, for example, is said by the later years of Nabonidus's reign in the mid-fifth century BCE to have been collecting produce on roughly 412.5–537.5 hectares of date groves and 1,250 hectares of barley fields—the two together totaling a little less than 6 sq. miles of arable land.[61] The Eanna produced a date crop equivalent to 100–125 typical households in Sippar.[62] Both temples, according to these documents, were engaged in moneylending and in trade for commodities that they themselves did not produce.[63] They also entered into business arrangements with entrepreneurial families such as the Murašû and Egibi clans, who themselves owned and rented large swaths of land in Babylonia.[64]

---

[59] On the Judean priests' struggles to raise sufficient revenue for themselves and the temple in Jerusalem, see Bedford, "Temple Funding," 336–51, and further discussion above in §1.2.
[60] See §1.1. The contrast has been pointed out by Albertz, *Israel in Exile*, 375–76.
[61] Jursa, *Aspects of the Economic History of Babylonia*, 357.
[62] Ibid., 441.
[63] Dandamayev, "An Age of Privatization in Ancient Mesopotamia," in *Privatization in the Ancient Near East* (op. cit.), 199–201, 208; "State and Temple in Babylonia," 589.
[64] Stolper, *Entrepreneurs and Empire*, esp. 152–56. On the Egibi archive, see Wunsch, "The Egibi Family's Real Estate in Babylon (6th Century BC)," in *Urbanization and Land Ownership* (op. cit.), 391–419; idem, *Das Egibi-Archiv I. Die Felder und Gärten* (2 vols.; Groningen: Styx, 2000), esp. 1–19 in vol. 1; and Abraham, *Business and Politics under the Persian Empire: The Financial Dealings of Marduk-nāṣir-apli of the House of Egibi (521–487 B.C.E.)* (Bethesda, MD: CDL Press, 2004), 9–10, 171–77.

In the Temple Vision, on the other hand, fiscal autonomy is to be achieved not by landholding but by establishing an effective support system for the temple and priesthood. This can explain why the sacred reserve is said in 48:14 to be non-sellable, non-exchangeable, and non-transferable.[65] It was to be an unprofitable landed asset, which also meant, we can presume, that it was to remain uncultivated, with Yahweh's altar to be nourished by produce emerging from the people's labor in the tribal territories alone. This point of view can explain why the only cultivable land mentioned in the vicinity of the sacred reserve is the city land, which was to be used for growing food for the workers of the city (Ezek 48:19).

Finally, the inclusion of the Levites within the sacred reserve, which is referred to among other things as *tĕrûmâ* (Ezek 45:1, 48:9), *tĕrûmât hāʾāreṣ* (48:12) and *rēʾšît hāʾāreṣ* (48:14), may have been a source of confusion to later tradents of MT Ezekiel. This is because by the end of the Second Temple period, the term *tĕrûmâ* came to refer to a specific token gift in kind, usually of wine, oil, or wheat, which was set aside exclusively for priests, not Levites.[66] Similarly, the term *rēʾšît hāʾāreṣ*, which is a unique phrase in the Hebrew Bible, calls to mind the first fruits, which also were gifted to priests rather than to Levites.[67] This issue can explain a glaring textual problem in MT Ezekiel's description of the sacred reserve: the garbled dimensions for it. Basic arithmetic dictates that two identically sized parcels of land for priests and Levites, each measuring 25,000 by 10,000, should form an area measuring 25,000 by 20,000. Yet whenever the MT refers to the sacred reserve, it reduces its total size to 25,000 by 10,000. This creates irresolvable discrepancies on three occasions in the text (45:1, 48:9, 48:13). None of these discrepancies appear in the LXX.[68] The textual changes behind the discrepancies are so egregious that they suggest a purposeful intervention.[69]

---

65 On the matter of transferability, note Num 27:6–7, which assumes that patrimonial land was transferable within the kin group under certain circumstances.
66 See §7.2.
67 The term *rēʾšît* is used in several places in the Hebrew Bible to describe them; see, e.g., Exod 23:19, 34:26; Deut 18:4.
68 In two of these (45:1, 48:13) one is best served to follow the LXX, which gives the appropriate number of 20,000 in both. While in 48:9, the nature of the required emendation depends on whether the verse refers to the sacred reserve or to the entire offering of land including the city land: the former would require a figure of 20,000, as above; the latter, 25,000. On the preference for the LXX on this matter, see, e.g., Zimmerli, *Ezekiel 2*, 523; and Kasher, *Ezekiel 2*, 874; but cf. Kalinda Rose Stevenson, *Vision of Transformation*, 31–32, for an argument on the primacy of the MT. Note also the absence of the dimensions entirely at Ezek 45:1 of P.967 of LXX Ezekiel, where they appear only in 48:9 and 48:13, suggesting harmonization in 45:1 toward 48:9 and 48:13—perhaps for clarity's sake—later in post-P.967 editions of the Old Greek. The MT change

Why was the MT altered in this way? Since the Temple Vision's sacred reserve was to include an allotment held by the Levites, later tradents of the text may have feared that one could read Ezek 48:12—where the reserve is called a *tĕrûmât hā'āreṣ*, or Ezek 48:14, where it is called *r'ēšît hā'āreṣ*—as envisioning a temple where the Levites received a portion of the *tĕrûmâ* and the first fruits too. The solution was to reduce the dimensions of the sacred reserve so that the terms *tĕrûmât hā'āreṣ* or *r'ēšît hā'āreṣ* could be read to refer exclusively to the priests' portion of land. Such an alteration fits a pattern of expansion, clarification, and harmonization in MT Ezekiel, some instances of which are geared towards early halakhah.[70] The issue of the temple pastureland, just discussed, is another instance. Here the alteration seems trifling, though it can speak nonetheless to the importance of the prophetic vision in matters of temple policy and the potential of that vision to be drawn upon for a program of reform.

---

of the dimension from 20,000 to 10,000 would occur as a separate textual process. See Jahn, *Papyrus 967*, 93, 116–17.

69 The alterations to letters required to move from *'eśrîm 'elep* (20,000) to *'ăśeret 'ălāpîm* (10,000) are simply too egregious to be unintentional: the tens number would need to be changed from the masculine plural form to the feminine singular, the respective endings of which look nothing alike and require the addition of an entirely new letter; and the thousands number similarly would need to be pluralized, requiring the addition of two new letters.

70 These emendations, while often intentional, do not qualify as a coherent redactional layer, according to Timothy Mackie; see *Expanding Ezekiel: The Hermeneutics of Scribal Addition in the Ancient Text Witnesses of the Book of Ezekiel* (Göttingen: Vandenhoeck & Ruprecht, 2015), esp. 212–13. Among the contradictions between Ezekiel's Temple Vision and rabbinic halakhah are the portrayal of steps on the south side of the temple altar (43:17), which are prohibited in Exod 20:33; see Sweeney, "The Problem of Ezekiel in Talmudic Literature," in *After Ezekiel: Essays on the Reception of a Difficult Prophet* (ed. Mein and Joyce; New York; London: T&T Clark, 2011), 11–23; see also Ego, "Reduktion, Amplifikation, Interpretation, Neukontextualisierung: Intertextuelle Aspekte der Rezeption der Ezechielschen Thronwagenvision im antiken Judentum," in *Das Ezechielbuch in der Johannesoffenbarung* (ed. Sänger; Neukirchen-Vluyn: Neukirchener, 2004), 31–60. A late Second Temple period date seems appropriate for the alterations discussed here, given the *terminus post quem* that the translation of the LXX provides for some point in the third to second centuries BCE; see O'Hare, *Translation and Vorlage of LXX Ezekiel 40–48*, esp. 189–90. On the expansive and exegetical style of the proto-Masoretic scribes who developed the text after the LXX of Ezekiel had been created, see Tov, "Recensional Differences between the MT and LXX of Ezekiel," *Ephemerides Theologicae Lovanienses* 62, no. 1 (1986), esp. 91–92. On other instances of intertextual exegesis in the book; see Stromberg, "Observations on Inner-Scriptural Scribal Expansion in MT Ezekiel," *VT* 58, no. 1 (2008), 68–86. For a discussion of similar pluses and glosses in MT (and LXX) in earlier chapters of Ezekiel, see Crane, *Israel's Restoration: A Textual-Comparative Exploration of Ezekiel 36–39* (Leiden; Boston: Brill, 2008), 265–70, esp. 269.

3.4 The Temple Collective and Sacred Property

There is also an ethic of collectivization and equal distribution of property in the Temple Vision. This is reflected foremost in the tribal land allotments (Ezek 48:1–35), which are to be distributed equally with respect to land area. These allotments contrast the allocation of land in Josh 13–19, where certain tribes enjoy much larger territories than others in a scheme that was still far from the reality of the actual geographic districts within the Persian economic system.[71] The Temple Vision's idealized tribal land allotments have an interesting parallel in Plato's *Laws* on how land was to be divided when a new city was settled; the population was to be split into twelve parts and an equal parcel of land was to be assigned to each (6.745b–c).[72] Moreover, the Temple Vision's allotments were to be established by the casting of lots, so that the geographic location of each tribe could be attributed to the deity (Ezek 45:1).[73] Clans would have periodically divided arable plots amongst themselves, usually marking them off with rope (e.g., Mic 2:5, Ps 16:6, Ps 105:11) to make sure allotments were similarly sized. After some time, they would redistribute the land. The advantages to such a system in promoting a sense of equitability are reflected in the famous line from Psalms, "How good and pleasant it is that brothers dwell together" (Ps 133:1), with its endorsement of communal landholding.[74] Phillip Guillaume has argued that the tribal allotment of the land of Israel is rooted in such a village-level approach, where plots would be assigned to clans and re-allotted periodically, as was customary in pre-Ottoman *musha'* systems.[75]

---

[71] On the Temple Vision's tribal land allotments, see Brodsky, "The Utopian Map in Ezekiel (48:1–35)," *Jewish Bible Quarterly* 34, no. 1 (2006), 21, 24–25; see also Greenberg, "Design and Themes," 200; and Wazana, *All the Boundaries of the Land*, 182. On the actual territories within Persian Yehud, whose sub-districts functioned within an overarching provincial system, see Lipschits, "The Rural Economy of Judah during the Persian Period and the Settlement History of the District System," in *Economy of Ancient Judah* (op. cit.), 237–64.

[72] Weinfeld, *Social Justice*, 236; see also Papazarkadas, *Sacred and Public Land*, 106–10. The tribal allotments also recall royal land grants in the ancient Near East; see Engelhard, "Ezekiel 47:13–48:29 as Royal Grant," in *"Go to the Land I Will Show You": Studies in Honor of Dwight W. Young* (ed. Coleson and Matthews; Winona Lake, IN: Eisenbrauns, 1996), 45–56.

[73] Guillaume, *Land, Credit and Crisis*, 28–55. On the view that lots were used as instruments in determining God's will for the division of property and other things, see Kitz, "Undivided Inheritance and Lot Casting in the Book of Joshua," *JBL* 119, no. 4 (2000), 601–18; and de Vos, "'Holy Land' in Joshua 18:1–10," in *The Land of Israel in Bible, History, and Theology. Studies in Honour of Ed Noort* (ed. Van Ruiten and de Vos; Leiden; Boston: Brill, 2009), 65–67.

[74] On this reading of Ps 133:1, see Westbrook and Wells, *Everyday Law*, 95.

[75] The primary comparandum from the Near East that Guillaume draws upon is the *musha'* system of pre-Ottoman Palestine; see Guillaume, *Land, Credit and Crisis*, 42–53, 152, 164–65. For

The communal ethic in the Temple Vision is reminiscent of the priestly system of dividing sacrifices at the altar. Since clan-based service rotations appear to have been the norm from the early Second Temple period, certain entitlements needed to be distributed equally among the priests on duty while others could be kept individually.[76] In the Priestly Source, those things that were to be distributed equally are the uncooked meal-offering (Lev 2:8–10; 6:7–9; 7:10) and the breast of the well-being offering (7:28–31). Things retainable by individual priests are the cooked meal offering (7:9), the hide of the burnt-offering (7:8), the meat of the sin-offering (6:19), the meat of the guilt-offering (7:6–7), the right thigh of the well-being offering (7:30–33), and the cakes accompanying the well-being offering of the thanksgiving type (7:14).[77] The potentially sensitive topic of distributing sacrificial shares communally was formalized with the assistance of a special ceremonial raising of the offering—the *tĕnûpâ* ritual as it is called in the Priestly Source. This added spectacle to the event but also signaled that the offering was to be consumed by all present.[78]

Interestingly, voluntary silver dedications and certain other kinds of cash payments to Yahweh appear not to have been shared among the clan. Deut 18:8 refers to the conferral of voluntary dedications to individual priests by their personal benefactors and asserts the right of those priests to hold a private claim over the offerings.[79] Num 5:9–10 rules that certain kinds of restitution pay-

---

further discussion on communal landholdings in ancient Israel and Persian Yehud, see Boer, *Sacred Economy*, 71–75; and Altmann, *Economics in Persian-Period Biblical Texts*, 186.

76 The number of 4,289 priests quoted in Neh 7:39–42 would have been large enough to have required a service rotation. There is a hint of a clan-based rotation system as part of the wood-tax for fueling the altar in Neh 10:35, where clans of priests, Levites, and laypeople are to take turns providing the wood based on lot. The full service rotation is laid out first in Chronicles (1 Chr 23:1–26:32).

77 This is a significantly more complex and formalized system than that described at the smaller sanctuary at Shiloh when it was run by Eli and his sons. According to the biblical account, the custom at that sanctuary was for the officiating priest to simply drop in on the meal that followed the sacrifice, stick a fork into the pot of stew, and settle for whichever piece of meat emerged from the pot (1 Sam 2:12–17).

78 Milgrom, *Cultic Theology and Terminology*, 159–70, esp. 168–70.

79 The verse reads: "They shall receive equal shares of the dues, without regard to his benefactors (*lĕbad mimkārāyw*) according to custom (*'al hā'ābôt*)." The second half of the verse is problematic, with both *mimkārāyw* and *'al hā'ābôt* presenting difficulties, the former perhaps referring to the sale of sacrificial shares and the latter to family possessions, leading to the alternative understanding (as in JPS and NRSV) that the rural Levites are assured equal portions even though they enjoy the income of the sale of patrimonial property. See also the notice in Deut 23:22–24 on the payment of vows to Yahweh; but it says nothing about the destination of the payments.

ments, as well as all private dedications, become the property of the individual priest who receives the money. "Each shall retain his sacred dedications (*qŏdāšāyw*): each priest shall keep what is given to him" (Num 5:10) is the stated rule.

This distinction between private and collective entitlements for the priesthood is at the heart of an account in 2 Kgs 12 regarding fiscal reforms carried out by King Jehoash (c. 837–796) to fund much-needed repairs to the Jerusalem sanctuary.[80] The discovery of the so-called "Jehoash inscription" in 2001—a fragmentary text telling of these very renovations—caught the attention of the mass media and seemed to authenticate the 2 Kgs 12 account, until the inscription was claimed to be a forgery.[81] According to the biblical account, the king first ruled that silver from the valuations of persons (*kesep napšôt ʿerkô*), the census tax (*kesep ʿôbēr ʾîš*), and voluntary donations (*kol kesep ʾăšer yaʿăleh ʿal leb ʾîš*) was to be set aside in its entirety for the purposes of the renovation (2 Kgs 12:5).[82] The revenues are described in 2 Kgs 12:6 as having been given over to individual priests by their "acquaintance" (*ʾîš mēʾēt makkārô*), a reading of the word *mkr* implying that social networks helped determine any given priest's private assets in silver.

According to the story, when the temple remained in disrepair—presumably because the priests were not setting aside their silver as requested—Jehoash established a special sanctuary fund for renovations. The priests were to pool silver in a special box placed next to the temple, as was done at temples elsewhere in

---

80 For a discussion of the account, see Davis, *Reconstructing the Temple: The Royal Rhetoric of Temple Renovation in the Ancient Near East and Israel* (Oxford; New York: Oxford University Press, 2019), 59–69. Marvin Sweeney has argued for the basic historicity of the reform and sees it as a "sign of national restoration" in the wake of the fall of the house of Omri and the renewed independence of the southern kingdom; *I & II Kings. A Commentary* (Louisville; London: Westminster John Knox Press, 2007), 351. Others have doubted its authenticity and tend to view it as a *de novo* composition from as late as the Second Temple period; Fritz, *1 & 2 Kings. A Continental Commentary* (trans. Hagedorn; Minneapolis: Fortress Press, 2003), 302–4; see also Wellhausen, *Die Composition des Hexateuchs und der historischen Bücher des Alten Testaments* (Berlin: Georg Reimer, 1889), 293–98; and Jones, *1 and 2 Kings, Based on the Revised Standard Version* (Grand Rapids, MI; London: W.B. Eerdmans; Marshall, Morgan & Scott, 1984), 487–88.
81 Cross, "Notes on the Forged Plaque Recording Repairs to the Temple," *IEJ* 53, no. 1 (2003), 119–22; Ephʿal, "The 'Jehoash Inscription': A Forgery," ibid., 123–28. But cf. Cohen, "Biblical Hebrew Philology in the Light of Research on the New Yehoʾash Royal Building Inscription," in *New Seals and Inscriptions, Hebrew, Idumean, and Cuneiform* (ed. Lubetski; Sheffield: Sheffield Phoenix Press, 2007), 239–68; and Shanks, *Freeing the Dead Sea Scrolls and Other Adventures of an Archaeology Outsider* (London; New York: Continuum, 2010), 193–202, 224–27.
82 On the valuations-of-persons dedications, see §§2.1, 2.2; on the census tax, see Exod 30:11–16.

the Near East.⁸³ The royal scribe and high priest would supervise the fund and allocate it as necessary to pay for the repairs. The only exceptions were the silver value of a guilt-offering or a sin-offering; these monies remained in the hands of individual priests (2 Kgs 12:17).⁸⁴ The narrative does not include the standard markers of etiologies that one finds in the Deuteronomistic History, such as "until this day" and the like.⁸⁵ And it does not seek to legitimize the reform for eternity by relating it to the legendary figures of David or Solomon, as the Chronicler is want to do.⁸⁶ So after the renovation was complete, priests could have presumably kept their individual sources of revenue, as the above-mentioned laws of Num 5:9–10 and Deut 18:8 require. The deposit into a common sanctuary fund of silver payments that once went into the coffers of individual priests appears to have been an ad hoc measure to raise funds for a particular renovation project in the reign of Jehoash, and the hallmark achievement of a king whose piety is remembered fondly (2 Kgs 12:3).

Therefore, the priests of Yahweh were likely holding precious metals they received privately, as they were doing with sacralized land, as established in the previous chapter. The Temple Vision's call to centralize priests and Levites in the sacred reserve, along with its equal distribution of land among the tribes, works toward an ideology of collectivization. That ideology is reflected too in an account in Nehemiah of a major temple reform in the mid-fifth century BCE (Neh 10:1–40, esp. 33–39). It consisted of the construction of temple store-

---

83 Oppenheim, "A Fiscal Practice of the Ancient Near East," 116–20. In Mesopotamia, cash boxes were set up in temples to collect either taxes or pious offerings. Officials in charge of them would have the silver smelted periodically in order to improve the quality of the metal and to establish the silver value of objects delivered to pay taxes. On a possible reference to such an official in Zechariah, see Schaper, "The Jerusalem Temple as an Instrument of the Achaemenid Fiscal Administration," 530–9. See also Lipschits, "On Cash-Boxes and Finding or Not Finding Books: Jehoash's and Josiah's Decisions to Repair the Temple," in *Essays on Ancient Israel in Its Near Eastern Context: A Tribute to Nadav Na'aman* (ed. Amit et al.; Winona Lake, IN: Eisenbrauns, 2006), 239–54.
84 Incidentally, this policy suits the legislation of Lev 6:19 and 7:6–7, where the meat of those offerings becomes the entitlement of the officiating priest. The evidence here and elsewhere (1 Sam 6 and Lev 5) supports the idea that at least in the First Temple period the guilt- and sin-offerings could be commuted into cash and given to the priest. See Milgrom, "Profane Slaughter and a Formulaic Key to the Composition of Deuteronomy," *HUCA* 47 (1976), 14–15, 142–43; and Wright, "MKR in 2 Kings XII 5–17 and Deuteronomy XVIII 8," *Vetus Testamentum* 39, no. 4 (1989), 445–49, n. 26.
85 Geoghegan, "'Until This Day' and the Preexilic Redaction of the Deuteronomistic History," *JBL* 122, no. 2 (2003), 201–27.
86 See, e.g., 1 Chr 26:20–28, 28:11–18 for instances where later organizational features of the temple are projected back onto Davidic history.

rooms for the collection of the offerings such as the tithe and the first fruits; the establishment of a lottery-based rotation system for the bringing of wood as fuel for the altar (just mentioned); and the introduction of the annual shekel tax for the upkeep of the temple and the regular cult of sacrifice.[87] This all suggests that the collection and redistribution of sacred dues had been fairly decentralized before this point. One is also struck by the fact that the priests and Levites are explicitly mentioned in Neh 10:29 as among those joining the covenant of individuals pledging to support the sanctuary in this way. This is in stark contrast to the description of the sacred dues in Ezek 44:28–30, which presents the dues in terms of their primary recipients, the priests, and as such follows in the footsteps of Num 18:19–20 and Deut 18:1–5. Now the dues are said to be for the house of Yahweh (10:36–37) and their collection centralized at the temple storerooms.

Collectivization may have been encouraged by Persian imperial administrators, who are known to have utilized local temple bureaucracies to streamline the extraction of resources.[88] Archival evidence from the Neo-Babylonian–Persian transitional period at the temple of Eanna at Uruk provides details on the involvement of royal authorities in temple affairs and the use of the temple assets for the benefit of the empire. Under Nabonidus a special royal commissioner was appointed to oversee the administration of the temple economy, with the improvement of agricultural profitability having been a key interest. Also established under Nabonidus was a tax-farming system where chief officials—referred to in the texts as *rab sūti* or *ša muhhi sūti* and often in modern scholarship as the *fermier générale* or *Generalpachter*—would commit to the delivery of a certain quantity of produce to the temple and would allocate temple lands to the highest bidders.[89] A similar position (the *ša muhhi ešrî*) oversaw the leasing of the right

---

[87] It is uncertain that Nehemiah's tax was a permanent fixture through the Persian and Hellenistic periods. Among the lengthy list of offerings Tobit is said to have brought to Jerusalem during his pilgrimages (Tobit 1:6–8)—a useful portrait of the sacred revenue system from the fourth–third centuries BCE—nothing is mentioned of the shekel tax. On the later history of the tax, see §5.3 below.

[88] On the Jerusalem temple as having served Persian imperial interests, see Schaper, "The Jerusalem Temple as an Instrument of the Achaemenid Fiscal Administration," 535; and Lemaire, "Administration of Fourth-Century B.C.E. Judah," 56–62. But for a more cautious view, see Bedford, "Economic Role of the Jerusalem Temple," 3*–20*; and Altmann, *Economics in Persian-Period Biblical Texts*, 181.

[89] For a general discussion on the position, see Michael Jursa's comprehensive study *Die Landwirtschaft in Sippar in neubabylonischer Zeit* (Wien: Institut für Orientalistik der Universität Wien, 1995), 85–116.

to collect the tithes, an arrangement applicable also to lands not under the direct ownership of a temple.[90]

At Uruk the chief officials were obligated to pay the temple a fixed amount annually, in silver or commodities. They would have managed extensive networks of lower ranking officials who had bid for the right to collect revenues from land. In the description of Nehemiah's reform, the Levites are responsible for collecting the tithe on the countryside—with oversight provided by a priest— and for bringing it to the storerooms of the temple (10:39). Perhaps these Levites were committing to pay a certain sum to the imperial authorities up front, in the manner of a tax farmer, while keeping any revenues left over after they finished collecting the tithe. They do not appear to have been successful in their attempts to raise revenue in any case, for according to Neh 13:10–14 they were forced to go back to their fields to earn a living once it became clear that the temple storerooms were inadequately supplied.[91]

Incidentally, the system at Uruk was adopted by Cyrus and Cambyses but was apparently annulled at some point during the reign of Darius I, when the administration over temple land there was fully taken over by the Eanna priesthood. During this period the Neo-Babylonian and Persian imperial regimes exacted levies from, and required valuations of, temple properties in a manner no different from private lands, though in some instances they could grant special concessions to sure up support of local leaders.[92] While at Uruk and Sippar the archival material becomes less useful on the question after the reigns of Darius I and Xerxes I, at Nippur the Murašû texts include evidence from the reigns of later Achaemenid kings of the continued extraction from temple revenues in the interests of the royal coffers.[93] An official at the Ebabbar managed a special tax meant to supply animals for sacrifices on behalf of the king; even the temple's own flocks and herds were subject to the tax.[94]

---

90 Ibid., 81–84, 191–97; Bongenaar, *The Neo-Babylonian Ebabbar Temple at Sippar: Its Administration and Its Prosopography* (Istanbul: Nederlands Historisch-Archaeologisch Instituut te Istanbul, 1997), 429–33.
91 For further discussion on Nehemiah's reforms in their historical context, see Altmann, *Economics in Persian-Period Biblical Texts*, 287–93.
92 Briant, *Cyrus to Alexander*, 74–76, 491–93, 891. On perquisites from royalty to priests in the Persepolis fortification tablets, see Williamson, "Ezra and Nehemiah in the Light of the Texts from Persepolis," *Bulletin for Biblical Research* 1 (1991), 50–54.
93 The "king's harvest" from the "land of Bel" is part of the rent received from one temple landlord; and the "king's share" is another; for sources and discussion, see Stolper, *Entrepreneurs and Empire*, 42–44, esp. 43, n. 29.
94 Dandamayev, "The Neo-Babylonian *rab ṣibti*," in *Assyriologica et Semitica. Festschrift für Joachim Oelsner* (ed. Marzahn and Neumann; Münster: Ugarit-Verlag, 2000), 29–31.

In Judea, it is conceivable that the most profitable agricultural land was appropriated by the Persian governor and divided into fiefs, akin to the system of *ilku* service that the Persian administration used elsewhere, as Lisbeth Fried has proposed.[95] The *ilku* service included periods of labor to the military or the Persian administration in exchange for the rights to tenancy on imperial land. Rent payments were also due. If land was indeed divided this way in Judea, one can expect dues owed to the Yahwistic priesthood to have been collected in some manner. Similarly, Persian administrators also parceled out colonized territory into collective units, which were often held by extended kinship groups. Each unit or *hadru* was led by a foreman who took responsibility for allocating the land, optimizing performance, and collecting taxes.[96] Judea's hilly agricultural territory, whose output paled in comparison to that of the more vast and fertile river-fed land in Mesopotamia, may not have merited such careful administrative attention by the Persian authorities. While there may have never been a true temple collective of the sort imagined in the Temple Vision, reforms by the Persian governor's office may have improved the fiscal standing of the temple nonetheless.

In the Book of Chronicles of the fourth century BCE, the Chronicler has King Hezekiah establishing a system in Jerusalem for collecting the dues of the priests and Levites (2 Chr 31:4–19). According to Sara Japhet, the account updates Pentateuchal precedent to reflect realities on the ground during the time the Chronicler lived, including a mechanism to incorporate dues at the temple, signalizing a further move toward collectivization.[97] The Chronicler's system clearly distinguishes the priests and Levites who lived in Jerusalem and worked year-round at the temple from those who came in from the countryside.

The Chronicler also shows awareness that priests continued to accumulate private wealth in the late Persian period. In 1 Chr 35:7–9, the Chronicler expands upon the brief Deuteronomistic account of the first Passover festival at Jerusalem (2 Kgs 23:21–23). He lists the main offerings brought by the wealthiest of society in order of prominence: King Josiah first, who is said to have donated 30,000

---

[95] "Exploitation of Depopulated Land," 151–64. For a more general discussion on land management under the Persians, see Edelman, "The Economy and Administration of Rural Idumea at the End of the Persian Period," ibid., 185–93.
[96] Bedford, "The Persian Near East," in *The Cambridge Economic History of the Greco-Roman World* (ed. Scheidel et al.; Cambridge: Cambridge University Press, 2007), 318–19; Fried, "Exploitation of Depopulated Land," 152.
[97] Japhet's main argument is that the Chronicler advocates for a strict position with respect to the right of priests' wives to partake of the priestly gifts; see "The Distribution of Priestly Gifts" in *From the Rivers of Babylon*, 289–306.

small cattle and 3,000 large cattle; his officers next, their donations consisting of an undisclosed sum of freewill offerings; the chief priests Hilkiah, Zechariah, and Jehiel third, offering a total of 2,600 small cattle and 300 large cattle to be used as sacrifices; and Levite officers together with the king's brothers last, their gift said to be 5,000 small cattle and 500 large cattle, also as sacrifices. This standard list of royal and priestly benefaction, projected back onto the reign of Josiah and unattested in the Chronicler's known primary source material from 2 Kgs, is best understood as an authorial elaboration rooted not in late Iron Age history but in the author's sense of what idealized euergetism should look like for his audience. Those with the highest status in the society—the priests and Levites among them—are depicted as giving generously to the sanctuary from the fat of their land. By the Chronicler's lifetime, there were those of the sacred class who had become men of great means, holders of significant herds of livestock and in the least pastureland, if not arable land as well.[98]

3.5 The "Plot of the House of Yeho" on a Land Survey from Idumea

The earliest archaeological evidence for the incorporation of land by the temple of God may be an Idumean ostracon of the late fourth century BCE, which appears to mention a "plot of the House of Yeho." The ostracon (Lemaire no. 283) emerged on the antiquities market as one of several hundred Aramaic ostraca thought to derive from the site of Khirbet el-Kôm—perhaps biblical Maqqedah—some 15 miles west of Hebron in the Judean lowlands and known to have been extensively looted in recent decades.[99] This group of ostraca is dated broadly to the fourth century BCE. They relate to a region that was part of the Persian province of Idumea and indicate that Maqqedah was an important administra-

---

[98] The Chronicler also gives special attention to the family lists of priests and Levites, among other tribal groups. For a discussion on the work's use of genealogical lists to further consolidate power in Jerusalem, see Jonker, "Agrarian Economy through City-Elites' Eyes: Reflections of Late Persian Period Yehud Economy in the Genealogies of Chronicles," in *Economy of Ancient Judah* (op. cit.), 77–101.

[99] Lemaire, *Nouvelles inscriptions araméennes d'Idumée II: Collections Moussaieff, Jeselsohn, Welch et divers* (Paris: Gabalda, 2002), 159–56 (No. 283); idem, "Nouveau Temple de Yahô (IVe S. AV. J.-C.)," in *"Basel und Bibel": Collected Communications to the XVIIth Congress of the International Organization for the Study of the Old Testament, Basel 2001* (ed. Augustin and Niemann; Frankfurt am Main: Peter Lang, 2004), 265–73; idem, "Another Temple to the Israelite God. Aramaic Hoard Documents Life in Fourth Century B.C.," *Biblical Archaeology Review* 30, no. 4 (2004), 38–44, 60.

tive center for the province. The individual ostracon in question is an undated land survey in six lines:¹⁰⁰

(1) The hillock, which is under the House of Uzza	(1) תלא זי תחת מן בית עזא
(2) And the plot [of land] of the House of Yeho	(2) וחיבלא זי בית יהו
(3) An unproductive plot of Zabi, the terrace(?) of the terebinth tree	(3) זבר זבי רפידא זי בטנא
(4) The devastated land of Sadu, the tomb of the Galgula (family)	(4) בזא שעדו כפר גלגול
(5) A basin, which belongs to the House of Nabu(?)	(5) רקק וי בית נבו
(6) The tomb of the Yinqam (family)	(6) כפר ינקם

As with the numerous other records among the corpus of ostraca, we can assume this document is a draft eventually recopied onto parchment or papyrus and kept among the imperial archives. Lemaire describes it as "apparently a list of estates that were not subject to taxes because they were not cultivated areas, either because the soil was bad or because they contained some kind of sacred building—that is, a tomb or temple."¹⁰¹ He prefers reading the word חיבלא in line 2 as a "ruin" and postulates that the ostracon is evidence of a heretofore unknown temple to the Judean God in Idumea, based on the assumption that Yeho was a common shortened appellation for Yahweh in this period.¹⁰² The other sanctuaries mentioned on the document are a "temple of Uzza," who was a north Arabian god appearing on Nabatean inscriptions; and Nabu, a Mesopotamian deity and son of the god Marduk. The other names appear to be those of families or individuals.¹⁰³ Perhaps boundary stones or ropes were prepared after the survey was taken to draw attention to the sacred parcels of land and to maintain whatever special protections were afforded them.

While Lemaire favors reading חיבלא as "ruin"—and incidentally is followed in that reading by Bezalel Porten and Ada Yardeni¹⁰⁴—the possible translation of that word as "a plot of land" is pointed out by Lemaire as a viable alternative,

---

100 Reading follows Lemaire; translation is adapted from his French and the English provided by Heltzer, "The Galgūla Family in South Judah and the Local Sanctuaries," in *Studien zu Ritual und Sozialgeschichte im Alten Orient: Tartuer Symposien, 1998–2004* (ed. Kämmerer; Berlin; New York: De Gruyter, 2007), 129. See in both sources discussions on questionable readings. For further discussion on the ostracon, see Edelman, "Economy and Administration of Rural Idumea," 186–87.
101 "Another Temple to the Israelite God," 42.
102 For other articulations of the theory, see Lemaire, "Nouveau Temple de Yahô," 265–73; and idem, "New Aramaic Ostraca from Idumea and Their Historical Interpretation," in *Judah and the Judeans in the Persian Period* (op. cit.), 417.
103 Ibid., 42–43; idem, *Nouvelles inscriptions araméennes*, 152–55.
104 "Why the Unprovenanced Idumean Ostraca Should Be Published," in *New Seals and Inscriptions* (op. cit.), 77.

and such is the preference of Michael Heltzer.¹⁰⁵ The use of the word חיבלא as referencing a plot of land is quite sensible in a cadastral survey of this sort, given the word's derivation from חבל, "rope." Ropes were commonly used to demarcate land and thus came to refer to plots or even entire districts.¹⁰⁶ Furthermore, a form of the word appears on another land-survey ostracon (Lemaire no. 250), which records two plots of an individual or family named Qosyahab (קוסיהב חבלן תרתין, "Qosyahab, plots: two"); there it is far more comprehensible as a reference to a plot of land rather than to a ruin.¹⁰⁷ One finds a close semantic parallel in the Greek ὄρια—itself deriving from a word for "boundary stone"—to refer to territories, as in those said in 1 Macc 10:43 to belong to the temple in Jerusalem.¹⁰⁸

If the ostracon does indeed mention land owned by the temple of Yeho, one can only speculate on which temple exactly is intended, whether at Jerusalem, Gerizim, or as Lemaire has proposed, at Maqqedah in Idumea. (This ostracon would be the sole evidence for such a temple.) The evidence for a significant Judean presence among the ethnic make-up of Idumea has long been apparent, as in Neh 4:6, for example, and in the numerous Yahwistic theophoric elements appearing on personal names on the Idumean ostraca, among other things.¹⁰⁹ And one need not expect an explicit mention of such a sanctuary to Yahweh in canonized Jewish texts; consider, for example, the total surprise among scholars upon the discovery of the Elephantine corpus from Upper Egypt and its multiple references to a previously unknown Yahwistic shrine there.¹¹⁰

One can also note based on this reading of the ostracon that the "House of Yeho" is explicitly mentioned as the organization with which the plot is affiliated. This language contrasts that used in the legislation of Lev 27, where plots are consecrated simply "to Yahweh," rather than to his house, and then taken over by priests. The ostracon fits chronologically with the reforms traditionally associated with Nehemiah: the further development of a fiscal arm of the Jerusalem temple that oversaw Yahweh's incorporated properties. The same system may

---

105 "The Galgūla Family," 129–30; for further discussion on the measuring rope as denoting a tract of land, see Boer, *Sacred Economy*, 73, n. 66.
106 On the use of ropes as property dividers, see, e.g., Deut 32:9, Josh 19:9, and 2 Sam 9:2; and Guillaume, *Land, Credit and Crisis*, 42–53.
107 *Nouvelles inscriptions araméennes*, 129.
108 See §4.5.
109 Stern, "The Population of Persian-Period Idumea According to the Ostraca: A Study of Ethnic Boundaries and Ethnogenesis," in *A Time of Change: Judah and Its Neighbours in the Persian and Early Hellenistic Periods* (ed. Levin; London; New York: T&T Clark, 2007), 213, 217–18.
110 This point was made by Lemaire; see "Another Temple to the Israelite God," 42.

have been adopted by a Yahwistic temple administration in Idumea, if Lemaire's supposition is correct that such a temple existed in this period.

3.6 Summary

The Temple Vision (Ezek 40–48) offers a blueprint for reforming temple operations in a new age. It may have been authored in the Persian province of Yehud in the late sixth or early fifth century BCE, as plans for a rebuilt temple to Yahweh were underway or had just been completed. The Vision's plan for reform includes a new role for priests with respect to land: it imagines them as non-agrarian, removed from all aspects of production and subsisting entirely from the offerings of the people. Rather than having the priests managing Yahweh's wealth in a productive way, inserting credit into the local economy or cultivating fields sacred to the deity, the Temple Vision extricates the priests from the countryside entirely.

Traditionally kings supported temples. Here the equivalent "prince" is a *primus inter pares* in his role as sustainer of the sanctuary. He provides a lion's share of animals and other produce for the cult of sacrifice, but the people join him in supporting the priesthood and in setting up the initial land endowment for the sacred reserve. Traditionally also Near Eastern temples would support themselves through the collection of rents on their land. In the Temple Vision the priests are to live in a single urban quarter in the shadow of the temple—an arrangement recalling the Levitical settlements of the Hebrew Bible. The priests' farming activity is limited to grazing the holy animals. This model also extricates priests from everyday interactions with the laity and wipes away the potentially unwieldy, burdensome, or even debasing transactions with benefactors or debtors.

The sacred reserve of the Temple Vision evokes not the crowded urban space that Jerusalem would become in the late Second Temple period, but rather a bucolic hilltop sanctuary at a remove from the city. It is to be unsullied by the affairs of the marketplaces; it is to remain uninvested in the economy of the hinterland. The model for this aspect of the Temple Vision appears to have been the relationship between Jerusalem and Ramat Rahel, the latter site having assumed more of a "city" role than Jerusalem did in this period, whether in terms of government administration, taxation, or commerce. When Jerusalem recovered over the centuries and came to take on those functions again with respect to its hinterland economy—the temple once again surrounded by a bustling urban scene—the Temple Vision of a sacred reserve at a remove from the city drifted further from reality. Its description of a *migrāš lammiqdāš*, "pastureland for the sanctuary," may have seemed strange to the tradents of MT Ezekiel. Its characterization as *těrûmât hāʾāreṣ* (48:12) and *rʾēšît hāʾāreṣ* (48:14), both terms that recall specific priestly perquisites of the land Second Temple period, may have confused halakhists interested in differentiating the entitlements of priests from those of Levites. Solutions appear to have been sought by altering slightly the text of MT Ezekiel.

The sacred reserve is part of a larger ethic in the Temple Vision where the land's resources are collectivized and distributed equitably, fully funding among other things the priests' ministration to the divine. How different things were for the priests in reality! A reform effort led by the Persian governor Nehemiah (Neh 10) addresses shortages in the temple revenues and seeks to centralize the collection of offerings at the temple. There is biblical precedent for the collectivization of offerings in silver at the temple in the fundraising initiative of King Jehoash (2 Kgs 12), but generally silver revenues and other sacred movables appear to have been held in a diffuse manner by individual priests. A crisis of administration with a growing priesthood, many of which lived scattered throughout the countryside, may have prompted Nehemiah's reform. The Persian imperial interest in streamlining temple revenue may have too, moving the temple administration toward true incorporation of sacred property. A fourth-century BCE ostracon from Idumea possibly mentioning the land of the temple of Yahweh may reflect the outcome of this process.

Chapter 4
Hellenistic Rulers, Jewish Temples, and Sacred Land

4.1 Introduction

The Yahwistic sanctuaries in Judea and Samaria were loci of political power and repositories of great wealth in the early Hellenistic period. Their priesthoods were embedded in the governing and administrative structures of their respective regions, approximating a theocracy. Similar "temple states" have been identified in Syria and Asia Minor, including Cappadocian Komana, Pontic Komana, Zela, Venasa, Olba, and Pessinus. The temple to Atargatis at Bambyke (Hierapolis) in northern Syria is another of the group. Such temple states were an alternative to the economic institutions of the Greek polis, whether in regard to production, distribution, or consumption. They could serve as economic centers in regions not yet impacted by Greek models of urbanization.[1]

With the coming of the Greeks, however, a new administrative regime took hold, and powerful regional temples became an object of imperial interests. The assumption had been that Hellenistic rulers systematically reduced the power of local priests and secularized temple land. Beate Dignas argues that such a view has been overstated, and that while Hellenistic rulers made judgments based on their own interests, they tended to work with local regimes productively. She holds that there was an "economy of the sacred" in the region—a distinct sphere of activity occupied by sanctuaries in the Hellenistic and Roman periods, and existing, for the most part, independent of the other social and political affiliations of the polis.[2] On the one hand, the epigraphic record from the Seleucid empire includes instances of royal largesse toward local temples. An inscription from Baetokaike in northern Syria, for example, commemorates a gift of land by a certain Antiochus, probably one of the late second-century BCE Se-

---

[1] On the "temple states" of Syria and Asia Minor, see Rostovtzeff, *The Social and Economic History of the Hellenistic World* (Oxford: Clarendon Press, 1959), 503–7, nn. 279–83; and Horden and Purcell, *Corrupting Sea*, 429–30. On Bambyke (Hieropolis), Lucian's *De Dea Syria*, a second-century CE description of the cult of Atargatis written in the style of Herodotus, is the most important source on its temple; see Bilde, "Atargatis/Dea Syria: Hellenization of Her Cult in the Hellenistic-Roman Period?," in *Religion and Religious Practice in the Seleucid Kingdom* (ed. Bilde et al.; Aarhus: Aarhus University Press, 1990), 151–87, esp. 162–66.
[2] *Economy of the Sacred*, 36, 271–78; and see further discussion above in §1.1.

leucid monarchs.³ On the other hand, temples could push back against unwanted encroachments by the Greeks. A group of "diachronic dossiers" from southwestern Asia Minor and Syria asserts various temples' ancient rights to sacred lands. The dossiers were engraved in stone and displayed prominently in temples, primarily in the Roman period, though the history they recount reaches back into the Hellenistic era. One dossier at the temple of Zeus at Labraunda records a dispute between its high priest and the nearby polis of Mylasa during the reign of Seleucus II (246–225 BCE). It accuses the polis of misappropriating lands that rightfully belonged to the temple.⁴ Similar disputes are recorded at Sinuri nearby.⁵

Meanwhile, in Egypt the Ptolemies appointed special officials to oversee temple finances. One such individual known from the extant sources was called Milon, and he was commissioned with managing the finances of the temples of Edfu in Upper Egypt in 225–222 BCE, the final years of the reign of Ptolemy III.⁶ The Ptolemies also instituted a regular cash grant to temples called a *syntaxis*, which helped supplement temple revenues from other sources.⁷ There are recorded instances of Ptolemaic largesse toward temples too. The construction

---

3 Ibid., 74–84; see also Wright, *Divine Kings and Sacred Spaces: Power and Religion in Hellenistic Syria (301–64 BC)* (Oxford: Archaeopress, 2012), 144–45.
4 Ibid., 59–66, 204–17; on Labraunda, see also Isager, "Kings and Gods in the Seleucid Empire: A Question of Landed Property in Asia Minor," in *Religion and Religious Practice in the Seleucid Kingdom* (op. cit.), 84–88. Isager thinks that the difference between the so-called "temple states" and other political arrangements such as city-states and monarchies was not pronounced (ibid., 88).
5 Dignas, *Economy of the Sacred*, 100–1.
6 Milon and his supervisor Euphronius were meant to resolve financial problems of the priests and the temple; his archive is rare because it was found in an excavation (at Elephantine in 1906). The receipts of the archives show the considerable incomes for the temple from rent payments—though it is impossible to know what they totaled—in addition to its profits from weaving activities, its mummification business, and freewill offerings. See Manning, *Land and Power in Ptolemaic Egypt: The Structure of Land Tenure* (Cambridge: Cambridge University Press, 2003), 83–85. Willy Clarysse has argued that these Ptolemaic officials were brought in temporarily to sort out affairs, while the permanently stationed official there overseeing financial matters was the high priest himself; "The Archive of the Praktor Milon," in *Edfu, an Egyptian Provincial Capital in the Ptolemaic Period* (ed. Vandorpe and Clarysse; Brussel: Koninklijke Vlaamse Academie van België voor Wetenschappen en Kunsten, 2003), 21–22.
7 Thompson, *Memphis*, 71–72; Manning, *Land and Power*, 237–38. On Ptolemaic support of its local temples and cult, including the granting of land, see §4.2. On temple land in general in Ptolemaic Egypt, see Monson, *From the Ptolemies to the Romans: Political and Economic Change in Egypt* (Cambridge; New York: Cambridge University Press, 2012), 77–78; and Clarysse, "Egyptian Estate-Holders in the Ptolemaic Period," in *State and Temple Economy* (op. cit.), 731–43, esp. 735–37.

by Ptolemy III Euergetes of a huge temple to Serapis is a case in point.[8] As are the Canopus and Rosetta decrees of 238 and 196 BCE, respectively, which confer rights and revenues to the Egyptian priesthood. The decrees reflect awareness by the Ptolemaic regime of the power of the local priesthood and the importance of pious munificence in negotiating with local authorities.[9] Similarly, a royal decree from the Tebtunis papyri (dated 229/8 or 187/6 BCE) concerns the assignment of a 2% tax as rent paid to priests around Alexandria and elsewhere, and shows the support by the Ptolemies of the Egyptian priesthood through their power to levy tax.[10]

Another reflection of Ptolemaic support for Egyptian temples is the Edfu Donation Text, an inscription of the first century BCE on the outer retaining wall of the temple of Horus at Edfu in Upper Egypt.[11] It is a hieroglyphic transcription of a dossier of temple holdings of land in the area of the temple. The list includes an apparently fictional donation of land given by Ptolemy X Alexander (110–109, 107–88 BCE) alongside real plots that the temple of Edfu held. Plots that were in possession of the temple for centuries appear to have been gifted anew, according to the Donation Text, at the beginning of the reigns of Ptolemaic rulers. In the words of J.G. Manning, the "religious act recorded by such texts is a record of pharaonic piety, an essential element in maintaining ritual order….Subsequent pharaohs merely 'reiterate' a donation of a previous king."[12]

The temple to the God of Israel at Leontopolis in Egypt was the beneficiary of Ptolemaic support too. As discussed in the first half of this chapter, Josephus's two descriptions of the founding of the temple have Ptolemy VI granting to the Judean priest Onias an old temple site and a nearby tract of land for the support of his priesthood and temple. The founding the temple can be dated to the mid-second century BCE. Josephus's account of it in *Jewish War* is one of several in his writings where foreign rulers are portrayed as benefactors of the temple of the God of Israel. Yet in *Antiquities* Josephus reveals a more disapproving tone in his description of the place, crafting a narrative that underscores the temple's

---

8 For a discussion of the Ptolemaic foundations of the Serapeum, see McKenzie, Gibson, and Reyes, "Reconstructing the Serapeum in Alexandria from the Archaeological Evidence," *The Journal of Roman Studies* 94 (2004), 79–84.
9 Jean Bingen sees these as a decline in royal influence; *Hellenistic Egypt: Monarchy, Society, Economy, Culture* (Berkeley: University of California Press, 2007), 262–66. J.G. Manning warns that it is not a zero-sum game; *Land and Power*, 68–69, n. 20, 177–78.
10 Ibid., 178.
11 Ibid., 74–79, 245–66.
12 Ibid., 76–77.

impurity, given its previous use by a pagan cult that was there before Onias's arrival. The temple's land may have had a parallel in a plot next to a synagogue at Arsinoe-Krokodilopolis.

As for Judea, by the late Persian period it had as its highest ranking figure a high priest, and its temple at Jerusalem may have even minted its own coins.[13] The Rainer papyrus's two royal ordinances issued by Ptolemy II Philadelphus in 261 BCE, which involve the economic administration of Syria and Phoenicia, reveal little on landed property in Judea specifically.[14] The documents from the personal archive of Zenon, the assistant to Ptolemy II's financial officer, from his visit to Palestine in 259 BCE, are similarly unhelpful on the matter of temple land.[15]

Moreover, Jewish literary works of the Hellenistic period that pay special attention to the geography of ancient Judea say nothing of temple land either. The romanticized picture of Judea in the *Letter of Aristeas*—a pseudonymous work likely by an Alexandrian Jew of the Ptolemaic period—has the temple towering above Jerusalem and a fertile well-watered countryside (§§83, 105–20). The third book of the Sibylline Oracles, the main corpus of which is probably another Egyptian Jewish work of the Ptolemaic period, describes the great wealth of the Jerusalem temple as consisting not of land but of gold, silver, and other fineries (3:656–60). Upon the salvation of the elect, the children of God will all live peacefully around the temple (3:702–5) and enjoy the gifts of peoples of all

---

[13] On Judean rule by a high priest in the Hellenistic period, see VanderKam, *From Joshua to Caiaphas*, 95–97, 125, 136–37, 167, 180–81, 190–91, 222–23. VanderKam puts forward a sustained argument against Deborah Rooke's thesis that the high priest had no political authority in the late Persian and early Hellenistic periods; cf. *Zadok's Heirs*, 243–65, esp. 250–52. One more piece of evidence can be added to VanderKam's observations: the seat of imperial authority in the Jerusalem area—the palatial complex at Ramat Rahel, a few kilometers south of the city—was abandoned in the late fourth century BCE presumably as tax collecting operations moved to the temple area and began to fall fully under the aegis of the high priest in office there; see Lipschits, Gadot, and Langgut, "The Riddle of Ramat Raḥel," esp. 76. On the matter of the temple perhaps minting its own coins, the coin issue in question bears a legend and minting authority reading "Yohanan the Priest," perhaps a reference to one of the high priests named Onias; see Barag, "A Silver Coin of Yohanan the High Priest and the Coinage of Judea in the Fourth Century B.C," *INJ* 9 (1986), 2–21.

[14] From the Rainer papyrus we can ascertain that Ptolemaic rule over the province of Syria and Phoenicia was in the hands of two leading figures—a *strategos* (military officer) and a *dioiketes* (financial officer). The province was subdivided into hyparchies, each with its respective military (*hyparchoi*) and financial (*oikonomoi*) officers. Tax collection was in the hands of tax farmers. Bagnall, *The Administration of the Ptolemaic Possessions outside Egypt* (Leiden: Brill, 1976), 18–19.

[15] Tcherikover and Fuks, *CPJ I*, 115–18; Pastor, *Land and Economy*, 33–34.

lands; the rugged terrain of the land will be transformed into a more traversable landscape (3:772–80).[16] But neither account makes mention of temple land.

A work of Hellenistic Jewish literature that does relate explicitly to temple land is 1 Maccabees, but the tract it references—the hinterland of Ptolemais as a source of revenue for the Jerusalem temple—was never actualized as such, if it was ever offered in the first place. The text in question, which is the subject of the second half of this chapter, is a letter from the Seleucid king Demetrius I to Jonathan (1 Macc 10:25–45), where the king offers Jonathan lucrative gifts in order to win his support in 153/2 BCE, including the offer of the Ptolemais hinterland for the upkeep of the Jerusalem temple. The gifts are rejected forcefully by Jonathan, who sides instead with Demetrius's rival to the Seleucid throne, Alexander Balas. As in Josephus's second description of the landed endowment for the temple at Leontopolis, in this account too we see a royal gift of land as signifying an inappropriate offering for the God of Israel. The message could relate to an ongoing debate among Jerusalem circles regarding the appropriateness of accepting funding from non-Jewish sources for the sake of the temple. The issue would resurface nearly two centuries after the composition of 1 Maccabees, when the refusal to receive offerings from Romans would, according to Josephus, help ignite the Jewish war with Rome.

4.2 The Land Endowment for the Oniad Temple at Leontopolis

Twice Josephus describes the temple of the God of Israel at Leontopolis, which is in the nome of Heliopolis in lower Egypt (*War* 7.423–36; *Ant.* 13.62–73).[17] The two descriptions disagree on who its founder was, whether Onias III or IV. Scholars

---

16 On the *Letter of Aristeas*, see Tcherikover, "The Ideology of the Letter of Aristeas," *HTR* 51, no. 2 (1958), 59–85; and Gruen, *Heritage and Hellenism: The Reinvention of Jewish Tradition* (Berkeley: University of California Press, 1998), 215–21. On the Ptolemaic date of the Sibylline Oracles, see Buitenwerf, *Book III of the Sibylline Oracles and Its Social Setting* (Leiden; Boston: Brill, 2003), 124–34; and Barclay, *Jews in the Mediterranean Diaspora from Alexander to Trajan (323 BCE–117 CE)* (Edinburgh: T&T Clark, 1998), 216–28.
17 A brief mention of the Oniad temple also appears in the early part of *War* during a description of the power struggles between Antiochus IV Epiphanes and Ptolemy VI (1.31–33), where Onias builds "a small town on the model of Jerusalem and a temple resembling ours"; and in Josephus's excursus on the high priesthood (*Ant.* 20.237), where he writes: "Onias...persuaded them to build a temple to God in the nome of Heliopolis, similar to the one at Jerusalem, and to appoint him high priest." Here the temple is built de novo; in the other *Ant.* passage it is cleansed.

tend to prefer the later Onias and place the foundation at some point after Onias III's death in 172 BCE.[18] A personal letter (*CPJ* I.132) to a certain Onias from an Egyptian administrator named Herodes, dated 164 BCE, encourages the cultivation of Onias's farmland in an economic crisis and would seem to indicate that the temple at Leontopolis had already been set up by then.[19] A papyrus that Gideon Bohak has dated to the middle of the second century BCE reflects local objection to the new Judean presence at Leontopolis.[20] Therefore, a founding date sometime in the early 160s BCE seems most likely. Archaeological work at Tell el-Yehoudieh, the site traditionally associated with Leontopolis, has yielded inconclusive results on the temple's whereabouts.[21] Meron Piotrkowski has proposed that Josephus's two accounts of the founding were based on an Oniad founding legend, which Josephus then altered to stress the illegitimacy of this breakaway temple.[22]

The temple would remain active until the end of the first Jewish war with Rome, when it was destroyed by the Roman authorities for fear that it would turn into a locus of sedition (*War* 7.423–36; *Ant.* 13.66–70; 20.237). In his retelling of this event, Josephus provides his first description of the temple's founding. He writes that Onias initially reached out to Ptolemy VI Philometer (c. 186–145 BCE) for assistance, noting that the temple could help in Ptolemy's struggles with the Seleucids by causing many Judeans to "flock to him for the sake of religious toleration." The account continues as follows (*War* 7.426–30):

---

[18] For a recent summary of the issues surrounding the founding of the temple and an argument for a date in the early part of the 160s BCE, see Wardle, *The Jerusalem Temple*, 120–29, esp. 129. For other literature on its foundation, see Kasher, *The Jews in Hellenistic and Roman Egypt: The Struggle for Equal Rights* (Tübingen: J.C.B. Mohr (Paul Siebeck), 1985), 119–35; Gruen, "The Origins and Objectives of Onias' Temple," in *Scripta Classica Israelica. Yearbook of the Israel Society for the Promotion of Classical Studies. Studies in Memory of Abraham Wasserstein II* (ed. Cotton et al.; Jerusalem: The Israel Society for the Promotion of Classical Studies, 1997); Modrzejewski, *The Jews of Egypt: From Rameses II to Emperor Hadrian* (trans. Cornman; Philadelphia: Jewish Publication Society, 1995), 129–33; Taylor, "A Second Temple in Egypt: the Evidence for the Zadokite Temple of Onias," *JSJ* 29 (1998), 297–321; and Capponi, *Il tempio di Leontopoli in Egitto: identità politica e religiosa dei Giudei di Onia, c. 150 a. C.* (Pisa: Edizioni ETS, 2007).

[19] Tcherikover and Fuks, *CPJ* I, 244–46. See also Wardle, *The Jerusalem Temple*, 127–28; Kasher, *Jews in Hellenistic and Roman Egypt*, 60–61; Gruen, "Onias' Temple," 55–56.

[20] Bohak, "CPJ III, 520: the Egyptian Reaction To Onias' Temple," *JSJ* 26 (1995), 32–41.

[21] For a summary of the archaeological exploration of the site, see Wardle, *The Jerusalem Temple*, 129–31.

[22] "Josephus on Onias and the Oniad Temple," *Jewish Studies Quarterly* 25, no. 1–16 (2018), 1–16.

(426) Induced by this statement, Ptolemy gave him a tract, a hundred and eighty furlongs distant from Memphis; this is the so-called nome of Heliopolis. (427) Here Onias erected a fortress and built his temple (which was not like that in Jerusalem, but resembled a tower) of huge stones and sixty cubits in altitude...
(430) The king, moreover, assigned him a large territory as a source of revenue, to yield both abundance for the priests and large provision for the service of God.

(426) Πεισθεὶς Πτολεμαῖος τοῖς λεγομένοις δίδωσιν αὐτῷ χώραν ἑκατὸν ἐπὶ τοῖς ὀγδοήκοντα σταδίους ἀπέχουσαν Μέμφεως νομὸς δ'οὗτος Ἡλιοπολίτης καλεῖται. (427) φρούριον ἔνθα κατασκευασάμενος Ὀνίας τὸν μὲν ναὸν οὐχ ὅμοιον ᾠκοδόμησε τῷ ἐν Ἱεροσολύμοις, ἀλλὰ πύργῳ παραπλήσιον λίθων μεγάλων εἰς ἑξήκοντα πήχεις ἀνεστηκότα...
(430) ἀνῆκε δὲ καὶ χώραν πολλὴν ὁ βασιλεὺς εἰς χρημάτων πρόσοδον, ὅπως εἴη καὶ τοῖς ἱερεῦσιν ἀφθονία καὶ τῷ θεῷ πολλὰ τὰ πρὸς τὴν εὐσέβειαν.

Josephus then notes that Onias's motives for founding the temple in Egypt involved his resentment toward the Jerusalem establishment and his desire to draw masses of worshippers away from the Jerusalem temple (*War* 7.431–32). How he managed the land that Ptolemy gave him is a matter of speculation. He could have divided up farmable plots and gardens among the priests who served at the temple, or he could have leased them out to the priests or to others. In any case, the land was clearly associated with him and his family line. This is evidenced not only in the above-mentioned papyrus (*CPJ* I.132) but also in the use of the moniker "the land of Onias" (ἡ Ὀνίου χώρα) to describe it in *War* §90 and *Ant.* 14.131, and in a comment by Strabo that refers to the Jews in the area as "those of the Oniad [district]" (οἱ ἐκ τῆς Ὀνίου γενόμενοι; *Ant.* 13.287).

Victor Tcherikover has identified the parcel set aside by Ptolemy VI for Onias as cleruchic land, which was a type of land awarded by the Ptolemies to soldiers as a reward for military service.[23] This relates to Tcherikover's theory that the Oniad temple and settlement was established for military purposes, and that its inhabitants were soldiers from Palestine, with some priests among them. It would thus make sense for the king to give shelter to Onias in hopes that one day he could take over the Jerusalem establishment and win over popular support. That there was a military colony around Leontopolis, and that the Judean presence there had a military character to it, is supported by the fact that Josephus refers to it as a fortress (ὀχύρωμα) in *Ant.* 13.66, that Onias's sons Helkias and Hananiah became prominent commanders under Cleopatra III (116–102 BCE; *Ant.* 13.287), that Judean inhabitants of the region would later protect the route from Pelusium to Memphis, and that there was a place in the vicinity called the "Judean camp" (*War* 1.190–91; *Ant.* 14.131–33).

---

23 *Hellenistic Civilization and the Jews* (Philadelphia: Jewish Publication Society of America, 1959), 278–81.

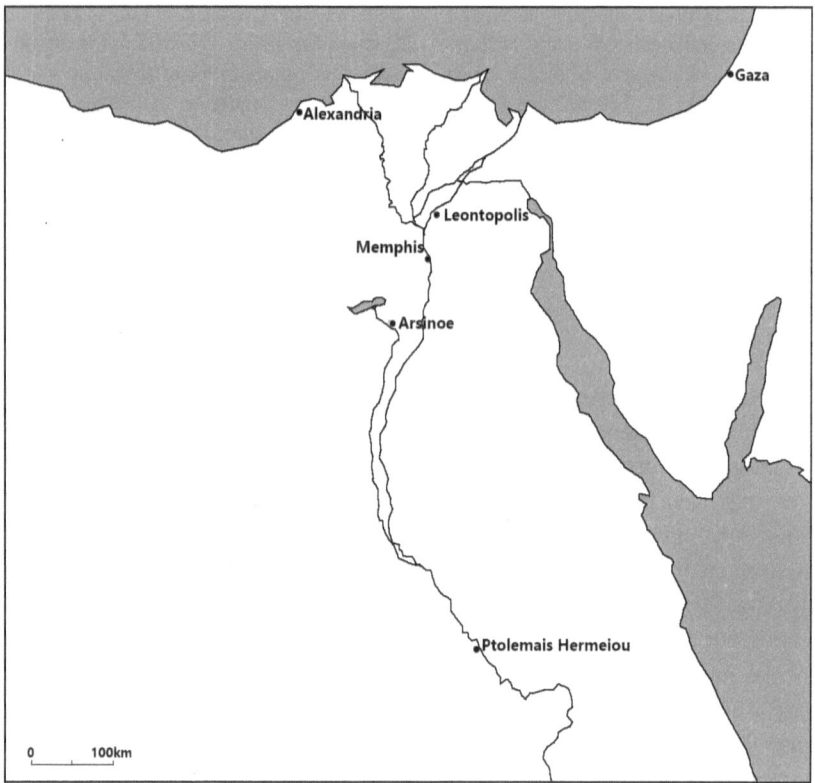

Figure 9. Map of Ptolemaic Egypt showing the location of Leontopolis in the Nile Delta.

Richard Last argues that the parcel was not cleruchic but ownerless (ἀδέσποτος) land.[24] As such it would have needed to be put up for auction and could not have technically been gifted by the king to a newcomer. Josephus would have been aware, claims Last, of the inappropriateness of Ptolemy VI's gesture of gifting ownerless land when the legal custom called for an auction. This would have further delegitimized Onias IV and his Egyptian holdings to Josephus's audience. Thus, according to Last the land endowment was not a rightful grant of cleruchic land but a wrongful seizure of a landed asset.

Regardless of the reasons behind Ptolemy VI's interest in supporting the temple, the parcel he granted to it likely carried the status of sacred land (ἱερὰ γῆ). Such land in Ptolemaic Egypt was, as Andrew Monson has put it, "a fiscal

---

[24] "Onias IV and the ἀδέσποτος ἱερός: Placing Antiquities 13.62–73 into the Context of Ptolemaic Land Tenure," *JSJ* 41, no. 4–5 (2010), 494–516.

category, within which land was either in private ownership or under various leaseholds of limited duration."[25] Along with cleruchic land, it was classified in Ptolemaic documents as "in release" (ἐν ἀφέσει). Such land was not exempt from taxes entirely but probably did not reach the tax burden approaching 50% per annum on the produce of typical peasant holdings on royal land, where landholders were viewed as tenants of the royal house and their heavy taxes seen as a kind of rent payment or tribute.[26] The Hauswaldt papyri (265–208 BCE) include land conveyances of sacred plots of pasturelands among the "servants of Horus of Edfu." Horus's herdsmen appear to have been given small plots of sacred land in exchange for their work. They could freely convey them to others and use them as they saw fit.[27]

The sacred status of the land at Leontopolis is hinted at in Josephus's second account of the founding of the temple there. In *Ant.* 13.66–71 he presents a correspondence between Onias IV and Ptolemy VI on the matter:[28]

(66) [Onias IV:] "I have found a most suitable place in the fortress called after Bubastis-of-the-Fields, which abounds in various kinds of trees and is full of sacred animals, (67) wherefore I beg you to permit me to cleanse this temple, which belongs to no one and is in ruins..."	... ἐπιτηδειότατον εὑρὼν τόπον ἐν τῷ προσαγορευομένῳ τῆς ἀγρίας Βουβάστεως ὀχυρώματι, βρύοντα ποικίλης ὕλης καὶ τῶν ἱερῶν ζῴων μεστόν, δέομαι συγχωρῆσαί μοι, τὸ ἀδέσποτον ἀνακαθάραντι ἱερὸν καὶ συμπεπτωκὸς...
(69) ...This, then, is what Onias wrote to King Ptolemy. And one may get a notion of the king's piety and that of his sister and wife Cleopatra from the letter which they wrote in reply, for they placed the blame for the sin and transgression against the Law on the head of Onias, writing the following reply:	...Καὶ ταῦτα μὲν ὁ Ὀνίας τῷ βασιλεῖ Πτολεμαίῳ γράφει. κατανοήσειε δ'ἄν τις αὐτοῦ τὴν εὐσέβειαν καὶ Κλεοπάτρας τῆς ἀδελφῆς αὐτοῦ καὶ γυναικὸς ἐξ ἧς ἀντέγραψαν ἐπιστολῆς, τὴν γὰρ ἁμαρτίαν καὶ τὴν τοῦ νόμου παράβασιν εἰς τὴν Ὀνίου κεφαλὴν ἀνέθεσαν.

---

25 *From the Ptolemies to the Romans*, 77.
26 Ibid., 77–78; Manning, *Land and Power*, 56–61. The *apomoira* tax was taken on vineyards and orchards and the *artabieia* on grain land; see Thompson, *Memphis*, 102, 111, 135.
27 Manning, *Land and Power*, 79–85.
28 Text and translation after Loeb, *Josephus IX* (Ralph Marcus, translator).

(70) "King Ptolemy and Queen Cleopatra to Onias, greeting. We have read your petition asking that it be permitted you to cleanse the ruined temple in Leontopolis in the nome of Heliopolis, called Bubastis-of-the-Fields. We wonder, therefore, whether it will be pleasing to God that a temple be built in a place so wild and full of sacred animals. (71) But since you say that the prophet Isaiah foretold this long ago, we grant your request if this is to be in accordance with the Law, so that we may not seem to have sinned against God in any way."

ἀντέγραψαν γὰρ οὕτως· "βασιλεὺς Πτολεμαῖος καὶ βασίλισσα Κλεοπάτρα Ὀνίᾳ χαίρειν. ἀνέγνωμέν σου τὴν ἐπιστολὴν ἀξιοῦντος ἐπιτραπῆναί σοι τὸ ἐν Λεόντων πόλει τοῦ Ἡλιοπολίτου ἱερὸν συμπεπτωκὸς ἀνακαθᾶραι, προσαγορευόμενον δὲ τῆς ἀγρίας Βουβάστεως. διὸ καὶ θαυμάζομεν εἰ ἔσται τῷ θεῷ κεχαρισμένον τὸ καθιδρυσόμενον ἱερὸν ἐν ἀσελγεῖ τόπῳ καὶ πλήρει ζῴων ἱερῶν. ἐπεὶ δὲ σὺ φῂς Ἡσαΐαν τὸν προφήτην ἐκ πολλοῦ χρόνου τοῦτο προειρηκέναι συγχωροῦμέν σοι, εἰ μέλλει τοῦτ'ἔσεσθαι κατὰ τὸν νόμον, ὥστε μηδὲν ἡμᾶς δοκεῖν εἰς τὸν θεὸν ἐξημαρτηκέναι."

In this account, Onias IV observes that the place is marked by its variety of trees and sacred animals, along with the dilapidated old temple itself. The implication is that the site could easily accommodate a new religious organization with a cult of sacrifice. The trees could have been used for growing fruit, producing oil and wine for the altar, or procuring timber for sanctuary construction; the animals could be designated for sacrifice on the altar, among other things; and the old sanctuary itself could be renovated and turned into a place of worship of the God of Israel. The surrounding fields that once grew produce for nourishing a pagan altar would now be set aside for the purposes of nourishing one for God. Josephus is crafting the story to underscore the fact that Onias's altar—his entire sacred economy, in other words—is being sustained by an impure source. It has all been sullied by its association with an earlier cult.

In an instance of deftly crafted irony, Josephus has Ptolemy and Cleopatra responding with incredulousness to Onias's request to build a sanctuary at this site. They wonder if the founding of a Judean temple there, with sacred animals from an earlier cult of worship still wandering around the place, would find favor in the eyes of the God of Israel. Their knowledge of Judean custom underscores Onias IV's transgression of it. Josephus's fashioning of the narrative works to delegitimize the Leontopolis temple, a sentiment that would continue into rabbinic writings as well.[29]

Josephus's negative attitude in *Antiquities* toward the land endowment at Leontopolis may relate to an aversion to the temple garden or the sacred grove, which were commonplace in Greco-Roman sanctuary precincts but absent

---

[29] The priests of Leontopolis were consigned by the rabbis a lesser status without altar privileges (*m. Menaḥot* 13:10). On Josephus's anti-Oniad polemicizing in the account, see Piotrkowski, "Josephus on Onias," 10–16.

from the Jerusalem temple. Philo of Alexandria voiced his disapproval of sacred groves in *Spec. Laws* 1.74–75, where he explains why the Jerusalem temple lacks one. A temple should be not about "providing pleasure and hours of easy enjoyment" as a sacred grove can provide, he writes, but should remind one of the "austerity of religion." He also notes that sacred trees would have required fertilizer, entirely inappropriate in his view for the temple, for "excrements of men and irrational animals cannot be brought (into the temple) without profanity." Furthermore, he notes that fruit-bearing trees would distract the fickle-minded from the respect due to the temple and the ceremonies conducted therein and were often where those seeking refuge would spend their time. The absence of a sacred grove in the Jerusalem temple is also pointed out by Pseudo-Hecataeus, as quoted by Josephus (*C. Ap.* 1.199).

The sacred animals that wandered about the Leontopolis temple area could have been a delegitimizing feature in the eyes of many Jews. Such animals, which were a prominent feature of Egyptian religion, were condemned on several occasions in the Second Temple source material (Philo, *Decalogue* 76–80; Josephus, *C. Ap.* 1.225; 2.66, 81, 86, 140; *Wisdom of Solomon* 15:18–16:1). The practice of keeping sacred animals in the temple precinct may have conjured images of bull worship as part of the old Canaanite cult, which was thoroughly denounced in biblical writings.[30] The repulsion may also relate to the anti-Semitic claim in classical antiquity that Jews worshipped an ass's head in their temples.[31]

Negative attitudes towards the Leontopolis temple, whether because it was a rival site to Jerusalem or because of its pagan origins, may have prompted a defensive, apologetic posture among those who worshipped there. Gideon Bohak has argued that the apocryphal Greek work *Joseph and Aseneth* was written to

---

30 The sin of the worship of the golden calf in Exod 32 is the most famous of the biblical polemics against it; see Sasson, "Bovine Symbolism in the Exodus Narrative," *VT* 18, no. 3 (1968), 380–87.

31 Mnaseas of Patara (*C. Ap.* 2.112–14) writes that a certain Idumean named Zabidus carried off the golden head of an ass from within the temple of the God of Israel and brought it to Dora. Tacitus (*Histories*, 5.3–4) relates that Moses discovered water in the wilderness by following a herd of wild asses; and Diodorus (*Bibliotheca Historica*, 34:2–4) states that Antiochus IV found in the temple a statue of a bearded man on an ass. See also *C. Ap.* 2.80; Stern, *Greek and Latin Authors on Jews and Judaism. Edited with Introductions, Translations and Commentary. Volume One: From Herodotus to Plutarch* (Jerusalem: Israel Academy of Sciences and Humanities, 1974), 97–98. Stern notes the association of the ass with Typhon-Seth, the enemy of Osiris, and the fact that the name Iao, the name of the God of Israel in pagan circles, resembles the sound of the Egyptian word for ass.

help legitimate the Judean presence at the site.[32] The story is a refashioning of the story of Joseph's marriage to Aseneth, a daughter of an Egyptian priest (Gen 41:45). It turns Aseneth into a righteous proselyte. Bohak points to the emphasis in the tale on Aseneth's field of inheritance (3:5, 4:2), which would then pass to Joseph once Aseneth married him.[33] The passage in 4:2 stresses all the good things that Aseneth would enjoy from the land—fruit, grapes, dates, doves, pomegranates, and figs. The tale thus extols the land while connecting it to the forefathers' generation. It recognizes that the land was once associated with the Egyptian priesthood, through the figure of Aseneth's father. But it portrays the land as the rightful holding of a Judean patriarch, by virtue of his marriage into Aseneth's family, in a period long before the Ptolemies. The tradition would serve to neutralize any notion that the land was impure. More importantly, the story in *Joseph and Aseneth* would retain the memory of this land having always associated with families of priests—once Egyptian, now Jewish.

Furthermore, Josephus's characterization of Ptolemy VI as a pious supporter of Judaism fits into a larger pattern in his works, regardless of Josephus's view on the Leontopolis temple and regardless of whether the temple's landed parcel was considered sacred in the eyes of the Ptolemaic authorities. As a beneficiary of Flavian patronage in Rome, Josephus wrote his histories, particularly *War*, with a degree of reverence for the Roman emperors.[34] He is careful to show a history of support by foreign regimes in the form of landed endowments that were

---

[32] Bohak, *Joseph and Aseneth and the Jewish Temple in Heliopolis* (Atlanta: Scholars Press, 1996), esp. 83–104.

[33] Ibid., 64–67. On a similar remark by the Hellenistic Jewish historian Artapanus, brought by Eusebius (*Praeparatio Evangelica* 9.23.1–4), see Frey, "Temple and Rival Temple: The Cases of Elephantine, Mt. Gerizim, and Leontopolis," in *Gemeinde ohne Tempel: Zur Substituierung und Transformation des Jerusalemer Tempels und seines Kults im Alten Testament, antiken Judentum und frühen Christentum* (ed. Ego et al.; Tübingen: Mohr Siebeck, 1999), 187, n. 99.

[34] On the view that Josephus saw patronage by ruling parties as the key element for Jewish prosperity during his post-bellum life in Rome, see Rajak, "Josephus in the Diaspora," in *Flavius Josephus and Flavian Rome* (ed. Edmondson et al.; Oxford; New York: Oxford University Press, 2005), 79–97. On the unequal power relations in Flavian Rome that underlie much of Josephus's writing and worldview, see Barclay, "The Empire Writes Back: Josephan Rhetoric in Flavian Rome," ibid., 315–32. On the thesis that during the period in which Josephus wrote *War* he was still engaged in Jewish apologetics, see Cohen, *Josephus in Galilee and Rome: His Vita and Development as a Historian* (Leiden: Brill, 1979), esp. 232–42. But cf. Steve Mason's argument challenging the view that *War* was written as propaganda to encourage submission to the Romans (but should be read first and foremost as an attempt at a fair treatment of his people) in "Of Audience and Meaning: Reading Josephus' *Bellum Judaicum* in the Context of a Flavian Audience," in *Josephus and Jewish History in Flavian Rome and Beyond* (ed. Sievers and Lembi; Leiden; Boston: Brill, 2005), 71–100.

meant to help the cult of the God of Israel subsist. The account of the founding of the Oniad temple at Leontopolis in *War*, for example, appears as an aside in a retelling of the temple's destruction at the hands of the Romans and thus provides an important counterpoint to it. Josephus wants his audience to know the entire Oniad enterprise there would have been impossible without foreign support, recalling other instances in his histories of a similar nature.

For example, in his account of Nehemiah's efforts to bolster the population of Jerusalem and the economic standing of its temple, he adds to the biblical account the detail that Nehemiah "had prepared houses for them [the priests and Levites] at his own expense and also told the people who cultivated the land to bring tithes of their produce to Jerusalem in order that the priests and Levites, having a perpetual source of livelihood, might not abandon the temple service" (*Ant.* 11.181–82). These measures are followed by the remark that Nehemiah had performed other "splendid and praiseworthy public services" and was a man of a "kind and just nature" (*Ant.* 11.183). These are elaborations by a historian interested in portraying Nehemiah as an ideal benefactor. The construction of houses for the priests and Levites in Jerusalem is not found in Josephus's source material in Neh 11:1–2 and could have been entirely imagined by him for the benefit of this characterization.

A similar portrait of imperial benefaction for the good of the Yahwistic cult emerges in Josephus's account of the founding of the Yahwistic sanctuary at Mt. Gerizim, which he erroneously dates to the reign of Darius III (338–331 BCE).[35] In his account he tells of the promise by Sanballat, governor of the Persian province of Samaria, of land grants for agriculture (χώραν εἰς γεωργίαν), dwelling places, and money for all those who followed the high priest Manasses to the new temple, priests included (*Ant.* 11.312). Josephus notes that Sanballat "enthusiastically supported" his new son-in-law Manasses as he established the new cult in Samaria.

A third instance involves Josephus himself, who relates an incident in *Life* 422 regarding his own parcel of land somewhere near Jerusalem. It is important testimony to the free holding of land by members of the Judean priesthood in the early Roman period, a subject to which I will return in Chapter 6. As part of his deal with the Roman authorities toward the end of the war, Josephus was compensated for this land because it had become unprofitable to him with the encampment of Roman soldiers in the area. Titus himself made sure that Josephus was given a fitting parcel near the Mediterranean coast. Josephus then describes

---

[35] For the historical issues surrounding Josephus's account, see Frey, "Temple and Rival Temple," 180–83.

Titus as having paid him "great respect" and even offering to let him sail with him on his ship back to Rome. Titus here assumes the role of patron to Josephus, as Nehemiah was for the priests and Levites who moved into Jerusalem, as Sanballat was for those priests who defected from Jerusalem to Gerizim, and as Ptolemy VI was in this account of the founding of the Oniad temple in Egypt. Similar accounts in Josephus and Second Temple literature relate to royal largesse toward the cult of the God of Israel but do not involve landed grants.[36]

Josephus's account of the gifting of a goodly plot of Onias IV at Leontopolis, with its emphasis on the munificence of leaders toward priests, has a parallel in Artapanus's work *Judaica*. There Moses rather than a foreign leader is said to have divided Egypt into territories, allotting special land exclusively for the use of Egyptian priests (Eusebius, *Praeparatio Evangelica*, 9.27.4). It has another parallel in the work of Hecataeus of Abdera, who portrays the biblical figure of Moses as a pious benefactor of priests. In the course of his retelling of the Exodus from Egypt in *Aegyptica* (as recorded by Diodorus Siculus, *Bibl. His.* 40.3), Hecataeus speaks of early Israelite history in a manner that confuses the biblical character of Moses with Joshua. It was Moses, writes Hecataeus, who "led out military expeditions against the neighboring tribes, and after annexing much land apportioned it out, assigning equal allotments to private citizens and greater ones to the priests, in order that they, by virtue of receiving more ample revenues, might be undistracted and apply themselves continually to the worship of God."[37] (Presumably the priests were absentee landlords.) As Menahem Stern points out, Hecataeus's vision of priests being allotted more land has parallels in Greek utopias, namely Euhemerus' comment that priests should get a double share of land.[38]

4.3 A Sacred Garden next to a Synagogue at Arsinoe

The endowment of land by Ptolemy VI for the benefit of the temple at Leontopolis—for the support of its priesthood and sanctuary expenses, as the comment in *War* 7.430 indicates—is the best evidence of sacred landholdings by the cult of

---

36 Shaye Cohen sees Josephus's characterization of the good and pious monarch as involving reverence for God, which can be expressed by votive offerings and other promises toward his temple; "Respect for Judaism by Gentiles According to Josephus," *HTR* 80, no. 4 (1987). Note also the example of Antiochus III, who according to *Ant.* 12.120 committed to support the expenses of the sacrificial cult.
37 Section 7 in Stern, *Greek and Latin Authors*, vol. 1, 26–29.
38 Ibid., 32.

4.3 A Sacred Garden next to a Synagogue at Arsinoe

the God of Israel in Egypt. However, a fragmentary land-survey papyrus of the second century BCE from Arsinoe-Krokodilopolis in the Fayum does mention a synagogue next to a sacred garden. The relevant part of the document reads as follows (*CPJ* I, no. 134, lines 18–21):[39]

Situated to the north, a Judean place of prayer represented by Pertollos, and a sacred garden cultivated by a tenant, Petesouchos son of Marres, of 3 13/16 arourai and 1 1/2 arourai planted with flowers and vegetables.	Βο(ρρᾶ) [ἐ]χ[ο(μένης)] προσευχῆς Ἰουδαίων διὰ Περτόλλου διὰ μι(σθωτοῦ) Πετεσούχου τοῦ Μαρρήους ἱερᾶς παρα(δείσου) γ (ἥμισυ) (τέταρτον) ι' ς', [σ]τεφά(νοις) καὶ λαχά(νοις) α (ἥμισυ).

The synagogue and adjacent garden are located on a tract of land in the northwestern area of the city. It is not clear from the survey whether the garden is part of the synagogue holdings. Tcherikover had suggested that the entire tract mentioned in the document was sacred, with the various sub-plots—that of the synagogue included—divided up among several parties. This would imply that the sacred garden adjacent to the synagogue was unrelated to it. The fact that the same survey notes another sacred garden, unrelated to the synagogue's, in the same tract of land serves for Tcherikover as evidence favoring this understanding, though he admits that the question is open for discussion.[40]

Aryeh Kasher notes the possibility that the garden belonged to the synagogue, which would imply that it "had a small income from it, for the land survey notes that flowers and vegetables were grown on it."[41] Though the names Petesouchos and Marres, who are mentioned in the document, are not Hebraic in origin, Kasher supposes that it would have been logical for Jews to hold the lands surrounding the synagogue based on the fact that it was given legal protection as a holy place.[42] But the circumstances of ownership are not made clear by the document, and it remains possible, following Tcherikover, that the Arsinoe synagogue in the second century BCE happened to sit next to a sacred garden with no connection to it.

---

39 Reconstructed text and translation follow Tcherikover and Fuks, *CPJ I*, 248–49 (no. 134).
40 Ibid., 249.
41 *Jews in Hellenistic and Roman Egypt*, 138–39.
42 On the sanctity conferred to synagogues in Ptolemaic Egypt, see ibid., 138, n. 95; and Levine, *The Ancient Synagogue: The First Thousand Years* (New Haven; London: Yale University Press, 2005), 78–80.

4.4 The Hasmoneans and Sacred Land in Judea

The Hasmonean takeover of Judea from the Seleucids led to sweeping changes in the settlement patterns of the region. By the second half of the second century BCE, the major cities that had been developed under the patronage of the Ptolemies and Seleucids were in decline, while Jerusalem was growing significantly.[43] Judea's territory was expanded into Iturea in the north and Idumea in the south. With the destruction of the competing Yahwistic shrine at Mt. Gerizim by John Hyrcanus (*Ant.* 13.255–58, 318), the worship of the God of Israel was centralized at Jerusalem, which also became the center for tax collection.[44] This would have increased pilgrimage to the city. The temple was enlarged significantly, the Southwestern Hill re-urbanized, and the expanded city fortified.[45] The military exploits of the Hasmoneans, as well as other state needs, appear to have been paid for by a 10% tax called the *dekate*, a holdover of older imperial tribute payments.[46] The appearance around the beginning of Hasmonean rule of a new type of stamped handle for jars probably used to transport tax revenue can be associated with these developments. The new stamped handles were inscribed with

---

[43] Tal, "Hellenism in Transition from Empire to Kingdom: Changes in the Material Culture of Hellenistic Palestine," in *Jewish Identities in Antiquity: Studies in Memory of Menahem Stern* (ed. Levine and Schwartz; Tübingen: Mohr Siebeck, 2009), 55–73. Tal has also examined the Ptolemaic and Seleucid policy regarding city foundations and concluded that generally the imperial authorities invested in existing centers with a strong Achaemenid past and conferred upon them minting rights; new city foundations were rare; "'Hellenistic Foundations' in Palestine," in *Judah between East and West: The Transition from Persian to Greek Rule (ca. 400–200 BCE)* (ed. Grabbe and Lipschits; London: T&T Clark, 2011), 242–54. On the extremely modest size of Jerusalem in the Persian and Early Hellenistic periods, see Finkelstein, "Territorial Extent," 44–54.
[44] On Hyrcanus's destruction of Gerizim and Judaization of Idumea and Aristobulus I's conquest and Judaization of Iturea, see Schürer, Vermes, and Millar, *The History of the Jewish People in the Age of Jesus Christ (175 B.C.–A.D. 135), Volume I, Revised and Edited* (Edinburgh: T&T Clark, 1973), 207, 217.
[45] 1 Macc 12:35–38, 14:37; *Ant.* 13.181–83, 213–18. The citadel hill is said by Josephus to have been lowered so that the temple would stand higher than it (*War* 1.50, 5.139). On the development of the Temple Mount concept in this period, see Eliav, *God's Mountain: The Temple Mount in Time, Place, and Memory* (Baltimore: Johns Hopkins University Press, 2005), 28–32.
[46] Bar-Kochva, "Manpower, Economics, and Internal Strife in the Hasmonean State," in *Armées et fiscalité dans le monde antique: [colloque] Paris 14–16 octobre 1976* (ed. Chastagnol et al.; Paris: C.N.R.S., 1977), 167–96, esp. 185–91. Bar-Kochva seeks to temper the earlier view of Shimon Applebaum, who had reconstructed an imposition by the Hasmoneans of a considerably increased taxation burden on the rural areas, the confiscation of tracts around cities settled by Greeks, and the rise of large estates owned by the Jerusalem aristocracy; see "The Hasmoneans—Logistics, Taxation, Constitution," in *Judaea in Hellenistic and Roman Times: Historical and Archaeological Essays* (ed. Applebaum; Leiden; New York: Brill, 1989), 9–29.

the word *yršlm* ("Jerusalem"). They replaced the well-established types that bore various formulations of the provincial name Yehud.[47]

The Hasmoneans may have re-instituted the shekel tax too, to help fund the regular cult of sacrifice at the Jerusalem temple. The initial use of such a tax, which was paid annually, is attributed to Neh 10:33–34 as part of his temple reforms. But from that point forward the sources are silent on the tax until the late Second Temple period. It is absent, for instance, from the lengthy list of dues that Tobit is said to have paid to the temple.[48] An ordinances text (4Q159) from Qumran, dated to around the end of the first century BCE, asserts that the shekel contribution should be paid not annually but once in a lifetime, in keeping with the practice attested in Exod 30:11–16. This led J. Liver to argue that the Qumran sectarians protested the reinstatement of the shekel tax by the Hasmoneans.[49]

As for temple land, Shimon Applebaum contended that all such land, as well as military holdings and royal estates, would have been subject to the *dekate* tax once the Hasmoneans instituted it.[50] He writes:

> Under the Hasmonaeans, however, the difference between the last two categories [royal and temple] would have been entirely theoretical, because the Jewish high priests now combined theocratic functions with secular government, and as we have observed elsewhere, Jewish records of the first and second centuries CE contain a number of references

---

47 On the evidence that the *yršlm* + star type postdates the latest of the YHD types, see Geva, "A Chronological Reevalution of Yehud Stamp Impressions in Palaeo-Hebrew Script, Based on Finds from Excavations in the Jewish Quarter of the Old City of Jerusalem," *Tel Aviv* 34, no. 1 (2007), 98–101; and Lipschits and Vanderhooft, *Yehud Stamp Impressions*, 668.

48 The list includes the following: the first fruits of crops, the firstborn of animals, the tithes of the cattle, and the shearing of the sheep to the priests; the tithe of corn, wine, olive oil, pomegranates, figs and other fruits to the Levites; a second tithe of money for distribution in Jerusalem; and a third tithe for orphans, widows, and converts (1:6–8). A mention in the *Letter of Aristeas* (§40) of "one hundred talents of silver for sacrifices and the other requirements" does not necessarily imply an obligatory tax.

49 Liver, "The Half-Shekel Offering in Biblical and Post-Biblical Literature," *HTR* 56, no. 3 (1963), 173–98, esp. 190–91; the view is followed by Broshi, "The Role of the Temple in the Herodian Economy," *JJS* 38 (1987), 34; and Schwartz, *Studies in the Jewish Background of Christianity* (Tübingen: J.C.B. Mohr, 1992), 104. The argument that Nehemiah's tax was a permanent fixture through the end of the Second Temple period is speculative; for this argument see Lemaire, "Administration of Fourth-Century B.C.E. Judah," 58–59; and Baesens, "Royal Taxation and Religious Tribute in Hellenistic Palestine," in *Ancient Economies, Modern Methodologies: Archaeology, Comparative History, Models and Institutions* (ed. Bang et al.; Bari: Edipuglia, 2006), 183–84. For more on the shekel tax, see §5.3.

50 "Hasmoneans," 9–29.

to Temple estates. It therefore becomes very probable that the δεκάτη was paid by Jewish military settlers and tenants of Temple and 'royal' land equally.[51]

Zeev Safrai argues in a similar vein:

> It may reasonably be assumed that if the Temple owned lands, then upon the Hasmoneans' ascent to power, the priestly and royal authorities in Judea would have been united, and the properties of the Temple would have been identified, at least partially, with all the properties of the kingdom.[52]

Regardless of how temple land was identified and taxed by Hasmonean authorities, one can expect sanctity protections to have been afforded to such plots.

A critically important source of the Hasmonean period, which can shed light on the question of temple land, is a halakhic section of the Damascus Document (CD 16:14–17 and parallels). The document suggests that by the second century BCE, Lev 27's laws on field consecrations were being read as regulations not on a secured lending operation but rather on donations for the upkeep of the temple in Jerusalem. The early rabbis would continue in this interpretive tradition. As we shall see below, the authors of the Damascus Document seem concerned that such donations were being misused. Landholders could dedicate their field to God to prevent a creditor, dependent, or ex-wife to lay claim to it, among other scenarios. The implication is not only that such dedications sent additional revenue to the incorporated assets of the temple in Jerusalem, but that sacred land was being held privately by non-priests. The topic will be explored in-depth in the following chapters. Given Hasmonean interests in bolstering the economic standing of Jerusalem and its temple, it would make sense for the landed assets profiting the temple to have increased in the period of their rule. Field consecrations may have been encouraged.

Nevertheless, the Temple Scroll mentions nothing of such plots. A work of utopian law from circa 100 BCE, the scroll is devoted to the proper construction and operation of the Jerusalem sanctuary in some future time.[53] It repackages biblical law in a manner that addresses halakhic issues of its time by presenting an alternative model for the layout and operation of the Jerusalem sanctuary. It

---

51 Ibid., 22.
52 Safrai, "The Agrarian Structure," 116.
53 Yigael Yadin dated the scroll to the reign of John Hyrcanus (134–104 BCE) or slightly earlier; *The Temple Scroll. The Hidden Law of the Dead Sea Sect* (New York: Random House, 1985), 220–39. The date has been refined by Lawrence Schiffman to 110–90 BCE; *The Courtyards of the House of the Lord. Studies on the Temple Scroll* (Leiden; Boston: Brill, 2008), 8–10.

thus offers criticism toward the current Hasmonean establishment. Generally speaking, the polemics of the Temple Scroll involve the minutiae of the correct observance of the temple cult within the sanctuary itself and other matters of ritual purity, in addition to a general disapproval of the integration of the kingship and priesthood into a single ruling figure.[54] Its legislation is not reluctant to innovate on matters of temple finances, but none of its extant portions relate to temple land.[55]

Meanwhile, priests appear to have continued to hold land privately, irrespective of whether that land was afforded sanctity protections.[56] According to Josephus, the Seleucid king Antiochus III exempted Judean priests and other temple staff from having to pay royal taxes upon his takeover of the region around 200 BCE (*Ant.* 12.138–44).[57] As the aristocracy continued to accumulate landed wealth in the Hellenistic period, certain wealthy priests may have come to own sizable estates.[58] Both Jason and Menelaus were able to promise higher tribute to the Seleucids, and in essence buy the high priesthood, their extraordinary income required to win the office perhaps deriving in part from their agricultural holdings.[59] It appears that priests of Hellenistic Samaria, in the words of the excavators of Mt. Gerizim, "constituted the highest class in Samaritan society."[60] The corpus of several hundred dedicatory inscriptions from the site, mostly of

---

54 Regev, *Sectarianism in Qumran: A Cross-Cultural Perspective* (Berlin; New York: De Gruyter, 2007), 141–43. Matters of sanctity and space center around maintaining the holiness of the Temple Mount area, for example (11Q19 45:7–46:16). On the notion that tribal territories may have been viewed as emanating from Jerusalem, see Schiffman, *Courtyards*, 287–88.
55 That the Temple Scroll's legislation on priestly revenue is not simply a regurgitation of Deut 18:3–5 is demonstrated by its conferral to the priesthood of the proceeds of a tariff on war booty and sacred donations (defined there as *tĕrûmâ*), both without scriptural precedent (11Q19 60:3–5); see Qimron, *The Temple Scroll: A Critical Edition with Extensive Reconstructions* (Beer Sheva; Jerusalem: Ben-Gurion University of the Negev; Israel Exploration Society, 1996), 85.
56 See §2.4.
57 On the taxation rate of Judea at the time of the Seleucid takeover, see Aperghis, *The Seleukid Royal Economy: The Finances and Financial Administration of the Seleukid Empire* (Cambridge: Cambridge University Press, 2004), 166–68; and Baesens, "Royal Taxation," 180–83.
58 On the conglomeration of landed wealth in the Hellenistic period more generally, see Kloppenborg, "The Growth and Impact of Agricultural Tenancy in Jewish Palestine (III BCE–I CE)," 31–66.
59 On the evidence that the Judean high priesthood was awarded on the basis of Greek tax-farming procedures, see Monson, "The Jewish High Priesthood for Sale: Farming out Temples in the Hellenistic Near East," *JJS* 67, no. 1 (2016), 15–35.
60 Magen, Misgav, and Tsfania, *Mount Gerizim Excavations Volume I: The Aramaic, Hebrew and Samaritan Inscriptions* (Jerusalem: Staff Officer of Archaeology—Civil Administration of Judea and Samaria, 2004), 28.

the third–second centuries BCE, records efforts by the priesthood there to raise money for temple construction and maintenance, sometimes drawing from the wealth of their own ranks. Seven of the nine inscriptions that mention titles record donations by priests.⁶¹ The Maccabean family of priests who successfully spearheaded the revolt against the Seleucids came from relatively modest beginnings, leaving behind all their holdings (ὅσα εἶχον) in their home village of Modiin in their flight to war (1 Macc 2:28; *Ant.* 12.271). A halakhic text from Qumran (4Q251) asserts the right of priests to herem property, and there is plenty of reason to believe that priests continued to hold land in the late Second Temple period, as will be discussed in Chapter 6.

4.5 The Ptolemais Hinterland and the Jerusalem Temple

In an era marked by an ethos of pious national pride and religious enthusiasm for Jerusalem, the Hasmoneans discouraged foreign involvement in temple affairs. The court history of the regime, 1 Maccabees, tells of its rise in the wake of a successful campaign against the Seleucids, which culminated in full autonomy under the high priest Simon in 140 BCE. Though extant in Greek, 1 Maccabees is thought to have been composed originally in Hebrew at some point during the reign of John Hyrcanus (134–104 BCE), whose rise to power marks the end of the work, or perhaps of his successor Alexander Janneaus (103–76 BCE).⁶² József

---

61 The inscriptions in question are brief and follow the standard formula די הקרב, "[The unnamed donation] that X offered..." Naveh and Magen reconstruct שורה דנה ("this wall") as the subject, based on the assumption that these inscriptions—appearing as they do on fine ashlar masonry, never *in situ*—would have been viewed from conspicuous places within the sacred precinct, perhaps on the barrier cordoning off the priestly court. See Gudme, *Before the God in This Place*, 52–90; Naveh and Magen, "Aramaic and Hebrew Inscriptions of the Second-Century BCE at Mount Gerizim," '*Atiqot* 32 (1997), 13*; and Magen, Misgav, and Tsfania, *Mount Gerizim Excavations I*, 16–20. For those mentioning priests, see ibid., 25–30, 34–35, Cat. Nos. 24, 25, 382, 388–89. The finances of Gerizim were further bolstered by donations from abroad. Two inscriptions from Delos from ca. 250–175 BCE and ca. 150–50 BCE, respectively, record Samaritans who refer to themselves as "Israelites who make offerings to hallowed, consecrated Argarizein"; Levine, *The Ancient Synagogue*, 110–11.
62 For a summary of the issues surrounding the dating of the book, see Bartlett, "1 Maccabees," in *The Oxford Encyclopedia of the Books of the Bible* (ed. Coogan; Oxford; New York: Oxford University Press, 2011), 5. Bartlett acknowledges that most scholars see the book coming together during the reign of Hyrcanus but he prefers a date in the reign of Janneaus, given the sense that the history told in the book is placed in a more distant past. Jonathan Goldstein dates it to the reign of Hyrcanus; *I Maccabees: A New Translation, with Introduction and Commentary* (New Haven: Yale University Press, 1976), 62–64.

Zsengellér sees "the purification, rededication, and preservation of the temple as an institution in an intact form" as the main theological issues of the book.[63] Similarly, Doron Mendels understands the book as working to achieve the rhetorical goal that the entire land has been cleansed of foreign peoples and been oriented towards the temple in Jerusalem and the Torah.[64] It is important to note that this religious "cleansing" was focused on specific non-Judean elements that had been introduced into the local culture, most notably syncretistic Hellenizing practices at the temple, rather than on Hellenism per se.[65]

Nowhere does 1 Maccabees have a foreign ruler making offerings at the altar of God. This is in stark contrast with 2 Maccabees, which was a product not of the Hasmonean court but of a diasporic Jew who reworked an original history written by Jason of Cyrene.[66] An early chapter of 2 Maccabees notes that "kings themselves honored the place and glorified the temple with the finest presents, even to the extent that King Seleucus of Asia defrayed from his own revenues all the expenses connected with the service of the sacrifices" (2 Macc 3:2–3). This is a prefacing remark to the story of Heliodorus, a Seleucid official sent by the king to inspect the temple treasury, prompting a miraculous intervention to prevent his entry. According to the story, Heliodorus learns to recognize the sovereignty of God, makes sacrifices, and vows a large sum to the temple (2 Macc 3:35). Later in the book, votive offerings that had been made in Jerusalem by kings are said to have been swept away by Antiochus IV Epiphanes (2 Macc 5:16), an act for which he repents before his death (9:16). These accounts join others brought by Josephus, where foreign leaders are said to have displayed great

---

[63] "Maccabees and Temple Propaganda," in *The Books of the Maccabees: History, Theology, Ideology. Papers of the Second International Conference on the Deuteronomical Books, Pápa, Hungary, 9–11 June, 2005* (ed. Xeravits and Zsengellér; Leiden; Boston: Brill, 2007), 194.
[64] Mendels, *The Land of Israel as a Political Concept*, 47–50; for a similar conclusion, see Williams, *The Structure of 1 Maccabees* (Washington, DC: Catholic Biblical Association of America, 1999), esp. 137.
[65] Erich Gruen argues that the Hasmoneans incorporated Greek cultural norms with Judean ones; *Heritage and Hellenism*, esp. 1–40. "The reciprocal benefits left a more enduring legacy than the intermittent antagonisms. Hasmonaean leaders practiced Hellenistic ways without compromising Jewish integrity," writes Gruen (40). Similarly, Doron Mendels has observed that the polemics in 1 and 2 Maccabees are against those who abandoned the covenant and married into the local population; the Hasmonean wars were similarly against the local population as well as the Seleucid invaders; "Memory and Memories: The Attitude of 1–2 Macc toward Hellenization and Hellenism," in *Jewish Identities in Antiquity* (op. cit.), 41–54.
[66] Schwartz, *2 Maccabees* (Berlin; New York: De Gruyter, 2008), 3–15.

piety toward the God of Israel, providing for his altar, as discussed above.[67] Such a point is never made in 1 Maccabees.

The only mention in 1 Maccabees of a foreign ruler visiting the temple is the account of Antiochus IV plundering of its treasury (1:21–24). Antiochus IV is said to have taken "the silver and the gold, and the costly vessels; he took also the hidden treasures that he found. Taking them all, he went into his own land" (1:23–24). This is the first of several perceived acts of dishonor and sacrilege committed against the temple by foreign rulers, setting the stage for the revolt and the ascent to power of the Hasmoneans. The story of Heliodorus's conversion, for example, was not included in 1 Maccabees.[68]

The rejection of foreign support for the benefit of the Jerusalem temple is also central to the story of 1 Macc 10, where the revenues from the port city of Ptolemais (Akko) and its hinterland are offered to the Hasmoneans as funding for the temple in Jerusalem. That chapter comes amid an extended chronicle on political dealings between Hasmonean and Seleucid authorities in the middle of the second century BCE.[69] The Seleucid king Demetrius I was being challenged for the crown by Alexander Balas in 153/2 BCE. Balas had occupied the city of Ptolemais, a bustling port on the northern coast of ancient Palestine.[70] This prompted Demetrius to prepare for battle. He is said to have approached the Judeans to garner further support for his efforts. Jonathan, who had succeeded his late brother Judah as Hasmonean king in 161 BCE, had taken residence in Jeru-

---

67 See §4.2.
68 The historicity of at least a visit to the temple by a Seleucid official is supported by the recently discovered Heliodorus stele of 178 BCE, which records efforts by Seleucus IV (187–175 BCE) for heightened administrative involvement in the financial affairs of the temples of Coele-Syria and Phoenicia, a responsibility that appears to have ultimately fallen to a certain Diophanes, upon the initial instructions of Heliodorus. The stele was found in conjoining pieces at Maresha and on the antiquities market. Cotton and Wörrle, "Seleukos IV to Heliodoros. A New Dossier of Royal Correspondence from Israel," *Zeitschrift für Papyrologie und Epigraphik* 159 (2007), 191–205.
69 For discussions of the events described in 1 Macc 10, see Schürer, Vermes, and Millar, *History of the Jewish People*, vol. I, 177–79; and Ehling, *Untersuchungen zur Geschichte der späten Seleukiden (164–63 v.Chr.): vom Tode des Antiochos IV. bis zur Einrichtung der Provinz Syria unter Pompeius* (Stuttgart: Steiner, 2008), 139–53. The other extant ancient source on the episode is Josephus's adaptation of the 1 Maccabees account in *Ant.* 13.48–57.
70 On the archaeological remains of Ptolemais in the Ptolemaic and Seleucid periods, see Tal, *The Archaeology of Hellenistic Palestine: Between Tradition and Renewal* (Jerusalem: The Bialik Institute, 2007) [Hebrew], 52–54, 74, 180–82, 300–7; on its history in the Hellenistic period in general, see Kasher, *Jews and Hellenistic Cities in Eretz-Israel: Relations of the Jews in Eretz-Israel with the Hellenistic Cities during the Second Temple Period (332 BCE–70 CE)* (Tübingen: J.C.B. Mohr, 1990), 34–37.

salem and had begun rebuilding the city after the devastating wars of the previous decade. Balas then offered honors of his own to Jonathan, including the high priesthood. Jonathan donned the sacred vestments and recruited an army for Balas, prompting a rejoinder from a now angry Demetrius: "I will write them words of encouragement and promise them honor and gifts, so that I may have their help" he said (1 Macc 10:24), addressing his letter to the Judean people.

The gifts Demetrius presented the people (1 Macc 10:25–45) are of extraordinary worth. They include a waiver on all tribute "for all time" for Judea, Samaria, and Galilee, including the 1/3 tax on all grains and the 1/5 tax on all fruit; the automatic release of all Judean captives anywhere in the Seleucid realm; the annexation of Samaria to the jurisdiction of the high priest; control of the Akra in Jerusalem; immunity for all Judeans in the Seleucid realm on festivals, sabbaths, and the new moon; the enrollment of 30,000 among the king's forces, including several in prominent positions; and the following list of offers regarding the temple in Jerusalem:[71]

(39) Ptolemais and the land adjoining it I have given as a gift to the sanctuary in Jerusalem, to meet the necessary expenses of the sanctuary.	Πτολεμαΐδα καὶ τὴν προσκυροῦσαν αὐτῇ δέδωκα δόμα τοῖς ἁγίοις τοῖς ἐν Ιερουσαλημ εἰς τὴν καθήκουσαν δαπάνην τοῖς ἁγίοις.
(40) I also grant fifteen thousand shekels of silver yearly out of the king's revenues from appropriate places.	κἀγὼ δίδωμι κατ᾿ἐνιαυτὸν δέκα πέντε χιλιάδας σίκλων ἀργυρίου ἀπὸ τῶν λόγων τοῦ βασιλέως ἀπὸ τῶν τόπων τῶν ἀνηκόντων.
(41) And all the additional funds that the government officials have not paid as they did in the first years, they give from now on for the service of the temple.	καὶ πᾶν τὸ πλεονάζον, ὃ οὐκ ἀπεδίδοσαν ἀπὸ τῶν χρειῶν ὡς ἐν τοῖς πρώτοις ἔτεσιν, ἀπὸ τοῦ νῦν δώσουσιν εἰς τὰ ἔργα τοῦ οἴκου.
(42) Moreover, the five thousand shekels of silver that my officials have received every year from the income of the temple, this too is canceled, because it belongs to the priests who minister there.	καὶ ἐπὶ τούτοις πεντακισχιλίους σίκλους ἀργυρίου, οὓς ἐλάμβανον ἀπὸ τῶν χρειῶν τοῦ ἁγίου ἀπὸ τοῦ λόγου κατ᾿ἐνιαυτόν, καὶ ταῦτα ἀφίεται διὰ τὸ ἀνήκειν αὐτὰ τοῖς ἱερεῦσιν τοῖς λειτουργοῦσιν.
(43) And all who take refuge at the temple in Jerusalem, or in any of its territories, because they owe money to the king or are in debt, let them be released and receive back all their property in my kingdom.	καὶ ὅσοι ἐὰν φύγωσιν εἰς τὸ ἱερὸν τὸ ἐν Ιεροσολύμοις καὶ ἐν πᾶσιν τοῖς ὁρίοις αὐτοῦ ὀφείλων βασιλικὰ καὶ πᾶν πρᾶγμα, ἀπολελύσθωσαν καὶ πάντα ὅσα ἐστὶν αὐτοῖς ἐν τῇ βασιλείᾳ μου.

This would confer onto the Jerusalem temple a fixed annual payment in cash from the king, a dynamic source of revenue from the agricultural land surround-

---

[71] Greek follows Rahlfs; English translation follows NRSV.

ing Ptolemais and any taxes procured at its active harbor, the remittance of taxes paid previously from temple funds to the Seleucids, and the granting of inviolable status to the temple and its ὅρια ("territories"). These gifts come on top of what is perhaps the most startling concession: the permanent remittance of annual tribute to the Seleucids on all agricultural produce from Judea, Samaria, and Galilee. The recipients of the letter recognize it for what it is—an empty and unrealistic gesture meant to bribe the Judeans into abandoning their leader Jonathan and his new ally Balas. "When Jonathan and the people heard these words, they did not believe or accept them," notes the author of 1 Maccabees, "because they remembered the great wrongs that Demetrius had done in Israel and how much he had oppressed them" (1 Macc 10:46). Their favor stayed with Balas, "because he had been the first to speak peaceable words to them, and they remained his allies all his days" (1 Macc 10:47).

Those who assert the authenticity of the letter in 1 Macc 10 tend to assume that the author of the book worked with an archive of royal letters that he incorporated into his work, the letter from Demetrius to the Judeans among them.[72] Those who question its authenticity point to the improbability of Demetrius's concessions, even for a ruler who is acting out of desperation and perhaps with no intention of following through on his offers.[73] Emil Schürer noted that

---

[72] Goldstein, *I Maccabees*, 405 (see also 90–103 for a general discussion of source material). Goldstein argues that the author of 1 Maccabees was unaware that the letter before him was anti-Hasmonean rhetoric meant to sway the people away from Jonathan. "The fact that our author misunderstood the text and used a document actually hostile to his own purposes would guarantee that he did not forge it," he writes (405). John Bartlett too seems positively inclined to the authenticity of the letter; *The First and Second Books of the Maccabees* (Cambridge: Cambridge University Press, 1973), 138; as do the following scholars: John Ma, "Seleukids and Speech-Acts: Performative Utterances, Legitimacy and Negotiation in the World of the Maccabees," in *Scripta Classica Israelica. Yearbook of the Israel Society for the Promotion of Classical Studies*. (ed. Cotton et al.; Jerusalem: The Israel Society for the Promotion of Classical Studies, 2000), 74, 98; Gauger, *Beiträge zur jüdischen Apologetik: Untersuchungen zur Authentizität von Urkunden bei Flavius Josephus und im I. Makkabäerbuch* (Köln: P. Hanstein, 1977), 42–44, 137–38; Stern, *The Documents on the History of the Hasmonean Revolt with a Commentary and Introductions* (Tel Aviv: Hakibbutz Hameuchad, 1965) [Hebrew], 97–106; and Aperghis, "Jewish Subjects and Seleukid Kings: A Case Study of Economic Interaction," in *Economies of Hellenistic Societies* (op. cit.), 27–29, 39. For a broad defense of the authenticity of letters from foreign sovereigns and peoples such as Sparta and Rome in 1 and 2 Maccabees and Josephus, see Bickerman, "A Question of Authenticity: The Jewish Privileges," in *Studies in Jewish and Christian History: A New Edition in English Including The God of the Maccabees* (Leiden; Boston: Brill, 2007), 295–314. Bickerman, however, does not relate to Demetrius's letter in particular in this discussion.

[73] Hugo Willrich had long ago argued that the document was a forgery; *Urkundenfälschung in der hellenistisch-jüdischen Literatur* (Göttingen: Vandenhoeck & Ruprecht, 1924), 36–41. Willrich

the concessions "exceed the bounds of probability." He understands the letter to be "similar to that of the speeches which ancient authors incorporated in historical works. The author makes Demetrius write what was appropriate to the situation at that time and of which he probably had some general knowledge."[74] A related theory is that the author of 1 Maccabees worked from an original letter from Demetrius but expanded it significantly.[75]

Further evidence supporting the inauthenticity of the letter has been brought by Kent Rigsby, who has made note of a glaring anachronism in it.[76] The conferral of the status of holy and inviolable to the cities of the Hellenistic East did not become common until the later part of the second century BCE, long after the dating of the letter (153/2 BCE). As a result, writes Rigsby, it would have been "improbable that Jerusalem and its god, among the less Hellenized of the important cities and cults of Palestine, achieved this honor at so early a date, before cities like Tyre or Seleuceia, or indeed at all."[77] To this can be added Schürer's observation that the number of 30,000 Judean troops to be enlisted into the army of Demetrius is identical to the number employed by Ptolemy to garrison his fortresses in the *Letter of Aristeas*, suggesting that the author was merely copying it from there.[78] And Jerome Murphy O'Connor has pointed out that the letter contains all the essential provisions of the *philanthropa basilika* of Antiochus III to

---

thought the document was inserted in the Roman period based on its seemingly anachronistic mention of the poll tax. Schürer disproves that notion but still recognizes it as the invention of the author of 1 Macc; Schürer, Vermes, and Millar, *History of the Jewish People*, vol. I, n. 14 on 178–79. For others who have adopted this approach, see Abel, *Les livres des Maccabées* (Paris: Gabalda, 1949), 184.

74 Schürer, Vermes, and Millar, *History of the Jewish People*, vol. I, n. 14 on 179.
75 Jerome Murphy O'Connor has noted inconsistency in style through the letter, with certain parts in first person singular, others first person plural, and others impersonal. The latter he sees as original and the others as the work of the author of 1 Maccabees or later redactions. "Demetrius I and the Teacher of Righteousness," *RB* 83, no. 3 (1976), 400–20. The non-original sections are according to this model the more improbable concessions—the full tax exemption on Judean land, the release of all Judean captives anywhere in the Seleucid kingdom, and the granting of all revenues from Ptolemais and its countryside for the Jerusalem temple. The original would according to Murphy O'Connor's reconstruction have granted sacred status to Jerusalem, reception of Judeans into the army, annexation of the three districts to the high priest, and right of sanctuary for those carrying debt.
76 *Asylia: Territorial Inviolability in the Hellenistic World* (Berkeley: University of California Press, 1996), 530–31.
77 Ibid.
78 Schürer, Vermes, and Millar, *History of the Jewish People*, vol. I, 179 n. 14.

the Jews (*Ant.* 12.142–44), which may similarly have been known to the author of 1 Maccabees.[79]

The letter of Demetrius is probably more reflective of the 1 Maccabee author's notion of an outrageous and ultimately unacceptable list of gifts than of an actual document he had in his possession from the Seleucid royal archives. Demetrius's character had already been much maligned prior to this point in the book. He had sent his forces into Judea a few years earlier, in a campaign that would result in the death of Judah Maccabee, Jonathan's brother and leader of the Judean cause (1 Macc 9:1–22). The Romans themselves, to whom the author of 1 Maccabees is positively inclined, end their treaty with the Judeans with a statement of special condemnation against Demetrius and ask, "Why have you made your yoke heavy on your friends and allies the Judeans? If now they appeal again for help against you, we will defend their rights and fight you on sea and on land" (8:31–32).[80] Thus when Demetrius comes to the Judeans with such an enticing list of gifts for them, the people face the question of whether the value of the gift could outweigh the character of the giver. Their unequivocal response is that it cannot.

Jonathan and the Judeans opt instead to ally with Balas, while Demetrius falls in battle (1 Macc 10:48–50). Jonathan would then enjoy military victories of his own, the chapter concluding with the notice that he was able to return to Jerusalem with a large amount of booty and even more honors bestowed upon him by Balas (10:87–89). The reward for the holy city eventually comes by virtue of success on the battlefield and the forging of a trusted alliance rather than through extravagant gifts from an inimical figure such as Demetrius. His letter earlier in the chapter comes in the service of this larger point.

Demetrius's offer of Ptolemais and its hinterland to the Judeans could have come across as patently unacceptable if not distasteful to the audience of 1 Maccabees.[81] The city was one of the most Hellenized areas of Syria-Palestine. The altar to Hadad (= Baal) and Astarte on Mt. Carmel towered over its countryside; to Judeans, the holy site may have conjured biblical images of the worship of

---

[79] "Demetrius I," 403.

[80] On the argument that the treaty between Rome and the Judeans in 1 Macc 8:1–32 is also a forgery meant to defend the respectability of the latter, see Gauger, *Beiträge zur jüdischen Apologetik*, 311–20.

[81] Scholars tend to view Demetrius's offer of Ptolemais as a form of punishment to the citizens of the city for siding with Balas, and as a way of enticing the Judeans into aiding him in his assault on the city; Bartlett, *Maccabees*, 137; Stern, *Documents*, 85–86; VanderKam, *From Joshua to Caiaphas*, 255, n. 49; Goldstein, *I Maccabees*, 413.

Baal and Asherah on the Carmel (1 Kgs 18:19, 31–33).[82] Jonathan himself would meet his demise at Ptolemais, after having been promised the city by a scheming Tryphon, who had him imprisoned and later killed there. Jonathan's troops were slaughtered by the inhabitants of the city as they entered its gates (1 Macc 12:44–53).[83] The author of 1 Maccabees could have had this all in mind in his choice of Ptolemais as part of Demetrius's offer to Jonathan in 10:39. Just as Demetrius was unfit to assume the role of benefactor for the house of Israel, so too the city of Ptolemais was unacceptable as a source of nourishment for its temple.

Also significant in this regard is the fact that of the five letters in 1 Maccabees from Seleucid rulers to the Judean people, that of Demetrius is the only one to offer a form of sustenance for the temple, and it is the only one to be rejected. Balas's offer in his letter to Jonathan involved friendship and the high priesthood to Jonathan (10:18–20). In another letter, Demetrius II would present Jonathan confirmation over the rights of possession of an enlarged territory and a remittance of taxes on agricultural produce (11:30–37). Several years later he would offer Simon sovereignty and further tax release (13:36–40). And Antiochus VII Sidetes would promise to Simon tax releases, permission to mint coinage, rights of possession of arms, debt forgiveness, and freedom for Jerusalem (15:2–9). None of these letters includes an offer that would result in the gifting of revenues destined for sacred purposes, as Demetrius I's letter does. They are all concerned with the conferral of honors or the remittance of taxes and debts for which Judeans were liable.[84]

Invoking the temple in Jerusalem in 1 Macc 10 as part of a list of scornful offers made by a hated king is aligned with the idea that foreign support is inappropriate for the temple. Whether it reflected actual Hasmonean policy is another matter. When the issue of foreign support for the temple surfaces in the writings of Josephus, it is presented as if to imply that the temple had been taking dedications and sacrifices throughout its history. Josephus writes that Eleazar, a high-ranking temple official and son of the high priest, decreed in 66 CE that the temple would no longer accept gifts or sacrifices from the Romans, an action that according to Josephus was one of the reasons behind the war with

---

82 For a general discussion on Ptolemais and its religious life in the Hellenistic period, see Kasher, *Jews and Hellenistic Cities in Eretz-Israel*, 34–37.
83 Ibid., 104. In 2 Macc 6:8 and 13:25 Ptolemais also shows hostility to the Judeans.
84 Mendels, "Was the Rejection of Gifts One of the Reasons for the Outbreak of the Maccabean Revolt? A Preliminary Note on the Role of Gifting in the Book of 1 Maccabees," *Journal for the Study of the Pseudepigrapha* 20, no. 4 (2011), 243–56. Mendels argues that from the rule of Jonathan onwards, the Hasmoneans were fully integrated into the gifting and reciprocity culture of Hellenistic rulers.

Rome (*War* 2.409–10). The response from the Judean elders and chief priests was as follows (2.412–13):

> Their forefathers, they said, had adorned the sanctuary mainly at the expense of aliens and had always accepted the gifts of foreign nations; not only had they never taken the sacrilegious step of forbidding anyone to sacrifice, but they had set up around the Temple the dedicatory offerings which were still to be seen and had remained there for so long a time.

The contrasting perspectives of Eleazar and the Judean aristocracy may have been anticipated by those of 1 and 2 Maccabees: the former would prefer that the temple be funded entirely by Judean sources of wealth, the latter readily accept foreign sources. Josephus would appear to fall in the latter camp, as his depiction of Ptolemy VI as pious benefactor of the cult of Yahweh alone attests, even if that cult was worshipped in a temple in Egypt of which he did not approve. The rabbis too would fall in the latter camp, deeming the gifts and sacrifices of non-Jews to be acceptable for the temple, as neither would have been used in relation to obligatory sacrifices.[85] For the same reason they stipulated that non-Jews could not contribute to the shekel tax fund (*m. Šeqalim* 1:5), for it was used to pay for sacrifices made on behalf of Jews alone.[86] Some among the Sadducees adopted the stringent position that the daily sacrifices could be funded individually by priests on altar duty rather than by the shekel tax fund, for fear that some of the money of that fund had been tainted somehow before it was contributed by Jews—all the more so that a non-Jew's contribution would be deemed inappropriate.[87] In 1 Macc 10, there are forerunners to this stringent position, whereby even a lucrative gesture of support by a foreign ruler is rejected forcefully, not only because of the character of the giver, but also because of the nature of the gift.

---

[85] Schürer et al., *History of the Jewish People*, vol. II, 309–11; Schmidt, *How the Temple Thinks*, 99–113; Schwartz, *Jewish Background of Christianity*, 102–16. Schwartz argues that Josephus has distorted somewhat Eleazar's decree to make Judaism seem a bit more universalistic, as he is wont to do; according to Schwartz, the original decree likely had to do with prohibiting sacrifice on behalf of Rome, rather than by foreigners. The latter had never been allowed. For one, non-Jews were not allowed close enough to the area of sacrifice.
[86] For more on the shekel tax, see §§4.4, 5.3.
[87] On the Sadducees and the shekel fund for the daily sacrifices, see Instone-Brewer, *Techniques and Assumptions in Jewish Exegesis before 70 CE* (Tübingen: J.C.B. Mohr (P. Siebeck), 1992), 114–15; Regev, *The Sadducees and Their Halakhah: Religion and Society in the Second Temple Period* (Jerusalem: Yad Ben-Zvi Press, 2005) [Hebrew], 132–39; and Klawans, *Purity, Sacrifice, and the Temple*, 196–98.

A final issue in 1 Macc 10 deserves attention. It is the offer by Demetrius of the right of security for debtors taking refuge in the Jerusalem temple or "in any of its territories" (ἐν πᾶσιν τοῖς ὁρίοις αὐτοῦ; 1 Macc 10:43). The right would be granted for those carrying royal debt and for any other kind of debtor in the Seleucid realm. The question of what these territories may refer to is an important one because it would reflect the historian's notion of property under the aegis of the temple.

In an earlier part of the letter (10:31), Demetrius uses the term *horia* ("territories") when he promises that Jerusalem "and its territories" (καὶ τὰ ὅρια αὐτῆς) be released from tithes and taxes. There the term seems to refer to the entire civic territory of Jerusalem—which is to say, the provincial area of Judea—and is thus equivalent to the term *chora* ("hinterland, city land").[88] The idea is supported by the use of the term *horia* elsewhere in 1 Macc to refer to the entire Land of Israel, as in 2:46 and 9:23, where it seems to be equivalent to the Hebrew *gĕbûl* ("boundary, territory").[89] The word *gĕbûl* would be an appropriate *Vorlage* for *horia* in 1 Macc 10:43 as well. If so, one could read that statement as granting debtors security in the temple and *bĕkōl gĕbûlôtāyw*—"in all its boundaries." Given the outlandishness of Demetrius's other offers to Jonathan, the right of debt asylum in such a huge territory, rather than in a temple and its immediate precinct, seems in keeping with the theme of the account.[90] Interestingly, a gloss on 1 Macc 10:43 by Josephus reads these "boundaries" of the temple as specific revenue-generating areas, rather than the entire region of Judea, as I will discuss in the next chapter.[91]

4.6 Summary

At some point likely in the late 160s BCE, Ptolemy VI Philometer and Cleopatra I gave the cult of the God of Israel in Egypt a tract of land to support the temple

---

[88] *Asylia*, 529. The verse in 1 Maccabees is difficult and Rigsby understands it to be granting asylum to Jerusalem and its territory as well as, following Goldstein, a release from certain taxes; see Goldstein, *I Maccabees*, 408.

[89] For other appearances of the term in 1 Maccabees, see 3:36, 3:42, and 5:9, all of which suit this understanding.

[90] Goldstein had understood the ὅρια as referring to areas within the sacred precinct, *I Maccabees*, 413. His notion is undermined by the use of the phrase in other parts of the book (particularly 10:31) to denote the borders of the Land, as well as the book's use of *temenos* to refer to the sacred precinct itself (as in 5:43–44).

[91] See §5.3.

founded there by Onias IV. It was probably considered sacred land (ἱερὰ γῆ) in the eyes of Ptolemaic fiscal administrators. Josephus depicts the Ptolemaic royalty as pious benefactors of Judaism, so knowledgeable of Judean customs that they express incredulousness that Onias would choose a place marked by its uncleanliness, given its previous use as a pagan sanctuary and the presence there of sacred animals and a grove. These depictions by Josephus support the notion that the temple enjoyed revenue from land, and they offer yet another instance in his writings of foreign leaders supporting the cult of the God of Israel through the gifting of real estate. Yet Josephus also delegitimizes the Oniad temple and its plot of land by emphasizing the place's pagan past.

Another instance in which a land endowment serves as an exemplar of an inappropriate source of revenue for a temple of God occurs in 1 Macc 10, where Demetrius I offers revenues from Ptolemais and its hinterland to the Jerusalem temple. In that instance the character of Demetrius and the nature of the city are to conjure for the audience of the book images of the foreign, the dangerous, and the inimical to Judea. This is in keeping with a larger theme in 1 Maccabees of cleansing the temple in Jerusalem of its foreign elements. The author of the book contrasts Demetrius's gifts, which were rejected by Jonathan and the Judean people, with those of foreign leaders who are portrayed in a more positive light in the book. Such leaders, however, are never said to offer sacrifice or voluntary contributions for the sake of the temple. This stance may relate to a rejection, from within the Hasmonean house, of support of the temple from foreign sources, a policy that would later be adopted in 66 CE and would lead to acrimonious debate among the Judean leaders of the time. Concern over the issue seems to reach back to at least the late second century BCE.

Chapter 5
Field Consecrations in the Late Second Temple Period

5.1 Introduction

The upheavals in Judea in the late 170s and 160s BCE led to the founding of a new temple to the God of Israel at Leontopolis in Egypt, the rise of the autocratic Hasmonean regime in Judea, and the formation of the breakaway Essene sect of Judaism who quarreled with the Jerusalem priestly establishment on matters of religious practice. In the previous chapter we considered the temple at Leontopolis, with its tract of land, as well as the question of sacred land in Hasmonean Judea. In this chapter we will continue to explore that question by considering a halakhic section of the Damascus Document that deals with field consecrations. The Damascus Document was a foundational text of a breakaway group of Jerusalem priests who would later develop into the Essenes. The document is dated to the middle or later part of the second century BCE.[1] After Lev 27:16 – 24, its section on field consecrations is the earliest extant halakhic text on the topic, and it raises intriguing points of comparison with early rabbinic writings on the sacralization of land for the benefit of the Jerusalem temple. Though the text is fragmentary, it suggests that by this point in Judean history the temple rather than the priesthood was profiting from the revenues generated by this form of

---

[1] On the nature of the sect and its architectural complex at Qumran, see Meyers and Chancey, *Alexander to Constantine*, 92–112. The most complete manuscript of the document (CD) is medieval in date and had been discovered in the Cairo Geniza; other sections were found in the Qumran library, the earliest of which is dated paleographically to the early first century BCE. The second-century BCE date of composition is based on internal historical references and comparative work with other literary and legal products of the sect. For a discussion of the date of the document and its role in the foundation of the sect at Qumran, see Schiffman, *Reclaiming the Dead Sea Scrolls: The History of Judaism, the Background of Christianity, the Lost Library of Qumran* (Philadelphia: Jewish Publication Society, 1994), 90–95. On the CD manuscript, see Baumgarten and Schwartz, "Damascus Document (CD)," in *The Dead Sea Scrolls: Hebrew, Aramaic, and Greek Texts with English Translations. Volume 2: Damascus Document, War Scroll, and Related Documents* (ed. Charlesworth; Tübingen; Louisville: J.C.B. Mohr (Paul Siebeck); Westminster John Knox Press, 1995), 6–7. On the Qumran manuscripts, see Baumgarten et al., "Damascus Document, 4Q266–273 (4QD^{a-h})," in *The Dead Sea Scrolls: Hebrew, Aramaic, and Greek Texts with English Translations. Volume 3: Damascus Document II, Some Works of the Torah and Related Documents* (ed. Charlesworth and Rietz; Tübingen; Louisville: Mohr Siebeck; Westminster John Knox Press, 2006).

consecration. In the discussion below, the text is presented alongside the early rabbinic comparanda, which can help in its interpretation.

The Damascus Document is one of a few late Second Temple period sources on the landed assets of the Jerusalem temple. Philo of Alexandria provides an explicit reference to temple estates in *Spec. Laws* 1.76, while Josephus interprets 1 Macc 10:34—from the story of the enticements offered by Demetrius to Jonathan, discussed in the previous chapter—as referencing plots of land that generated revenue for the temple (*Ant.* 13.56). These three sources anticipate numerous references in early rabbinic teachings to hekdesh ("consecrated property"), a term that usually refers to property devoted to the temple but can also be used to connote the temple as an economic agent.[2] Conceptually the term hekdesh has a close parallel in the rabbinic word *hefqēr*, which denotes ownerless property.[3] Hekdesh does not appear in pre-rabbinic texts, including the Dead Sea Scrolls, though it does have a noteworthy antecedent in a peculiar form in 1 Chr 26:28.[4] Theoretically speaking, dedications to the temple through the mechanism of consecration should have become defunct after 70 CE, but the institution of hekdesh appears to have continued to be observed in a post-temple world, as the rabbis faced the issue of persons consecrating coins or other valuables in their day. The rabbinic solution in such instances was for the hekdesh thing to remain forbidden from use—taboo, hidden away, buried, or thrown into the Dead Sea.[5] Later in Jewish history it would come to refer to a home of the destitute in European shtetls.[6]

---

2 For further discussion, see §1.2.
3 The word hekdesh derives from the transitive-causative (*hipîl*/*hopāl*) of קדש ("to be holy"); and *hefqēr* from the transitive-causative of פקר ("to be free"), translatable "ownerless." On both terms as legal concepts, see Herzog, *The Main Institutions of Jewish Law. Volume I: The Law of Property* (London; New York: Soncino Press, 1965), 287–92, 295–96. For marginal and usually unproductive land of a similar "ownerless" status in ancient Greece, see Papazarkadas, *Sacred and Public Land*, 241.
4 The form in the phrase *wĕkōl hahiqdîš Šĕmû'ēl* ("and all that Samuel consecrated") approximates the substantive form while remaining verbal; on the usage of the definite article in relative constructions, a late feature of biblical Hebrew, see Waltke and O'Connor, *An Introduction to Biblical Hebrew Syntax* (Winona Lake, IN: Eisenbrauns, 1990), 339.
5 The default position of the Mishnah is that shekels are to be set aside for the temple only when it stands, as in *m. Šeqalim* 8:8. According to rabbinic halakhah, their holy status should stand if they are set aside and they must be hidden away or preferably thrown into the Dead Sea; see *b. 'Arakin* 29a. On a possible coin hoard found along the Dead Sea shoreline and understood to be related to the practice, see Eshel and Zissu, "A Note on the Rabbinic Phrase: 'Cast Them into the Dead Sea'," in *Judea and Samaria Research Studies* (ed. Eshel; Ariel: College of Judea and Samaria, 2003) [Hebrew], 91–96. The proposal has been accepted by Magness, *Stone and Dung*, 103–6. Cf. Hirschfeld and Ariel, "A Coin Assemblage from the Reign of Alexander Jan-

5.1 Introduction — 149

Comparative rabbinic texts on hekdesh are discussed throughout this chapter, as well as Chapters 6 and 7. But the objective of the following three chapters is not to speculate on the origins of rabbinic texts, nor to argue for a linear evolution in early Jewish interpretation of Lev 27 or in practical halakhah regarding field consecrations from the Second Temple period into the rabbinic era. The focus is resolutely on the Second Temple source material itself. Though a very large amount of early rabbinic tradition is devoted to matters of priestly law and the temple, scholars recognize the extent to which rabbis reshaped and even invented older traditions in order to establish preeminence in a post-temple world.[7] While it is clear that early rabbinic texts are the outcome of a long oral tradition of rulings on sacred law, and that they include some older priestly halakhic traditions, separating out inherited from invented tradition is a difficult task and it is not the objective of the following discussion.[8]

The objective is simply to enlighten our understanding of the source material on field sacralization from the Second Temple period. This follows in the tradition established by other scholars who have sought out instructive comparisons between Second Temple sources and early rabbinic tradition on other topics.[9] On

---

naeus Found on the Shore of the Dead Sea," *IEJ* 55, no. 1 (2005), 72, n. 7. On the argument that a hoard of edibles and valuables from the "Patrician House" at Meiron in the Galilee were declared hekdesh, stored away, and the edibles burnt in the fourth century CE, see Goodman, "The Purpose of Room F," in *Excavations at Ancient Meiron, Upper Galilee, Israel 1971–72, 1974–75, 1977* (ed. Meyers et al.; Cambridge, Mass: The American Schools of Oriental Research, 1981), 71–72.

6 Meir, "The Labor of Schnorring," *AJS Perspectives* (Fall 2013), 16–17.
7 Cohn, *The Memory of the Temple and the Making of the Rabbis* (Philadelphia: University of Pennsylvania Press, 2013); Neusner, "Map without Territory: Mishnah's System of Sacrifice and Sanctuary," *History of Religions* 19, no. 2 (1979), 103–27; and Fonrobert, "The Political Symbolism of the Eruv," *Jewish Social Studies* 11, no. 3 (2005), 9–35.
8 On the possibility that older priestly halakhic traditions survive within early rabbinic texts, see Cohen, "The Judaean Legal Tradition and the *Halakhah* of the Mishnah," in *The Cambridge Companion to the Talmud and Rabbinic Literature* (ed. Fonrobert and Jaffee; Cambridge; New York: Cambridge University Press, 2007), 131–34; Hezser, *The Social Structure of the Rabbinic Movement in Roman Palestine* (Tübingen: Mohr Siebeck, 1997), 69–74; and Greengus, *Laws in the Bible*, 2, 7. On the oral culture behind early rabbinic writings, including its development in a Second Temple period setting, see Jaffee, *Torah in the Mouth: Writing and Oral Tradition in Palestinian Judaism, 200 BCE–400 CE* (New York: Oxford University Press, 2001), 15–62; Alexander, *Transmitting Mishnah: The Shaping Influence of Oral Tradition* (Cambridge: Cambridge University Press, 2006), 9–23; and idem, "The Orality of Rabbinic Writing," in *Cambridge Companion to the Talmud* (op. cit.), 38–57.
9 Shemesh, *Halakhah in the Making: The Development of Jewish Law from Qumran to the Rabbis* (Berkeley: University of California Press, 2009); Schiffman, "The Dead Sea Scrolls and Rabbinic Halakhah," in *The Dead Sea Scrolls as Background to Postbiblical Judaism and Early Christianity:*

the topic of field sacralization, the rabbinic texts offer insight into questions of how consecrated fields were managed, a topic for this chapter; how priests monetized in-kind herem gifts, a topic for the next chapter; and how organic outgrowths and derivatives of consecrated things on the farm—such as milk from a sacred cow—were to be treated, a topic for Chapter 7.

5.2 Fields in the Freewill-Offering Laws of the Damascus Document

Consecrated fields are legislated upon in the section of the Damascus Document called "The Law of Freewill Gifts," parts of which are preserved in three fragmentary manuscripts (CD 16:14–17; 4Q266, 8ii:1–3; 4Q271, 4ii:15–16). The section immediately follows laws on oaths (CD 16:6b–12) and precedes laws on the declaration of a person as herem (CD 9:1–8). It resembles other sections of laws that were grouped thematically and given a formulaic heading.[10] The section's first few laws, which are the relatively well preserved of the section and the ones relevant to field consecrations, read as follows:[11]

Papers from an International Conference at St. Andrews in 2001 (ed. Davila; Leiden; Boston: Brill, 2003), 27–33; Fraade, "Shifting from Priestly to Non-Priestly Legal Authority: A Comparison of the Damascus Document and the Midrash Sifra," *DSD* 6 (1999), 109–25; idem, "A New View on Comparative Midrash: From the Dead Sea Scrolls to Midrash of the Sages," in *Higayon L'Yona: New Aspects in the Study of Midrash, Aggadah and Piyut in Honor of Professor Yona Fraenkel* (ed. Levinson et al.; Jerusalem: Hebrew University Magnes Press, 2006) [Hebrew], 261–84; and Sanders, *Judaism, 63 BCE–66 CE*, passim, esp. 465–72.

10 Other examples include the laws "Concerning purification in water" (CD 10:10) and "Concerning the Sabbath" (CD 10:14). On the notion that Folio 9 follows Folio 16 in CD, see Hempel, *The Laws of the Damascus Document: Sources, Tradition, and Redaction* (Leiden; Boston: Brill, 1998), 30–32, n. 24; this order is presented by Baumgarten and Schwartz, "Damascus Document," 40–43. But see Qimron, "The Text of CDC," in *The Damascus Document Reconsidered* (ed. Broshi; Jerusalem: Israel Exploration Society, 1992), 41–43, where Folio 16 is followed by Folio 19. Disagreements emerge because the bottom of Folio 16 is not preserved in CD or in the Qumran fragments.

11 The text brought here is based primarily on CD 16:14–17, whose line breaks it follows, after Baumgarten and Schwartz, "Damascus Document," 40; but it also utilizes 4Q266, particularly for line 6 above, after Baumgarten et al., "Damascus Document," 50; and 4Q271, particularly for lines 4–5 above, after ibid., 166. See also Qimron, "The Text of CDC," 40–41. The translation is mine in consultation with the above editions and Murphy, *Wealth in the Dead Sea Scrolls and in the Qumran Community* (Leiden; Boston: Brill, 2002), 61. Changes to the document in the period between the Qumran manuscripts and the medieval CD do not appear to have affected this section; on the redaction, see Hempel, *Laws*, 21–22.

(1) על משפט הנדבות אל ידור איש למזבח מאום אנוס וגם
(2) [הכ]הנים אל יקחו מאת ישראל [ ] אל[ ] יקדש איש את מאכל
(3) פ[יהו לא]ל כי הוא אשר אמר איש את רעיהו יצ[ו]דו חרם ואל
(4) יקדש איש מכל[ ]   [ואם מש]דה[ ] אחזתו
(5) יקדש לאל גם המשפט[ ] הזה   ו[נענש
(6) הנודר חמישית כסף ערכו

(1) Concerning the law of freewill offerings: Let no man vow to the altar anything forcibly seized, nor shall (2) [the pr]iests take it from an Israelite. [Let no] man consecrate the food of (3) [his] wor[ker][12] for this is what he said, "Each one t[ra]ps his neighbor (with) herem" [Mic 7:2]. And (4) a man shall not consecrate any [...] And if of the fie[ld of] his holding (5) he shall consecrate to God, also this law [...] [And] the one who vows (6) shall be punished by a fifth of the money of his valuation...

The full legal apparatus here is unknowable given the frequent lacunae, yet the following regulations can be surmised: first, that nothing stolen or unlawfully seized should be dedicated to the altar of God, here perhaps used as a metonymy for incorporated sacred wealth; second, that the food apparently of one's worker should also not be dedicated; and third, that anyone who violates the law in this manner should be fined at a rate of an additional fifth of the value of the principle of the property in question.[13] This last component is more speculative than the first two, as will be discussed below. The primary message of the pericope is about prohibiting consecration as a means of dispossession. Individuals who otherwise could have benefited in some way from a property might feel their hands were tied if it were now set apart for sacred purposes. Any effort to get hold of it might be perceived as a slight against God or even worse—an act of sacrilege.

Commentators on the text usually point to Matt 15:5 and Mark 7:11 for comparison, where Jesus criticizes the Pharisees for allowing one to consecrate their property to God in order to absolve themself of providing support to their parents.[14] The renunciation of parental support is but one way in which consecration could have been used as a form of dispossession. Others include preventing

---

12 On this reading, see discussion in §5.2.2.
13 For a preliminary discussion of the text, see Gordon, "Debt Fraud," 258–60.
14 Rabin, *The Zadokite Documents. I. The Admonition. II. The Laws. Edited with a Translation and Notes* (Oxford: Clarendon Press, 1958), 76–77; Ginzberg, *An Unknown Jewish Sect* (New York: Jewish Theological Seminary of America, 1976), 101; Baumgarten, *Qumran Cave 4. The Damascus Document (4Q266–273)* (Oxford: Clarendon Press, 1996), 179–80; Baumgarten and Schwartz, "Damascus Document," 41; Davies, *The Damascus Covenant: An Interpretation of the "Damascus Document"* (Sheffield: JSOT Press, 1983), 129; Sanders, *Judaism, 63 BCE–66 CE*, 185; Murphy, *Wealth in the Dead Sea Scrolls*, 65.

Figure 10. A halakhic section of the Damascus Document on freewill offerings and field consecrations. 4Q271, Col. 4ii (= CD 16). Courtesy of The Leon Levy Dead Sea Scrolls Digital Library; Israel Antiquities Authority. Photo: Shai Halevi.

a creditor from seizing property put up as security on a loan, or an ex-wife from claiming property promised her in a marriage contract. The latter scenarios emerge from the early rabbinic sources, which are similarly vexed by the use of consecration as a means of blocking access to property, as we shall see below.

Moreover, this section of the Damascus Document seems to deal with the consecration of agricultural plots, or the products growing on them, as freewill offerings to the temple. The reference to Lev 27 comes in line 4, with the phraseology "field of his holding" (as in Lev 27:16). This suggests that the authors of the document were interpreting Lev 27 as regulating freewill offerings rather than a secured lending operation, which was argued in Chapter 2 as its original objective. The following discussion will consider what forcibly seized assets might refer to in the Damascus Document, what kinds of scenarios might have given rise to this unseemly form of sacralization, and how the dedicant may have been penalized for trying to dispossess someone in this way.

5.2.1 Consecration of Forcibly Seized Assets

The opening lines of the section prohibit one from vowing to the altar anything stolen or otherwise wrongfully acquired. One can assume that this was attempted to avoid penalty or at least render the goods unrecoverable.[15] Consecration effectively dared the rightful owner to risk liability for sacrilege. In order to prevent such a situation, the authors of the Damascus Document prohibit such vows to be taken; they also forbid priests from taking anything seized in this way. Scenarios of the sort could have resulted in litigation involving jurists who were expert on Judean sacred law.

Interestingly, an ossuary inscription in Aramaic from Jerusalem, of the first century BCE or CE, attests to the use of altar dedication as a threat to prevent wrongful seizure. The inscription reads: "Whatever benefit a man may derive from this ossuary is a *qorban* [sacrificial offering] to God from him who is in it" (כל די אנש מתהנה בחלתה דה קרבן אלה מן דבגוה). This formula is meant to prevent not only the theft of the ossuary itself but also the disruption of the bones contained therein. According to Moshe Benovitz, the formula has the consecrated status of the ossuary taking effect only once theft is attempted. In that case, the thief would find himself guilty of sacrilege with an object now technically owned by God, its consecration having been realized by his own act of theft.[16]

The slightly different scenario about which the Damascus Document legislates, namely the vowing to the altar of something wrongfully seized, could apply to property in land. The noun מאום, "nothing, anything," is general enough to refer to both real and movable property.[17] The passive participle אנוס, "forcibly seized," can also denote the seizure of land and should not be taken as necessarily synonymous with outright stealing or robbery, for which the Damascus

---

15 On this reading, see Sanders, *Judaism, 63 BCE–66 CE*, 184, 186. For a similar concern in Philo, see *Spec. Laws* 1.204.
16 *Kol Nidre*, 27–29. See also Cotton et al., eds., *Corpus Inscriptionum Iudaeae/Palaestinae. Volume I: Jerusalem, Part 1: 1–704* (Berlin: De Gruyter, 2010), no. 287, 307–9. The ossuary was found in the area of Jebel Khallet et-Turi in the Kidron Valley.
17 See, e.g., Deut 24:10, where pledges on any kind of loan (משאת מאומה) are referred to.

Document uses the terms גנב (9:11) and גזל (6:16).[18] On the contrary, the wrongful seizure implied here appears to be of a more wide-ranging sort, as shown by the use of the word אנס elsewhere in the Damascus Document—4Q266 5i:2, 8ii:4; 4Q270 4:3, 6iii:14. Of these, one can note the law of the false oath from the continuation of the freewill offering section. In that law the אונס would appear to refer to one committing the full gamut of crimes listed in Lev 5, on which the law of the false oath is based; among those crimes are the wrongful seizure of a deposit (פקדון) and the wrongful seizure of a pledge or security of some sort (תשומת יד; Lev 5:21).[19]

Early rabbinic halakhah can shed light on the practices underlying this section of the Damascus Document. The early rabbis simply require consecrated land that is found to be serving as a lien on a loan or another contract—such as a marriage contract—to be forcibly put up for public auction once it is dedicated to God. The Damascus Document, on the other hand, would prohibit its consecration in the first place. The rabbinic concern is that the owner could prevent the creditor or wife from laying claim to the hypothecated field by conferring upon it sacred status. The issue is given considerable attention in tractate *'Arakin*, which lays out the details of the ensuing auction. The fullest tradition on the matter is in *t. 'Arakin* 4:1, with parallels in the Mishnah and the Babylonian Talmud:[20]

The proclamation process [for the sale of property] of orphans is 30 days, and the proclamation process of consecrated property is 60 days. The announcement is made in the morning and in the evening—when the workers are brought in and when the workers are brought out. They state its features, its worth, and how much it demands for redemption in order to pay a woman her marriage contract and a creditor his debt.	שום היתומים שלשים יום ושום הקדש ששים יום ומכריזין בבקר ובערב—בהכנסת פועלין ובהוצאת פועלין. אומרין כמה סימניה, כמה היתה יפה, וכמה היא רוצה לפדות על מנת ליתן לאשה כתובתה ולבעל חוב את חובו.

---

18 See, e.g., *m. Kil'ayim* 7:6, where the אנס has seized a field.
19 These crimes call for full restitution plus the addition of the fifth (Lev 5:24), the catchword linking this topic to ours regarding consecrations; for further discussion on this topic, see §5.2.3.
20 See *m. 'Arakin* 6:1 and a *baraita* in *b. 'Arakin* 21b. The association of the pre-auction proclamation process with the settlement of debts is never stated explicitly in the Mishnah but emerges from the more expansive Toseftan version given here, where the nature of the advertisement includes a mention of the amount of debt on which the land serves as a lien.

Just as any person has precedence [of a claim to property] over another, and this precedence is forever [binding]—so too any person can have precedence [of a claim to property] over the Most High, and this precedence is forever [binding].	כשם שההדיוט קדם את הדיוט, הרי זו קדימה לעולם—כך הדיוט קדם את הגבוה, הרי זו קדימה לעולם.

The orphan's property, like consecrated property, was serving as a lien on an outstanding debt from before the death of the last surviving parent, requiring the liquidation of the parental estate.[21] The proclamation process (שום) would seem to have included not just the public advertisement of the land but also an appraisal of its value by a committee, as indicated by *t. Ketubot* 11:2 and *b. Baba Batra* 107a. According to *m. Sanhedrin* 1:3, the appraisal of consecrated property required a committee of three for movables and ten for real estate.[22] The proclamation process has a comparandum in the Roman custom of *proscriptio*—the posting of written notices giving details on the sale; a herald could also have been used.[23]

According to the rabbinic teaching, the proclamation would occur in the morning and evening, presumably so that field workers could investigate the property on behalf of their employers and report back to them.[24] Its relatively long duration would help ensure that the property is sufficiently marketed, in hopes that heightened interest will result in more and higher bids during the auction. In the case of consecrated property, the creditor and the temple stand to benefit. The rabbis were also concerned that the creditor not lay claim to the property prior to its redemption (*m. 'Arakin* 6:2); otherwise they could become liable for misappropriation.

The didactic saying appended to *t. 'Arakin* 4:1 stresses the importance of a contractually binding claim to the land, even if it is to the detriment of God's holdings. The rabbis are thus legislating against any claims of the temple's ex-

---

[21] Had the father not left the child with debt, one might reconstruct a system resembling the *misthosis oikou* in classical Greece, whereby the property of orphans could be rented out until the child reached adulthood, freeing up land for the rental market; see Burford, *Land and Labor*, 179, 260, n. 32.

[22] Sharfman, "Valuation in Jewish Law," 178–79. Sharfman understands the principle of appraisal by committee as a measure meant to add expertise to the equation and prevent cases of expensive appeals and further litigation; the ten-person panel would have been necessary in the more complicated cases of land appraisal.

[23] Learmount, *A History of the Auction* (London: Barnard & Learmount, 1985), 7.

[24] Herzka, "Tractate Arachin Chapter 6," in *The Schottenstein Edition. Talmud Bavli. The Artscroll Series. Tractate Arakhin* (ed. Schorr and Malinowitz; New York: Menorah Publications, Ltd, 2004), n. 3 on 21b.

ceptionality in these affairs, ruling out the view that the temple should take precedence over a previous claim. Yet the rabbinic constraints on the temple exist alongside efforts to ensure its proper compensation. It is for this reason apparently that the longer proclamation process is used for consecrated property as compared to that of the orphan. This question was a matter of dispute among the early rabbis.[25]

Land auctions were particularly popular among the Romans, but the practice is attested in the ancient world from as early as the Babylonian empire.[26] In classical Greece leases involving sacred land and deme and phratry holdings were regularly auctioned off to the highest bidder; the process may have relied on previously established overbids, which can explain the appearance of "rounded" numbers in the sources, such as an inscription regulating leases on one of the goddess Athena's territories called the Nea.[27] In the Greek polis, the public auction of land often concerned instances of estates confiscated to repay public debt or in punishment of political crimes, with the purchase of such lands seen as a civic duty. The auctioning of public property including deme-owned land or temple holdings was the main responsibility of a board of public officials called the *poletai*.[28]

Rounded overbids are also apparent in the rabbinic teachings that outline how the public auction of consecrated real estate was to be carried out (*m. 'Arakin* 8:2–3). Two hypothetical auctions are considered: one (8:2) in which the landowner does not participate, and one (8:3) where he does. In both the auction seems fashioned in the rabbinic imagination to serve as a kind of communal fundraiser for the temple, with the overbids reaching a price that far exceeds the market value of the land in question. Furthermore, each participant who retracts their bid must pay the difference between their overbid and the next highest bid. The result is a community of individuals participating in the giving of an

---

[25] A *baraita* in *b. 'Arakin* 22a preserves a dispute regarding the lengths of the proclamation process for the respective types of property, with R. Meir reflecting the Mishnah's view, R. Judah increasing each period by 30 days, and the sages calling for a 60-day proclamation process in both cases.

[26] On the earliest attestations of auctions in Babylonia (involving slaves not land), see Learmount, *A History of the Auction*, 6–11; on Roman public auctions, see Gargola, *Lands, Laws, & Gods: Magistrates & Ceremony in the Regulation of Public Lands in Republican Rome* (Chapel Hill; London: The University of North Carolina Press, 1995), 116–19.

[27] Sosin, "Two Attic Endowments," *Zeitschrift für Papyrologie und Epigraphik* 138 (2002), 125, n. 17. See also Papazarkadas, *Sacred and Public Land*, 55–56.

[28] Burford, *Land and Labor*, 49–50; Langdon, "Public Auctions in Ancient Athens," in *Ritual, Finance, Politics: Athenian Democratic Accounts Presented to David Lewis* (ed. Osborne and Hornblower; Oxford: Clarendon Press, 1994), 253–65.

exorbitant sum of money to the temple under the pretense of a land auction. The land functions as little more than an apparatus measuring the size of multiple donations in cash. Of course, the rabbinic teachings on the auction of consecrated property with a lien would be moot if the consecration had been forbidden in the first place, which is precisely the strict measure that the Damascus Document adopts.

5.2.2 Consecration of Assets Claimable by Household Dependents

The use of consecration as a means of blocking access to property carries through to the next law in the Damascus Document (lines 2–3, above). The law prohibits one from consecrating to God the food of [...]פ, which is reconstructed פיהו ("his mouth") or, following Louis Ginzberg, פעלו ("his worker").[29] According to the first option, the individual may have sought to deny a member of his family or a guest in his household from laying hands on something he owns. He thus declares it sacred to God. According to the second option, he does this to prevent one of his workers from touching it.[30] In either case, the use in the document of the prooftext from Mic 7:2, "one traps his neighbor with herem"—a wordplay on a phonetically similar biblical word for net[31]— shows that consecration is being used as a form of entrapment or a snare. This is because one who enjoyed something that was devoted to God might unwittingly commit sacrilege, the repercussions for which could have been severe.[32] Dedication would then become, in the words of Catherine Murphy, "a sort of prophylactic against sharing."[33] The food in question could have derived from anywhere on the farm: pantries, storerooms, fruit trees, or fields. The potential for sacrilege thus links this case with the previous one. There the sacred status of the asset kept its rightful claimant from gaining access to it; here a dependent

---

[29] Baumgarten and Schwartz, "Damascus Document," 40; Ginzberg, *An Unknown Jewish Sect*, 100–1.
[30] Employers would customarily allow those working for them to partake of some of the food of the field and farm; see *m. Baba Meṣʿia* 7:2–8.
[31] That verse in its plain meaning reads: "All lie in wait to commit crimes; one traps the other in his net." For a similar use of this word, see Ezek 32:3 and Hab 1:15–17.
[32] On the crime of sacrilege, its repercussions, and rabbinic protections working to prevent it, see §7.3.
[33] Murphy, *Wealth in the Dead Sea Scrolls*, 65, n. 91.

or another on the farm appears to be the one against whom the obstruction has been placed.

Early rabbinic teachings bear directly on this issue of how the consecration of real estate could result in instances of unwitting acts of sacrilege on the farm. A tradition in the name of R. Simeon in *m. Meʿilah* 3:6 notes that laborers working on consecrated property are forbidden to eat even the least valuable of produce on that property; cows are even muzzled lest they partake of it. The Toseftan parallel (*t. Meʿilah* 1:21) appears to note that a special donation would be made to provide the necessary food to make sure the sacred produce goes untouched (ואחרים מתנדבין להן).[34] In the Babylonian Talmud (*b. Meʿilah* 13a), a teaching by a certain R. Ahadboi bar Ami uses Deut 25:4 ("You shall not muzzle an ox while it is threshing") creatively as a prooftext for this Mishnaic teaching. Such teachings reflect rabbinic concerns over how to prevent acts of sacrilege on a farm where property has been declared sacred to God.

But the rabbinic teachings are more lenient than the Damascus Document is on the topic, for that document appears to forbid consecration altogether if one's dependent or employee regularly enjoys food from the farm's produce. In a similarly disapproving view, Matt 15:3–6 and Mark 7:9–13 have Jesus condemning the Pharisees and scribes for allowing persons to renounce all support of their parents by declaring their property a "sacrifice" or gift to God, in language recalling the ossuary described above. It appears that this maneuver was used in the context of petty family disputes. To Jesus, this is in flagrant opposition to the biblical commandment to honor one's parents.

5.2.3 Forced Redemption of Consecrated Assets

After presenting these two cases in which consecration is forbidden because of its use as an impediment, the extant manuscripts of the Damascus Document leave us only fragments. Though the poor state of preservation does not allow for a confident reconstruction of the text, it would seem that the law relating to the consecrated field in lines 4–5 prohibits the consecration of a field in a scenario resembling that of the antecedent laws, i.e., as a response to rightful claims to the property. This is supported by the appearance of the phrase

---

[34] On this reading of the parallel, see Neusner, *A History of the Mishnaic Law of Holy Things. Part Five: Keritot, Meilah, Tamid, Middot, Qinnim. Translation and Explanation* (Leiden: Brill, 1980), 115. And for more on the text and a discussion of its context, see §7.3.

"also this law" (גם המשפט הזה)—an explicit attempt at connecting the law to something else in the pericope, probably the legal ground already covered.

There is also a mention in lines 5–6 of a punishment for the vow-taker in the amount of one-fifth of the valuation of the property in question. This is an explicit reference to Lev 27. As argued in Chapter 2, the fifth was in its original conception an interest payment on loans from God, as well as the difference between the holy shekel standard and the common shekel standard. This meant that properties valued in the holy standard could be redeemed in the common standard and the same "number" of shekels would change hands. In the Damascus Document, however, from roughly half a millennium later, the reasons for the biblical fifth are significantly different. Since the fifth appears in Lev 5:24 as part of a restitution payment for various offenses involving misappropriated property, including sacrilege, it can be surmised that the authors of the document assumed that in Lev 27 too it was mentioned as a penalty.[35] Therefore, they concluded that in instances of wrongful or otherwise fraudulent consecration, the one who vowed their property over to sacred purposes is to be punished by the addition of the fifth. Presumably, the lacuna in line 5 included some ordinance calling for the forced redemption of the consecrated asset, the fifth adding to the redemption cost as a penalty. Incidentally, Philo understands the fifth as a penalty too, but for different reasons. He sees it as legislated by God for the rashness of making a vow for which one would come to regret, and for one's lustfulness of possession in wishing the property back (*Spec. Laws* 2.37).[36]

A teaching in the Tosefta describing the public auction of a consecrated field (*t. ʿArakin* 4:22) has the original owner of the field compelled to open the bidding, as if their participation in the auction is obligatory. They are also forced to add the fifth supplement to the overbid ("If one said, 'Lo it is mine for twenty-one,' they force the owners to give twenty-six...") in keeping with the biblical injunction that redemption by the owner should come with the supplement.[37] There is no explicit mention in the teaching that the fifth functions as a punishment, but the language of compulsion (i.e., כופין את הבעלים) would suggest as much. The teaching ends with a mention of a dispute between the houses of Hillel and Shammai on the matter: the former holds that the fifth should remain fixed at the owners' opening bid, the latter that it should increase proportionally with the overbid. As noted, the Mishnah (*m. ʿArakin* 6:1–2) includes a similar

---

35 For further discussion on Lev 5:24, see §5.2.2.
36 For more on the exegetical tradition viewing the "fifth" in Lev 27 as a penalty, see §2.2.2.
37 Rabbinic tradition would have the supplement at 25% rather than 20% presumably on the logic that the "fifth" refers to one of five parts *including* the supplement. The understanding is reflected in the calculations of *m. ʿArakin* 8:3; see also *b. Baba Meṣʿia* 53b–54a.

auction process in its examination of the consecrated field of Lev 27, but offers no suggestion that the owner was compelled to participate, fashioning the event more as a fundraising auction for the temple than as a means for settling a debt.[38] The editors of the Tosefta may have introduced the element of legal coercion into the Mishnaic teaching or merely brought a parallel teaching that retained it. In either case the Tosefta demonstrates that redemption with the added fifth is attested in rabbinic memory too as punitive in nature, as it appears to have been understood by the authors of the Damascus Document.

The laws in the Damascus Document regarding freewill offerings work towards inhibiting them. This is a key difference between its legislation and the halakhic traditions of the early rabbis, who did not prohibit these consecrations at the outset. The more stringent approach of the Damascus Document may be related to its authors' negative disposition to the temple and its wealth. Their view that the business transactions involving the temple had been corrupted is reflected in a statement in the opening, non-legal section of the document. There the new covenant community is told, among other things: "to separate from the sons of the pit (בני השחת) and to refrain from the wicked wealth (הון הרשע) that is impure due to oath, herem dedication, and the temple wealth (הון המקדש), for they steal from the poor of his people, preying upon the widows and murdering orphans" (CD 6:15–17).[39] The "wicked wealth that is impure" is thought to have become so by the moral failings of the temple institution, among which the authors of the document would presumably include the abuse of consecrations as a means of blocking rightful claimants to a property or of depriving needy dependents.

5.3 The Proceeds from Agricultural Consecrations

An important implication of these texts in the Damascus Document is that by the time of its composition in the second century BCE the temple treasuries were receiving proceeds of field consecrations. This supposition is rooted foremost in the fact that the document places its discussion of field consecrations in a section on freewill offerings, rather than on the priests' perquisites from agricultural

---

38 See §5.2.1.
39 A similar line in the Rule of the Community (4Q258 1:12) reads, "All those who scorn his word shall be obliterated from the earth…oaths, herem declarations, and vows in their mouths…" See also the complaint in *Testament of Moses* 5:5–6. On the view that this section of the Damascus Document deals with the moral failings of the temple cult, see Regev, *Sectarianism in Qumran*, 111–12, 340; and Murphy, *Wealth in the Dead Sea Scrolls*, 77–78.

produce, which appear elsewhere (4Q266, 6iii, iv; 4Q270, 2ii:6–10; 4Q271, 2:1–6).⁴⁰ The term for freewill offerings (נדבות) is alone suggestive of altar-bound gifts.⁴¹ It is important to note that the authors of the Damascus Document appear to have viewed the altar as existing in Jerusalem rather than in the imagined alternative community of the sect. It is true that in the Rule of the Community the terms הנדבים and המתנדבים ("those who give freewill offerings") are applied in a technical sense to refer simply to adherents of the sect; and generally speaking the Rule of the Community presents offerings that once would have been designated for the altar as wealth now meant to sustain the sect itself, in keeping with the sect's self-perception as an alternative temple community.⁴² But the perspective of the Damascus Document is different from the Rule of the Community and from other sectarian writings from a later period in the development of the sect. As Joseph Baumgarten and Daniel Schwartz write, "While other Qumran texts usually either ignore the Temple cult (e. g. 1QH), spiritualize it (e. g. 1QS), or criticize the way it is currently maintained (1QpHab 12.8–9), CD (11:19–12:2, 16:13–20) [i. e., the Damascus Document] suggests that the temple is pure, shows a concern to maintain its purity, and reflects participation in its cult."⁴³ Furthermore, even as the Essene sect developed later in history, members of the sect sent money to the temple.⁴⁴

---

40 That section mentions the fourth-year produce, the animal tithe, ransom for the firstborn of the unclean animal and of the flocks, and the valuations-of-persons payments; for a discussion on these laws, see Hempel, *Laws*, 50–58.

41 Later in line 1 above the altar is explicitly mentioned as the destination for them. See also Ezra 1:4, "the freewill gifts of the house of God"; 1QS 9:5, "the freewill grain offering." For a discussion of the term as one of several kinds of freewill offerings given at the temple, see Levine, *In the Presence of the Lord: A Study of Cult and Some Cultic Terms in Ancient Israel* (Leiden: Brill, 1974), 42–44. The term does not appear anywhere else in the Damascus Document and its sole use in the Rule of the Community (1QS, 9:5) is in a metaphorical sense: "...and the perfect of the Way (are as) a pleasing freewill offering." Rabbinic tradition would include a special donative offerings (נדבה) chest in the temple treasury, which was drawn upon to pay for various sacrifices (*m. Šeqalim* 6:5–6, 7:1).

42 Murphy, *Wealth in the Dead Sea Scrolls*, 63, 155–61; Wardle, *The Jerusalem Temple*, 139–62.

43 "Damascus Document," 7. Also setting the Damascus Document apart from the Qumran library is the fact that it reflects a community of families living in villages with individuals earning private income—from which persons were required to contribute two days' worth of their wages to the communal funds per month (CD 14:12–13); see Murphy, *Wealth in the Dead Sea Scrolls*, 63. It is important to keep in mind that the sectarian complex at Qumran was only constructed in the early first century BCE, over a generation or two after the composition of the Damascus Document; see Magness, *The Archaeology of Qumran and the Dead Sea Scrolls* (Grand Rapids, MI; Cambridge, U.K.: William B. Eerdmans, 2002), 66, 90–100; and Meyers and Chancey, *Alexander to Constantine*, 92.

There is further support for the notion that the authors of the Damascus Document saw field consecrations as benefitting the temple in Jerusalem rather than individual priests. Catherine Murphy has proposed that the temple officials condemned in the document were called the "sons of the pit" because those in charge of collecting much of the produce in kind or selling items for sacrifice at the temple would likely have worked out of underground storage spaces accessed from the sacred esplanade.[45] She points to the use of the Aramaic term מנקרה ("pit") in fourth-century BCE ostraca from Idumea as referring to storage places for various commodities.[46] Therefore, since in CD 6:15–17 the sons of the pit are seen as dealing with wealth that was incorporated, among which are numbered the oath and the herem dedication, it is logical to presume that the property dedicated by oath in the section on freewill offerings—field consecrations included—was understood by the authors of this document as having been bound for the temple.

In addition to the laws from the Damascus Document, there are other reasons to believe that by the late Second Temple period the proceeds of agricultural consecrations were being diverted to the incorporated assets of the temple in Jerusalem. Philo of Alexandria makes note of the temple's revenues from land in a passing remark (*Spec. Laws* 1.76) in a compendium of legal material organized around the Decalogue. It reads:

---

[44] Josephus notes that the Essenes send votive offerings (ἀναθήματα) to the temple (*Ant.* 18:19); a hoard of 561 Tyrian tetradrachms found at Qumran could reflect collection of the tax. On the latter, see Magness, *Stone and Dung*, 102–3. On the question of the Essenes' participation in the cult of sacrifice at the temple in Jerusalem, see Hempel, *Laws*, 38; Wardle, *The Jerusalem Temple*, 145–50; Heger, *Cult as the Catalyst for Division: Cult Disputes as the Motive for Schism in the Pre-70 Pluralistic Environment* (Leiden; Boston: Brill, 2007), 349–54; and Angel, *Otherworldly and Eschatological Priesthood*, 238, n. 128.

[45] Murphy, *Wealth in the Dead Sea Scrolls*, 76–77. The buying and selling of goods from these individuals is prohibited again in CD 13:14 if we read בני השחת there as well rather than בני השחר ("sons of dawn"); for an argument for the former reading and a presentation of the textual issues at hand, see Stroup, "A Reexamination of the Sons of the Pit in CD 13:14," *DSD* 18, no. 1 (2011), 45–53.

[46] Murphy, *Wealth in the Dead Sea Scrolls*, 373; Eph'al and Naveh, *Aramaic Ostraca of the Fourth Century BC from Idumaea* (Jerusalem: Magnes Press; Israel Exploration Society, 1996), 72–73.

The temple has for its revenues not only plots of land, but also other possessions of much greater extent and importance, which will never be destroyed or diminished; for as long as the race of mankind shall last—and it shall last for eternity—the revenues likewise of the temple will always be preserved, being coeval in their duration with the universal world.	Προςόδους δ'ἔχει τὸ ἱερὸν οὐ μόνον ἀποτομὰς γῆς ἀλλὰ καὶ πολὺ μείζους ἑτέρας, αἳ μηδενὶ χρόνῳ φθαρήσονται· ἐφ'ὅσον γὰρ τὸ ἀνθρώπων γένος διαμενεῖ—διαμενεῖ δ'εἰς ἀεί— καὶ αἱ πρόσοδοι τοῦ ἱεροῦ φυλαχθήσονται συνδιαιωνίζουσαι παντὶ τῷ κόσμῳ.

Philo offers no details on the nature of these "plots of land" (*apotomai gēs*) of the temple: where they were located, how they functioned, and who managed them. He notes that the value of the land is no comparison to that of the temple's "other possessions," which appear to refer to its holdings in coin. That is because immediately after this comment, Philo summarizes the law of Exod 30:13–16— that every adult male over the age of twenty should bring the shekel tax to Jerusalem. He would later describe banking places for the collection of the tax (1.77–78), a comment that is corroborated in early rabbinic tradition, which speaks of special collection vessels throughout the provinces for gathering the coins (*m. Šeqalim* 2:1). However, Philo's dependency on proto-rabbinic halakhic tradition in *Spec. Laws* has been called into question on other matters, and one can hardly assume that Philo was drawing on such material in making these comments.[47]

He then transitions into various sources of income for the priests, covering topics such as the eligibility for the priests' portions (1.117) and the special honor due to priests (1.131). But he would never again mention the temple land to which he refers in 1.76. Philo may have chosen to emphasize this mark of honor of the Jerusalem temple since his audience in Alexandria would have been familiar with temple land in Egypt. The Oniad temple at Leontopolis, for example, held a fine tract, as discussed above; and others in Egypt continued to hold land in the Early Roman period as well.[48]

---

[47] Hecht, "Preliminary Issues in the Analysis of Philo's *De Specialibus Legibus*," *Studia Philonica* 5 (1978), 1–55, esp. 41–42. Hecht examines also the case-study of the red heifer in Philo's *Spec. Laws*, which he determines to be free of significant parallels with rabbinic materials on the subject.

[48] On the sacred land at the temple of Leontopolis, see §4.2. On the continued importance of Egyptian sanctuary landholdings in the Early Roman period, see Monson, *From the Ptolemies to the Romans*, 218–27. Monson challenges earlier reconstructions of widespread desacralization from the Augustan period onward. On the taxation of sanctuary landholdings, see Capponi, *Augustan Egypt: The Creation of a Roman Province* (New York: Routledge, 2005), 112.

Philo's comment has an analogue in Josephus's version of the events told in 1 Macc 10, where Demetrius I attempts to entice Jonathan and the Judeans with extravagant offers for the temple. One such offer is the liberation of all who take refuge in the temple in Jerusalem or within its territories (1 Macc 10:43), which is told in Josephus's version as follows (*Ant.* 13.56):[49]

And all those taking refuge in the temple in Jerusalem or in any place belonging to it, whether because they owe money to the king or for any other reason, shall be set free, and their possessions shall be left untouched.	Καὶ ὅσοι δ'ἂν φύγωσιν εἰς τὸ ἱερὸν τὸ ἐν Ἱεροσολύμοις καὶ εἰς τὰ ἀπ'αὐτοῦ χρηματίζοντα, ἢ βασιλικὰ ὀφείλοντες χρήματα ἢ δι'ἄλλην αἰτίαν, ἀπολελύσθωσαν οὗτοι καὶ τὰ ὑπάρχοντα αὐτοῖς σῶα ἔστω.

The key difference is that Josephus has Demetrius referring to asylum-seekers in places "belonging" to the temple (τὰ ἀπ'αὐτοῦ χρηματίζοντα), while 1 Maccabees has them in places within the temple's territories (ἐν πᾶσιν τοῖς ὁρίοις αὐτοῦ). In the context of 1 Maccabees, the temple's territories are best understood as referring to the entire Judean ethnic territory under the auspices of the Hasmoneans, as discussed in the above chapter.[50] But Josephus seems to be interpreting that phrase to mean plots of land that are linked financially to the temple or are providing revenue for it. While the word χρηματίζω could also mean being nominally associated with something,[51] here the proprietary relationship seems clear by Josephus's use of the derivative form χρήματα ("money") in the same sentence.

Furthermore, in Josephus's version of 1 Macc 10:31, where Demetrius offers a remission of the tithes and taxes for Jerusalem and its territories (ὅρια), Josephus translates ὅρια with the closely related ὅροι ("borders," *Ant.* 13.51)—a term referring to the stone markers commonly erected along administrative borders. The use of χρηματίζω in his adaptation of 10:43, in other words, seems quite intentional. Josephus understands Demetrius to be offering freedom to those seeking asylum in places funding the Jerusalem temple. These places must have been meaningful to him and reflective of some institution with which he was familiar, perhaps consecrated fields or orchards in the Judean hinterland. It bears mentioning also that Josephus refashions the Chronicler's description of the tribal apportionment of the house of Levi by making special note of the fact that the

---

49 Text and translation (slightly adapted) after Loeb, Josephus IX (Ralph Marcus, transl.). Josephus's version seems entirely dependent on 1 Macc 10. See Sievers, *Synopsis of the Greek Sources for the Hasmonean Period: 1–2 Maccabees and Josephus, War 1 and Antiquities 12–14* (Roma: Pontificio Istituto Biblico, 2001), 161–64.
50 See §4.5.
51 Rengstorf, *Concordance to Josephus*, 4:369. For the former meaning, see, e.g., *Ant.* 16.310; for the latter, see, e.g., *Ant.* 13.318.

keepers of the treasury of God and of royal offerings are descendants of Moses rather than of Levi (*Ant.* 7.367). This could reflect his perception that temple finances had by his day become fully separate from the interests of individual priestly clans.

How were consecrated plots managed and how were their revenues collected by the temple authorities? The source material does not allow for definitive answers to these questions, but the model of a simple land lease, commonly adopted by ancient temples,[52] may point us in the right direction. If my reading of the fraudulent practices underlying the legislation in the Damascus Document is correct, the implication would be that field consecration resulted in forfeiture of rights of alienation, and of much if not all of the proceeds of the harvest, but not the responsibility for cultivation and sale costs. The property remained physically within the domain of the dedicant, in other words, who would then have been obligated to pay a certain amount of the harvest as rent to the temple.

Though it is impossible to know whether rabbinic ordinances regulating these conveyances are at all relevant to a pre-70 CE context, they are worth mentioning nonetheless. A brief statement in *t. Baba Meṣiʻa* 8:30 involves the case of a renter whose landlord consecrates his house to the temple.[53] The rent payment according to the teaching goes toward hekdesh, or consecrated property. It comes amidst a group of teachings on renting rights. One should note, however, that good evidence for the leasing of land of any sort in ancient Judea is sparse and relatively late, coming in the form of leases on papyri from the early second century CE in the Judean desert caves and in early rabbinic writings; this despite the fact that land leasing appears to have become commonplace in the region already from the Ptolemaic period, as John Kloppenborg has argued.[54]

According to early rabbinic law, the voluntary application of consecrated status to property does not require its immediate transfer into the hands of the temple authorities.[55] Even though hekdesh can remain within the physical domain of

---

[52] See §1.1.
[53] See also a parallel *baraita* in *b. Baba Meṣ'ia* 21a.
[54] There is, in fact, no evidence in the Hebrew Bible for the leasing of land, but it would be central to the parable of the tenants in Mark 12:1–9, the basis for Kloppenborg's study; see his discussion of the evidence on leasing arrangements in Judea and a list of sources in *Tenants in the Vineyard*, 290–95. On rabbinic terms for tenancy and their application to an Early Roman context in Judea, see Applebaum, "Economic Life in Palestine," in *The Jewish People in the First Century*, vol. 2 (op. cit.), 659–60.
[55] Coins can become hekdesh, for example, as soon as they are designated by their owner for some sacred use, such as purchasing an animal for sacrifice; see *m. Keritot* 6:8, which deals with the question of leeway in purchasing holy offerings once one has set aside money for that pur-

Figure 11. A laborer on a threshing board drawn by a horse at Saffourieh (Sepphoris) near Nazareth, 1940. Library of Congress Prints and Photographs Division. G. Eric and Edith Matson Photograph Collection.

the dedicant, the dedicant is absolved from certain responsibilities regarding it since it technically has become the holding of the temple; they are not required to pay a penalty, for example, should they use it for some profane or otherwise inappropriate purpose.[56] Anything deemed hekdesh can be freely monetized or exchanged, the original consecrated asset losing its sanctity entirely and transferring to the cash or exchanged property.[57] In the case of land dedicated specif-

---

pose. Likewise, animals can become hekdesh by simple declaration; see *m. Ḥullin* 10:2; *m. Bekorot* 2:2–3.

[56] Even paying the temple tax or the redemption fee for the firstborn son with hekdesh coins is prohibited; see *m. Šeqalim* 2:2 and *m. Bekorot* 8:8. On the punishment for the misuse of hekdesh, see *m. Meʿilah* 5:1–2 and *m. Makkot* 3:2; for uncertain cases of misuse, see *m. Keritot* 5:2–3. On allowances with regard to oath procedures involving hekdesh, see *m. Šebuʿot* 6:5.

[57] The case of *m. Meʿilah* 6:2 involves a messenger sent to purchase something with hekdesh coins; in order to preempt the inevitable transgression of sacrilege, the owner of the coins can set aside the same value in coin or kind and thus desanctify the coins in the possession of the messenger. Far stricter regulations pertain to items sanctified for the altar, as delimited,

ically for the altar, its usable products would presumably have been offered up and other things sold for the benefit of the sacrificial cult. A discussion in *m. Šeqalim* 4:6–8 considers instances in which consecrated properties include things suitable for the altar. A disagreement there between R. Eliezer and R. Akiva relates to the question of whether the altar or the temple-upkeep fund is to be preferred in such instances. These principles would allow for a system whereby the cultivation and harvesting responsibilities for land consecrated to the temple were assumed by the tenant, as was common in land leases.

According to the rabbis, the management of hekdesh, real or movable, lies not with the priests but with the "temple revenuer" (גזבר). The revenuer can in certain instances come onto one's property to deal with hekdesh. One who dedicates the produce of his threshing floor to the sanctuary, for instance, will according to the rabbis have the revenuer even out the grain (*m. Pe'ah* 1:6).[58] A tradition in *m. Šeqalim* 5:2 claims that three revenuers at the temple were charged with managing hekdesh and with collecting valuation payments and other vowed monies. The tradition reads: "The three revenuers: What do they do? Through them [people] would redeem [pay off] valuations, declarations of herem, acts of consecration, and second tithe. And all the work of hekdesh was done by them...." The text accords with the rabbinic tradition in *m. Sanhedrin* 1:3, and its parallel in *m. Megillah* 4:3, requiring the presence of three for the appraisal of movable temple properties, and of ten for the appraisal of temple real estate.

Similarly, early rabbinic exegesis of Lev 27 replaces the anonymous priest, who is mentioned throughout that chapter as the appraiser and economic agent of Yahweh, with the temple revenuer (Sifra, *Beḥuqotai* 10:10 [273:15]). The matter of where the unredeemed consecrated field is to go at the Jubilee (Lev 27:21) perplexed the rabbis since scripture would explicitly note that it is to go to the priest; an unresolved disagreement in *m. 'Arakin* 7:4 has the temple either selling the field to a priest, gifting it to him, or making sure it remains abandoned until the end of time. In other words, in rabbinic thought there is a clear division between revenue for priests and the temple, with hekdesh falling into the latter category. According to *m. Temurah* 7:1–3, for example, priests can derive economic benefit from altar offerings—with their valuable hides, cuts of meat, and other foodstuffs—but in *m. Temurah* 7:2 they are deprived of any benefit from offerings made explicitly for the upkeep of the temple. The distinction

---

e.g., in *m. Temurah* 7:1–3. On the matter of redeemed consecrations losing their sanctity, see *m. Berakot* 7:1, where it figures into the issue of who can participate in a *zimmûn*.
58 See also *m. Ḥallah* 3:3–4.

of priestly and temple revenues in early rabbinic tradition is also reflected in the category of "the heave-offering of hekdesh" (תרומת הקדש), which is the consecration by a priest of some of his heave-offering to the sanctuary (*m. Terumot* 6:4); and of "the value dedication" (הקדש עלוי), which is the donation by a supplicant of the market-value of an animal due for sacrifice to a temple-upkeep fund (*m. Temurah* 7:3).[59]

While the plot, grove, tree, or other consecrated asset enjoyed sacred status, one can assume that physical markers were put up to call attention to it. The Mishnah preserves teachings recalling the practice of marking fourth-year vineyards with clods of earth, 'orlâ trees with clay, and ripe first fruits by tying reedgrass around them (*m. Ma'aser Šeni* 5:1; *m. Bikkurim* 3:1). A similar kind of marking such as a boundary stone or low fence may have been useful in the case of consecrated fields.[60]

Finally, we can do little more than speculate on the taxation policy regarding such real estate, though probably whatever taxes were drawn from them would have been handled locally by tax farmers or other authorities.[61] The Hasmonean system of tax collection is notably obscure, though one might expect a break for consecrated fields on the *dekate*, which replaced the older imperial taxes.[62] The same may have been the case for taxes under the Herodians. By the time of Herod much of the fertile land in the country was in the hands of the royal family and other agricultural areas were taxed directly, with temple revenues probably deducted from those sums.[63]

---

[59] On the latter concept, see Neusner, *A History of the Mishnaic Law of Holy Things. Part Four: Arakhin, Temurah. Translation and Explanation* (Leiden: Brill, 1979), 145.

[60] On the use of boundary stones for marking agricultural space apparently for taxation purposes, including perhaps the collection of sacred dues, see Rosenfeld, "The 'Boundary of Gezer' Inscriptions and the History of Gezer at the End of the Second Temple Period," *IEJ* 38, no. 4 (1988), 235–45; Reich and Greenhut, "Another 'Boundary of Gezer' Inscription Found Recently," ibid. 52, no. 1 (2002), 58–63. On low fences surrounding sacred trees dedicated to Athena, see Todd, *A Commentary on Lysias, Speeches 1–11* (Oxford: Oxford University Press, 2007), 485–87.

[61] Extremely little can be said on Seleucid policy toward sacred landholdings in the region. The Apollonia-Salbake (Asia Minor) decree from the reign of Antiochus III (222–187 BCE) relates to the question but does not reveal much; see Aperghis, *Seleukid Royal Economy*, 288, 324–25.

[62] For discussions on the Hasmonean *dekate*, see Applebaum, "Hasmoneans," 21–22; and Bar-Kochva, "Manpower, Economics, and Internal Strife," 185–87.

[63] Such is Emilio Gabba's supposition with regard to the dues of the priests and Levites; see "The Finances of King Herod," in *Greece and Rome in Eretz Israel: Collected Essays* (ed. Kasher et al.; Jerusalem: Yad Ben-Zvi, 1990), 161–62. For another discussion on taxes in the time of the Herodians and the argument that taxation was not as burdensome as many have made it seem, even considering the levying of sacred dues, see Sanders, *Judaism, 63 BCE–66 CE*, 146–69.

5.4 Land Donations among the Yahad and the Jesus Movement

The sectarian community of the Yahad, as well as the Jesus movement, may have been sustained in part by landed donations. An ostracon (KhQOstracon) found in 1996 at Qumran may be evidence for an agricultural consecration to the Yahad, a movement promoting a cult of worship quite different from that dominated by the Zadokite priesthood at Jerusalem. Discovered during archaeological work directed by James Strange on the Qumran plateau, the ostracon was read by Frank Moore Cross and Esther Eshel as recording the gift of a house, figs, and olives by a certain Honi from Holon to an Elazar son of Nahamani. Cross and Eshel understood one line of the deed of gift as having read "when he fulfills (his oath) to the community (ליחד = for the Yahad)."[64] The recipient of the gift would then be the administrator in charge of the communal funds of the Yahad. In fact, a section of the Rule of the Community (1QS 9:7–9) limits the community's resources to the men of the Yahad and stipulates clearly that they should never be mixed with the funds of the "men of deceit" (אנשי הרמיה), which may refer to Judean priests not of the Yahad community.[65] The mention of "figs" and "olives" probably refers to the trees themselves, as Cross and Eshel claim. Paleographic analysis of the ostracon indicates a Late Herodian date, somewhere in the years 30–68 CE.[66]

The problem, however, is that the reading of the linchpin form ליחד—the word that would associate the deed with the Yahad community—is debatable. The word appears on the bottom left of the broken edge of the ostracon, the breakage erasing the lower half of the last three letters of the word, and the ink itself badly faded and smudged.[67] Yardeni reads the end of that line not as וכמלותו ליחד but as וכול אילן אח]ר ("and every oth[er] tree").[68] Frederick Cryer

---

64 Cross and Eshel, "KhQOstracon," in *Qumran Cave 4: Cryptic Texts and Miscellanea* (Oxford: Clarendon Press, 2000), 497–507. See also Murphy, *Wealth in the Dead Sea Scrolls*, 383–89; and Magness, *Stone and Dung*, 98.
65 On approaches to wealth and its management in the Qumran community, see Murphy, *Wealth in the Dead Sea Scrolls*, 447–55.
66 On the metonymic use of the plural form of the fruit product as a reference to the tree itself in an Early Roman Aramaic document from the Judean Desert, see Cross and Eshel, "KhQOstracon," 503. On the paleography, see ibid., 497–98.
67 Ibid., Pl. XXXIII.
68 Yardeni, "A Draft of a Deed on an Ostracon from Khirbet Qumrân," *IEJ* 47, no. 3/4 (1997), 233–37.

reads ליחד as לנאחז "to take possession of."⁶⁹ Either of these alternate readings would mean that the document does not record a field consecration but a simple deed of gift from one individual to another; nor would it have any bearing on the question of whether the archaeological site can be linked with the scrolls found in the caves below. Of course, the deed could still be related to the Yahad or to whatever group lived at Qumran, as Catherine Murphy has discussed, but merely involve the transfer of land from one member to another.[70]

From the realm of the Jesus movement come testimonies regarding the practice of field consecration, though they indicate that land donations for sacred purposes in that context were regularly monetized rather than exploited as real estate. In Acts 4:34–37, the followers of Jesus are extolled for selling off their land and other assets and for laying the proceeds at the feet of the apostles. Barnabas the Cypriot Levite is singled out for his pious observance of the practice. And in Acts 5:1–11, the characters of Ananias and Sapphira are said to have not contributed the true value of their land and to have met their death as a result.[71] In both cases, the religious purposes of the gift are obvious, linking them conceptually with the acts of consecration made for the benefit of the temple.

5.5 Agricultural Consecrations and the Herodian Temple Economy

Despite these scattered testimonies to the practice of field consecration, land does not appear to have been a major part of the temple economy in the Herodian period. When the temple needed raw materials or agricultural products such as animals, wheat, oil, and wine, it seems to have relied not on its own estates but on donations from the people and on certain private suppliers with which it regularly did business. As a major consumer of animals and other agricultural products, the temple played a large role in the local economy.[72] It pur-

---

69 Cryer, "The Qumran Conveyance: A Reply to F.M. Cross and E. Eshel," *Scandinavian Journal of the Old Testament* 11, no. 2 (1997), 232–40.
70 *Wealth in the Dead Sea Scrolls*, 383–89.
71 Richard Ascough has argued that Luke's presentation of the event is meant as a "cautionary tale about wanting honours for benefaction," since the apostles distribute the goods to others and prevent a situation in which honors are passed back onto the benefactors; see "Benefaction Gone Wrong: The 'Sin' of Ananias and Sapphira in Context," in *Text and Artifact in the Religions of Mediterranean Antiquity: Essays in Honour of Peter Richardson* (ed. Wilson and Desjardins; Waterloo, Ontario: Wilfrid Laurier University Press, 2000), 91–110, quote on 105.
72 Lapin, "Temple, Cult, and Consumption in Second Temple Jerusalem," in *Expressions of Cult in the Southern Levant* (op. cit.), 241–53.

chased flour and wine from private estates known for producing superior products. The fine flour of Mikhmas, Mezonihah and Hafarayim is praised in *m. Menaḥot* 8:1; and the fine wine of Kerutim, Hatulim, Bet Rimah, Bet Lavan, and Kefar Signa extolled in *m. Menaḥot* 8:6.[73] The Mishnah notes in both cases that products from all the provinces (כל הארצות) are suitable for the altar, though it was customary to bring from those specific places. It also appears to be the case that the Hatulim winery supplied products to the Qumran sectarians, based on the inscription יוחנן חטלא on four jars from Qumran.[74] Wood for fuel on the altar was donated regularly by the people for an event that would occur around the 15th of Av.[75]

For construction the temple purchased wood from private suppliers too. In *War* 5.35–36, for example, John of Gischala is said to have wrongfully used the timber that had been brought by King Agrippa II from Mt. Libanus for a sanctuary renovation project. The people and the chief priests apparently initiated the project, but the raw materials were procured at the king's expense. The scenario recalls a rabbinic ruling in *m. Meʿilah* 3:8 regarding trees consecrated only for the use of their timber in temple construction.[76]

According to *m. Šeqalim* 4:3, the temple could use surpluses remaining after the basic needs of the temple cult are met to purchase wine, oil, and fine flour, which in turn can be sold to pilgrims for profit. But there is a dissenting view on the practice expressed by R. Akiva, who says there that "one should not engage in business dealings with consecrated property (hekdesh) or the property of the poor." This perspective would have effectively ended any profit-making endeavors on the part of the temple with movables or land.

In the end, it seems that the temple's main revenues from the people derived not from landed wealth but from the shekel tax. The tax was collected from adult males on an annual basis by the late Second Temple period. It was used foremost as a source of funding for the daily sacrifices—allowing the regular Tamid service to be for the atonement of the entire house of Israel, both in

---

[73] See also *t. Menaḥot* 9:5–13; and Safrai, *Seeking Out the Land*, 132. And see ibid., 160, for a discussion on a passage in *y. Ḥagiga* 79c (= *b. Ḥagiga* 25a) that has the people of Judea selling their produce to the temple.

[74] Demsky, "Qumran Epigraphy and Mishnaic Geography: The Identification of ḤTL' with Ḥaṭtulim (Menaḥoth 8:6)," *DSD* 4, no. 2 (1997). For a general discussion on the supply of agricultural products for the temple cult, see Safrai, "The Temple," 881–82.

[75] On the wood-offering and its relationship to the Jewish holiday Tu b'Av, see Schürer et al., *History of the Jewish People*, vol. II, 273; and Safrai, "The Temple," 882–84.

[76] See §7.3. For a discussion of a rabbinic passage (*y. Pesaḥim* 30d) on sanctity protections given to a forest of acacia trees because of the belief that the temple in Jerusalem cut down trees there to use in construction, see Safrai, *Seeking Out the Land*, 379.

Judea and abroad—and other sabbath and festival offerings for which animals and other goods needed to be procured. The tax could also be used to pay for the maintenance of buildings, salaries, support of the needy, and municipal services.[77] The data do not allow for one to begin to quantify the revenues and expenditures of the Jerusalem temple, but the sheer volume of mentions in the sources of the shekel tax and particularly the extraordinarily large sums it appears to have generated suggest that the temple treasury remained the single greatest deposit of cash and valuables in Judea—even greater than Herodian and Roman-provincial treasuries, and any public funds—though much of it would have remained unproductive.[78] Josephus claims in *Ant.* 14.113 that there is no such thing as public money in Judea "except that which is God's," a reference to the large sums generated by this tax.[79]

The vast wealth of the temple treasury was drawn upon by local leaders for certain urban projects. In one case, Pontius Pilate is said to have funded the construction of a new aqueduct with funds from the temple treasury (*War* 2.175; *Ant.* 18.60). In another instance, Agrippa II used these funds to repave the streets in white stone after the temple was finished, a measure according to Josephus that was meant to help mitigate against unemployment problems once the major work on the temple had been completed (*Ant.* 20.219–22). Given the treasury's great wealth, various Roman officials plundered it on occasion. One infamous such incident was Crassus's acquisition of 2,000 talents of silver and a considerable amount of gold from the temple to help fund his Parthian campaign in 54 BCE (*Ant.* 14.105–9; see also *War* 1.179). The monies he took had been spared by Pompey a decade earlier (*War* 1.152–53; *Ant.* 14.72). Sabinius, when procurator of Syria during the Varus uprising in 4 BCE, secured 400 talents for himself from the temple treasury, with Roman soldiers said to have fallen

---

[77] For general discussions on the tax, see Liver, "The Half-Shekel Offering in Biblical and Post-Biblical Literature," 173–98; Schürer et al., *History of the Jewish People*, vol. II, 270–74; Applebaum, "Economic Life," 677–78; and Levine, *Jerusalem: Portrait of the City in the Second Temple Period (538 B.C.E.–70 C.E.)* (Philadelphia: The Jewish Publication Society, 2002), 247. For a rabbinic understanding of how the tax was used, see m. *Šeqalim* 4:1–2. On the tax in the Persian period, see §3.4; and in the Hasmonean period, §4.4.

[78] On the use of the Hasmonean and Herodian desert fortresses as store-places of great wealth, see Strabo, *Geog.* 16.40. Presumably royal deposits such as these were more usable and productive for the economy than the temple funds; on another deposit of generally untouchable wealth, see Josephus's mention of the great valuables stored in King David's tomb in Jerusalem, which he claims were used by both Hyrcanus and Herod in times of need (*Ant.* 7.393–94, 16.171; *War* 1.61).

[79] However, one must note how he contradicts himself in *Life* 199 when he refers to public funds used to pay for John of Gischala's mission into Galilee.

5.5 Agricultural Consecrations and the Herodian Temple Economy — 173

Figure 12. Map of King Herod's Judea at its peak in the late first century BCE.

upon the treasury as well (*War* 2.50; *Ant.* 17.264). Florus, procurator of Syria in 64–66 CE, took from the temple 17 talents, provoking local outrage (*War* 2.293–94).[80]

One should note that the shekel tax was collected not only from Judeans in this period but from diaspora Jews as well.[81] The requirement that pilgrims pay-

---

[80] On the financial resources of the Jerusalem temple, see Wardle, *The Jerusalem Temple*, 23–27; and Levine, *Jerusalem*, 235–37.
[81] Cicero recalls the confiscation at Apamea, Laodicea, and Adramyttium of this sacred tax bound for Jerusalem (*Pro Flacco* 28.66–69); and Josephus quotes Strabo regarding an incident in which Mithridates VI Eupator took 800 talents deposited at Cos apparently in an attempt to protect it from Mithridates (*Ant.* 14.110–13). Marcus Agrippa would issue a decree ordering foreign cities to ensure the proper treatment of sacred Jewish monies at Ephesus, Cyrene, and Sardis (*Ant.* 16.166–73). The Qumran sectarians called for the payment of the tax once in a lifetime,

ing the tax convert their currency into the Tyrian tetradrachm standard would have benefitted the temple treasury; resistance to the surcharge may have led to the famous disturbance at the moneychangers' tables by Jesus of Nazareth (Matt 21:12–13; Mark 11:15–17; Luke 19:45–46; John 2:13–17).[82] After the fall of Jerusalem in 70 CE, the Roman provincial authorities would inherit the temple's collection apparatus for the shekel tax and rename it the Fiscus Iudaicus. According to Josephus, the Romans directed the funds to the Capitoline Hill in Rome (*War* 7.218), apparently a reference to the temple of Jupiter there, which had just burned in 69 CE.[83] Receipts of payment from Edfu in Upper Egypt show that special tax collectors were appointed by the Romans for the task.[84]

The temple had other sources of support in addition to the shekel tax, such as benefaction by royalty and aristocrats. Nothing can compare to Herod's largesse to the temple. The rebuilding project he financed transformed Jerusalem into a pilgrimage center of international renown (*War* 1.401, *Ant.* 15.380–402), regularly drawing masses from foreign lands.[85] Herod needed to convince the temple officials of the merits of the rebuilding project, which would have required the demolition of the standing structure. Josephus relates that during Herod's speech to them on the matter he described the project as capable of being "the most notable of all things achieved" by him (*Ant.* 15.380) and "a return for the gift of the kingdom" (387). He decorated the temple with spoils he had taken from foreign lands (402) and would quite controversially put up a golden eagle over the great gate of the temple (*War* 1.648–55, *Ant.* 17.151–63). When Herod defended the eagle to Judean officials at Jericho, he is said by Josephus to have reminded them of his good works for the temple and to have claimed that the Hasmoneans could never have done "anything so great for the honor of God"

---

as a form of ransom (4Q159, Frag. 1ii 9:7), apparently following Exod 30:11–16. The Temple Scroll mentions the tax but is unclear on the frequency of payment (11Q19 39:8–9). Paul encouraged the payment of a similar tax for the Christian community in Jerusalem (1 Cor 16:1–4).

82 Sanders, *Judaism, 63 BCE–66 CE*, 86–87.

83 Stern, *Greek and Latin Authors*, vol. 1, 198–99. Famously much of the temple valuables were marched ceremoniously through the streets of Rome after the war, some put on display by Vespasian in the Templum Pacis (*War* 7.161–62).

84 Tcherikover and Fuks, *Corpus Papyrorum Judaicarum* (vol. 2; Cambridge, MA: The Magnes Press; Harvard University Press, 1960), 111–16, 119–36, 204–8 (Nos. 160–229, 421).

85 On the positive economic impact of Herod's efforts to transform Jerusalem into an international pilgrimage center, see Goodman, "Pilgrimage Economy of Jerusalem," 69–76; Applebaum, "Economic Life," 683; and Wardle, *The Jerusalem Temple*, 23–27. On the economic benefits of such a massive temple construction project in general, see Davies, "Rebuilding a Temple: The Economic Effects of Piety," in *Economies beyond Agriculture in the Classical World* (ed. Mattingly and Salmon; London: Routledge, 2001), 209–29.

(*Ant.* 16.161–62). Nothing in Josephus's reports of Herod's acts of benefaction toward the temple includes the endowment of a sacred plot of land, even though Herod himself was likely the largest single landowner in Judea during his reign.[86]

Similarly, there are several other examples of prominent displays of aristocratic support for the temple in the late Second Temple period, but none involve land grants.[87] Josephus mentions gifts of precious metal and other fine vessels to the Jerusalem temple by Roman sovereigns, who were following in the footsteps of Hellenistic rulers.[88] Herod's ally Sossius dedicated a crown of gold (*War* 1.357). Temple offerings brought by Augustus and other Roman sovereigns were melted down by John of Gischala during his occupation of the temple in the war with Rome, prompting Josephus to remark that "the Roman sovereigns ever honored and added embellishment to the temple, whereas this Jew now pulled down even the donations of foreigners…" (*War* 5.562). As mentioned in the above chapter, the question of dedications to the temple by non-Jews was one of several controversies plaguing the local authorities on the eve of the war (*War* 2.411–17).[89] One of the chief priests had stopped accepting them, leading to a forceful defense of the practice by other priests and notable Pharisees. "The Words of the Luminaries" from Qumran tells of "all the countries" carrying their offerings of silver, gold, and precious stones to the Jerusalem temple (4Q504a, Frags. 1–2iv, 8–11).

---

86 On Herod's land, see Applebaum, "Economic Life," 664–65; Gabba, "The Finances of King Herod," 162–63; and Oakman, *Jesus and the Economic Questions of His Day* (Lewiston, NY: The Edwin Mellen Press, 1986), 44–45, 69–71. For Herod's other benefaction at home and abroad, see *War* 1.402–28; and *Ant.* 15.328–30, 16.146–49. Another prominent instance of Herod's benefaction toward his people is the Egyptian grain he provided to many of his subjects, among other things, during the drought in the mid-20s BCE (*Ant.* 15.310–15).

87 Queen Helena's gifts of a golden candlestick and golden tablet inscribed with a section of Torah discussing the adulteress (Num 5:12–31) are mentioned in rabbinic tradition (*m. Yoma* 3:10). On Izates and Helena's support of Jerusalem and the needy, see *Ant.* 20.51–53. See also Pseudo-Philo's *LAB* 29:3, where the judge Zebul (Ehud) is said to have established a treasury for Yahweh at Shiloh and encouraged the people to donate silver and gold to it. On rabbinic praise for offerings from the poor and from aristocrats, see Klawans, *Purity, Sacrifice, and the Temple*, 188–90. On evidence for a rejection of civic euergetism among certain Jewish circles, see Schwartz, *Were the Jews a Mediterranean Society? Reciprocity and Solidarity in Ancient Judaism* (Princeton; Oxford: Princeton University Press, 2010), esp. 173–74. A remark by Josephus in *Ant.* 16.157–59 is central to Schwartz's argument. There Josephus notes that Herod's euergetism was solely in pursuit of honor, an endeavor thought by Josephus to be in opposition to Jewish sentiment, which prefers righteousness to glory (16.158).

88 On benefaction by Seleucid rulers toward the temple, see Aperghis, "Jewish Subjects and Seleukid Kings," 38–39.

89 See §4.5.

Persons of more modest means could make contributions to the so-called Qorban ("sacrifice") fund.⁹⁰ Apparently cash gifts marked as Qorban were given over to individual priests, as Josephus notes (*Ant.* 4.73), in continuation of the practice of the valuation of persons from Lev 27:2–8. The priests' right to this kind of valuation payment is asserted as well in the Damascus Document (4Q270 2ii), where it is referred to as "the valuation money for the redemption of their soul" (כסף הערכים לפדוי נפשם); perhaps this was a word of protest against the temple for laying claim to these gifts. There is evidence of a similar disagreement regarding the proper destination of fourth-year produce and of herem offerings, as we will see in the following chapter.⁹¹ It would appear that the practice of dedicating money in lieu of dedicating one's person to sacred purposes would remain far more common than consecrating fields, leading the temple authorities to begin laying claims to the incoming cash and resulting in protest from those who preferred to see these monies remaining in the hands of the priests.⁹² No such protest is evident for income from field consecrations, perhaps because of its relative infrequency among the types of voluntary dedications in this period.

---

90 According to Josephus the Qorban fund was drawn upon by Pontius Pilate when he wished to build a new aqueduct into the city (*War* 2.275; see also *Ant.* 18.60). Judas's payment for the betrayal of Jesus was deemed inappropriate for this fund in Matt 27:6. There are references to vessels labeled in such a manner in *m. Ma'aser Šeni* 4:10–11 (see also *m. Nedarim* 1:2–3). A stone vessel from the Herodian period excavated at the foot of the Temple Mount is inscribed with the word קרבן (Qorban); see Cotton et al., eds., *CII/P I:1*, 52–53. An ossuary inscribed with the same word as a part of a formula to prevent its theft was mentioned above (§5.2.1). Phoenician oaths involving freewill gifts appear to have employed a similar terminology: In *Life* 167 Josephus relates the anecdote of Theophrastus, the student of Aristotle (fourth–early third century BCE), that the laws of the Tyrians prohibit the use of foreign oaths, among which he includes the Qorban. Josephus takes this to refer to the Jewish oath, though Menahem Stern argues that a Phoenician practice of the same name was probably intended; *Greek and Latin Authors*, vol. 1, 12–13.

91 See §6.2.1. The sectarians—as well as the Karaites and Samaritans—saw fourth-year produce as a priestly entitlement, the rabbis as equivalent to the second tithe, calling for it to be consumed or its monetary equivalent spent in Jerusalem rather than handed over to the priests; see Shemesh, "The Laws of First Fruits in the Dead Sea Scrolls," in *Meghillot: Studies in the Dead Sea Scrolls* (ed. Bar-Asher and Dimant; Jerusalem; Haifa: The Byalik Institute; University of Haifa, 2003) [Hebrew], 152–53.

92 After the mention of the ערך of the consecrated field in the Damascus Document (see §5.2), the other two occurrences of the word in the non-biblical scrolls from Qumran where the context is ascertainable refer to the valuations of persons (4Q159 1ii:6, 4Q270 2ii:9; 4Q513 17:3 and PAM 43.668 4:1 are too fragmentary to be of any assistance).

5.5 Agricultural Consecrations and the Herodian Temple Economy — 177

In addition to the proceeds from the shekel tax, from voluntary offerings, and from the Qorban fund, the temple also had revenue from fines levied for various offenses, such as sacrilege and the introduction of non-kosher animals or hides into Jerusalem.[93] The temple treasury was used to store private funds set aside for sacrifices too, such as that pooled together and sent to Jerusalem by Judah and his men after they discovered that their fallen comrades had been hiding idols under their tunics (2 Macc 12:43). There were also funds deposited there for safe-keeping.[94] The rabbinic tractate *Šeqalim* discusses, among other things, the proper uses of cash held in the temple treasury (*m. Šeqalim* 4:1–5, 7:1).[95] Interestingly, these rabbinic teachings do not mention the revenues from hekdesh holdings among the various chests in the treasury chamber. Influxes of cash from offerings and the shekel tax appear to have been the common revenues in the sacred economy of Jerusalem, far eclipsing income from consecrated real estate. This can help explain the elusiveness of temple-owned land on the historical record.

Furthermore, evidence for the involvement of the Jerusalem temple in the local real estate market is sparse at best. In Matt 27:3–10, the chief priests are said to have purchased a burial site in the Akeldama ("Blood Field") area of Jerusalem for the interment of foreigners; for the purchase they used the blood money received by Judas for betraying Jesus, which Judas had deposited in the temple treasury into the Qorban fund. But an alternative version has Judas himself purchasing the field after his act of betrayal (Acts 1:18–19), calling into question the historicity of the involvement of the priests in the purchase in Matt

---

[93] Among Antiochus III's decrees in 198 BCE was the right of the local authorities to fine anyone who brought non-kosher meat into Jerusalem, including hides (*Ant.* 12.145–46). On rabbinic ordained fines for sacrilege with consecrations, see *m. Meʿilah* 5:1–2.

[94] In 2 Macc 3:10, the high priest asserts to Heliodorus that the temple contained only the personal deposits of widows and orphans. In 4 Macc 4:1–14, there are "tens of thousands" of private funds said to be in the temple. Josephus calls the temple the "general repository of Jewish wealth" at the time of the war with Rome; many had sold off much of their property and deposited its value there (*War* 6.282). The royal palace in Jerusalem was also where many deposited their cash during the crisis (*War* 6.358). A rabbinic teaching in the name of Hillel has the owners of a house using the temple treasury as part of a scheme to purchase back their property after they had sold it (*m. ʿArakin* 9:4).

[95] According to *m. Šeqalim* 4:1–5, funding the daily service is of foremost importance, followed by various other weekly and festival offerings. At the bottom of the list come the needs of the city, such as its aqueduct and fortifications. The latter point recalls the use by Pontius Pilate of sacred money for building a new aqueduct in Jerusalem (*War* 2.175; *Ant.* 18.65); and Agrippa II's use of it to repave some of the city (*Ant.* 20.220). In *m. Šeqalim* 7:1, a donative offerings (נדבה) chest and shekels chest are mentioned in a teaching on the question of what to do if coins were found lying on the chamber floor.

27:3–10. The fact that the excavated tombs in the Akeldama area appear to have been inhumed with the bodies of foreigners in the first century CE can hardly prove the details of the account in Matthew.[96] Even if the account were true, it would attest to little more than the purchasing and holding of a tomb complex by the temple authorities. Though sellable or rentable, this would not have been a particularly profitable asset.

Consecrated land was not significant enough, either as an asset or a symbol of temple wealth, to merit mention by Josephus in his lengthy descriptions of the temple and its priesthood. We recall however his interpretation of 1 Macc 10:43 to connote areas providing revenue for the temple, described above. (Josephus presumably saved many details on the temple organization for a work he planned to write on Judaism.[97]) In his summary of the priests' dues (*Ant.* 4.67–75, 240–243), he makes mention only of the valuations-of-persons payments of Lev 27:2–8 (*Ant.* 4.73) and says nothing of field consecrations as a source of revenue, perhaps because the latter was no longer among the priests' perquisites and were being used to fund temple operations. But the failure to mention any of these plots in his descriptions of the geography and fertility of Judea and Galilee (*War* 3.35–58, 518; 4.451–74) would seem to attest to a lack of prominence. The closest he comes in these texts to a mention of consecrated land is the following statement on the fertility of the Jericho plain: "it would be no misnomer to describe as 'divine' (θεῖον) this spot in which the rarest and choicest plants are produced in abundance" (*War* 4.469). Yet this could be merely a turn of phrase reflecting Josephus's belief in the inherent sanctity of the Land of Israel—its holiness intrinsic to the land and not limited to consecrated plots.[98]

Finally, there is no indication regarding the fate of sacred landholdings of the Jerusalem temple after the fall of the city in 70 CE. Small consecrated plots were likely monetized quickly, while temple land of any significance could have been left desolate under the force of Roman law or possibly appropriated by the Roman imperial cult. The notice by Josephus that the Roman em-

---

96 France, *The Gospel of Matthew* (Grand Rapids, MI: William B. Eerdmans, 2007), 1038–45. The names of the interred include members of the Eros and Ariston families, both perhaps having come to Jerusalem from Apamea; see Avni and Greenhut, *The Akeldama Tombs. Three Burial Caves in the Kidron Valley, Jerusalem* (Jerusalem: Israel Antiquities Authority, 1996), 33–35.

97 On his interpretation of 1 Macc 10:43, see §5.3. On his planned work on Judaism, see *War* 5.237, where he describes the project as relating to the customs and laws on the city of Jerusalem and its temple.

98 On Josephus's writings and attitude to the Land of Israel, see Amaru, *Rewriting the Bible*, 95–115.

peror "farmed out" all of Judea (*War* 7.216–17) is probably an exaggeration but reflects nevertheless the appropriation by Roman imperial authorities on a massive scale of Judean private land—royal land and any consecrated properties included.[99]

5.6 Summary

Since Jonathan and the Judeans are said in 1 Macc 10:46 to have rejected the offer of Demetrius of the revenues from Ptolemais and its hinterland as a source of revenue for the temple, the freewill offerings section of the Damascus Document offers the only evidence from the Hasmonean period of agricultural plots consecrated to the temple. It anticipates a couple references to temple land in Philo, Josephus, and the rabbinic teachings. The freewill offering section of the Damascus Document is concerned, among other things, with the use of consecration as a means of blocking access to property. The first law of the section prohibits dedicating to the altar forcibly seized assets, which indeed can involve goods taken through larceny but also hypothecated properties. The second law of the section, while fragmentary, seems to forbid consecration for the purposes of denying provisions to dependents or laborers. The sacralization of such provisions could render those persons liable for a sacrilege penalty. While early rabbinic law notes measures taken to prevent sacrilege trespasses, the Damascus Document forbids consecration altogether in such instances.

In this section of the document, there is a mention of the consecrated "field of holding" from Lev 27:16. Though speculative given the poor state of preservation of the document here, it would seem most appropriate that the scriptural verse is invoked to justify a law requiring the redemption of a consecrated field when the land is needed to settle a debt or to provide sustenance to dependents. In such cases the redemption comes with the "penalty" of an added fifth, presumably because consecration should not have happened in the first place. This in turn would prompt a discussion of the false oath, another transgression for which the added fifth is understood as a penalty. The mention of the consecrated field in the text is thus a vital component of the document, providing scriptural backing for one of its principles, working to apply these principles to the case of an entire field, and serving as a link between the cases of con-

---

[99] The presence of new occupants in the region is reflected in rabbinic texts by the term סיקריקון, which refers to property confiscated by the Romans (e.g., *m. Gittin* 5:6); see Rosenfeld and Perlmutter, "Landowners in Roman Palestine," 340–41, nn. 65–66.

secrations and the false oath. The document also shows that by the second century BCE, Judeans were interpreting Lev 27 as regulations on gifts to the deity, fields included, rather than on loans from him.

The association in the Damascus Document of the revenues of field consecrations with the "altar" in Jerusalem suggests that the temple rather than the priesthood was receiving proceeds from such offerings. This reflects a viewpoint entrenched in later Jewish legal thought—albeit free of the vitriol toward the temple that is seen in the Damascus Document. Philo's remark that the Jerusalem temple profited from tracts of land suits this picture, as does Josephus's take on a specific offer by Demetrius in 1 Macc 10:43. But the Damascus Document also implies that consecrated fields were not alienated from the holdings of the dedicant. This suits rabbinic notions that individuals took personal responsibility over the management and protection of consecrated property, while directing its revenues toward the temple treasury. The implication is that sacred plots were dispersed across the countryside among private landholders, who probably paid rent to the temple. Yet the degree to which their everyday management—including proprietary arrangements, crop cultivation, and market sale of produce, among other things—was in the hands of temple officials or remained the responsibility of the owners of the field is unknown.

In any case, field consecrations were likely a small part of the Jerusalem temple economy in the late Second Temple period. The temple relied primarily on the shekel tax and other donations in the form of movables and cash and probably benefitted only modestly from income from consecrated land. Rather than growing its own produce, it appears to have relied on voluntary offerings or purchased products in kind from sellers on the countryside. Meanwhile, certain groups such as the Yahad and the followers of Jesus used donations of land to further their organizational aims.

Chapter 6
Herem Property and Landholding by Priests in the Late Second Temple Period

6.1 Introduction

The biblical war herem, where an enemy population was annihilated in dramatic fashion, could have resulted in the conferral of sacrosanct status to cultivable land.[1] But the war herem appears to have been relegated to the literary imagination by the late Second Temple period. It is invoked, for example, in the account of Judah Maccabee's rout of a pocket of Idumeans living in the Acraba district of Samaria (1 Macc 5:3–5; 2 Macc 10:15–17). According to 1 Macc 5:5 the Judean victors "anathematized them" (ἀνεθεμάτισεν αὐτοὺς; 1 Macc 5:5).[2] The version in 2 Macc 10:15–17 differs slightly in the details of the event but too appears to have utilized biblical models of a war herem.[3] Yet this one instance is an outlier and could have been little more than a turn of phrase to underscore the severity of the military blow the Idumeans received.[4] Generally one is struck by how rare the language of the wartime herem is in 1 Maccabees, given its many descriptions of battles and its reliance on biblical models.[5]

---

[1] On the biblical war herem, see §2.5.
[2] The district's major city, Acraba, commanded over the main route leading from Shechem down to the Jordan River valley and would become a toparchy of Herodian Judea (Pliny, *Natural History* 5:70; Josephus, *War* 3.55); see Kasher, *Jews, Idumaeans, and Ancient Arabs: Relations of the Jews in Eretz-Israel with the Nations of the Frontier and the Desert during the Hellenistic and Roman Era (332 BCE-70 CE)* (Tübingen: J.C.B. Mohr, 1988), 25–26; and Eshel and Erlich, "The Fortress of Acraba in Kh. Urmeh," *Cathedra* 47 (1988) [Hebrew], 24.
[3] That account alludes to a wartime herem oath (as that taken in Num 21:1–3 and Judg 11:29–31) by noting that Judah and his men offered up prayer and asked God to be their ally. Appropriately, the oath is taken before the campaign commences.
[4] The Greek translator of the conjectured Hebrew original of 1 Maccabees probably encountered a *hipîl* form of the verb *ḥ-r-m*, which had been written in the style of Deuteronomistic and prophetic accounts of war, and provided the usual equivalent; see Batsch, *La guerre et les rites de la guerre dans le judaïsme du deuxième Temple* (Leiden: Brill, 2005), 418–21. The particularly harsh language of 1 Maccabees can be connected to its notice in 5:4–5 that the Idumeans were committing brigandage against Jews along the trading routes; their thorough defeat thus comes as a form of punishment. Those accused are actually the Baianites, apparently a biblically inspired reference to Idumeans from their territorial homeland; see Kasher, *Jews, Idumaeans, and Ancient Arabs*, 28–29; and Goldstein, *I Maccabees*, 294–95.
[5] While 1 Maccabees draws inspiration from the conquest narratives of Joshua in presenting its protagonists as the divine elect cleansing the land of heresy, it diverges from the Deuteronomis-

The dramatic imagery conjured by biblical accounts of the war herem appealed to authors of the Dead Sea Scrolls as well.[6] In the Damascus Document (CD 9:1, 4Q266 8ii:8–9) the herem appears in a polemic against a certain kind of execution.[7] In the eschatological visions of the War Scroll, the language of herem is used to underscore the absolute finality of the defeat of the Sons of Darkness. One noteworthy instance is at the very end of the seven battles on the decisive day of the battle with the Kittim, "When the great hand of God shall be raised up against Belial and all the army of his dominion for eternal defeat...and the Kittim shall be smashed without [remnant]." The priests' trumpets will sound, and the entire multitude will spread out against the army of the Kittim "to devote them to herem destruction" (להחרימם; 1QM 18:1–5).[8] The other instance is at the end of Yadin's "Battle Serekh Series," a description of tactical maneuvers to be employed during the war, concluding with the final defeat of the enemy. In this case the text uses a rare instance of the substantive form of the term to indicate extermination, reading that the enemy will be rolled back at the sides "until the herem [destruction]" (עד החרם; 1QM 9:7).[9]

However, the war herem is absent in the histories of Josephus in places where one would expect to find it. He leaves it out for example in his version of the account of Judah's defeat of the Idumeans at Acraba (*Ant.* 12.328).[10] When he notes that he took the spoils from surrounding Syrian cities and sent

---

tic History in its sparing use of the language of herem. Accounts where one would expect the invoking of the biblical wartime herem, had it been regularly practiced, include 1 Macc 5:43, Judah's burning of the sacred precinct at Karnaim; 5:58, Judah's destruction the sacred precincts at Azotus; and 10:83–84, Jonathan's rout of the Dagon temple at Azotus. Katell Berthelot has made a similar observation and concludes that the Hasmoneans did not in fact see themselves as fulfilling God's command to Joshua; "The Biblical Conquest of the Promised Land and the Hasmonaean Wars according to 1 and 2 Maccabees," in *Books of the Maccabees* (op. cit.), 45–60. On 1 Maccabee's indebtedness to Deuteronomy in general, see Borchardt, "The Deuteronomic Legacy of 1 Maccabees," in *Changes in Scripture: Rewriting and Interpreting Authoritative Traditions in the Second Temple Period* (ed. von Weissenberg et al.; Berlin: De Gruyter, 2011), 297–319. See also Goldstein, *I Maccabees*, 4–26.

6 Ibid., 417–26, 429–46.
7 The text reads "Any man who destroys (יחרים) a man among men by the statutes of the gentiles..." and could refer to the practice of death by stoning; see ibid., 411–12. On a reference to herem vows in CD 6:15–17, see above, §5.2.2.
8 Yadin, *The Scroll of the War of the Sons of Light against the Sons of Darkness. Edited with Commentary and Introduction* (London: Oxford University Press, 1962), 10–13.
9 Ibid., 8–10, 183. Interestingly, the Temple Scroll understands war booty to be an entirely separate category from herem property, conferring upon the priesthood a levy on both (11Q19 60:5).
10 Park, *Finding Herem?: A Study of Luke-Acts in the Light of Herem* (London: T&T Clark, 2007), 98–106; Batsch, *La guerre*, 424–25.

them home to Jerusalem (*Life* 81), he does not call them herem, though the context of the story suggests that he had the priests' entitlements in mind, for it comes just after he bragged about piously refusing those entitlements. During his struggles with John of Gischala (*Life* 370), he threatens to confiscate the property and burn to the ground the houses of those siding with his rival. The process is akin to the biblical herem and may derive from it, but in Josephus's telling there is no hint of sacralization nor is the deity invoked in any way.

Yet while the old war herem was rarely if ever practiced by the late Second Temple period, the herem did continue in the context of votive procedures and alimentary offerings. For example, there is an oath procedure recorded in 1 Enoch 6:4–6 (4Q201 III:1–3) where the participants bound one another by threat of herem.[11] A similar procedure appears in Acts 23:12–14, when Jews made a pact (ἀνεθεμάτισαν ἑαυτοὺς) not to eat or drink until they had killed Paul; their pact was under the force of a herem oath rendered in the Greek as anathematization.[12] The principle behind the enforcement mechanism is expressed well in *m. Nedarim* 5:4, where one person prohibits himself from deriving any benefit from or having any contact with another by saying, "I am herem to you."[13]

As for alimentary offerings, it is recalled from Chapter 2 that in Lev 27 the herem is a means of giving full ownership rights of a plot of land to the deity, which effectively conveyed the plot to a priest. The owner simply declared the field herem and it became anathema to them. The best evidence for the continuation of the practice in the late Second Temple period is a fragmentary halakhic text from Qumran, 4Q251 (4Qhalakha A), which will be the focus of this chapter. The text's paleography indicates a date of composition in the mid- to late first century BCE, if not slightly thereafter.[14] Aharon Shemesh argues that the document is a commentary on Exod 21:1–23:19, prompting him to refer to it as "Midrash Mishpatim."[15] Those verses in Exodus include a law conferring firstborn animals to priests (Exod 22:29), which one can assume is the reason 4Q251 includes a broader discussion of the priests' perquisites, including the priests' rights to

---

11 Nickelsburg, *1 Enoch 1: A Commentary on the Book of 1 Enoch, Chapters 1–36; 81–108* (Minneapolis: Fortress Press, 2001), 177; Nickelsburg has also examined the sanctity of the area of Mt. Hermon in classical antiquity given its use for pagan cult activity; see ibid., 239–47; and Park, *Finding Herem*, 91–92.
12 Ibid., passim, and see Benovitz, *Kol Nidre*, 92–94 for other examples from the New Testament.
13 See also, e.g., *m. Nedarim* 2:4–5; *m. ʿArakin* 8:4–7; and *t. ʿArakin* 4:23–25, 29–34.
14 On its paleography and date, see Larson, Lehmann, and Schiffman, "4QHalakha A," in *Qumran Cave 4, XXV: Halakhic Texts* (Oxford: Clarendon Press, 1999), 27–28.
15 "4Q251: Midrash Mishpatim," *DSD* 12, no. 3 (2005), 290–302.

herem property. Among the prooftexts invoked are the regulations concerning the herem field in Lev 27.

4Q251 offers an important link in the chain of Judean legal tradition on herem property. As argued below, it can be read as a response to two main developments in late Second Temple society with regard to herem property: First, in some instances persons were dedicating property to the temple treasury by virtue of a herem decree, an idea that patently contradicts scripture's bestowal of the property to a priest, giving rise to a word of protest on the matter in 4Q251. A similar affirmation of the priests' right to herem is made in 11Q19 60:5 (the Temple Scroll) and 4Q379 Frag. 3:6 (apocrJosh[b]). Second, lenient approaches allowing for the desanctification of herem once it joined the holdings of the priest may have provoked the authors of 4Q251, who affirm herem's status as eternally sacred and provide regulations on how to protect that sanctity. A more lenient approach with respect to herem finds expression in rabbinic literature.

6.2 The Herem Field in a Halakhic Text from Qumran

4Q251 mentions herem in three non-adjoining fragments (Frags. 10, 14, and 15), all of which deal with the issue of the priests' entitlements. Roughly one-third of the extant text of 4Q251 is about those entitlements (including Frags. 9, 11, 12, and 16). Shemesh has rearranged the conventional ordering of the document's fragments based on his theory that they comprise a work of exegesis on Exod 21:1–23:19.[16] The single verse of Exod 22:29, "You shall not put off the skimming of the first yield of your vats. You shall give me the firstborn among your sons" is the catalyst for this lengthy consideration of the priests' entitlements, suggesting to Shemesh the following reconstruction and new organization of the fragments: The skimming of the vats and firstborn concept is expanded to include firstfruits, the loaf offering, and the fruit of the fourth-year; the expansion draws on the priests' entitlements in Num 18:14–17 (Frags. 9, 10).[17] Num 18:14 includes the notice that "everything herem in Israel," prompting the authors of 4Q251 to launch into a discussion of herem property:[18]

---

[16] Ibid., 295–98; Larson, Lehmann, and Schiffman, "4QHalakha A," 25–51.
[17] Frag. 9 is mislabeled as Frag. 17 in Shemesh, "4Q251: Midrash Mishpatim," 17.
[18] Text follows and translation based on Larson, Lehmann, and Schiffman, "4QHalakha A," 37, 42–43. Shemesh has placed these three fragments in this order, understanding herem as the catchword; see "4Q251: Midrash Mishpatim," 288, 290.

Fragment 10 (final 2 lines):

(1) [וכול עץ מאכל התאנה והר]מון והזית בשנה הרביעית
(2) [יהיה כול פריו קודש הילולים כ]תרומה כל חרם לכוהן

(1) [and every edible tree, the fig, the pome]granate, and the olive in the fourth year, (2) all its fruit shall be a holy praise-offering, like] a heave-offering. Everything ḥerem is the priest's...

Fragment 14:

(3) [והבהמה הטמאה אשר]
(4) לוא יקריבו ממנה י[גאלו ושדה החרם תהיה אחזת [הכוהן
(5) [ת נפשו לשמ ל

(3) ...and the impure animal, of which [... (4) one may not sacrifice it, he] shall redeem it. And a ḥerem field will be the holding of [a priest...(5)] himself....

Fragment 15:

(6) קדש קד[שים הוא והי]ה
(7) ה[חרימו לכוהן לעוברו][19]
(8) והיה [לו] [לכוהן והאיש אש]ר
(9) אל [יאכל איש]

(6) ...It is most ho]ly and it [...] (7) They shall declare it ḥerem for a priest, for passersby (?) [... (8) And it shall be] for him [...] for the priest and the person wh[o... (9) No] one shall eat...

Shemesh summarizes the organizational scheme of this section as follows: "Having listed the presents given to the priests on the basis of Exod 22:29, the author added the dedication [i.e., ḥerem] offering, discussed in frags. 14 and 15, which also belongs to the priest, even though this halakhah's source is Leviticus 27."[20] In other words, in a comment on a verse on firstborn animals the authors of the document included a lengthy excursus on ḥerem, which incorporates Num 18:14 and verses from Lev 27 and includes a ruling of some sort on the ḥerem field.

---

[19] See §6.2.2 for other suggestions on how to read and translate this form.
[20] "4Q251: Midrash Mishpatim," 290.

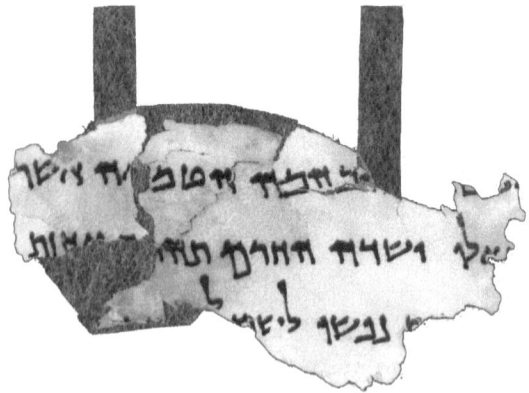

Figure 13. A halakhic text from Qumran commenting on a herem field. 4Q251, Frag. 14. Courtesy of The Leon Levy Dead Sea Scrolls Digital Library; Israel Antiquities Authority. Photo: Shai Halevi.

6.2.1 Herem and the Priests' Entitlements

The affirmation that "everything herem is the priest's..." in Frag. 10 may be an appeal to scripture to reestablish the priests as the rightful beneficiaries of these dedications. Several lines of evidence suggest that persons were handing over herem to the temple treasury rather than to priests in the late Second Temple period. The mention of herem vows in the Damascus Document (CD 6:15) comes in a section that appears to be criticizing the temple administration, for example; it resembles a similar complaint in the Rule of the Community (4Q258 1:12). But most compelling is the appearance of herem goods in the Copper Scroll, a document likely of the late first century CE that lists the whereabouts of temple treasures on the Judean countryside.[21] It places one cache of

---

[21] Scholars initially considered the Copper Scroll to be little more than imaginative folklore, greatly exaggerating the wealth of the temple. But others now view the list as a reflection of reality, hardly utopian given what we know of the temple's wealth in this period; see McCarter, "The Copper Scroll Treasure as an Accumulation of Religious Offerings," in *Methods of Investigation of the Dead Sea Scrolls and the Khirbet Qumran Site* (ed. Wise et al.; New York, NY: The New York Academy of Sciences, 1994); Lefkovits, *The Copper Scroll 3Q15: A Reevaluation. A New Reading, Translation, and Commentary* (vol. XXV; Leiden: Brill, 2000), 443–70; and Wolters, "Copper Scroll," in *Encyclopedia of the Dead Sea Scrolls* (ed. Schiffman and VanderKam; Oxford; New York: Oxford University Press, 2000). The dating is supported by the late Herodian writing style and the archaeological context in Cave 3; see ibid., 144.

herem goods (9:14–16) in a cistern near a place called Beth Tamar, apparently near the Jericho plain; and another (11:5–7) in a rock near the "garden of Zadok."²² There is nothing on the details of the herem deposits other than the fact that they were kept together and separated from the more than 60 other caches appearing in the Copper Scroll and bearing no special status. The scroll contains no mention of the priests' entitlements such as the heave-offering or redemption fees, for example. Following Judah Lefkovits, the difficult term כלי דמע is best rendered as "dedicated vessels" rather than vessels containing shares for priests.²³ In the two cases where the caches were situated on properties possibly associated with priests, they could have been deposited with the priests for safekeeping or they may have been dedicated by the priests for the temple.²⁴

Also relevant is the apparent confusion in early rabbinic circles regarding the proper beneficiaries of herem dedications. It is true that the majority view among the early rabbis follows scriptural precedent and confers these properties to priests, as reflected in this anonymous tradition (*t. Temurah* 1:5):

Which properties are deemed herem? When one says, "This herem is for a priest." Which properties are deemed hekdesh [consecrated property]? When one says, "This hekdesh is for the upkeep of the Temple."	אלו הם חרמים? האומר: חרם זה לכהן. אלו הם הקדשות? האומר: הקדש זה לבדק הבית.

This simple bifurcation would allow the donor to earmark gifts for priests as herem and gifts for the temple as hekdesh. And we see a similar perspective with regard to herem in the Mishnah, which discusses whether priests and Levites can themselves declare something to be herem given that it is their rightful due (*m. 'Arakin* 8:5).²⁵ Yet in the subsequent teaching the Mishnah changes course slightly when it addresses the question of where property dedicated by a herem vow should go when the dedicator does not specify its destination. The Mishnah refers to these kinds of dedications as סתם חרמים, "inexplicit

---

22 Park, *Finding Herem*, 81–82; Lefkovits, *The Copper Scroll 3Q15*, 306–7.
23 Ibid., 461, 505–45.
24 This depends on the assumption that Zadok's courtyard of 10:17 and Zadok's garden of 11:6 refer to properties of a priest, and that *byt ḥqṣ* in 7:9 should be read as the "house of the Hakkots family," one of the priestly divisions (Ezra 2:61; Neh 7:63; 1 Chr 24:7–10); but see Lefkovits, *The Copper Scroll 3Q15*, 225–31, where the latter is read as a "summer house."
25 A debate is framed between R. Judah and R. Simeon regarding whether Levites can declare things herem, R. Judah holding that they do not and R. Simeon that they do. The solution is that R. Judah refers to landed property, for the Levites could not dedicate anything from their inalienable pasturelands (Lev 25:34b), and that R. Simeon refers to movables.

herem dedications" (*m. 'Arakin* 8:6). According to R. Judah b. Beterah, they should go to the temple treasury—a view, one should note, that would openly contradict Num 18:14 (and Ezek 44:29). According to the sages, they are to go to the priests.[26]

The Tosefta also recognizes that some rabbis held a position similar to that of Judah b. Beterah and conferred these properties to the temple, offering a nice synthesis of the range of rabbinic understandings of things and persons declared herem as referring to gifts for priests, temple offerings, and individuals sentenced to death (*t. 'Arakin* 4:34). The teaching reads: "There are three kinds of herem: 'However, anything which a man declares herem for the Lord...' [Lev 27:28a]—these are the herem properties of the priests. 'Everything herem is a most sacred thing to the Lord' [Lev 27:28b]—these are the herem properties of the Most High. 'Any person declared herem shall not be ransomed" [Lev 27:29] —these are individuals sentenced to death by a court'." Thus, this midrash understands Lev 27:28's characterization of herem property that is "most holy to Yahweh" as referring to something pledged to the altar rather than given to a priest. It could be the case that the authors of 4Q251 were similarly aware of the problem—that one might think herem goods were to be designated for the temple treasury based on the language of scripture—and thus ruled explicitly otherwise.

A similar ambivalence is expressed in the Sifra's commentary on Lev 27, which like the Mishnah associates the dissenting view (that some herem properties can go to the temple) with Judah b. Beterah (*Behuqotai* 12:4–5).[27] In *m. Nedarim*'s discussion of the inexplicit herem dedication, the point of view is associated not with a particular rabbi but with the entire Jewish population of Galilee. Should one mark property as herem and not indicate the intended recipient, it can be assumed that the intention was for the temple, "for the Galileans are not familiar with the herem property of the priests" (2:4).[28] The Judeans of the Second Temple period, in contrast, would have been.

---

26 The disagreement between Judah b. Beterah and the sages is never unequivocally resolved, though the explanatory addendum to the sages' argument, combined with the mishnaic teaching's opening statement and its assertion of herem as the priest's individual holding, strongly suggest an inclination toward the latter; see Instone-Brewer, *Techniques and Assumptions*, 72–73.
27 Neusner, *Sifra: An Analytical Translation. Volume III: Aharé Mot, Qedoshim, Emor, Behar, and Behuqotai* (Atlanta: Scholars Press, 1988), 403.
28 The case is brought as one of several exemplars of the following principle: "Inexplicitly declared vows are more stringent, and their explanation lenient." Here the stringency is the marking of assets for the temple; the leniency would come if the dedicator explained that they are meant for priests. In the latter case one could treat the property with less scrupulousness.

Figure 14. Jerusalem with its enlarged temple complex in the first century CE. Illustration by Balage Balogh.

In short, the assertion of the right of priests to herem in 4Q251 stands in tension with other sources of its period, as well as with sources of the early rabbinic era that associate it with the temple. This is not to imply that the temple authorities were necessarily laying claim to herem in a forceful way, though one should not rule out that possibility. Rather it could have been the case that the reform came from the people, with donors voluntarily handing over movables and real estate carrying herem status to the temple rather than to priests, prompting this point of clarification in 4Q251.

This is not the only instance in this section of 4Q251 in which the rights to a priests' perquisite are reasserted on scriptural grounds. Immediately preceding the paraphrase of Num 18:14 on herem is the stipulation that fruits of the fourth-year—that is, the first year in which the fruit of a tree is permitted for consumption according to Lev 19:23–25—are to be given over to priests as a holy offering (line 1 above). Some have observed that the Qumran sectarians' claim on this issue differs from rabbinic halakhah, which has the fourth-year fruits consumed by their owners in Jerusalem or their monetary equivalent spent in its markets rather than given to the priests (as in 11Q19 60:3–4, 4QMMT B 62–63;

cf. *m. Ma'aser Šeni* 5:1–5).²⁹ On the priests' right to herem the sectarians are also submitting a word of protest, favoring the interests of individual priests over that of the municipal authorities in Jerusalem.

From Frag. 14 (line 4 above) we see that support for the notion was also drawn from Lev 27:21's characterization of the herem field as a priest's holding. The scholars who published 4Q251 thought that the herem field is mentioned merely as a comparandum for the consecration of the non-kosher animal. As they write, "Rather, it is most probable that all this line [with regard to the herem field] says is that a 'non-kosher' animal which is not redeemed by its owner (despite the requirement of the previous line that it must be redeemed) is to be considered like a donated field which becomes the property of the priests."³⁰ But placing Frag. 14 after Frag. 10, following Shemesh, allows us to recognize the extent to which the document is concerned with matters of herem. The impure consecrated animal is relevant, to be sure, given that the entire legal excursus is related to the firstborn animals of Exod 22:29, but it is not as directly on point as Lev 27's treatment of herem.

6.2.2 Sanctity Protections for Herem Property

This section of 4Q251 on the priests' entitlements moves from a consideration of what they are, affirming that herem is among them, to a discussion of their proper management once they move into the domain of a priest. That the latter topic was a matter of interest is established by the paraphrase in Frag. 16 of Lev 22:11–13, which has to do with the priest's wife and daughter and the access they enjoy to the holy offerings. The fragment reads:³¹

---

29 Larson, Lehmann, and Schiffman, "4QHalakha A," 38; Shemesh, "Laws of First Fruits," 152–53; Regev, *Sectarianism in Qumran*, 139; Yadin, *Temple Scroll*, 162–63. Another notable difference between the two is the Qumran sectarians' assertion—again following scriptural precedent (Lev 27:32)—that the animal tithe is to be gifted to priests rather than consumed by their owners in Jerusalem as the rabbis would hold (4QMMT B 63–64; cf. *m. Zebaḥim* 5:8); see Regev, *Sectarianism in Qumran*, 139; and Sanders, *Judaism, 63 BCE–66 CE*, 150.
30 Larson, Lehmann, and Schiffman, "4QHalakha A," 42.
31 On the placement of Frag. 16 after 15, see Shemesh, "4Q251: Midrash Mishpatim," 297. Lev 22:11–13, which the fragment paraphrases, reads: "No lay person should eat of the sacred donations (*wĕkol zār lō' yō'kal qōdeš*). No bound or hired laborer of a priest shall eat of the sacred donations; but a person who is a priest's property by purchase may eat of them; and those that are born into his household may eat of his food. If a priest's daughter marries a layman, she may not eat of the sacred gifts (*tĕrûmat haqqodāšîm*); but if the priest's daughter is widowed or di-

...when a woman is married to a priest, she may ea]t the food of her husband...one purchased by him and one born into his household the]se may eat of his food. A prostitute [or a profaned woman may not eat of the sanctified food. And] any sacrilege which [a person] shall commit [...] to eat, for [it] is an abomination [...] owner who has no redeemer.

But before Frag. 16 is our Frag. 15, which shall be our primary concern because of its mention of herem. It may be an important link between 4Q251's regulations on entitlements and its regulations on how those entitlements were to be managed. Its first line (line 6 above; "...It is most ho]ly and it [...]") may serve as a reminder of herem's sanctity.

Its second line (line 7 above; "They shall declare it herem for a priest so that it passes [...]") is enigmatic due to its strange final form: לעוברו. The English translation given by the editors for the form ("to make him transgress"[32]) is hardly satisfactory, for it would call for an infinitive construct *hipîl* in the Hebrew. The form may have been a participle instead. Participles of the root '-b-r do appear in the Qumran library in reference to passersby (e.g., 4Q368 10ii:6; 4Q432 13:1) or sinners (e.g., 1QS I:24, V:7). The former option is attractive given the context here, allowing perhaps for [דרך] לעוברי ("for passersby"), since the reading of the final *waw* is uncertain and what remains of the letter could in fact be *yod*. The issue of whether a guest in the house of a priest should partake of holy offerings was taken up by Philo, who in *Spec. Laws* 1.122 notes that the practice is prohibited "for the privilege belongs not to a dwelling-house but to a caste."

Another possibility is to read in the final form of the line a *dalet* instead of a *resh*, giving לעובדו ("to his laborer") or לעובדי [ביתו] ("to the laborers of his house").[33] In the same passage in *Spec. Laws*, Philo notes that assets gifted to a priest are not to be used for the wages of a hired laborer, "for he will sometimes use the gift for improper purposes..." (1.123). Only the priest's slave is free to partake of the sacred dues, "for the master's estate consists of the sacred gifts of charity by which the slave must necessarily be maintained" (1.126), following the law of Lev 22:11. Both this and the above reading are not without their problems: in both we would expect a prefixed conjunction of some sort. But both solutions would relate more directly to the rights of the priest's household to herem property, the larger issue of this part of the document.

---

vorced and without offspring, and is back in her father's house as in her youth, she may eat of her father's food. No lay person may eat of it."

32 Ibid., 43. This alternative suggestion is rooted in the text's mentioning of consecration as a trap or stumbling block (e.g., Matt 15:5, Mark 7:11), as discussed above (§5.2.2).
33 The *resh* or *dalet* is precisely on the edge of the fragment and is partially damaged; the editors place the reading of it in some doubt; ibid., 43, Pl. IV.

The third and fourth lines of Frag. 15 (lines 8 and 9 above; "And it shall be] for him [...] for the priest and the person wh[o... (9) No] one shall eat...") would appear to continue this discussion, leading into the recapitulation of Lev 22:11–13. If we assume that 4Q251 is interested in placing protections on herem property and maintaining its sanctity in the priest's home, then once again we see a noteworthy contrast with the early rabbis. After all, the rabbis were comfortable removing the sanctity of herem altogether once it moved into the domain of the priest. Consider the following teaching in *t. 'Arakin* 4:31:

"Things which are declared herem by altar priests are not subject to redemption" (*m. 'Arakin* 8:6); and they are not released in the Jubilee. Things declared herem by Israel [i.e., non-priests]—if the owners want to redeem them, the priest can allow it. Regarding things declared herem by Israel, once they come into the domain of the priest, they are like ordinary [i.e., non-sacred] things in every respect.

חרמי כהנים אין להם פדיון; ואין יוצאין ביובל. חרמי ישראל—רצו הבעלים לגאל הרשות ביד כהן. חרמי ישראל—כיון שבאו ליד כהן הרי הן כחולין לכל דבר.

Consider also its very close parallel brought as a *baraita* in *b. 'Arakin* 29a:

Our sages taught [on Tannaitic authority]: Things which are declared herem by priests are not subject to redemption, and one gives them to a priest. So long as herem properties are in the owners' house, they are like hekdesh [consecrated property] in every respect, as it is said, "Everything herem is a most sacred thing to the Lord" (Lev 27:28b). Once they are given to the priest, they are like ordinary [non-sacred] things in every respect, as it is said, "Everything herem in Israel shall be yours" (Num 18:14).

תנו רבנן: חרמי כהנים אין להן פדיון ונותנין לכהן. חרמים כל זמן שהן בבית בעלים—הרי הן כהקדש לכל דבריהן, שנאמר: כל חרם בישראל קדש קדשים הוא לה'. נתנן לכהן—הרי הן לכל דבריהן כחולין, שנאמר: כל חרם בישראל לך יהיה.

There is a deft exegetical move made in both teachings. It involves reading the phrase חרמי כהנים in *m. 'Arakin* 8:6 as referring not to herem properties declared as such *for* priests, as the Mishnah would seem to understand it, but to properties declared as such *by* priests. This would allow one to understand Lev 27:28, which prohibits the redemption of herem property and its automatic release in the Jubilee, as referring only to herem dedications made by priests themselves on their own property. (In such cases, one priest gives a gift to another, renouncing all ownership and redemption rights over it.) Once Lev 27:28 can be read in this quite limited way, these teachings would argue, scripture is left with absolutely no comment on the redemption rights for properties declared herem by everyone else. The properties can then be understood as redeemable and their status as herem revocable. As a result, the priest has the option of allowing them to be monetized.

Moreover, and even more striking given Lev 27:28's description of herem property as "most holy to Yahweh," these two teachings hold that such property takes on *ḥullîn* or non-sacred status once it moves into the domain of the priest. He is permitted to do what he sees fit with the property, including using it to pay the wages of laborers under his employ or serving its products at meals with non-priests present. In addition, herem land could be rented out to non-priests or cultivated for profit, and herem produce could be mixed or stored together with unsacred produce or consumed in a state of impurity. While the Mishnah does not include this perspective in its commentary on herem dedications in *m. 'Arakin* 8:4–7, it notes elsewhere that herem dedications can be trusted with priests of dubious status (*m. Ḥallah* 4:9), reflective of a similar tendency to lessen restrictions on such property if not divest it of sanctity altogether.

Contrast this with 4Q251, which juxtaposes the teachings on herem in Lev 27 with the rulings in Lev 22 on how the priests' dues are to be consumed by members of the household. Though 4Q251's precise regulations on the matter remain elusive, its general approach seems clear enough. The very inclusion of Lev 22 demonstrates its interest in protecting the sanctity of the priests' entitlements, while its mention of the herem field could work to apply the approach to land. The matter must have been a sufficiently pressing one to justify such a lengthy excursus (at 17 extant lines) to the law of the firstborn. The next longest excursus in 4Q251 would be the six lines of Frag. 18, which is a recapitulation of Num 35:9–11.[34]

The concern in 4Q251 over sanctity protections for herem property is mirrored in the anonymous early Jewish work of rewritten Bible called *Liber Antiquitatum Biblicarum* (*LAB*). That work contains a fascinating tale involving herem, which like 4Q251, advocates for stringent protections to it. The work itself was penned by a Judean or Galilean author referred to as Pseudo-Philo (because his work was preserved together with Philo's writings) likely in the first century CE or shortly thereafter.[35] The setting of the tale is just after the Israelite conquest

---

34 Shemesh, "4Q251: Midrash Mishpatim," 296–98.
35 For a summary of views on the dating of the work and an argument for an early second century CE date for it, see Jacobson, *A Commentary on Pseudo-Philo's Liber Antiquitatum Biblicarum, with Latin text and English Translation, Volume One* (Leiden; New York: Brill, 1996), 199–210; for a discussion of the author's provenance, which is unknowable, see ibid., 210–11.

of Canaan. It is part of a series of narratives expanding upon the character of Cenaz, who is mentioned only in passing in Judg 3:9–10 as the father of Othniel.[36]

The tale involves seven golden idols inlaid with luminescent gems that had been taken from the Amorites by Asherites and hidden on Mt. Gerizim (*LAB* 25:10). Pseudo-Philo has Cenaz identifying the Asherite miscreants by lot, putting them to trial, and burning them alive together with the stolen valuables in a *wadi* bed (*LAB* 25:2–26:2). This all recalls the account in Josh 7:1–26 of Achan, an Israelite who stole from the herem valuables that were taken by the Israelites during their conquest of Jericho; there are also echoes here of the story of Israelite apostasy in Judg 2:10–23. The book of Joshua never addresses the question of what happened to the herem valuables stolen by Achan; the initial instructions were for them to be taken from Jericho and placed in the treasury of Yahweh (*'ôṣar YHWH*; Josh 6:19). Pseudo-Philo, in his reworked account, advocates a far more stringent position. He addresses the issue of what to do with the herem valuables in an exchange between Cenaz and God, just before Cenaz is to have the Asherites executed (26:1–2):[37]

Cenaz said, "Shall we burn those precious stones in the fire or sanctify them to you, for among us there are none like these?" God said to him, "If God takes anything for his own sake from what was proscribed, what will man do?"	Et dixit Cenez: Numquid et lapides hos preciosos comburimus igni, aut sancitificamus eos tibi, quoniam non sunt in nobis similes his. Et dixit ad eum Deus: Si Deus aliquid accipit in suo nomine de anathemate, quid faciet homo?

Pseudo-Philo then has God assure Cenaz that the stones are to be destroyed, bringing into clear focus the contrast with Josh 7: The biblical account had herem going into the treasury of God, but here even God refutes any claim to property carrying that status. And the formulation of his response advocates the position quite explicitly that, in imitation of him, persons too are to refrain from deriving any benefit from herem.

Assuming that certain halakhists in Judean society were not only allowing individual priests to benefit from herem but were also ruling that once they

---

36 Othniel is the first judge called by name in the book of Judges. Pseudo-Philo has a relatively large amount of material on Cenaz (*LAB* 25:2–26:15).
37 The Latin text, likely a translation of a Greek version of an original Hebrew, follows Kisch, *Pseudo-Philo's Liber Antiquitatum Biblicarum* (Notre Dame, IN: University of Notre Dame, 1949), 184; translation follows Jacobson, *Commentary on Pseudo-Philo's LAB*, vol. 1, 135–36; on manuscript issues, see ibid., 760 (vol. 2); on the question of the Hebrew and Greek *Vorlagen*, see ibid., 215–24 (vol. 1).

moved into the priest's domain they could be treated like *ḥullîn* or entirely desanctified property, Pseudo-Philo's message can be read as a forceful appeal to scripture in hopes of reforming practices of which he disapproved. His insistence that herem be treated as entirely sacrosanct would surpass in its stringency even the point of view of 4Q251, for the authors of the latter would allow herem to enter the priest's household and be exploited there if its sanctity is protected. The early rabbinic view has them stripped of this sanctity altogether in the priest's home and farm—the most lenient view of all. Perhaps some in Second Temple Judea foreshadowed this rabbinic approach by treating herem leniently as well, giving rise to these affirmations of its sanctity in 4Q251.

6.3 Landholding by Priests

The biblical notion that God's holy men were given no portion of arable land and were sustained by the offerings of the people is expressed in later Second Temple rhetoric.[38] Ben Sira's encomium of Aaron, the founding patriarch of the priestly caste, includes a close echo of the perspective of Num 18:20 and Deut 18:1–2, both of which affirm the caste's landless status: "He added glory to Aaron and gave him a heritage; he allotted to him the best of the first fruits, and prepared bread of first fruits in abundance; for they eat the sacrifices of the Lord, which he gave to him and his descendants. But in the land of the people has no inheritance, and he has no portion among the people; for the Lord himself is his portion and inheritance" (45:20–22). The Greek Testament of Levi conveys the same message. When an angel appears to Levi in a dream, he says to him: "Your life shall be from the Lord's provision; he shall be to you as field and vineyard and produce, as silver and gold" (2:12). The fruits of labor in the field are to be replaced by the offerings of God's table.[39]

This rhetoric may be responding to the economic reality of a Judean priesthood that held land in the late Second Temple period, as they had done in earlier eras, to supplement their income from temple service.[40] Already we have seen how Lev 27 conferred to priests full ownership rights of portions of land by virtue of a herem decree. 4Q251 suggests that this practice continued through the Second Temple period. Regardless of whether priests were affording herem property

---

[38] On its use in earlier rhetoric of the era, see §§3.2–3.
[39] See also the Temple Scroll, 11Q19 60:1, which restates the message of Deut 18:1–2.
[40] See §3.3.

any special sanctity protections, we can suppose that such dedications, when they consisted of real estate, were supplementing their landholdings.

Josephus was a priest and landholder, his plot located somewhere near Jerusalem. As mentioned in Chapter 4, he recounts efforts by Titus to compensate him for his land after the war with Rome, for it had become unprofitable to him when Roman troops garrisoned in the area.[41] Titus gave him land "in the plain" instead (*Life* 422). He is silent on how he procured his land near Jerusalem, but presumably he inherited it from his father, who he calls one of "the most notable men" in the city (*Life* 7).[42] Perhaps due to the sustenance his own land provided he was able to proudly refuse offerings entitled to him as a priest during his stay in the Galilee during the war (*Life* 80). There is no hint in his writings that his ownership of land was somehow improper because he was a priest.

In one account Josephus remarks that at the time of the Samaritan schism the priests and others who followed Manasses to Gerizim were provided money, houses, and land for cultivation (*Ant.* 11.312), as if landed property was to be taken for granted as part of a priest's livelihood.[43] In another account he notes that the priests who defected to the Roman side during the siege of Jerusalem (*War* 6.113–17) agreed to do so only with the promise of protection at Gophna and the restoration of every man's property (τὰς κτήσεις; 115). These resources would have been particularly crucial to the priests with the demise of the temple and the termination of their entitlements in exchange for service at the altar. Josephus also makes note of the high priest Ananias's great wealth and reputation (*Ant.* 20.205).[44]

Though the rabbis were certainly aware of the biblical notice that the tribe of Levi received no land in biblical history,[45] they were quite comfortable neverthe-

---

41 See §4.2.
42 Adolf Büchler thinks that many of the Jehoiarib clan of priests, of which Josephus as well as the Hasmonean line was a part, originated in Jerusalem with only a faction having moved to Modiin for a period, the Maccabean family among them (1 Macc 2:1); see *The Priests and Their Cult in the Last Decade of the Temple in Jerusalem. Translated from the German by Naphtali Ginton* (Jerusalem: Mossad Harav Kook, 1966 (1895)), 135–37; see there (n. 45) his evidence showing the prominence of the Jehoiarib clan.
43 For further discussion on this passage in Josephus, see §4.2.
44 Ananias was later condemned by Josephus (*Ant.* 20.206–7) for sending servants to the threshing floors to forcibly take tithes; on this passage, see Levine, *Jerusalem*, 360; Stern, "Aspects of Jewish Society: The Priesthood and Other Classes," in *The Jewish People in the First Century*, vol. 2 (op. cit.), 587; and VanderKam, *From Joshua to Caiaphas*, 458–59.
45 See, e. g., the disagreement in *m. Ma'aser Šeni* 5:14 between R. Meir and R. Yose regarding whether priests and Levites should be included among the classes of people who need not recite the "*ma'aser* confession" stipulated in Deut 26:13–15 because they received no share in the land

less with the notion that priests could own land. The priest Eleazar ben Harsom is said in rabbinic tradition to have owned 1,000 villages in the Har Ha-melekh area (*y. Ta'anit* 69a, *b. Yoma* 35b), which was part of the Ephraim mountains south of the Carmel. Shimon Applebaum suggested that the Hasmoneans, who traditionally owned this area of Har Ha-melekh, made grants to notables of Judean society, priests among them, and in this way Eleazar ben Harsom's ancestors began accumulating wealth.⁴⁶ R. Tarfon, a priest who participated in the temple service as a young boy, is said to have held land in Galilee (*b. Nedarim* 62a).⁴⁷ In *m. Demai* 6:3–5 and *t. Demai* 7:1–15, the rabbis discuss various sharecropping arrangements between priests, Levites, and non-priests. Among the situations they consider are priests or Levites leasing their land to tenants, who in turn could be priests themselves. The teachings are specifically interested in the question of who is obligated to contribute what as a holy offering in these leasing arrangements. There is no concern expressed over whether priests and Levites should be holding land in the first place.

One should keep in mind that priests enjoyed positions not only as cultic officials in Judea but also as prominent figures in civil and judicial life, even as armed law enforcers in the Second Temple period. Josephus gives a clear sense of the power they wielded when he calls the priests of God "punishers of those who were condemned to suffer punishment" (*C. Ap.* 2.187). The concern that gifts to priests, including land grants and other valuables, could be used as a means of currying favor may lie behind condemnation of herem dedications and other vows in some of the Qumran literature. The disapproval of such dedications in the Damascus Document (CD 6:15) and the Rule of the Community (4Q258 1:12) has already been noted, though these may refer to gifts dedicated to the temple.⁴⁸ In addition to these condemnations, we find in the Temple Scroll a ruling that the priest "shall not pervert justice, and he shall not accept a bribe to perfect righteous judgment. And he shall not crave a field, a vineyard, any wealth, a house or any valuable thing in Israel" (11Q19 57:19–21). This joins other texts reproving the Jerusalem temple administrators and Judean priests

---

(i.e., proselytes and freed bondmen are exempted by all authorities). Meir exempts the priests and Levites; Yose obligates them based on their holding of the ערי מגרש, the Levitical pasturelands. Halakhah follows Yose (as in Rambam, *Hilkhot Ma'aser Šeni* 11:17). The discussion is pure theory: in the very next teaching the Mishnah notes that the *ma'aser* confession had been abolished by a certain high priest named Yohanan, perhaps one of the Oniads.

46 "Economic Life," 636; see also Fiensy, *The Social History of Palestine in the Herodian Period: The Land is Mine* (Lewiston, NY: E. Mellen Press, 1991), 36–38, 52.
47 Ibid., 52, n. 141.
48 See §6.2.1.

for misappropriating sacred revenues and committing other acts of impiety. Pesher Habakkuk, for example, condemns the "wicked priest" for amassing the people's money (1QpHab 8:6–13) and plundering the people's possessions on the countryside and in the towns of Judah (12:9–10). And the Testament of Levi portrays the priesthood as corrupt and self-serving, its members dealing illegally with sacred offerings (14–17). It predicts the progressive debasement of the priesthood in seven stages or Jubilees; in the last stage, the priests "shall be in captivity and will be preyed upon; both their land and their possessions shall be stolen" (17:9–10).[49]

Irrespective of the circumstances behind landed gifts to priests, real estate could have been held communally within priestly clans, in a manner resembling the Levitical pasturelands of the Iron Age.[50] One way such gifts could have been distributed is described in the Palestinian Talmud (y. Ḥallah 60b):[51]

(1) R. Aha, R. Abbahu in the name of R. Yohanan: "'Everything herem is a most holy thing to the Lord' (Lev 27:28b). Just as Most Holy Things are given to men of the priestly division on duty, so properties declared herem are given to men of the priestly division on duty."	(1) רבי אחא רבי אבהו בשם רבי יוחנן: כל חרם קודש קדשים הוא לה. מה קדשי קדשים לאנשי משמר, אף חרמים לאנשי משמר.
(2) Does this apply also to movable properties? For it is taught: What is the difference between landed and movable property? Landed property is given to men of the priestly division on duty, and movable property to any altar priest.	(2) מעתה אף המטלטלין? דתני: מה בין הקרקעות למטלטלין אלא שהקרקעות לאנשי משמר והמטלטלין לכל כהן.

---

49 Ecclesiastes appears to be condemning evil priests in a passing remark in 8:10: "And I saw scoundrels coming from the Holy Site and being brought to burial, while such as had acted righteously were forgotten in the city." The Psalms of Solomon have various references to the improper behavior of the cult personnel in Jerusalem (1:8, 2:3–5, 8:11–12, 8:22). The "pens" of the Qatros clan of priests are denounced in a rabbinic teaching (y. Taʿanit 69a), perhaps in a reference to land theft through the use of fraudulent contracts and bills-of-sale. See Schwartz, "Bar Qatros and the Priestly Families of Jerusalem," in *Jewish Quarter Excavations in the Old City of Jerusalem Conducted by Nahman Avigad, 1969–1982. Volume IV: The Burnt House of Area B and Other Studies. Final Report.* (ed. Geva; Jerusalem: Israel Exploration Society, 2010), 316 n. 5.
50 On the pasturelands of the Levitical settlements, see §3.2.1.
51 Text follows Guggenheimer, *The Jerusalem Talmud. First Order, Zeraïm. Tractates Maʿaser Šeni, Ḥallah, ʿOrlah, and Bikkurim. Edition, Translation, and Commentary* (Berlin; New York: De Gruyter, 2003), 383–84; translation is based on Guggenheimer.

(3) R. Yose b. R. Bun, R. Hiyya in the name of R. Sheshet: "'They shall live off the Lord's offerings by fire and his portion [of land]' (Deut 18:1). Just as offerings by fire are given to men of the priestly division on duty, so a portion of land is given to the priestly division on duty."

(3) רבי יוסי בי רבי בון רבי חייה בשם רב ששת: אשי ה' ונחלתו יאכלון. מה אישים לאנשי משמר אף נחלה לאנשי משמר.

The implication of the teaching is that clans of priests received gifts of land marked as herem and then assuming responsibility for them as communal holdings. Movables could be conferred to any priest without consideration for the service rotation schedule at the altar.

Indeed, earlier source material suggests, however remotely, that priests were holding property in communal clan-based arrangements. That clans of priests could hold their own sacred wealth, apart from the temple treasury, is indicated by the refusal of certain Sadducees to use the shekel-tax fund from the treasury for the payment of the daily sacrifices during their periods of altar service, preferring instead to provide their own animals for sacrifice lest the collected shekels have been tainted in some way.[52] The evidence for a decentralization of the tithe collection system in the Early Roman period would also suggest that clans of priests were taking individual responsibility for the collection of their entitlements.[53] One might also view the "Woe is me" traditions in *t. Menaḥot* 13:21, as well as Josephus's report (*Ant.* 20.179–81) on the infighting among clans of priests and the resulting impoverishment of certain priests, against the backdrop of a decentralized system for the collection of entitlements.[54] Certain wealthy

---

[52] The dispute is framed in *b. Menaḥot* 65a as involving whether an individual can bring the Tamid offering on his own. The Sadducees argue that it is possible, while the Pharisees require that the offering be made by the entire people via purchase using funds in the temple treasury; see Instone-Brewer, *Techniques and Assumptions*, 114–15; Regev, *The Sadducees*, 132–39; and Klawans, *Purity, Sacrifice, and the Temple*, 196–98.

[53] Aharon Oppenheimer makes this argument based on the notice regarding John Hyrcanus's tithe reforms in *y. Maʿaser Šeni* 56d, which suggest royal prerogative over the system; and on later evidence (e.g., Josephus, *Life* 80) that tithe collection would become decentralized; *ʿAm Ha-Aretz*, 30–38. See also Udoh, *To Caesar What is Caesar's: Tribute, Taxes, and Imperial Administration in Early Roman Palestine (63 B.C.E.–70 C.E.)* (Providence, RI: Brown University, 2005), 263–73; and Schmidt, *How the Temple Thinks*, 208–9, 227–29. Schmidt points out that decentralization may have been necessary merely because of the shear amount of produce that would have needed to be brought to Jerusalem.

[54] The "Woe is me" traditions of *t. Menaḥot* 13:21 condemn the houses of Boethus, Qatros, Elhanan, and Ishmael ben Phiabi for various forms of corruption. Part of the sumptuous residence of a member of the Qatros clan may have been excavated in the Jewish Quarter Area B ("the Burnt House"); Schwartz, "Bar Qatros," 308–19.

clans of priests must have succeeded in procuring not only more of the sacred shares, but also lucrative private assets, land included.

The priests' settlement patterns also point in this direction. Most lived dispersed throughout the towns and villages of the countryside but in many cases in discrete settlements or quarters within villages. Evidence for the latter from rabbinic sources has been gathered by Adolf Büchler and B.Z. Luria, though the source material makes it difficult to distinguish between realities of life in Late Roman and Early Byzantine Palestine and those of pre-70 CE history.[55] Sources quoted in these studies include a tradition in *y. Berakot* 9d referring to a "city entirely of priests" (עיר שכולה כהנים) and another in *b. Sota* 38b involves a halakhic case regarding a synagogue entirely composed of priests. A *baraita* in *y. Ta'anit* 69a appears to Büchler to be a list of statements regarding settlements with significant numbers of priests, among which are the villages of Caphrabis and Dikhrin (Kefar Zechariah), both located in the Judean lowlands, an area largely depopulated of Jews in the period of the wars with Rome.[56] Another tradition in *y. Ta'anit* 69a (and its parallel in *b. Berakot* 44a) involves the marriage at Gophna of eighty pairs of brothers, all of whom were priests, to eighty pairs of sisters, all of whom were daughters of priests.[57] Gophna, some 15 miles north of Jerusalem and a prominent town in the Herodian period, happens to be where the chief priests who defected to Rome sought shelter, as told in *War* 6.115.[58] None of this proves that priests were holding land communally, but it does show that their settlement patterns would have accommodated it.

Jericho appears to have been home to a significant number of priests, as Joshua Schwartz has discussed.[59] He relates traditions on a large priestly pres-

---

[55] Büchler, *The Priests and Their Cult*, 119–54; Luria, "Priestly Cities in the Second Temple Period," *HUCA* 44 (1973) [Hebrew], 1–18. See also Kahane, "The Priestly Courses and Their Geographical Settlements," *Tarbiz* XLVIII, no. 1–2 (1978–1979) [Hebrew], 9–30.

[56] *The Priests and Their Cult*, 139–44. Both Caphrabis and Dikhrin are in the area of Maresha/Beit Guvrin; Caphrabis is said by Josephus to have been taken in 69 CE (*War* 4.552). On the villages, see Tsafrir, Di Segni, and Green, *Tabula Imperii Romani. Iudaea-Palaestina: Eretz Israel in the Hellenistic, Roman and Byzantine Periods. Maps and Gazetteer* (Jerusalem: The Israel Academy of Sciences and Humanities, 1994), 97, 99–100. On the movement of the priests northward into the Galilee in this period, see Trifon, "Did the Priestly Courses (Mishmarot) Transfer from Judaea to Galilee after the Bar Kokhba Revolt?," *Tarbiz* 59 (1989–1990) [Hebrew], 77–93; and Safrai, "When Did the Priests Transfer to the Galilee? A Response to Dalia Trifon," ibid. 62 (1993), 287–92.

[57] Büchler, *The Priests and Their Cult*, 120.

[58] Tsafrir, Di Segni, and Green, *TIR Iudaea-Palaestina*, 137.

[59] "On Priests and Jericho in the Second Temple Period," *The Jewish Quarterly Review* 79, no. 1 (1988), 23–48.

Figure 15. The desert oasis of Jericho in the Jordan River valley, ca. 1867–1885. Many Judean priests lived at Jericho in the Second Temple period. Museum für Kunst und Gewerbe Hamburg. Photograph by Félix Bonfils.

ence at Jericho to its role as a major Hasmonean and Herodian royal administrative center. The Babylonian Talmud (*b. Taʿanit* 27a) notes in a *baraita* that half of the priestly divisions in the Land of Israel lived at Jericho. The comment is explained by the Stammaim as referring to the practice of sending half of a priestly division to Jericho during their period of service at the altar, in order to provide water and food for their brethren in Jerusalem. Based in part on this teaching, Zeev Safrai has made the argument that Jericho was home to significant temple holdings in land.⁶⁰ He also notes an early rabbinic teaching involving caprification branches attached to sycamore trees at Jericho consecrated to the temple (*m. Pesaḥim* 4:8; *t. Pesaḥim* 3:19); and the discovery at Jericho of a Persian-period YHD seal bearing the name אוריו (Uriah/Ario), which happens to be the same name of a priest whose son Meremoth is said to have been charged with weighing the silver, gold, and other vessels in the temple (Ezra 8:33 and Neh 3:3, 21).⁶¹

---

60 "The Agrarian Structure," 115–16.
61 On the caprification branches, see §7.4. The latter association suggested to Nahman Avigad that a temple estate was located at Jericho, though he would admit there was no way to confirm the identification of this אוריו with the father of the temple official; see *Bullae and Seals from a Post-Exilic Judaean Archive* (Jerusalem: Hebrew University Institute of Archaeology, 1976), 22.

Oded Lipschits and David Vanderhooft have noted that the name is quite common and could have referred to any number of persons.[62]

As for the *baraita* on the priestly divisions, Safrai interprets it to mean that during a division's service at the altar in Jerusalem, some of the priests of that division went to Jericho to work on temple estates.[63] But it could also retain a memory of a large concentration of priests having lived there. Further archaeological evidence for their presence comes from the Jericho necropolis, where a tomb of the Goliath family of priests has been excavated.[64]

Communal settlements would suit the priests' endogamous tendencies. Josephus draws attention to the great care priests take to marry within their race. He writes that there were archives in Jerusalem recording every marriage and priestly lineage, and that priests paid no regard to wealth or distinction, but only to family pedigree (*C. Ap.* 1.31–36). The Qumran sectarians advocated strict endogamy for priests, as reflected in the legislation of the Temple Scroll (4Q11 57), which stipulates that each priest should find a wife from his father's house and father's family; and in a halakhic letter (4Q396 4:11), which condemns priests for defiling the holy seed by intermarrying with non-priests.

Furthermore, the priests' communal settlements patterns are evidenced in late antiquity as well, in the form of Byzantine synagogue inscriptions and Jewish liturgical poems preserving memories of the old priestly divisions for temple service. In some cases these sources list the priestly divisions together with their corresponding settlements in the Galilee, to which they apparently moved after the wars with Rome.[65] These Byzantine testimonies seem to represent a cultural

---

62 *Yehud Stamp Impressions*, 108.
63 "The Agrarian Structure," 116.
64 Hachlili, "The Inscriptions," in *Jericho: The Jewish Cemetery of the Second Temple Period* (ed. Hachlili and Killebrew; Jerusalem: Israel Antiquities Authority; Civil Administration in Judea and Samaria, Staff Officer for Archaeology, 1999), 152–55.
65 The Caesarea-Maritima synagogue inscription, for example, gives the numbered priestly courses followed by the Galilean settlement with which each was identified; see Naveh, *On Stone and Mosaic: The Aramaic and Hebrew Inscriptions from Ancient Synagogues* (Jerusalem: Israel Exploration Society, 1978) [Hebrew], nos. 51, 52, 56; and Ameling et al., eds., *Corpus Inscriptionum Iudaeae/Palaestinae. Volume II: Caesarea and the Middle Coast* (Berlin: De Gruyter, 2011), 66–68. Two lamentations for Tisha b'Av by Eleazar ha-Qallir mention the priestly divisions; and liturgical poems by Yose ben Yose, Yannai, Yehuda, and Hadutha ben Abraham deal with priestly themes. For further discussion, see Kahane, "The Priestly Courses and Their Geographical Settlements," 9–30; Fleisher, "Regarding the [Priestly] Courses in Piyyutim," *Sinai* 62 (1968) [Hebrew], 13–40, 142–62; "The Piyyutim of Yannai the Hazzan on the Priestly Courses," *Sinai* 64 (1969) [Hebrew], 176–84; Hachlili, *Ancient Synagogues—Archaeology and Art: New Discoveries and Current Research* (Boston: Brill, 2013), 530, 669–71; and Leibner, *Settlement and History*

memory of clans of priests re-establishing themselves or remaining in new settlements in the north of Palestine. Their family- and clan-based organization could have had economic ramifications as well, with private holdings and their profits possibly incorporated across the larger circle of priests in any given settlement. These realities may be vestiges of the social and economic organization of the Judean priesthood prior to the destruction of the temple.

6.4 Summary

The institutions involving herem underwent an evolution in the Second Temple period. The old wartime and punitive anathematization for heretics, whereby persons were excommunicated or killed, and objects confiscated or destroyed in a kind of whole-burnt offering to the deity, appear to have fallen out of regular use. The war herem was drawn upon for literary effect, however, as in the books of the Maccabees and in the Qumranic literature. The taboo around anathematization led to its effectiveness as an enforcement mechanism for individuals taking vows. The herem was also used as a means of marking something as the eternal property of the deity.

Traditionally priests were entitled to properties of value that had been declared herem. Fields could be declared herem too, as we have seen in Lev 27. A fragmentary halakhic text from Qumran (4Q251) contains a rather long excursus on the matter of the priests' entitlements, including several extant lines relating to the conferral and management of herem property. Drawing on Shemesh's argument that 4Q251 is connected to Exod 21:1–23:19, we can recognize 4Q251's discussion of herem as a lengthy excursus to the issue of the firstborn in Exod 22:29. The concerns of the authors of the document surrounding herem must have been pressing enough to justify the excursus.

One noteworthy concern of 4Q251 is to assert the priests' claim to herem as their private property—a claim backed by scripture but apparently ignored or reinterpreted by some who were donating such property to the temple. The inclusion of herem goods among the treasury deposits of the Copper Scroll attests to the practice against which the authors of 4Q251 may have been filing this protest. Some early rabbinic teachings also have these dedications going not to priests but to the temple; R. Judah b. Beterah is associated with this halakhic approach. The assertion of the priests' right to herem in 4Q251 could have been in response

---

in Hellenistic, Roman, and Byzantine Galilee: An Archaeological Survey of the Eastern Galilee (Tübingen: Mohr Siebeck, 2009), 404–19.

to persons in late Second Temple Judea who were dedicating herem property to the temple.

Another concern of 4Q251 appears to have been that the sanctity of herem be maintained even after it moved into the domain of the priest. The document cites scriptural verses that seek to protect the sanctity of the priest's dues after they come into his household (Lev 22:11–13), while one of its poorly preserved sections relates to the rights of non-priests to derive benefit from herem. The tendency in rabbinic thought is to remove all special sanctity protections from this kind of property once it becomes the priest's holding. The authors of 4Q251 may have been responding to a similar leniency among halakhists active in their day. An even stricter view on herem's exploitability in the home, farm, and market is reflected in Pseudo-Philo's *LAB*, where God himself forswears all benefit from herem and asks himself, "If God takes anything for his own sake from what was proscribed, what will man do?" (26:1).

Dedications of herem fields to priests would have supplemented their income from temple service and any other landholdings in their possession. The biblical ideal of a landless priesthood subsisting on the offerings of the period continued to be far from the reality in the late Second Temple period. The clan-based settlement patterns of priests likely continued throughout the period and well into late antiquity; there may have been ramifications on how they managed the land they held, including property resulting from herem dedications. Such dedications to individual priests, or to an entire enclave of priests, must be considered against the esteem, social influence, and civic power the priests enjoyed in Judean society.

Chapter 7
An Allusion to a Sacred Tree in Paul's Letter to the Romans

7.1 Introduction

The sacralization of fields, animals, and other goods on the farm in late Second Temple Judea implies that measures would be taken to protect that sanctity. A violation could render one liable for a sacrilege penalty, which in Lev 5:15–16 is established as one unblemished ram or the monetary value thereof. We have seen how property consecrations can be weaponized by the threat of such a penalty. An individual seeking to block access to a rightful claimant to property might dedicate it to God to prevent the claimant from laying hands on it. A thief could do this with stolen goods, so could a debtor in default, a husband with property due to his wife, or the owner of a household with provisions meant for their dependents or laborers. As discussed in Chapter 5, a halakhic section of the Damascus Document works to prevent such an untoward use of the consecration mechanism by prohibiting one from vowing to the altar anything wrongfully seized; rabbinic sources deal with such a scenario by calling for the property to be desanctified somehow. The underlying threat in all cases is that one might misappropriate sacred property and thus commit an act of sacrilege.

Judean source material of the late Second Temple period rarely relates to cases of sacrilege and when it does its focus is on instances of movables wrongfully taken from temples.[1] References to sacrilege (*hierosulia*) in Josephus, for example, have to do with the robbing of temples (*War* 1.654, 5.562; *Ant.* 12.359; *C. Ap.* 1.249, 318–19) and the stealing of coins collected as part of the shekel tax (*Ant.* 16.45, 16.164, 168). A similarly generalized understanding is apparent in Philo (*Spec. Laws* 2.13, 3.83, 4.87; *Decal.* 133). The ample epigraphic, legal,

---

[1] Gordon, "Debt Fraud," 255–64; Newman, "Sacrilege," in *Encyclopaedia Judaica, Second Edition*, vol. 17 (ed. Skolnik and Berenbaum; Farmington Hills, MI: Thomson Gale, 2006), 649–50. For a summary of sacrilege in the Dead Sea Scrolls, see Milgrom, "The Concept of Maʻal in the Bible and the Ancient Near East," *Journal of the American Oriental Society* 96, no. 2 (1976), 240, nn. 29–30.

and rhetorical material on the subject from the Greco-Roman sphere is similarly concerned with the misappropriation of sacred objects from the temple.[2]

However, for ancient Jewish discussions on acts of sacrilege in an agrarian setting, outside of the context of the Jerusalem temple, we must turn to the early rabbinic material. The Mishnaic tractate of *Me'ilah* ("Sacrilege") provides a rare glimpse into some of the legal issues involved when the violation is against something growing on a farm. The teachings of *m. Me'ilah* 3:6–8, which will be explored in depth in this chapter, consider the issue of the organic derivatives of sacred fruit-bearing trees and arable fields. A debate among two students of R. Akiva in *m. Me'ilah* 3:6 has to do with the transference of sanctity from—among other things—a consecrated tree to its branches. A related teaching in 3:7 considers the perplexing case of a sacred root belonging to a non-sacred tree. In these instances, the driving question is whether the sanctity of the consecration applies to its offshoots and outgrowths.

Interestingly, a brief saying quoted by Paul in Rom 11:16b—"if the root is holy, so too the branches"—seems to relate to the same question.[3] Paul mentions the saying at the opening of a new vision for how non-Jewish Christ believers and nonbelieving Jews can join in a community of faith in the church. The allegory has non-Jewish Christ believers represented by wild branches grafted onto an olive tree, an agricultural technique used to stimulate fruit production. The nonbelieving Jews in the metaphor are broken-off branches that can be easily reattached to the tree. The allegory pushes back against presumptions among Paul's gentile audience that nonbelieving Jews had no potential for salvation and should thus be excluded entirely from the church. It also affirms the ties

---

[2] On the difficulties in distinguishing legally and practically between *hierosulia*, *asebia*, and *klope*, see Cohen, *Theft in Athenian Law* (München: C.H. Beck, 1983), 93–115. On simple protections given to trees and groves associated with sanctuaries in Classical Greece, see Lupu, *Greek Sacred Law: A Collection of New Documents* (Leiden; Boston: Brill, 2005), 26–28, 189–90; Dillon, "The Ecology of the Greek Sanctuary," *Zeitschrift für Papyrologie und Epigraphik* 118 (1997): 113–27; and Jordan and Perlin, "On the Protection of Sacred Groves," in *Studies Presented to Sterling Dow on His Eightieth Birthday* (ed. Rigsby; Durham, NC: Duke University, 1984), 153–59. For a brief treatment of Roman *sacrilegium*, see Watson, *The State, Law and Religion: Pagan Rome* (Athens, GA; London: The University of Georgia Press, 1992), 55–57; and Burriss, "The Misuse of Sacred Things at Rome," *The Classical Weekly* 22, no. 14 (1929): 105–10.

[3] An earlier and more condensed version of the discussion presented in this chapter appears in Gordon, "On the Sanctity of Mixtures and Branches: Two Halakhic Sayings in Romans 11:16," *JBL* 135, no. 2 (2016).

of the church's non-Jewish members to Israel. Scholarship on the allegory has focused almost exclusively on these important themes that emerge from Rom 11.[4]

As argued below, Paul's statement on the sanctity of the root extending to the branches is crucial evidence that proto-rabbinic sacrilege law on agricultural consecrations circulated among halakhic authorities of the late Second Temple period. The statement is, in fact, the second part of a couplet in Rom 11:16 on the concept of extended sanctity, the first of which is understood by scholars to involve the loaf from which the dough offering was taken. That part of the couplet is better read as a reference to the mixing of unsacred produce with the heave-offering. Since both sayings have to do with things consecrated for holy purposes, one can surmise that when Paul compares the Jewish and non-Jewish members of the church to the branches of an olive tree in Rom 11:17–24, he is envisioning a consecrated tree.

7.2 Sacred Admixtures

Paul uses two metaphors in Rom 11:16 to convey the notion that the sanctity of one part of something can extend to the whole. They read:

εἰ δὲ ἡ ἀπαρχὴ ἁγία, καὶ τὸ φύραμα· καὶ εἰ ἡ ῥίζα ἁγία, καὶ οἱ κλάδοι.

If the offering is holy, so too the mixture; if the root is holy, so too the branches.

While the metaphorical sense of the two sayings may be clear—that the holiness of Israel extends to new members of the church—their literal sense is not. The first statement has been erroneously taken to refer to a religious practice that

---

[4] For recent scholarship on this passage, see the compilation Wilk and Wagner, eds., *Between Gospel and Election: Explorations in the Interpretation of Romans 9–11* (Tübingen: Mohr Siebeck, 2010), XI–XXVII; and see Kruse, *Paul's Letter to the Romans* (Grand Rapids, MI: William B. Eerdmans, 2012), 421–59; Jewett, *Romans: A Commentary* (Minneapolis: Fortress Press, 2007), 650–93; Nanos, "Romans 11 and Christian-Jewish Relations: Exegetical Options for Revisiting the Translation and Interpretation of This Central Text," *Criswell Theological Review* 9, no. 2 (2012): 3–21; idem, "'Broken Branches': A Pauline Metaphor Gone Awry? (Romans 11:11–24)," in *Between Gospel and Election: Explorations in the Interpretation of Romans 9–11* (ed. Wilk and Wagner; Tübingen: Mohr Siebeck, 2010), 339–76; Johnson Hodge, "Olive Trees and Ethnicity: Judeans and Gentiles in Rom. 11.17–24," in *Christians as a Religious Minority in a Multicultural City: Modes of Interaction and Identity Formation in Early Imperial Rome* (ed. Zangenberg and Labahn; London; New York: T&T Clark International, 2004), 77–89; and Bourke, *A Study of the Metaphor of the Olive Tree in Romans XI* (Washington, D.C.: The Catholic University of America Press, 1947), esp. 65–75.

does not suit Paul's overall message. The second is hardly recognized as a statement of practical halakhah.

The standard reading of 11:16a ("if the offering is holy, so too the mixture") is that it refers to the custom when baking bread of setting aside a small part of the dough for a priest, as decreed in Num 15:18–20 and legislated upon in *m. Ḥallah.*[5] Paul's intention would then be that the offering itself sanctifies the loaf, as reflected in the NRSV translation for 11:16a: "If the part of the dough offered as first fruits is holy, then the whole batch is holy." However, the reading is problematic. This would hardly be a feasible approach for those observing basic Judean religious laws, where the marking of foodstuffs as sacred usually meant they became the rightful property of priests or Levites.[6] For if the entire loaf becomes sacred once the dough offering is set aside, not only would the sanctity of the offering become irrelevant, but the entire loaf would then be forbidden for consumption by anyone outside of the holy caste. Indeed, nowhere in ancient Jewish legal exegesis on the dough offering do halakhic authorities adopt such a ruling.[7] Reading 11:16a as a reference to the practice of Num 15:18–20 means that Paul is quoting some heretofore unattested stringent and impractical position on the dough offering, forbidding the entire loaf from regular use. Alternatively, it has been argued that Paul is using the term *hagios* to denote the ritually pure, but this would be inconsistent with his use of the term elsewhere and it would be similarly impractical.[8]

---

[5] Nanos, "Romans," in *The Jewish Annotated New Testament* (ed. Levine and Brettler; Oxford; New York: Oxford University Press, 2011), 277; Jewett, *Romans: A Commentary*, 681–82; Bourke, *The Olive Tree in Romans XI*, 65–76. On the dough offering in ancient Judaism, see Instone-Brewer, *Prayer and Agriculture* (Grand Rapids, MI; Cambridge, U.K.: William B. Eerdmans, 2004), 365–66; and Baumgarten, "The Laws of Orlah and First-Fruits in the Light of Jubilees, the Qumran Writings, and Targum P. Jonathan," *JJS* 38 (1987), 195–202.

[6] On the dedication of movables to the temple and priesthood and their concomitant sacralization, see Safrai, "Religion in Everyday Life," 817–28; Oppenheimer, *'Am Ha-Aretz*, 29–51; Schürer et al., *The History of the Jewish People*, vol. II, 257–74; Sanders, *Judaism: Practice and Belief*, 146–90; Schmidt, *How the Temple Thinks*, 191–244; and Wardle, *The Jerusalem Temple*, 23–27.

[7] On the dough offering, see Philo, *Spec. Laws* 1.132; Josephus, *Ant.* 4.71. The Mishnah in facts prohibit one from declaring an entire loaf of dough to be set aside for a priest, in keeping with the language of Num 15:21, "…the *first* of your dough" (*m. Ḥallah* 1:9). Mentions of the offering in halakhic documents of the Dead Sea Scrolls are too vague to be of any assistance. Some of them concern the separate requirement to bring to Jerusalem two baked loaves of bread at Pentecost, after Lev 23:17; i.e., 4Q251, frag. 5:4; and 4Q270, frag. 3:19.

[8] On the reading of *hagios* as denoting ritually pure, see, e.g., Bourke, *The Olive Tree in Romans XI*, 68–72. It may be true that in some cases the word approximates in New Testament usage the concept of ritual purity (טהרה), but there is no reason to suppose that purity status was affected

The second problem with the typical reading of 11:16a is the fact that the imagery it conjures would not quite suit the overall message of the chapter. The sanctification of the loaf, once the offering is set aside from it, would run precisely counter to Paul's message regarding the inalienability of Israel's heritage to the church. Applying its logic to the metaphor that follows would result in the sanctification of the olive tree only once its sacred root is removed from it. Rather, most fitting to the context would be a saying that illustrates how something is sanctified when it is added to a holy entity, not detached from it.

A solution to these issues is to understand Paul's reference in Rom 11:16a as having been to mixtures of unsacred and sacred food. In rabbinic thought, this issue was of particular significance with the heave-offering (תרומה), which was a donation to the priesthood usually consisting of batches of wine, oil, or bread and given in addition to the tithes and first fruits.[9] According to the rabbis, if a certain amount of regular food got mixed in with a batch of the heave-offering, the entire mixture remained forbidden to anyone but a priest and thus took on a level of sanctity beyond that of normal food.[10] The mixing of profane with consecrated is referred to in these teachings using verb forms of the root דמע, a word that appears in a sectarian halakhic text (4Q251, 9:3) and regularly in the Copper Scroll.[11] In Rom 11:16a Paul's reference is quite possibly to an admixture of profane and consecrated dough, given his language here, but it could also have been a batch of wine or olive oil.[12] He is saying that the sanctity transfers when something profane is added to a consecrated batch. Read in this fashion, the metaphor fits Paul's larger message on the sanctification of non-Jewish Christians once they join in the house of Israel.

---

by the separation of an offering. On the contrary, ritual purity would likely have been a sine qua non for all foodstuffs from which offerings were made; see Magness, *Stone and Dung*, 5–8.

9 See §3.3; Milgrom, *Studies in Cultic Theology*, 159–70. On the evolution of the term into the Roman era, see Sanders, *Jewish Law from Jesus to the Mishnah: Five Studies* (London; Philadelphia: SCM Press; Trinity Press International, 1990), 196. See also Schürer et al., *History of the Jewish People*, vol. II, 262–63.

10 For the general principles involving these heave-offering mixtures, see *m. Terumot* 3:1–2, 5:1–9; and Instone-Brewer, *Prayer and Agriculture*, 276–82. For a case involving a mixture of dough, see *m. Ṭebul Yom* 3:4, *t. Ṭebul Yom* 2:7, and *b. Niddah* 46b.

11 In the Dead Sea Scrolls the term seems to be a synonym of תרומה, connoting merely a dedication in the form of produce or perhaps even the vessel containing the dedication, depending on how one reads כלי דמע in 3QCopper Scroll (e.g., 11:4). See Lefkovits, *The Copper Scroll 3Q15*, 461, 505–45; and Larson, Lehmann, and Schiffman, "4QHalakha A," 35–36.

12 The term *phurama* probably has as its Hebrew equivalent עיסה, which also refers to something mixed together, usually by kneading. The Greek word is used in Rom 9:21 to refer to a lump of potters' clay and in 1 Cor 5:6 and Gal 5:9 to dough. See Strack and Billerbeck, *Kommentar zum Neuen Testament aus Talmud und Midrasch*, vol. III (München: Oskar Beck, 1922), 290.

7.3 Protecting Derivatives of Agricultural Consecrations

As for the saying in Rom 11:16b ("if the root is holy, so too the branches"), the tradition in scholarship is to read it figuratively, with Paul's inspiration thought to have come from the Hebrew Bible, where Israel is compared to an olive tree (e. g., Jer 11:16), a root (Hos 14:6), or a righteous plant (e. g., Jub 1:16).[13] But the tight parallelism of the verse would indicate that, like the first saying, this too is halakhic in nature. And there are indeed compelling similarities between the saying and early rabbinic halakhah in *m. Meʿilah* 3:6 – 8.[14] The halakhic question at the heart of Paul's statement on the holiness of the root extending to the branches involves outgrowths and byproducts of consecrations—גדולי הקדש in the parlance of the Mishnah.

The Mishnah considered the question once it has established the distinction between altar properties (קדשי מזבח) and temple-upkeep properties (קדשי בדק הבית). While only nominal protection is afforded to the byproducts of altar properties, such as the eggs of a chicken that has been set aside for sacrifice, the Mishnah confers full protection under the law of sacrilege to the byproducts of agricultural consecrations designated for temple upkeep (*m. Meʿilah* 3:5). Underlying the teaching is the recognition that consecrations for the purpose of supporting the temple derive their value from their economic worth. Things dedicated to the altar, on the other hand, are valued for other reasons, such as their ability to facilitate expiation or to serve as a gesture of gratitude in the form of a sacrifice. Since temple-upkeep consecrations are important as a source of revenue, their altar suitability is irrelevant in the eyes of the Mishnah.

The distinction is also outlined in *m. Temurah* 7:1 – 3 (=*t. Temurah* 4:12 – 13), which is the final chapter of a tractate dealing with the substitution or exchange of consecrated movables. According to these teachings, once animals and products are designated for altar sacrifice, they incur a status of intrinsic, unalterable holiness. They cannot be slaughtered outside the temple, substituted for another

---

[13] See, e. g., Jewett, *Romans: A Commentary*, 682 – 83; Maurer, "Rhíza," in *Theological Dictionary of the New Testament, Translated and Abridged* (ed. Kittel et al.; Grand Rapids, MI: Eerdmans, 1985), 986. See also n. 4 above.

[14] Mark Nanos has acknowledged a connection here to the ancient Jewish practice of consecrating agricultural real estate, though he does not make the connection with rabbinic literature on the topic; see Nanos, "Romans," 277. Bourke too alludes to the same practice; see *The Olive Tree in Romans XI*, 76 – 77. Otherwise, I have found no mention of the connection between Rom 11 and *m. Meʿilah* 3 in analyses by rabbinicists or New Testament scholars; see, e. g., Boyarin, *A Radical Jew: Paul and the Politics of Identity* (Berkeley: University of California Press, 1994), 201 – 9; Chilton and Neusner, *Judaism in the New Testament: Practices and Beliefs* (London; New York: Routledge, 1995), 62 – 70; and Strack and Billerbeck, *Kommentar III*, 290.

animal, or used to pay the wages of craftsmen; their sacred status carries through to their offspring. Animals designated for the upkeep of the temple, on the other hand, derive their holiness not intrinsically but from their value.[15] Therefore, the products of sacred things designated for temple-upkeep —such as eggs, milk, and other agricultural produce—are protected by the laws of sacrilege, while those of altar offerings are not.[16] Moreover, there is no problem exchanging one such animal for another, given that their value is the same (*t. Temurah* 1:6).

The same distinction is worked out in *m. Meʿilah* 3:6, which continues the Mishnah's discussion on the byproducts of agricultural consecrations designated for temple upkeep:

"Whatever is appropriate for the altar but not for the upkeep of the temple, for the upkeep of the temple and not for the altar, and not for the altar and not for the upkeep of the temple—the laws of sacrilege apply thereto. How so? If one consecrated a cistern full of water, a dung enclosure full of manure, a dovecote full of pigeons, a tree full of fruit, a field full of grass—the laws of sacrilege apply to them and to what is in them. But if one consecrated a cistern and later it filled with water, a dung enclosure and later it filled with manure, a dovecote and later it filled with pigeons, a tree and later it filled with fruit, a field and later it filled with grass: The laws of sacrilege apply to them but not to what is in them," the words of R. Judah.	כל הראוי למזבח ולא לבדק הבית, לבדק הבית ולא למזבח, לא למזבח ולא לבדק הבית, מועלין בו. כיצד? הקדיש בור מלא מים, אשפה מלאה זבל, שובך מלא יונים, אילן מלא פירות, שדה מלאה עשבים—מועלין בהם ובמה שבתוכן. אבל אם הקדיש בור ואחר כך נתמלא מים, אשפה ואחר כך נתמלאה זבל, שובך ואחר כך נתמלא יונים, אילן ואחר כך נתמלא פירות, שדה ואחר כך נתמלאה עשבים—מועלין בהן ואין מועלין במה שבתוכן; דברי רבי יהודה.
R. Simeon says: "One who consecrated a field or a tree—the laws of sacrilege apply to them and to their products, because they are the products of sacred property...Laborers should not eat from dried figs of sacred property. Likewise, a cow should not eat vetches of sacred property."	רבי שמעון אומר: המקדיש שדה ואילן—מועלין בהם ובגדוליהם מפני שהן גדולי הקדש...הפועלים לא יאכלו מגרוגרות של הקדש. וכן פרה לא תאכל מכרשיני הקדש.

---

15 Neusner, *History of Mishnaic Law of Holy Things: Arakhin, Temurah*, 145. On the Mishnah's teaching regarding the 13 chests for coin donations set out in the temple, see *m. Šeqalim* 6:5–6.
16 However, *b. Meʿilah* 12b would introduce an exception to the latter case, which involves the consecration of the *value* of an animal for the altar, in which case its byproducts as well are to be protected by the laws of sacrilege.

The discussion is framed as a disagreement between R. Judah and R. Simeon, who were two students of R. Akiva from the mid-second century CE.[17] R. Judah first lays out five types of landed property whose produce may not be suitable for the altar but whose sanctity is to be protected nonetheless given their economic value. They include a cistern full of water, a dung enclosure full of dung, a dovecote full of pigeons, a tree full of fruit, and a field full of crops. These are standard features on a farmstead, in keeping with the rabbinic tendency to view the independent family farm as the basic social and economic unit of society.[18] Each offers a distinct and quantifiable commodity of potential value to the temple. Moreover, the organizing principle of the teaching appears to be spatial rather than conceptual, moving from the vicinity of the house out towards farmland.[19]

R. Judah then veers into territory that would prove divisive. Should any these forms of property be empty of their respective commodities at the time of consecration—as in the case of a cistern consecrated when it had no water—the law of sacrilege according to R. Judah should only apply to the property itself rather than to its associated commodity. One could be subject to the sacrilege penalty for cutting down a consecrated tree but not for selling fruit that grows on it after the point of consecration; or for using a dovecote as a storehouse but not for selling the pigeons that are later brought into it. The view establishes that protection applies only to those commodities present at the time of consecration.

---

[17] R. Judah's opinion is attributed to R. Meir in a parallel teaching in *t. Meʿilah* 1:20, and that of R. Simeon to R. Yosé in parallel versions in *t. Meʿilah* 1:20 and *b. Meʿilah* 13a; see Epstein, *Introduction to the Mishnaic Text* (2 vols.; Jerusalem: Hebrew University Magnes Press, 2001) [Hebrew], 124, 1157.

[18] Neusner, *The Economics of the Mishnah* (Chicago: University of Chicago Press, 1990), 63–68. See also Ben Zion Rosenfeld and Haim Perlmutter's discussion of the economic status of the landowner in the rabbinic conscience; "Landowners in Roman Palestine," 338–47. They understand the term בעל הבית ("owner of the house") to refer to a widespread class of middle-income farmers who owned houses and fields and were a backbone of Jewish society in the Roman and Byzantine periods, particularly on the countryside. Tenant farming, monoculture, and *latifundia* are not the paradigms in the rabbinic materials; freeholding and polycropping are.

[19] Some commentaries view the first three commodities as exemplars of the three-part heading of the teaching; see, e.g., Neusner, *A History of the Mishnaic Law of Holy Things. Part Five*, 114; Albeck, *Shishah Sidre Mishnah: Seder Qodashim* (Jerusalem: Mossad Bialik, 1952) [Hebrew], 279; and Kehati, *Seder Kodashim. Vol. 3: Temurah, Keretot, Meʾilah, Tamid, Middot, Kinnim. A New Translation with a Commentary by Rabbi Pinhas Kehati. Translated by Rabbi Nahum Wengrove.* (Jerusalem: Eliner Library, 1995), 33–34. But this does not account for their order of presentation or for the presence of the tree and field.

R. Simeon claims otherwise. He holds that natural derivatives of the consecration that grew after the point of dedication should also be protected. He says, "One who consecrated a field or a tree—the laws of sacrilege apply to them and to their products, because they are the products of sacred property (גדולי הקדש)." He recognizes here the equivalency between agricultural produce and the eggs of a chicken donated for temple-upkeep, as established in the previous teaching (*m. Meʿilah* 3:5). But he also distinguishes between agricultural produce and the commodities associated with a cistern, dung enclosure, and dovecote. The former are organic outgrowths and fundamental components of the property's value in a way that commodities associated with the latter properties—water, dung, and pigeons—are not. Cisterns, after all, cannot produce water on their own.

As support for his opinion, R. Simeon quotes halakhic traditions holding that laborers on consecrated property should not eat the dried figs from fig trees, while cows put to work on such property should be muzzled lest they eat even vetches among the produce.[20] The protection of these products of relatively minimal value implies, according to the approach of R. Simeon, that all those of greater value should be similarly subject to the laws of sacrilege. The Mishnah does not resolve his dispute with R. Judah, but by placing his view at the end of the discussion on the matter, it seems to be pushing its audience toward him.[21] Halakhic tradition would indeed follow R. Simeon.[22]

How does this relate to Paul's statement in Rom 11:16b? Its verbatim equivalent is absent in the Mishnaic discourse, but its underlying principle is indeed present. The maxim that a holy root sanctifies the branches is one way to articulate the view—in the typically rabbinic style of casuistic discourse—that all outgrowths and byproducts of sacred real estate become sanctified by virtue of their association with the consecration, as illustrated in the Mishnah through the cases of fruit that grows on a tree and crops in a field. R. Simeon represents the point of view holding that these organic outgrowths are an essential aspect of the value of the property at the time of consecration. The sanctity of the endowment extends to its derivatives. In the case of Paul's root (*riza*), he probably

---

[20] See also *t. Meʿilah* 1:21 and a statement by R. Ahadboi bar Ami in *b. Meʿilah* 13a, both of which are discussed above, §5.2.2.
[21] For a discussion on the use of disputes and borderline cases in the Mishnah, see Alexander, *Transmitting Mishnah*, 155–67.
[22] Maimonides, *Trespass* 5:6.

Figure 16. An olive tree is trimmed in Ottoman Palestine. G. Eric and Edith Matson Photograph Collection. Library of Congress Prints and Photographs Division.

had in mind the roots and trunk of an olive tree. The word *riza* can connote both, and with olive trees the two are often indistinguishable.[23]

In the continuation of the Mishnah's discussion of the topic, there may be another thematic connection to Rom 11:16b. The subsequent cases fall under a category for which the following ruling applies: "they may not be used but are not subject to sacrilege" (לא נהנין ולא מועלים). The ruling is a linking device hold-

---

[23] In Jud 6:13 the word is used for the base of a mountain, and in 1 Tim 6:10 and Heb 12:15 for the foundation of things; see Maurer, "Rhíza," 985–86.

ing together much of the material of the chapter. The cases are as follows (*m. Meʿilah* 3:7):

[If] the roots of a privately owned tree grow into sacred property, or that in sacred property grows into privately owned property—they may not be used but are not subject to sacrilege. A well gushing forth from a sacred field—it may not be used but is not subject to sacrilege. [But if] it goes outside of the field, it may be used.	שרשי אילן של הדיוט באין בשל הקדש, ושל הקדש באין בשל הדיוט—לא נהנין ולא מועלין. המעין שהוא יוצא מתוך שדה הקדש—לא נהנין ולא מועלין. יצא חוץ לשדה—נהנין ממנו.
Water which is in a golden pitcher—it may not be used but is not subject to sacrilege. [If] one put it into the flask [for pouring onto the altar for the Water Libation on Sukkot]—it is subject to sacrilege. The willow-branch [set beside the altar on Sukkot]—it may not be used but is not subject to sacrilege. R. Eleazar b. Tsadoq says: "The elders would take some of it for their *lulab*s."	המים שבכד של זהב—לא נהנין ולא מועלין. נתנו בצלוחית—מועלין בהם. ערבה—לא נהנין ולא מועלין. רבי אלעזר ברבי צדוק אומר: נותנין היו ממנה זקנים בלולביהם.

The cases relevant to this discussion include the roots of a sacred (*hekdesh*) tree extending into non-sacred property, the roots of a non-sacred tree extending into sacred property, and a stream of water pouring forth from a spring on sacred property.[24] In the Mishnah, these kinds of marginal outgrowths are deemed an insufficiently vital component of the initial endowment to justify protection under the laws of sacrilege, and their usage is merely ruled improper rather than punishable.[25] Nevertheless, once the roots are sacred, the tree itself be-

---

[24] The consecrated stream recalls the river Ilissos adjacent to the sacred field of Herakles at Kynosarges by Athens; and a moat consecrated to Athena next to the bath of Diochares in the city; see Papazarkadas, *Sacred and Public Land*, 21–23, n. 38. In *b. Baba Batra* 26b, Rabina is recorded as introducing the principle of a minimum length between the roots and tree; anything extending up to 16 cubits is considered identical to the tree in every regard and anything beyond 16 cubits follows the rulings of the Mishnah; see also Maimonides, *Trespass* 5:6.

[25] One does not normally consecrate a tree because of the use-value of its roots, as significant in extent and weight as olive tree roots may have been; on an olive tree in post-war France with roots weighing over 2,300 kg, see Todd, *Lysias, Speeches 1–11*, 486. And usage fees for a spring were likely collected at its source rather than downstream. The point is further illustrated in the continuation of *m. Meʿilah* 3:7 by the distinction between the water in any consecrated golden pitcher and that in the golden flask used to draw water up to the temple in the rite of Sukkot (*m. Sukkah* 4:9). In the first case, the act of consecration was intended to confer to the temple a valuable golden pitcher; the water it contains is inconsequential and thus undeserving of protection. In the second case, the water for the Sukkot rite is an essential part of the religious act,

comes off-limits for regular use and as such is imbued with the sanctity extending from the roots. Here too the sanctity of a core or foundational component extends to its outgrowths, even though the sacrilege penalty is remitted by the Mishnah. This may be another permutation of the teaching quoted by Paul.

From this point until the end of the chapter, the Mishnah discusses cases demonstrating that the intention behind the consecration matters when establishing protections for it. The pericope ends with the following teaching: "One who consecrates a forest—the whole of it is subject to sacrilege. Temple treasurers who bought wood—the wood is subject to the law of sacrilege, but the chips and foliage are not" (m. Meʿilah 3:8b–c).[26] The difference involves purpose and intent. In the first instance, the forest is consecrated as a long-term source of income for the treasury and thus all its valuable products are to be protected, wood chips and foliage included. In the second, however, the temple needs wood beams for a construction project. This does not automatically consecrate the forest whence they came, but only the products whose value is consecrated for the altar. Incidentally, later rabbis would be uncomfortable with the idea that the consecration of building materials was a necessary part of temple construction, mostly because the (non-priestly) laborers would be vulnerable to sacrilege penalties for deriving any benefit from them, such as resting on the sacred beams.[27] Generally speaking, however, in rabbinic thought the sacred source does not generate protectable derivatives when those derivatives were obviously never intended or expected to be a part of the consecration.

Post-Mishnaic sources continue working out the potential use-value of consecrated land. A Toseftan teaching reads: "[In the case of] one who lives under the covering of a [sacred] dovecote or cave—they may not be used but the laws of sacrilege do not apply. One who lives on landed [sacred] property—the laws of sacrilege apply" (t. Meʿilah 1:24). Here the benefit derived from the shade-cover of a natural cave or of a dovecote is deemed insufficiently correlated with the purpose of the original consecration. A cave or dovecote could have been designated for use as a burial chamber, a place of storage, or an animal

---

given its use in an altar libation, and thus its consecration-value is worthy of protection. In order to demonstrate that the water is not consecrated in the golden flask because of touching, the Mishnah brings the final case of the willow branches set beside the altar at Sukkot in order to decorate it (m. Sukkah 4:5). Even the sanctity of the altar does not transfer onto the branches—for the altar was, after all, not consecrated to hold up branches, but as the table of God.

26 See a nearly identical parallel in t. Meʿilah 1:25.
27 See b. Meʿilah 14a for a discussion and R. Shmuel's resolution: בונים בחול ואח"כ מקדישים ("One builds first and then consecrates"). See discussion above (§5.3) on wood brought down from Lebanon by King Agrippa for temple construction (War 5.35–36).

pen, among other things, but the fact that they can provide shade to a squatter is ruled to be too far from its inherent value to warrant special protection. However, in the case of landed property, part of its value lies in its ability to be built upon and lived upon, thus calling for special protection and justifying the distinction in the Toseftan teaching.

A further refinement occurs in an anonymous early rabbinic tradition quoted in *b. Meʿilah* 13a, which recognizes the value of a sacred (i.e., hekdesh) field not just as arable land but also as a workspace. The teaching reads: "One who stamps *qalʿîlîn* in a sacred field [שדה הקדש] commits sacrilege." The word *qalʿîlîn* is probably a corruption of *qalʿîlon*, a special kind of bluish wool imitating the color of *tĕkēlet*, though Haas (following Rashi) understands the word to refer to a legume.[28] The point of the teaching is that stomping or threshing on a sacred field can render one liable for sacrilege. The Stammaim relate this teaching to the regulation established in *m. Meʿilah* 5:1 that "plucking" is a prerequisite for sacrilege to occur, apparently because they read *qalʿîlîn* to be a type of plant. Rabina provides an artful solution to the potential contradiction by noting that the dirt of the ground is not technically attached to it, and so by using the ground in industrial activity one is actually benefiting from something that is plucked.[29] The teaching unit demonstrates a further effort by the early rabbis to place protections on sacred fields in recognition of their potential value.

This survey of teachings on sacrilege as it relates to sacred landholdings can be taken as another instance of the rabbinic concern with what Eyal Regev has called the cognitive category of intention.[30] The approach is not one that sees sanctity as transferrable, dynamic, and capable of effecting cosmic change, as evidenced in priestly writings of the Hebrew Bible and in certain works of the

---

28 Jastrow, *A Dictionary of the Targumim, the Talmud Babli and Yerushalmi, and the Midrashic Literature* (New York: Pardes, 1950), 1372; see *t. ʿAbodah Zarah* 6:1 for another use of the word. Haas translates it as "*qlʿylyn* wood"; *The Talmud of Babylonia, An American Translation. XXXII: Meilah and Tamid* (Atlanta: Scholars Press, 1986), 68.
29 See also Maimonides, *Trespass* 5:5: "If one threshed in a consecrated field, he committed sacrilege, because its dirt helped the threshing and consequently he benefited from the dirt and reduced the value of the field."
30 "The Sadducees, the Pharisees, and the Sacred: Meaning and Ideology in the Halakhic Controversies between the Sadducees and the Pharisees," *Review of Rabbinic Judaism* 9 (2006), 136–40; see also Neusner, *Judaism: The Evidence of the Mishnah* (Chicago: University of Chicago Press, 1981), 270–83; Eilberg-Schwartz, *The Human Will in Judaism: The Mishnah's Philosophy of Intention* (Atlanta: Scholars Press, 1986); and Comstock, "A Behavioral Approach to the Sacred: Category Formation in Religious Studies," *Journal of the American Academy of Religion* 49, no. 4 (1981).

Qumran sectarians.³¹ Rather it is one with ad hoc and flexible definitions of sanctity, which serve a deeper religious purpose, of growing closer to God or of working to fulfill his will. The perspective is evidenced already in Hag 2:10–13.³² There the prophet answers in the negative regarding whether the sanctity of a piece of sacrificial meat transfers to food touching it, reflecting a rejection of the holiness contagion. The result is an ethic of great personal responsibility with regard to the protection of holiness.

The rabbinic teachings on sacrilege surveyed here fall into this category because they place the greatest importance on the intention behind the endowment and they reject the conferral of sanctity merely because of proximity, association, or touch. Agricultural products of consecrated properties are sacred because their consecration—the rabbis hold—was meant to set aside those very products for sacred purposes. In other words, the root sanctifies the branches not because holiness transfers by touch between the two but because future outgrowths and byproducts were intended to be a part of the original endowment.

The closeness of the halakhic sayings in Rom 11:16 to the Mishnah's teachings may be explained by Paul's own literacy in proto-rabbinic tradition.³³ More specifically, it is possible that the saying on the holy root sanctifying the branch is an early attestation of halakhic discourse whose evolution in the first and second centuries CE would result in the teachings of *m. Meʿilah* 3:6–8. Jacob Neusner has posited that the teachings of Tractates *ʿArakin* and *Meʿilah*—in fact the entire order of *Qodašim*, for that matter—reach no further back in time than the rabbinic circles of Yavneh and Usha from the late first

---

31 Regev hypothesizes that Sadducean halakhah resembled the latter; see "The Sadducees, the Pharisees, and the Sacred," 137; idem, "Priestly Dynamic Holiness and Deuteronomic Static Holiness," *VT* 51, no. 2 (2001): 243–61; and idem, "Reconstructing Qumranic and Rabbinic World-Views: Dynamic Holiness vs. Static Holiness," in *Rabbinic Perspectives: Rabbinic Literature and the Dead Sea Scrolls. Proceedings of the Eighth International Symposium of the Orion Center for the Study of the Dead Sea Scrolls and Associated Literature, 7–9 January, 2003* (ed. Fraade et al.; Leiden; Boston: Brill, 2006), 99–112.
32 As Carol Meyers and Eric Meyers have written in their commentary on this verse, "Each individual becomes responsible for adherence to standards that lead toward holiness"; *Haggai, Zechariah 1–8*, 56. They too note the ideological similarity to rabbinic halakhah.
33 For Paul's possible background in Pharisaic circles, see Acts 22:3. On the "re-Judaized" Paul as portrayed in scholarly understandings of him, see Gager, *Reinventing Paul* (Oxford; New York: Oxford University Press, 2000), 54–57; Andrew S. Jacobs, "A Jew's Jew: Paul and the Early Christian Problem of Jewish Origins," *The Journal of Religion* 86, no. 2 (2006), 258–65; and the various contributions in Nanos and Zetterholm, eds., *Paul within Judaism: Restoring the First-Century Context to the Apostle* (Minneapolis: Fortress Press, 2015).

to the middle of the second century CE.³⁴ The two halakhic sayings in Rom 11:16 would thus join the limited halakhic material from the Dead Sea Scrolls and other sources pre-dating 70 CE, surveyed in earlier chapters, to suggest that these teachings on agricultural consecrations were being worked out as part of a broader intellectual tradition reaching back into the days of the Second Temple.³⁵

7.4 Sacred Olive Trees and the Allegory of Romans 11

In addition to reflecting Paul's connectedness to proto-rabbinic scholastic discourse, this reading of Rom 11:16b can help contextualize the olive tree allegory that follows in 11:17–24. In the allegory, the non-Jewish Christ believers are represented by wild branches grafted onto an olive tree, while nonbelieving Jews are detached branches that can easily be reconnected to the tree. The allegory is conceptually and rhetorically linked to 11:16b by its opening phrase—"If some of the branches were broken off"—with the conditional particles *ei de* recurring across both verses and the linking word *klados* signaling a continuous line of thought. These points of connection suggest that throughout the teaching Paul has in mind the same olive tree, which has been consecrated to God. The grafting of new branches would then have as its primary goal the rejuvenation of the tree, while symbolically it would stand for the joining of all of Israel together as a holy church regardless of the stock from which its branches derive. The allegory, in other words, is governed by 11:16b and it seems to involve a sacred (hekdesh) tree.

This reading calls into question the view that Paul is intentionally subverting the usual practice of grafting domesticated branches onto wild trees as an argument against anti-Jewish bias on the part of his gentile audience.³⁶ The notion is

---

34 On *Meʿilah* he has written that "the tractate begins its history at Yavneh and rests not only on facts supplied by Scripture but also on conceptions contributed by Yavneans"; *A History of the Mishnaic Law of Holy Things. Part Six: The Mishnaic System of Sacrifice and Sanctuary*, 239. And on *ʿArakin* he writes that it "is the work of Ushans who chose to create a tractate on Temple-income and property"; ibid., 263.
35 For a summary of studies that take this longer view on the development of proto-rabbinic halakhic discourse, see §3.1.
36 W.D. Davies "Paul and the Gentiles: A Suggestion Concerning Romans 11:13–24," in *Jewish and Pauline Studies* (Philadelphia: Fortress Press, 1984), 153–63. Philip Esler argues similarly that it is meant to assert the superiority of the Judeans; "Ancient Oleiculture and Ethnic Differentiation: The Meaning of the Olive-Tree Image in Romans 11," *JSNT* 26, no. 1 (2003): 103–24. Sigurd Grindheim understands it as furthering Paul's position that gentile Christians should

that his audience would have been familiar with the usual practice of grafting domesticated branches onto wild trees, rather than vice versa, and would have recognized the message underlying Paul's subversion of it. But there is nothing suggesting irony in Paul's language here and, if the root and trunk were consecrated, new branches from undomesticated trees could indeed have been grafted into trees to assure their productivity, as A.G. Baxter and J.A. Ziesler have shown.[37] A comment by Columella (ca. 4–70 CE) says as much.[38] This suits Robert Jewett's claim that Paul was envisioning equality between the Jewish and gentile members of the church, as well as arguments by E.P. Sanders and Daniel Boyarin regarding the centrality of faith in Christ as the great equalizer within the community.[39]

Interestingly, the grafting of branches onto sacred olive trees was practiced in classical Greece as a means of propagating olive trees called *moriai*, as discussed by Nikolaos Papazarkadas and S.C. Todd.[40] The *moriai* are said to derive from a primordial olive tree planted by Athena on the sacred rock of the Acropolis. Through the classical period, certain trees in Attica were recognized as *moriai* and their products regulated by the polis. They provided among other things the prizes of oil at the Panathenaic festival.[41] A speech of Lysias, a Greek orator of the fifth century BCE, records the trial of a certain Nikomakhos who was accused of pulling up the low fence that surrounded one of these trees to mark it as

---

not be prideful with respect to nonbelieving Jews; *The Crux of Election: Paul's Critique of the Jewish Confidence in the Election of Israel* (Tübingen: Mohr Siebeck, 2005), 158–68; Grindheim was anticipated by Havemann, "Cultivated Olive—Wild Olive: The Olive Tree Metaphor in Romans 11:16–24," *Neotestamentica* 31, no. 1 (1997): 87–106. Mark Nanos has articulated a similar argument in "Broken Branches," 339–76.

37 Baxter and Ziesler, "Paul and Arboriculture: Romans 11:17–24," *JSNT* 24 (1985): 25–32.
38 Forster and Heffner, *Lucius Junius Moderatus Columella on Agriculture* (Cambridge: Harvard University Press, 1968), 85.
39 Jewett, *Romans: A Commentary*, 685. Sanders has written that "Jew and Gentile may be 'in' the olive tree only on the condition of faith"; *Paul, the Law, and the Jewish People* (Minneapolis: Fortress Press, 1983), 180–98, esp. 193–94. Boyarin asserts that Paul's vision of particularist univeralism would have all others as dead wood, signifying the Jewish tribe now replaced by a community defined by grace; *A Radical Jew: Paul and the Politics of Identity*, 201–9. For a similar view, see Chilton and Neusner, *Judaism in the New Testament: Practices and Beliefs*, 62–70.
40 Papazarkadas, *Sacred and Public Land*, 260–84; Todd, *Lysias, Speeches 1–11*, 482–87. See also Burford, *Land and Labor*, 24, n. 23.
41 Aristotle, *Athenaion Politeia*, 60.1–3. See Papazarkadas's argument that the trees were a kind of sacred realty conceptually and legally distinct from other forms of polis property; *Sacred and Public Land*, 277–84.

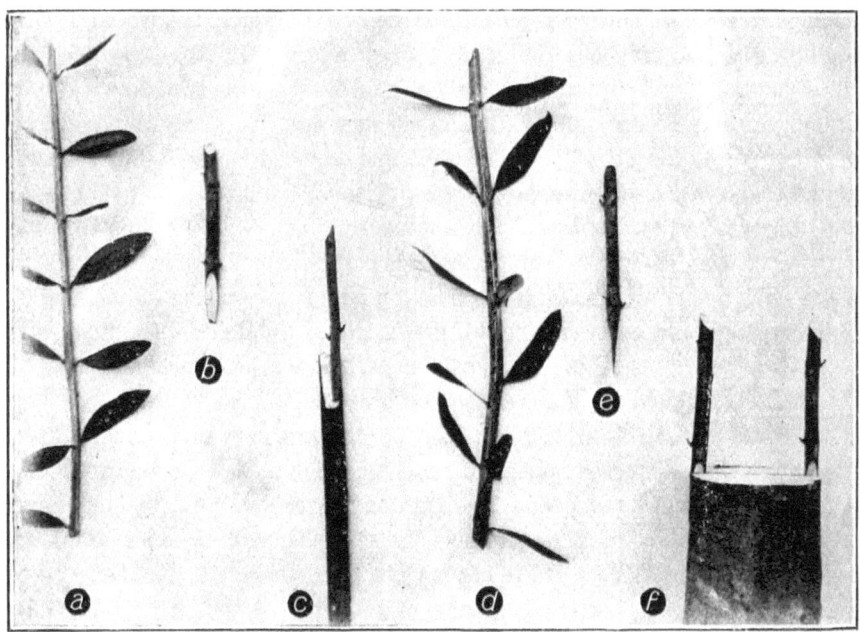

Figure 17. The grafting process for an olive branch using the tongue (a–c) and cleft (d–f) techniques. *Journal of the Department of Agriculture, Victoria* 1912, 128, Fig. 8.

sacred.[42] His act was taken as a crime of sacrilege. Todd has suggested that the grafting of new branches onto the venerable *moriai* was meant to preserve them once they had ceased to be productive on their own.[43] Perhaps Paul had a similar custom in mind when he formulated this allegory.

A second ramification of reading Rom 11:17–24 as involving a consecrated tree regards early Jewish halakhah on agricultural consecrations. Paul's message would imply that the sanctity of the roots and trunk transfer not only to natural outgrowths of the tree but also to branches grafted onto it. In fact, an anecdote in *m. Pesaḥim* 4:8 draws on that principle. It involves instances in which sages of the late Second Temple period condemned the anonymous "men of Jericho" for, among other things, allowing the non-sacred use of caprification branches that were attached to consecrated sycamore trees.[44] The branches would have assist-

---

[42] The defendant may have pulled up the stump instead, depending on how one understands the term *sēkos*; see Todd, *Lysias, Speeches 1–11*, 485–87.

[43] Ibid., 482.

[44] The Toseftan version (*t. Pesaḥim* 3:19) provides, in place of the difficult word גמזיות ("caprification branches"), the word גזויות ("branches"); see Jastrow, *Dictionary*, 252.

ed in pollination and the overall health of the tree.⁴⁵ As such they would be similar in function to branches grafted onto an olive tree. The sages saw these caprification branches as fundamental to the value of the consecrated tree and thus prohibited their use according to the laws of sacrilege. Branches grafted onto an olive tree would presumably be given the same protection, even if they were not natural outgrowths of consecrated property.

Incidentally, grafting as an agricultural technique was well known to the early rabbis, who referred to it as הרכבה. It is particularly relevant to Tractate *Kil'ayim*, which is concerned with the possibility that the grafting of one species onto another could be in violation of the scriptural prohibition against mixing seeds (Lev 19:19; see, e.g., *m. Kil'ayim* 1:7). Thus, we hear in *t. Kil'ayim* 1:10 that sages prohibited the grafting of palm branches onto olive trees. (No such issue would have arisen with the grafting of olive branches onto an olive tree.)

The metaphorical use of this grafting technique in the Jewish context did not end with Paul. In *b. Pesaḥim* 49a, vine grafting between high-quality grapes and wild grapes is compared to the marriage of a scholar into an uneducated family; and in *b. Yebamot* 63a, the image of vine grafting is used in a statement attributed by R. Eleazar to describe the joining of Ruth and Naomi to Israel. Marc Rastoin has suggested a connection between the latter and Rom 11:17–24.⁴⁶ His argument is that the Babylonian Talmud preserves a haggadic tradition that circulated among Jewish literati already in the days of Paul; and that Paul drew inspiration from the tradition in his formulation of the allegory. The argument is perhaps undermined by the terminology of R. Eleazer's statement, which calls upon grafting techniques in vine cultivation (as in *m. Šebi'it* 2:6) rather than olive tree cultivation.⁴⁷ Paul's connection to proto-rabbinic oral tradition is far better attested by the two halakhic sayings he quotes in Rom 11:16, both of which relate to much larger and chronologically closer bodies of rabbinic tradition.

---

45 Mudge et al., "A History of Grafting," *Horticultural Reviews* 35 (2009), 441–45.
46 "Une bien étrange greffe (Rm 11, 17): Correspondances rabbiniques d'une expression paulinienne," *RB* 114, no. 1 (2007), 73–79. The relevant statement reads: אמר ליה הקדוש ברוך הוא לאברהם: שתי ברכות טובות יש לי להבריך בך, רות המואביה ונעמה העמונית ("The Blessed Be He said to Abraham: Two good blessings I have to engraft for you: Ruth the Moabite and Naomi the Ammonite...").
47 The relationship to the root ברך ("to bend, bend a knee, bless") is explained by the fact that the vine can be bent over and drawn into the ground to promote the growth of an independent plant; see Jastrow, *Dictionary*, 195. For tree grafting, the term is the causative form הרכיב; see *m. Pesaḥim* 4:8 and *m. Šebi'it* 2:6.

7.4 Sacred Olive Trees and the Allegory of Romans 11 — 223

An even more compelling association between the metaphor of Rom 11:17–24 and rabbinic allegory appears in the Palestinian Talmud. A curious midrash by the Amora R. Levi, who lived ca. 300 CE, reads as follows (*y. Kil'ayim* 27b):[48]

"Your wife shall be like a fruitful vine within your house; your sons, like olive saplings around your table" (Ps 128:3). Just as there is no grafting with olive trees, so may there not be any worthlessness among your children.

אשתך כגפן פוריה בירכתי ביתך בניך כשתילי זתים סביב לשולחנך. מה זיתים אין בהן הרכבה, אף בניך לא יהא בהן פסולת.

Though the early rabbis were indeed familiar with olive grafting as an agricultural technique, as evidenced by the above-mentioned teaching in *t. Kil'ayim* 1:10, R. Levi takes notice of the fact that the Psalmist speaks only of saplings regarding the olive tree and not of grafted branches. To him this demonstrates that Jewish families should never be adulterated through the engrafting of foreign branches. In sharp contrast to Paul, where foreign branches sustain the tree, R. Levi has them polluting it.

The neat subversion of the message of Rom 11:16–24 begs the question of whether R. Levi was intentionally engaging in anti-Christian polemic here. It is true that R. Levi's statement has been fully incorporated into another matter, leaving no overt reference in the redacted text to Paul's allegory.[49] Furthermore, the purity of bloodlines was a matter of general interest in rabbinic circles, as similar figurative uses of the term פסולת ("worthlessness") attest.[50] Yet it is also the case that in at least one other place R. Levi is invoked in an oral tradition (Lev. Rabbah 6:6) grounded in anti-Christian polemic, as Burt Visotsky has discussed.[51] If R. Levi's statement in *p. Kil'ayim* 27b indeed relates to Rom 11:16–24, it would be one of a string of ancient comments on it that glosses over its association with agricultural consecrations.[52] It appears that already in

---

[48] Text and translation follow Mandelbaum, *The Talmud of the Land of Israel: A Preliminary Translation and Explanation. Volume 4: Kilayim* (Chicago: University of Chicago Press, 1990), 38–39.
[49] The teaching unit is interested in whether R. Levi's statement contradicts *t. Kil'ayim* 1:10, which speaks of the grafting of olive branches onto a palm tree. See ibid., nn. 176–77.
[50] See, e.g., *Sifre Deuteronomy* 312 and *Genesis Rabbah* 68.
[51] "Anti-Christian Polemic in Leviticus Rabbah," in *Fathers of the World: Essays in Rabbinic and Patristic Literatures* (Tübingen: J.C.B. Mohr, 1995), 95–96.
[52] For texts and discussion, see Bourke, *The Olive Tree in Romans XI*, 73–76.

antiquity the ancient Jewish practice to which Paul refers in Rom 11:16b was falling into obscurity.

7.5 Summary

When Paul introduces the olive tree allegory of Rom 11:17–24 with an axiom on a root sanctifying the branches (11:16b), he is quoting a halakhic teaching on agricultural consecrations. It is immediately preceded by another teaching in 11:16a, that one reinterpreted here as involving the sanctification not of the loaf once the dough offering is set aside, but of an admixture of a heave-offering and non-sacred food. Both sayings set up the allegory that follows by establishing the principle of extended or transferrable sanctity: just as the heave-offering sanctifies the batch when it is intermixed with the non-sacred, so too a holy root sanctifies the branches of a tree. The latter statement is rhetorically linked to the allegory that follows, suggesting that Paul is envisioning the grafting of non-sacred branches onto a sacred olive tree. The practice of agricultural consecrations of this sort is a little-known feature of early Judean life, which has a parallel in the sacred *moriai* trees of classical Greece, where the grafting of new branches was a means of perpetuating them.

By quoting a halakhic saying relevant to the practice of consecrating trees, Paul is offering some proof—limited though it may be—that proto-rabbinic circles were discussing the matter of offshoots and outgrowths of agricultural consecrations long before the codification of the Mishnah. The disagreement in *m. Meʻilah* 3:6 between two students of R. Akiva involves the very issue at the center of Rom 11:16b. R. Simeon has the roots sanctifying the branches and rules that misuse of the latter should be subject to the sacrilege penalty; R. Judah disagrees. The Mishnah presents R. Simeon's argument as the preferred position and it would later become standard halakhah. Paul and Rom 11:16b have never received due credit for being the earliest known evidence of the viewpoint. Regarding the letter to the Romans, this new reading may do little more than help us appreciate the rhetorical artistry of Paul's language and his connectedness to proto-rabbinic scholastic discourse. On the Judean practice of consecrating agricultural real estate, however, the saying is a vital piece of evidence among rare pre-Mishnaic attestations.

Summary and Conclusions

Judean priests in the Second Temple period (516 BCE–70 CE) took an active role in the farming life on the countryside, far beyond the temple precinct in Jerusalem. Among their ranks were individuals engaged in agrarian finance, which called for land survey and appraisal. There were priests who were landholders themselves, hiring labor, trading their goods in the local markets, and acquiring new land through gifts or purchase. Some cultivated relationships with patrons who supported them, while others served in the role of patron to farmers in need, providing them with loans. The priests' role was also to maintain the integrity of agricultural spaces set apart as sacred. The temple, after all, was not the only place in which an ancient worshipper of Yahweh encountered sacred space. The sacralization of plots, trees, or plants on the farm could infuse generic, undifferentiated space with deep spiritual meaning. It could forge a connection between the farmer, the deity, and the temple. Priests helped facilitate that connection and protect it.

Three types of sacred land emerge from the Judean source material: (1) land hypothecated to the deity as security on debt; (2) land whose produce was meant to sustain the temple, including small plots, trees, or plants consecrated as in-kind offerings; and (3) herem land, which was viewed as the eternal holding of the deity but was effectively the property of priests. By the late Second Temple period there appears to have been debates over whether herem property, real or movable, was an entitlement of priests or was to join the incorporated assets of the temple.

The first type—land hypothecated to the deity as security on debt—is reflected in Lev 27, which is a late source of the Pentateuch that was likely appended to the Holiness Code in the Persian period. It was argued above that the chapter helps regulate indebtedness to the deity. When a Judean farmer needed subsistence credit to make it through a harvest season, he could turn to the priests of Yahweh. The priests would then call for a vow of consecration to be taken by the landowner, at which point the field is pledged to Yahweh in a manner approximating a regular sale. Like sales in the Holiness Code, these conveyances expired at the Jubilee. In exchange for the field, Yahweh's priests issued to the landowner a sum of silver equal to the property's valuation; this is the loan. Repayment required an additional fifth on top of the valuation amount. The fifth was an interest payment, but it could be masked because the holy shekel standard, at 20 gerahs, was 20% lighter than the common shekel standard, at 24 gerahs. This allowed priests to lend out and collect the same number of shekels, even if repayment called for 20% more in silver weight (or its in-kind equivalent). The 20% rate of interest was standard for silver loans in the ancient Near East.

The 50-shekel valuation benchmark given in Lev 27:16 for a field with a capacity of a bushel of barley seed allowed for neat payments in installments annually or even monthly. At full repayment the land was "redeemed," which meant the title returned to the farmer and the field's sacred status was removed. This kind of fiscal arrangement, which could have been quite long term, is but one of several that is implied by the laws of Lev 27 and predicated upon the use of hack-silver currency. Deities were regularly appealed to in the ancient world as sources of credit, their temple treasuries often the main repositories of local cash and valuables. The loan-giving operations of the temple of Apollo at Delos offer a well-documented example.

By the late Second Temple period, Lev 27 appears to have been interpreted as regulating a donative mechanism consisting of the commutation into cash of in-kind offerings. This interpretation of Lev 27 has persisted in scholarship too, obscuring field sacralization as hypothecation to secure a loan. Yet it must be noted that a state of indebtedness to the deity could have arisen from reasons extending beyond the receipt of a silver loan from him. It could have come about from services rendered by a priest, for example, or as part of a conditional vow made to the deity. In any case, the extent to which the fiscal mechanisms of Lev 27 were put into practice in the Persian period (or later) is unknown.

The second type of sacred land evidenced from the sources is temple land. This refers to a plot designated for temple upkeep. In the ancient world, temples could activity manage production in the environment through the large estates they owned. They could rent out their plots to help fund their cult of worship or to grow their deity's treasuries as a mark of honor. The phenomenon stretches back to the early days of large temple organizations in the ancient Near East but is particularly well attested in the archives of the mid-first millennium BCE from Uruk and Ebabbar. Babylonian temple land could be leased out to agricultural entrepreneurs in complex business arrangements. In the ancient Greek world, sacred land that was associated with temples or cult organizations was bestowed a distinct status and was managed through specific administrative channels within the city economy.

The Hebrew Bible knows virtually nothing of temple land. The pasturelands of the Levitical settlements and herem land are both holdings of individual priests or clans of priests, not the incorporated assets of a temple administration. The closest thing to temple land in the Hebrew Bible is the sacred reserve of Yahweh in Ezekiel's Temple Vision (Ezek 45:1–6; 48:8–14)—an imaginary blueprint for how the Jerusalem temple was to function in an idyllic age. Likely authored in the Persian period, the Temple Vision has the sacred reserve consisting of a beautiful tract surrounding the temple, with houses for the priests and Levites, and pasture for the holy animals. It appears to have been inspired somewhat by the Levitical settlements (Num 35:1–8, Josh 21:1–40). In the Vision the holy men of Yahweh are to be freed of all self-sufficiency endeavors, the temple is to be entirely supported by the people too, and the sacred reserve is not to be cultivated. This program of reform would have been a stark contrast with the realities on the ground in the late sixth and fifth centuries BCE, when Judea was still reeling from the Babylonian wars.

Nehemiah's reforms in the mid-fifth century BCE incorporated Yahweh's wealth in the city and, through the implementation of the shekel tax, led the temple on a path toward institutional self-sufficiency (Neh 10:1–40, esp. 33–39). By the late Persian period, surveyors in Idumea were associating tracts in the countryside with the incorporated assets of the God of Israel, as shown by an ostracon (Lemaire no. 283). The ostracon is a geographic survey of the fourth century BCE that seems to refer to a "plot of the House of Yeho." This would be the earliest known archaeological attestation of Yahwistic temple land. Whether the plot was under the auspices of a heretofore unattested temple in Idumea is not clear.

As evidenced in a papyrus of the mid-second century BCE from Egypt, a synagogue at Arsinoe-Krokodilopolis was abutted by a sacred garden that may have been associated with it (*CPJ* I, no. 134, lines 18–21). Meanwhile, the Yahwistic temple at Leontopolis in Egypt appears to have had land affiliated with it too. The founding of the temple can be attributed to Ptolemy VI Philometer, who gave the Judean priest Onias IV, scion of the line of Jerusalem high priests now displaced by the Hasmoneans, an old pagan sanctuary site and an adjacent tract of land in the mid-second century BCE. The account of the founding is brought twice by Josephus (*War* 7.430, *Ant.* 13.66–71). The attributes of the temple's tract of land, as they emerge from Josephus's account, suggest that it was considered sacred by the Ptolemaic fiscal authorities—a status that would have brought certain tax benefits. In the *Antiquities* version of the tale of the temple's founding, Josephus has Ptolemy VI and Cleopatra I incredulous that a Jew would set up a sanctuary in such an impure place with sacred animals roaming about. In Josephus's eyes these holdings were stained by the impurity of the place's pagan past.

Concerns over appropriate sources of revenue for the Jerusalem temple pervade an account in 1 Macc 10, where the Seleucid ruler Demetrius tries to entice the Hasmonean ruler Jonathan and the Judean people to side with him in his struggles with Alexander Balas. Among a list of enticements, Demetrius writes: "Ptolemais and the land adjoining it I have given as a gift to the sanctuary in Jerusalem, to meet the necessary expenses of the sanctuary" (1 Macc 10:39).

The offer was likely the product of the imagination of the author of 1 Maccabees, and it would have been seen by many Judeans as an unacceptable source of revenue for the temple. Ptolemais was a major center of foreign, Hellenizing culture in the region—a cosmopolitan space enjoying close economic ties with the western world—whose population had shown hostility to Jonathan and the Judeans. Had Jonathan accepted it as a gift for the temple, he would have been working precisely counter to the efforts of his Maccabean forebears, who went to war to drive out the foreign, non-Judean presence from Jerusalem. The ethic of purification from foreign influence is at the heart of the narrative in 1 Maccabees. While other offers by Seleucid kings, such as tax concessions, are received favorably in the book, 1 Maccabees includes no instance of a Hasmonean king accepting foreign gifts for the temple. Resistance to foreign support for the temple would later resurface in the policy adopted in 66 CE of rejecting all gifts and offerings made by Romans to the God of Israel (*War* 2.409–10).

As for actual land that profited the Jerusalem temple in the late Second Temple period, the Egyptian-Jewish philosopher Philo of Alexandria proclaims its existence when he writes, "The temple has for its revenues not only plots of land, but also other possessions of much greater extent and importance, which will never be destroyed or diminished" (*Spec. Laws* 1.76). A remark by Josephus in his paraphrase of 1 Macc 10:43 is noteworthy too. He writes that liberation was to be granted by the Seleucid authorities to all asylum-seekers within the temple "or in any place belonging to it" (*Ant.* 13.56). Finally, there are clues in the halakhic literature of the late Second Temple period of a scholastic interest in the category of consecrated land. They include a section of the Damascus Document (CD 16:14–17 and Qumranic parallels) and a saying quoted by Paul in Romans 11:16. These are forerunners to a larger group of teachings on hekdesh ("consecrated property") in rabbinic texts, particularly in tractates *'Arakin* and *Me'ilah*.

The Damascus Document, which is a foundational text of the Essenes of the mid-second century BCE, reads the field consecrations of Lev 27 not as hypothecary pledges on a loan from the priests of God but as freewill offerings to his temple. Though fragmentary, the laws in CD 16:14–17 appear to reflect a concern over the use of consecration as a means of blocking access to forcibly seized property or to provisions that household dependents enjoyed. A similar practice is denounced in Mark 7:9–13, where support for parents is cut off once that support is offered to God. Early rabbinic commentary on field consecrations is concerned with this kind of untoward behavior too. The rabbis consider the case of a debtor who had hypothecated his land to secure a loan and then later consecrated that land to the temple in Jerusalem, perhaps to keep the creditor from seizing it. In such a case, the temple is to put the land up for public auction and the creditor is to be paid with the proceeds of the sale (*t. ʿArakin* 4:1 and parallels).

According to rabbinic sources, anything of value in the home and farm could be declared hekdesh for the temple. The protection of its sanctity is the responsibility of the dedicant. A common way to desacralize such property was to sell it, the sanctity of the object or plot of land now transferring to the coins or other currency resulting from the sale. Though the word hekdesh is unattested in Jewish source material prior to the Mishnah, we see in the Damascus Document the setting of parameters for the category. Concerns over unwitting acts of sacrilege must have pervaded farms where agricultural property had been consecrated. We are without any kind of data, however, on the extent of such consecrations in Judea or where they were located.

The short statement by Paul in Rom 11:16 is critically significant as a link between Second Temple practice and rabbinic teachings. When Paul uses the phrase "if the root is holy, so too the branches," he is quoting a teaching of practical halakhah on agricultural consecrations. The teaching holds that sanctity transfers to outgrowths of consecrated trees. According to rabbinic halakhah, the transference only occurs with endowments meant for temple-upkeep purposes, not for offerings meant to be consumed at the altar. The difference is worked out in a disagreement between R. Judah and R. Simeon (*m. Meʿilah* 3:6). Paul offers evidence that the legal tradition on agricultural consecrations has a history reaching long before the teachings of these early rabbinic sages were put into writing ca. 200 CE.

How the temple authorities managed the upkeep and revenues of such plots —whether they were involved in any way, for that matter, prior to the conferral of the harvests or their monetary equivalent—is impossible to ascertain. One would expect harvest-time payments to the temple and some sort of regular oversight by its officials, in the least, and of course more thoroughgoing intervention in cases where property was consecrated to dispossess a rightful claimant. One would also expect boundary stones, ropes, signs, or other forms of demarcation to call attention to these plots. In any case, when raw materials for construction were necessary, or agricultural products such as animals, wheat, oil, and wine were needed for the cult of sacrifice, the temple appears to have relied not on its own estates, but rather on donations from the people and on certain private suppliers with whom it regularly did business. Moreover, it used the shekel tax as its primary source of revenue. Theologically, this meant that support for the temple was to come from all members of the house of Israel, whose sustenance and succor the altar assures and for whose transgressions the altar atones. This value system stressed funding from a diffuse system of giving rather than through revenue-generating estates.

The development of the shekel tax as a means for the entire people to contribute to the sustenance of their sanctuary in Jerusalem led, by all accounts, to significant surpluses in the sacred treasury by the late Second Temple period. It more than covered the cult's regular operating experiences in that period, helping too with the municipal needs of Jerusalem. Moreover, the three annual week-long pilgrimages to the temple city would have injected the temple with cash, swelled its storerooms with produce, and sustained the city's markets. In addition to this form of resource extraction from the Judean economy, the sacralization of individual plots presumably fed the holy coffers too, however modestly.

The third type of sacred land—herem land—connotes eternal, irrevocable possession by the deity. Such land effectively became the private property of priests, supplementing the income they received from agricultural dues such as the heave-offering, the first fruits, and the firstborn. That a herem field became the private landholding of a priest is made clear from Lev 27:21. The conferral of herem to the priesthood as an entitlement is also affirmed by Num 18:14 and Ezek 44:29. In the Iron Age, herem anathematization had been a mechanism of warfare, akin to a whole-burnt offering to the deity given up in exchange for victory on the battlefield and assuring total annihilation of the enemy population. It was also used against heretics. In the Second Temple period, properties confiscated from excommunicated individuals may have been given herem status, as suggested by Ezra 10:8. And the priesthood's claim to any property marked in this way continued to be asserted, as evidenced in a halakhic text from Qumran (4Q251, Frags. 10, 14, 15). The text is a running commentary of a section of Exodus. The length of the excursus and its marginal relevance to the Exodus passage attest to the urgency of the issue to the authors of 4Q251. While the conferral of herem to the priesthood is scripturally backed, it would appear to have been undermined by persons who were gifting such properties to the temple, prompting this word of protest in 4Q251.

The authors of 4Q251 also offer legislation on how the priest is to protect the sanctity of herem property once it moved into his domain. These regulations may have come in response to a leniency among certain circles allowing for the desacralization of herem property, which would have facilitated its sale or the sale of its proceeds in the local markets. There is a rejection of this lenient approach in a story told in Pseudo-Philo (*LAB* 25:2–26:2), where it is written, "If God takes anything for his own sake from what was proscribed, what will man do?"

The Second Temple priesthood was a loosely regulated firm consisting of administrators in Jerusalem and many priests spread throughout Judea. While the Levitical settlements of the Hebrew Bible appear to have not been a formal feature of the Judean administrative regime in the Second Temple period, as they were in the era of the late Judahite monarchy, priests continued to dwell together and perhaps even hold land together in the period. Their coalitions were strictly endogamous and founded upon shared values, but their manner of subsistence may have diverged considerably from clan to clan. The same goes for their involvement in the cultivation of land. Landed gifts to priests may have been given out of a desire to support a local clan of priests, or to bless an area's farmland through the permanent presence there of a priest. They may also have been out of rank self-interest, given the social power priests enjoyed in Second Temple society. Individuals may have gifted land to them to curry favor, to dispossess an heir, or to rid oneself of the responsibilities of land ownership. There would have been similar motivations behind the gifting of movables to them.

The priests' involvement in the agrarian economy of Second Temple Judea is but one element of their embeddedness in society. Their dispersal throughout the region had been a feature of the late Iron Age monarchy and it would continue to be so through late antiquity. The patterns of social and economic interaction that governed their relationship with villagers resulted from the failures of the temple to adequately provide for them, pushing them into land ownership. The biblical ideal of a priesthood free from the responsibilities of the farming life or working as if in quarantine within the confines of the sacred precinct in the city gives a false impression. These priests were fully entrenched in the Judean landscape. The self-subsistent communal farming life of the Essenes can provide some insight into how many of them lived. So can the agrarian economies of monastic farms in late antiquity.

Bibliography

Abel, P.F.-M. *Les livres des Maccabées*. Paris: Gabalda, 1949.
Abraham, Kathleen. *Business and Politics under the Persian Empire: The Financial Dealings of Marduk-nāṣir-apli of the House of Egibi (521–487 B.C.E.)*. Bethesda, MD: CDL Press, 2004.
Adams, Samuel L. *Social and Economic Life in Second Temple Judea*. Louisville: Westminster John Knox Press, 2014.
Ahlström, G.W. *Royal Administration and National Religion in Ancient Palestine*. Studies in the History of the Ancient Near East I. Leiden: Brill, 1982.
Albeck, Chanoch. *Shishah Sidre Mishnah: Seder Qodashim*. Jerusalem: Mossad Bialik, 1952 [Hebrew].
Albertz, Rainer. *A History of Israelite Religion in the Old Testament Period. Volume I: From the Beginnings to the End of the Monarchy*. Louisville: Westminster John Knox Press, 1994.
Albertz, Rainer. *A History of Israelite Religion in the Old Testament Period. Volume II: From the Exile to the Maccabees*. Louisville: Westminster John Knox Press, 1994.
Albertz, Rainer. *Israel in Exile: The History and Literature of the Sixth Century B.C.E.* Society of Biblical Literature, Studies in Biblical Literature 3. Leiden; Boston: Brill, 2004.
Alexander, Elizabeth Shanks. *Transmitting Mishnah: The Shaping Influence of Oral Tradition*. Cambridge: Cambridge University Press, 2006.
Alexander, Elizabeth Shanks. "The Orality of Rabbinic Writing." Pages 38–57 in *The Cambridge Companion to the Talmud and Rabbinic Literature*. Edited by Charlotte Elisheva Fonrobert and Martin S. Jaffee. Cambridge; New York: Cambridge University Press, 2007.
Alles, Gregory. "Religion and Economy." Pages 601–12 in *Religion, Theory, Critique: Classic and Contemporary Approaches and Methodologies*. Edited by Richard King. New York: Columbia University Press, 2017.
Alt, Albrecht. "Festungen und Levitenorte im Lande Juda." Pages 306–16 in *Kleine Schriften zur Geschichte des Volkes Israel*. Vol. 2. München: Beck'sche Verlagsbuchhandlung, 1953.
Altmann, Peter. *Economics in Persian-Period Biblical Texts: Their Interactions with Economic Developments in the Persian Period and Earlier Biblical Traditions*. FAT 109. Tübingen: Mohr Siebeck, 2016.
Altmann, Peter. "Tithes for the Clergy and Taxes for the King: State and Temple Contributions in Nehemiah." *The Catholic Biblical Quarterly* 76, no. 2 (2014): 215–29.
Altmann, Peter. "Ancient Comparisons, Modern Models, and Ezra-Nehemiah: Triangulating the Sources for Insights on the Economy of Persian Period Yehud." Pages 103–20 in *The Economy of Ancient Judah in Its Historical Context*. Edited by Marvin Lloyd Miller, Ehud Ben Zvi, and Gary N. Knoppers. Winona Lake, IN: Eisenbrauns, 2015.
Amaru, Betsy Halpern. *Rewriting the Bible: Land and Covenant in Post-Biblical Jewish Literature*. Valley Forge, PA: Trinity Press International, 1994.
Ameling, Walter, Hannah M. Cotton, Werner Eck, Benjamin Isaac, Alla Kushnir-Stein, Haggai Misgav, Jonathan Price, and Ada Yardeni, eds. *Corpus Inscriptionum Iudaeae/Palaestinae. Volume II: Caesarea and the Middle Coast*. Berlin: De Gruyter, 2011.
Anderson, Gary A. *Sacrifices and Offerings in Ancient Israel: Studies in Their Social and Political Importance*. Harvard Semitic Monographs 41. Atlanta: Scholars Press, 1987.

Anderson, Gary A. *Sin: A History.* New Haven: Yale University Press, 2009.
Andrew S. Jacobs. "A Jew's Jew: Paul and the Early Christian Problem of Jewish Origins." *The Journal of Religion* 86, no. 2 (2006): 258–86.
Aperghis, G. G. *The Seleukid Royal Economy: The Finances and Financial Administration of the Seleukid Empire.* Cambridge: Cambridge University Press, 2004.
Aperghis, G.G. "Jewish Subjects and Seleukid Kings: A Case Study of Economic Interaction." Pages 19–41 in *The Economies of Hellenistic Societies, Third to First Centuries BC.* Edited by Zofia Archibald, John Kenyon Davies, and Vincent Gabrielsen. Oxford; New York: Oxford University Press, 2011.
Applebaum, Shimon. "The Hasmoneans—Logistics, Taxation, Constitution." Pages 9–29 in *Judaea in Hellenistic and Roman Times: Historical and Archaeological Essays.* Edited by Shimon Applebaum. Studies in Judaism in Late Antiquity 40. Leiden; New York: Brill, 1989.
Applebaum, Shimon. "Economic Life in Palestine." Pages 631–700 in *The Jewish People in the First Century: Historical Geography, Political History, Social, Cultural and Religious Life and Institutions.* Vol. 2. Edited by Shemuel Safrai, Menahem Stern, David Flusser, and W. C. van Unnik. Compendia rerum Iudaicarum ad Novum Testamentum 2. Assen: Van Gorcum, 1976.
Ascough, Richard S. "Benefaction Gone Wrong: The 'Sin' of Ananias and Sapphira in Context." Pages 91–110 in *Text and Artifact in the Religions of Mediterranean Antiquity: Essays in Honour of Peter Richardson.* Edited by Stephen G. Wilson and Michel Desjardins. Studies in Christianity and Judaism 9. Waterloo, Ontario: Wilfrid Laurier University Press, 2000.
Ashkenazi, Jacob and Mordechai Aviam. "Monasteries and Villages: Rural Economy and Religious Interdependency in Late Antique Palestine." *Vigiliae Christianae* 71, no. 2 (2017): 117–33.
Auld, A. Graeme. "Cities of Refuge in Israelite Tradition." Pages 37–48 in *Joshua Retold: Synoptic Perspectives.* Edinburgh: T&T Clark, 1998.
Avigad, Nahman. *Bullae and Seals from a Post-Exilic Judaean Archive.* Qedem 4. Jerusalem: Hebrew University Institute of Archaeology, 1976.
Avni, Gideon and Zvi Greenhut. *The Akeldama Tombs. Three Burial Caves in the Kidron Valley, Jerusalem.* IAA Reports 1. Jerusalem: Israel Antiquities Authority, 1996.
Baden, Joel S. "The Violent Origins of the Levites: Text and Tradition." Pages 103–16 in *Levites and Priests in Biblical History and Tradition.* Edited by Mark A. Leuchter and Jeremy M. Hutton. Ancient Israel and Its Literature 9. Atlanta: Society of Biblical Literature, 2011.
Baesens, Viviane. "Royal Taxation and Religious Tribute in Hellenistic Palestine." Pages 179–200 in *Ancient Economies, Modern Methodologies: Archaeology, Comparative History, Models and Institutions.* Edited by Peter F. Bang, Mamoru Ikeguchi, and Hartmut G. Ziche. Pragmateiai 12. Bari: Edipuglia, 2006.
Bagnall, Roger S. *The Administration of the Ptolemaic Possessions outside Egypt.* Columbia Studies in the Classical Tradition IV. Leiden: Brill, 1976.
Bar-Kochva, Bezalel. "Manpower, Economics, and Internal Strife in the Hasmonean State." Pages 167–96 in *Armées et fiscalité dans le monde antique: [colloque] Paris 14–16 octobre 1976.* Edited by André Chastagnol, Claude Nicolet, and Henri van Effenterre.

Colloques nationaux du Centre national de la recherche scientifique 936. Paris: C.N.R.S., 1977.
Barag, Dan. "The Coinage of Yehud and the Ptolemies." *INJ* 13 (1999): 27–38.
Barag, Dan. "A Silver Coin of Yohanan the High Priest and the Coinage of Judea in the Fourth Century B.C." *INJ* 9 (1986): 2–21.
Barclay, John M. G. *Jews in the Mediterranean Diaspora from Alexander to Trajan (323 BCE–117 CE)*. Edinburgh: T&T Clark, 1998.
Barclay, John M.G. "The Empire Writes Back: Josephan Rhetoric in Flavian Rome." Pages 315–32 in *Flavius Josephus and Flavian Rome*. Edited by J. C. Edmondson, Steve Mason, and J. B. Rives. Oxford; New York: Oxford University Press, 2005.
Bartlett, John R. *The First and Second Books of the Maccabees*. Cambridge: Cambridge University Press, 1973.
Bartlett, John R. "1 Maccabees." Pages 1–15 in *The Oxford Encyclopedia of the Books of the Bible*. Vol. 2. Edited by Michael D. Coogan. Oxford; New York: Oxford University Press, 2011.
Batsch, Christophe. *La guerre et les rites de la guerre dans le judaïsme du deuxième Temple*. Supplements to the Journal for the Study of Judaism 93. Leiden: Brill, 2005.
Baumgarten, Joseph M. "The Laws of Orlah and First-Fruits in the Light of Jubilees, the Qumran Writings, and Targum P. Jonathan." *JJS* 38 (1987): 195–202.
Baumgarten, Joseph M. *Qumran Cave 4. The Damascus Document (4Q266–273)*. Discoveries in the Judaean Desert XVIII. Oxford: Clarendon Press, 1996.
Baumgarten, Joseph M., James H. Charlesworth, Lidija Novakovic, and Henry W. L. Rietz. "Damascus Document, 4Q266–273 (4QD^{a-h})." Pages 1–185 in *The Dead Sea Scrolls: Hebrew, Aramaic, and Greek Texts with English Translations. Volume 3: Damascus Document II, Some Works of the Torah and Related Documents*. Edited by James H. Charlesworth and Henry W. L. Rietz. Tübingen; Louisville: Mohr Siebeck; Westminster John Knox Press, 2006.
Baumgarten, Joseph M. and Daniel R. Schwartz. "Damascus Document (CD)." Pages 1–185 in *The Dead Sea Scrolls: Hebrew, Aramaic, and Greek Texts with English Translations. Volume 2: Damascus Document, War Scroll, and Related Documents*. Edited by James H. Charlesworth. Tübingen; Louisville: J.C.B. Mohr (Paul Siebeck); Westminster John Knox Press, 1995.
Baxter, A.G. and J.A. Ziesler. "Paul and Arboriculture: Romans 11:17–24." *JSNT* 24 (1985): 25–32.
Bedford, Peter R. "The Economic Role of the Jerusalem Temple in Achaemenid Judah: Comparative Perspectives." Pages 3*–20* in *Shai le-Sara Japhet. Studies in the Bible, its Exegesis and its Language*. Edited by Moshe Bar-Asher, Dalit Rom-Shiloni, Emanuel Tov, and Nili Wazana. Jerusalem: The Bialik Institute, 2007.
Bedford, Peter R. "The Persian Near East." Pages 302–29 in *The Cambridge Economic History of the Greco-Roman World*. Edited by Walter Scheidel, Ian Morris, and Richard Saller. Cambridge: Cambridge University Press, 2007.
Bedford, Peter R. "Temple Funding and Priestly Authority in Achaemenid Judah." Pages 336–51 in *Exile and Return: The Babylonian Context*. Edited by Jonathan Stökl and Caroline Waerzeggers. Beihefte zur Zeitschrift für die alttestamentliche Wissenschaft 478. Berlin/Boston: De Gruyter, 2015.

Ben-Arieh, Yehoshua. "Perceptions and Images of the Holy Land." Pages 37–53 in *The Land that Became Israel: Studies in Historical Geography*. Edited by Ruth Kark. New Haven; Jerusalem: Yale University Press; Magnes Press, 1989.

Ben-David, Arye. *Talmudische Ökonomie: die Wirtschaft des jüdischen Palästina zur Zeit der Mischna und des Talmud*. Hildesheim; New York: Georg Olms, 1974.

Ben-Yehuda, Eliezer. *Milon Ha-Lashon Ha-Ivrit*. Berlin: Langenscheidt, 1908–1959 [Hebrew].

Ben Zvi, Ehud. "Introduction: Writings, Speeches, and the Prophetic Books." Pages 1–30 in *Writings and Speech in Israelite and Ancient Near Eastern Prophecy*. Edited by Ehud Ben Zvi and Michael H. Floyd. SBL Symposium Series 10. Atlanta: Society of Biblical Literature, 2000.

Ben Zvi, Ehud. "The Concept of Prophetic Books and Its Historical Setting." Pages 73–95 in *The Production of Prophecy: Constructing Prophecy and Prophets in Yehud*. Edited by Diana V. Edelman and Ehud Ben Zvi. London; Oakville, CT: Equinox, 2009.

Benovitz, Moshe. *Kol Nidre: Studies in the Development of Rabbinic Votive Institutions*. Brown Judaic Studies 315. Atlanta: Scholars Press, 1998.

Bergsma, John S. "The Restored Temple as 'Built Jubilee' in Ezekiel 40–48." *Proceedings, Eastern Great Lakes and Midwest Biblical Societies* 24 (2004): 75–85.

Bergsma, John Sietze. *The Jubilee from Leviticus to Qumran: A History of Interpretation*. Supplements to Vetus Testamentum 115. Leiden; Boston: Brill, 2007.

Berlinerblau, Jacques. *The Vow and the 'Popular Religious Groups' of Ancient Israel*. JSOT Supp. 210. Sheffield: Sheffield Academic Press, 1996.

Berthelot, Katell. "The Biblical Conquest of the Promised Land and the Hasmonaean Wars according to 1 and 2 Maccabees." Pages 45–60 in *The Books of the Maccabees: History, Theology, Ideology. Papers of the Second International Conference on the Deuteronomical Books, Pápa, Hungary, 9–11 June, 2005*. Edited by Géza G. Xeravits and József Zsengellér. Supplements to the Journal for the Study of Judaism 118. Leiden; Boston: Brill, 2007.

Bickerman, E.J. "A Question of Authenticity: The Jewish Privileges." Pages 295–314 in *Studies in Jewish and Christian History: A New Edition in English Including The God of the Maccabees*. Vol. 1. Ancient Judaism and Early Christianity 68/1. Leiden; Boston: Brill, 2007.

Bilde, Per. "Atargatis/Dea Syria: Hellenization of Her Cult in the Hellenistic-Roman Period?" Pages 151–87 in *Religion and Religious Practice in the Seleucid Kingdom*. Edited by Per Bilde, Troels Engberg-Pederson, Lise Hannestad, and Jan Zahle. Studies in Hellenistic Civilization 1. Aarhus: Aarhus University Press, 1990.

Bingen, Jean. *Hellenistic Egypt: Monarchy, Society, Economy, Culture*. Hellenistic Culture and Society 49. Berkeley: University of California Press, 2007.

Bintliff, John. "The Implications of a Phenomenology of Landscape." Pages 27–45 in *Die Landschaft und die Religion: Stuttgarter Kolloquium zur Historischen Geographie des Altertums 9, 2005*. Edited by Eckart Olshausen and Vera Sauer. Geographica Historica 26. Stuttgart: Franz Steiner, 2009.

Blenkinsopp, Joseph. "Did the Second Jerusalemite Temple Possess Land?" *Transeuphratène* 21 (2001): 61–68.

Block, Daniel I. *The Book of Ezekiel, Chapters 25–48*. The New International Commentary on the Old Testament. Grand Rapids, MI: W.B. Eerdmans, 1997.

Boer, Roland. *The Sacred Economy of Ancient Israel*. Library of Ancient Israel. Louisville: Westminster John Knox Press, 2015.
Bohak, Gideon. "CPJ III, 520: the Egyptian Reaction To Onias' Temple." *JSJ* 26 (1995): 32–41.
Bohak, Gideon. *Joseph and Aseneth and the Jewish Temple in Heliopolis*. Society of Biblical Literature: Early Judaism and Its Literature 10. Atlanta: Scholars Press, 1996.
Bongenaar, A. C. V. M. *The Neo-Babylonian Ebabbar Temple at Sippar: Its Administration and Its Prosopography*. Uitgaven van het Nederlands Historisch-Archaeologisch Instituut te Istanbul 80. Istanbul: Nederlands Historisch-Archaeologisch Instituut te Istanbul, 1997.
Borchardt, Francis. "The Deuteronomic Legacy of 1 Maccabees." Pages 297–319 in *Changes in Scripture: Rewriting and Interpreting Authoritative Traditions in the Second Temple Period*. Edited by Hanne von Weissenberg, Juha Pakkala, and Marko Marttila. Beihefte zur Zeitschrift für die alttestamentliche Wissenschaft 419. Berlin: De Gruyter, 2011.
Borowski, Oded. *Agriculture in Iron Age Israel*. Winona Lake, IN: Eisenbrauns, 1987.
Bourke, Myles M. *A Study of the Metaphor of the Olive Tree in Romans XI*. The Catholic University of America Studies in Sacred Theology, Second Series 3. Washington, D.C.: The Catholic University of America Press, 1947.
Boyarin, Daniel. *A Radical Jew: Paul and the Politics of Identity*. Berkeley: University of California Press, 1994.
Boyle, Brian. "The Figure of the Nāśî' in Ezekiel's Vision of the New Temple (Ezekiel 40–48)." *Australian Biblical Review* 58 (2010): 1–16.
Briant, Pierre. *From Cyrus to Alexander: A History of the Persian Empire*. Translated by Peter T. Daniels. Winona Lake, IN: Eisenbrauns, 2002.
Brin, Gershon. *Studies in Biblical Law: From the Hebrew Bible to the Dead Sea Scrolls*. Journal for the Study of the Old Testament. Supplement Series 176. Sheffield: JSOT Press, 1994.
Brodsky, Harold. "The Utopian Map in Ezekiel (48:1–35)." *Jewish Bible Quarterly* 34, no. 1 (2006): 20–26.
Brodsky, Harold. "Ezekiel's Map of Restoration." Pages 17–29 in *Land and Community: Geography in Jewish Studies*. Edited by Harold Brodsky. Studies and Texts in Jewish History and Culture 3. Bethesda, MD: University Press of Maryland, 1997.
Broshi, Magen. "The Role of the Temple in the Herodian Economy." *JJS* 38 (1987): 31–37.
Brown, Peter. *Through the Eye of a Needle: Wealth, the Fall of Rome, and the Making of Christianity in the West, 350–550 AD*. Princeton, NJ: Princeton University Press, 2012.
Brueggemann, Walter. *The Land: Place as Gift, Promise, and Challenge in Biblical Faith*. Philadelphia: Fortress Press, 1977.
Büchler, Avraham (Adolf). *The Priests and Their Cult in the Last Decade of the Temple in Jerusalem*. Translated from the German by Naphtali Ginton. Jerusalem: Mossad Harav Kook, 1966 (1895).
Buitenwerf, Rieuwerd. *Book III of the Sibylline Oracles and Its Social Setting*. Studia in Veteris Testamenti Pseudepigrapha 17. Leiden; Boston: Brill, 2003.
Bula, Menachem. *Sefer Vayikra*. Jerusalem: Mosad ha-Rav Kook, 1992 [Hebrew].
Burford, Alison. *Land and Labor in the Greek World*. Ancient Society and History. Baltimore; London: Johns Hopkins University Press, 1993.
Burkert, Walter. "Greek Temple-Builders: Who, Where and Why?" Pages 21–29 in *The Role of Religion in the Early Greek Polis: Proceedings of the Third International Seminar on Ancient Greek Cult, Organized by the Swedish Institute at Athens, 16–18 October 1992*.

Edited by Robin Hägg. Skrifter utgivna av Svenska institutet i Athen 14. Stockholm: Paul Åströms, 1996.

Burriss, Eli Edward. "The Misuse of Sacred Things at Rome." *The Classical Weekly* 22, no. 14 (1929): 105–10.

Busink, Th. A. *Der Tempel von Jerusalem von Salomo bis Herodes. Band II. Von Ezechiel bis Middot.* Leiden: Brill, 1980.

Cahill, Kevin. *Who Owns the World: The Hidden Facts behind Landownership.* Edinburgh; London: Mainstream Publishing, 2006.

Campbell, Brian. *The Writings of the Roman Land Surveyors: Introduction, Text, Translation and Commentary.* Journal of Roman Studies Monograph 9. London: Society for the Promotion of Roman Studies, 2000.

Capponi, Livia. *Augustan Egypt: The Creation of a Roman Province.* Studies in Classics. New York: Routledge, 2005.

Capponi, Livia. *Il tempio di Leontopoli in Egitto: identità politica e religiosa dei Giudei di Onia, c. 150 a. C.* Pubblicazioni della Facoltà di lettere e filosofia dell'Università di Pavia 118. Pisa: Edizioni ETS, 2007.

Carlsen, Jesper. "*CIL* X 8217 and the Question of Temple Land in Roman Italy." Pages 9–15 in *Landuse in the Roman Empire.* Edited by Jesper Carlsen, Peter Ørsted, and Jens Erik Skydsgaard. Analecta Romana Instituti Danici Supplementum XXII. Rome: "L'Erma" di Bretschneider, 1994.

Cartledge, Tony W. *Vows in the Hebrew Bible and the Ancient Near East.* JSOT Supp. 147. Sheffield: JSOT Press, 1992.

Chankowski, Véronique. *Athènes et Délos à l'époque classique: recherches sur l'administration du sanctuaire d'Apollon délien.* Bibliothèque des écoles françaises d'Athènes et de Rome 331. Athènes: Ecole française d'Athènes, 2008.

Chankowski, Véronique. "Divine Financiers: Cults as Consumers and Generators of Value." Pages 142–65 in *The Economies of Hellenistic Societies, Third to First Centuries BC.* Edited by Zofia Archibald, John Kenyon Davies, and Vincent Gabrielsen. Oxford; New York: Oxford University Press, 2011.

Charpin, Dominique. *Gods, Kings, and Merchants in Old Babylonian Mesopotamia.* Publication de l'Institut du Proche-Orient Ancien du Collège de France 2. Paris; Leuven; Bristol: Peeters, 2015.

Chilton, Bruce and Jacob Neusner. *Judaism in the New Testament: Practices and Beliefs.* London; New York: Routledge, 1995.

Christian, Mark A. "Middle-Tier Levites and the Plenary Reception of Revelation." Pages 173–98 in *Levites and Priests in Biblical History and Tradition.* Edited by Mark A. Leuchter and Jeremy M. Hutton. Ancient Israel and Its Literature 9. Atlanta: Society of Biblical Literature, 2011.

Clarysse, W. "Egyptian Estate-Holders in the Ptolemaic Period." Pages 731–43 in *State and Temple Economy in the Ancient Near East: Proceedings of the International Conference Organized by the Katholieke Universiteit Leuven from the 10th to the 14th of April 1978.* Vol. II. Edited by Edward Lipiński. Orientalia Lovaniensia Analecta 6. Leuven: Departement Oriëntalistiek, 1979.

Clarysse, Willy. "The Archive of the Praktor Milon." Pages 17–27 in *Edfu, an Egyptian Provincial Capital in the Ptolemaic Period.* Edited by Katelijn Vandorpe and Willy

Clarysse. Brussel: Koninklijke Vlaamse Academie van België voor Wetenschappen en Kunsten, 2003.
Clay, Rachel. "The Tenure of Land in Babylonia and Assyria." *University of London Institute of Archaeology, Occasional Papers* 1 (1938): 7–30.
Clines, David J. A. *The Dictionary of Classical Hebrew*. Sheffield: Sheffield Academic Press, 1993.
Cody, Aelred. *A History of Old Testament Priesthood*. Rome: Pontifical Biblical Institute, 1969.
Cohen, Chaim. "Biblical Hebrew Philology in the Light of Research on the New Yeho'ash Royal Building Inscription." Pages 222–84 in *New Seals and Inscriptions, Hebrew, Idumean, and Cuneiform*. Edited by Meir Lubetski. Hebrew Bible Monographs 8. Sheffield: Sheffield Phoenix Press, 2007.
Cohen, David. *Theft in Athenian Law*. Münchener Beiträge zur Papyrusforschung und antiken Rechtsgeschichte 74. München: C.H. Beck, 1983.
Cohen, Shaye J. D. *Josephus in Galilee and Rome: His Vita and Development as a Historian*. Columbia Studies in the Classical Tradition 8. Leiden: Brill, 1979.
Cohen, Shaye J. D. "Respect for Judaism by Gentiles According to Josephus." *HTR* 80, no. 4 (1987): 409–30.
Cohen, Shaye J. D. "The Judaean Legal Tradition and the *Halakhah* of the Mishnah." Pages 121–43 in *The Cambridge Companion to the Talmud and Rabbinic Literature*. Edited by Charlotte Elisheva Fonrobert and Martin S. Jaffee. Cambridge; New York: Cambridge University Press, 2007.
Cohn, Naftali S. *The Memory of the Temple and the Making of the Rabbis*. Divinations: Rereading Late Ancient Religion. Philadelphia: University of Pennsylvania Press, 2013.
Collins, John J. "The Zeal of Phinehas: The Bible and the Legitimation of Violence." *JBL* 122, no. 1 (2003): 3–21.
Comstock, W. Richard. "A Behavioral Approach to the Sacred: Category Formation in Religious Studies." *Journal of the American Academy of Religion* 49, no. 4 (1981): 625–43.
Cotton, Hannah M., Leah Di Segni, Werner Eck, Benjamin Isaac, Alla Kushnir-Stein, Haggai Misgav, Jonathan Price, Israel Roll, and Ada Yardeni, eds. *Corpus Inscriptionum Iudaeae/Palaestinae. Volume I: Jerusalem, Part 1: 1–704*. Berlin: De Gruyter, 2010.
Cotton, Hannah M. and Michael Wörrle. "Seleukos IV to Heliodoros. A New Dossier of Royal Correspondence from Israel." *Zeitschrift für Papyrologie und Epigraphik* 159 (2007): 191–205.
Cowley, A. *Aramaic Papyri of the Fifth Century B.C*. Oxford: Clarendon Press, 1923.
Cowley, A.E. *Gesenius' Hebrew Grammar as Edited and Enlarged by the Late E. Kautzsch*. Oxford: Clarendon Press, 1910.
Crane, Ashley S. *Israel's Restoration: A Textual-Comparative Exploration of Ezekiel 36–39*. Supplements to Vetus Testamentum 122. Leiden; Boston: Brill, 2008.
Cross, F.M. and E. Eshel. "KhQOstracon." Pages 497–507 in *Qumran Cave 4: Cryptic Texts and Miscellanea*. Discoveries in the Judaean Desert XXVI. Oxford: Clarendon Press, 2000.
Cross, Frank Moore. "Notes on the Forged Plaque Recording Repairs to the Temple." *IEJ* 53, no. 1 (2003): 119–22.
Cryer, Frederick H. "The Qumran Conveyance: A Reply to F.M. Cross and E. Eshel." *Scandinavian Journal of the Old Testament* 11, no. 2 (1997): 232–40.

Dahm, Ulrike. *Opferkult und Priestertum in Alt-Israel: ein kultur- und religionswissenschaftlicher Beitrag.* Beihefte zur Zeitschrift für die alttestamentliche Wissenschaft 327. Berlin: De Gruyter, 2003.

Dandamaev, Muhammad A. *Slavery in Babylonia: From Nabopolassar to Alexander the Great (626–331 B.C.).* Translated by Victoria A. Powell. DeKalb, IL: Northern Illinois University Press, 1984.

Dandamayev, M.A. "State and Temple in Babylonia in the First Millennium B.C." Pages 589–96 in *State and Temple Economy in the Ancient Near East: Proceedings of the International Conference Organized by the Katholieke Universiteit Leuven from the 10th to the 14th of April 1978.* Vol. II. Edited by Edward Lipiński. Orientalia Lovaniensia Analecta 6. Leuven: Departement Oriëntalistiek, 1979.

Dandamayev, Muhammed. "An Age of Privatization in Ancient Mesopotamia." Pages 197–221 in *Privatization in the Ancient Near East and Classical World.* Vol. I. Edited by Michael Hudson and Baruch A. Levine. Peabody Museum Bulletin 5. Cambridge, MA: Peabody Museum of Archaeology and Ethnology, 1996.

Dandamayev, Muhammed. "The Neo-Babylonian rab şibti." Pages 29–31 in *Assyriologica et Semitica. Festschrift für Joachim Oelsner.* Edited by Joachim Marzahn and Hans Neumann. Alter Orient und Altes Testament 252. Münster: Ugarit-Verlag, 2000.

Dauphin, Claudine M. "A Byzantine Ecclesiastical Farm at Shelomi." Pages 43–48 in *Ancient Churches Revealed.* Edited by Yoram Tsafrir. Jerusalem: Israel Exploration Society, 1993.

Davies, John K. "Rebuilding a Temple: The Economic Effects of Piety." Pages 209–29 in *Economies beyond Agriculture in the Classical World.* Edited by David J. Mattingly and John Salmon. London: Routledge, 2001.

Davies, John K. "Temples, Credit, and the Circulation of Money." Pages 117–28 in *Money and Its Uses in the Ancient Greek World.* Edited by Andrew Meadows and Kirsty Shipton. Oxford; New York: Oxford University Press, 2001.

Davies, Philip R. *The Damascus Covenant: An Interpretation of the "Damascus Document".* JSOT Supp. 25. Sheffield: JSOT Press, 1983.

Davies, W. D. *The Gospel and the Land. Early Christianity and Jewish Territorial Doctrine.* Berkeley: University of California Press, 1974.

Davies, W. D. "Paul and the Gentiles: A Suggestion Concerning Romans 11:13–24." Pages 153–63 in *Jewish and Pauline Studies.* Philadelphia: Fortress Press, 1984.

Davies, W. D. *The Territorial Dimension of Judaism.* Berkeley: University of California Press, 1982.

Davis, Andrew R. *Reconstructing the Temple: The Royal Rhetoric of Temple Renovation in the Ancient Near East and Israel.* Oxford; New York: Oxford University Press, 2019.

Davis, Ellen F. *Scripture, Culture, and Agriculture: An Agrarian Reading of the Bible.* New York: Cambridge University Press, 2009.

Davis, Raymond. *The Book of Pontiffs (Liber Pontificalis). The Ancient Biographies of the First Ninety Roman Bishops to AD 715.* Translated Texts for Historians, Latin Series 5. Liverpool: Liverpool University Press, 1989.

de Vos, J. Cornelius. "'Holy Land' in Joshua 18:1–10." Pages 61–72 in *The Land of Israel in Bible, History, and Theology. Studies in Honour of Ed Noort.* Edited by Jacques Van Ruiten and J. Cornelius de Vos. Supplements to Vetus Testamentum 124. Leiden; Boston: Brill, 2009.

Decker, Michael. *Tilling the Hateful Earth: Agricultural Production and Trade in the Late Antique East*. Oxford Studies in Byzantium. Oxford; New York: Oxford University Press, 2009.

Demsky, Aaron. "Qumran Epigraphy and Mishnaic Geography: The Identification of ḤTL' with Ḥaṭṭulim (Menaḥoth 8:6)." *DSD* 4, no. 2 (1997): 157–61.

des Courtils, Jacques. "From Elyanas to Leto: The Physical Evolution of the Sanctuary of Leto at Xanthos." Pages 63–67 in *Sacred Landscapes in Anatolia and Neighboring Regions*. Edited by Charles Gates, Jacques Morin, and Thomas Zimmermann. BAR International Series 2034. Oxford: Archaeopress, 2009.

Dignas, Beate. *Economy of the Sacred in Hellenistic and Roman Asia Minor*. Oxford; New York: Clarendon Press; Oxford University Press, 2002.

Dillon, Matthew P. J. "The Ecology of the Greek Sanctuary." *Zeitschrift für Papyrologie und Epigraphik* 118 (1997): 113–27.

Douglas, Mary. *Leviticus as Literature*. Oxford: Oxford University Press, 1999.

Driel, G. van. *Elusive Silver: In Search of a Role for a Market in an Agrarian Environment. Aspects of Mesopotamia's Society*. Uitgaven van het Nederlands Instituut voor het Nabije Oosten te Leiden 95. Leiden: Nederlands Instituut voor het Nabije Oosten, 2002.

Durkheim, Émile. *The Elementary Forms of Religious Life*. Translated by Carol Cosman. Oxford World's Classics. Oxford: Oxford University Press, 1912.

Edelman, Diana. "The Economy and Administration of Rural Idumea at the End of the Persian Period." Pages 175–204 in *The Economy of Ancient Judah in Its Historical Context*. Edited by Marvin Lloyd Miller, Ehud Ben Zvi, and Gary N. Knoppers. Winona Lake, IN: Eisenbrauns, 2015.

Edzard, Deitz Otto. "Private Land Ownership and its Relation to 'God' and the 'State' in Sumer and Akkad." Pages 109–28 in *Privatization in the Ancient Near East and Classical World*. Vol. I. Edited by Michael Hudson and Baruch A. Levine. Peabody Museum Bulletin 5. Cambridge, MA: Peabody Museum of Archaeology and Ethnology, 1996.

Ego, Beate. "Reduktion, Amplifikation, Interpretation, Neukontextualisierung: Intertextuelle Aspekte der Rezeption der Ezechielschen Thronwagenvision im antiken Judentum." Pages 31–60 in *Das Ezechielbuch in der Johannesoffenbarung*. Edited by Dieter Sänger. Biblisch-theologische Studien 76. Neukirchen-Vluyn: Neukirchener, 2004.

Ehling, Kay. *Untersuchungen zur Geschichte der späten Seleukiden (164–63 v. Chr.): vom Tode des Antiochos IV. bis zur Einrichtung der Provinz Syria unter Pompeius*. Historia Einzelschriften 196. Stuttgart: Steiner, 2008.

Eichrodt, Walther. *Ezekiel: A Commentary*. The Old Testament Library. Philadelphia: The Westminster Press, 1970.

Eilberg-Schwartz, Howard. *The Human Will in Judaism: The Mishnah's Philosophy of Intention*. Atlanta: Scholars Press, 1986.

Ekelund, Robert B., Robert F. Hébert, Robert D. Tollison, Gary M. Anderson, and Aubrey B. Davidson. *Sacred Trust: The Medieval Church as an Economic Firm*. Oxford; New York: Oxford University Press, 1996.

El-Gamal, Mahmoud A. *Islamic Finance: Law, Economics, and Practice*. Cambridge: Cambridge University Press, 2008.

Eliade, Mircea. *The Sacred and the Profane: The Nature of Religion*. Translated by W.R. Trask. New York: Harcourt, Brace and World, 1959.

Eliav, Yaron Z. *God's Mountain: The Temple Mount in Time, Place, and Memory.* Baltimore: Johns Hopkins University Press, 2005.

Ellickson, Robert C. and Thorland, Charles DiA. "Ancient Land Law: Mesopotamia, Egypt, Israel." *Chicago-Kent Law Review* 71 (1995–1996): 321–411.

Elliott, M.W. *Engaging Leviticus: Reading Leviticus Theologically with Its Past Interpreters.* Eugene, OR: Cascade Books, 2012.

Ellis, Maria deJ. *Agriculture and the State in Ancient Mesopotamia: An Introduction to Problems of Land Tenure.* Occasional Publications of the Babylonian Fund 1. Philadelphia: Babylonian Fund, University Museum, 1976.

Engelhard, David H. "Ezekiel 47:13–48:29 as Royal Grant." Pages 45–56 in *"Go to the Land I Will Show You": Studies in Honor of Dwight W. Young.* Edited by Joseph E. Coleson and Victor H. Matthews. Winona Lake, IN: Eisenbrauns, 1996.

Eph'al, Israel and Joseph Naveh. *Aramaic Ostraca of the Fourth Century BC from Idumaea.* Jerusalem: Magnes Press; Israel Exploration Society, 1996.

Eph'al, Israel. "The 'Jehoash Inscription': A Forgery." *IEJ* 53, no. 1 (2003): 123–28.

Epstein, J.N. *Introduction to the Mishnaic Text.* 2 vols. Jerusalem: Hebrew University Magnes Press, 2001 [Hebrew].

Eshel, H. and Zeev E. Erlich. "The Fortress of Acraba in Kh. Urmeh." *Cathedra* 47 (1988): 17–24 [Hebrew].

Eshel, Hanan and Haggai Misgav. "A Fourth Century B.C.E. Document from Ketef Yeriḥo." *IEJ* 38, no. 3 (1988): 142–57.

Eshel, Hanan and Haggai Misgav. "Jericho papList of Loans ar." in *Miscellaneous Texts from the Judaean Desert.* Edited by James Charlesworth et al. Discoveries in the Judaean Desert XXXVIII. Oxford: Clarendon Press, 2000.

Eshel, Hanan and Boaz Zissu. "A Note on the Rabbinic Phrase: 'Cast Them into the Dead Sea'." Pages 91–96 in *Judea and Samaria Research Studies.* Vol. 12. Edited by Ya'acov Eshel. Ariel: College of Judea and Samaria, 2003 [Hebrew].

Esler, Philip Francis. "Ancient Oleiculture and Ethnic Differentiation: The Meaning of the Olive-Tree Image in Romans 11." *JSNT* 26, no. 1 (2003): 103–24.

Fager, Jeffrey A. *Land Tenure and the Biblical Jubilee: Uncovering Hebrew Ethics through the Sociology of Knowledge.* JSOT Supp. 155. Sheffield: JSOT Press, 1993.

Falkenstein, Adam. *The Sumerian Temple City.* Translated by Maria deJ Ellis. Monographs in History: Ancient Near East 1/1. Los Angeles: Undena Publications, 1974.

Fantalkin, Alexander and Oren Tal. "The Canonization of the Pentateuch: When and Why?" *Zeitschrift für die Alttestamentliche Wissenschaft* 124, no. 1 (2012): 1–18.

Faust, Avraham. *The Archaeology of Israelite Society in Iron Age II.* Winona Lake, IN: Eisenbrauns, 2012.

Feliks, Jehuda. "Agriculture." Pages 483–93 in *Encyclopaedia Judaica, Second Edition, Vol. 1.* Edited by Fred Skolnik and Michael Berenbaum. Farmington Hills, MI: Thomson Gale, 2006.

Fiensy, David A. *The Social History of Palestine in the Herodian Period: The Land is Mine.* Studies in the Bible and Early Christianity 20. Lewiston, NY: E. Mellen Press, 1991.

Fine, John V.A. *Horoi: Studies in Mortgage, Real Security and Land Tenure in Ancient Athens.* Hesperia Supplement 9. Baltimore: American School of Classical Studies at Athens, 1951.

Fine, S. "Between Liturgy and Social History: Priestly Power in Late Antique Palestinian Synagogues?" *Journal of Jewish Studies* 56, no. 1 (2005): 1–9.

Fine, Steven. *Art and Judaism in the Greco-Roman World: Toward a New Jewish Archaeology* Book, Whole. Cambridge; New York: Cambridge University Press, 2005.

Finkelstein, Israel. "The Territorial Extent and Demography of Yehud/Judea in the Persian and Early Hellenistic Periods." *RB* 117, no. 1 (2010): 39–54.

Finley, Moses I. *Studies in Land and Credit in Ancient Athens, 500–200 B.C. The Horos Inscriptions*. New Brunswick, NJ: Rutgers University Press, 1952.

Fishbane, Michael A. *Biblical Interpretation in Ancient Israel*. Oxford; New York: Clarendon Press; Oxford University Press, 1985.

Fleisher, Ezra. "The Piyyutim of Yannai the Hazzan on the Priestly Courses." *Sinai* 64 (1969): 176–84 [Hebrew].

Fleisher, Ezra. "Regarding the [Priestly] Courses in Piyyutim." *Sinai* 62 (1968): 13–40, 142–62 [Hebrew].

Fonrobert, Charlotte Elisheva. "The Political Symbolism of the Eruv." *Jewish Social Studies* 11, no. 3 (2005): 9–35.

Forster, E. S. and Edward H. Heffner. *Lucius Junius Moderatus Columella on Agriculture*. Cambridge: Harvard University Press, 1968.

Fox, Nili Sacher. *In the Service of the King: Officialdom in Ancient Israel and Judah*. Monographs of the Hebrew Union College 23. Cincinnati: Hebrew Union College Press, 2000.

Fraade, Steven D. "Shifting from Priestly to Non-Priestly Legal Authority: A Comparison of the Damascus Document and the Midrash Sifra." *DSD* 6 (1999): 109–25.

Fraade, Steven D. "A New View on Comparative Midrash: From the Dead Sea Scrolls to Midrash of the Sages." Pages 261–84 in *Higayon L'Yona: New Aspects in the Study of Midrash, Aggadah and Piyut in Honor of Professor Yona Fraenkel*. Edited by Joshua Levinson, Jacob Elbaum, and Galit Hasan-Rokem. Jerusalem: Hebrew University Magnes Press, 2006 [Hebrew].

France, R.T. *The Gospel of Matthew*. The New International Commentary on the New Testament. Grand Rapids, MI: William B. Eerdmans, 2007.

Frankel, David. *The Land of Canaan and the Destiny of Israel: Theologies of Territory in the Hebrew Bible*. Siphrut: Literature and Theology of the Hebrew Scriptures 4. Winona Lake, IN: Eisenbrauns, 2011.

Fratantuono, Lee. *Madness Triumphant: A Reading of Lucan's Pharsalia*. Lanham, MD: Lexington Books, 2012.

Freedman, David Noel and K.A. Mathews. *The Paleo-Hebrew Leviticus Scroll (11QpaleoLev)*. Winona Lake, IN: American Schools of Oriental Research, 1985.

Frey, Jörg. "Temple and Rival Temple: The Cases of Elephantine, Mt. Gerizim, and Leontopolis." Pages 171–203 in *Gemeinde ohne Tempel: Zur Substituierung und Transformation des Jerusalemer Tempels und seines Kults im Alten Testament, antiken Judentum und frühen Christentum*. Edited by Beate Ego, Armin Lange, and Peter Pilhofer. Wissenschaftliche Untersuchungen zum Neuen Testament 118. Tübingen: Mohr Siebeck, 1999.

Friberg, Jöran. *A Remarkable Collection of Babylonian Mathematical Texts. Manuscripts in the Schøyen Collection. Cuneiform Texts I*. Sources and Studies in the History of Mathematics and Physical Sciences. New York; London: Springer, 2007.

Fried, Lisbeth S. "Exploitation of Depopulated Land in Achaemenid Judah." Pages 151–64 in *The Economy of Ancient Judah in Its Historical Context*. Edited by Marvin Lloyd Miller, Ehud Ben Zvi, and Gary N. Knoppers. Winona Lake, IN: Eisenbrauns, 2015.

Fried, Lisbeth S. and David N. Freedman. "Was the Jubilee Year Observed in Preexilic Judah?" Pages 2257–71 in *Leviticus 23–27: A New Translation with Introduction and Commentary*. Edited by Jacob Milgrom. The Anchor Bible 3B. New York: Doubleday, 2001.

Fritz, Volkmar. *1 & 2 Kings. A Continental Commentary*. Translated by Anselm Hagedorn. Continental Commentaries: Old Testament. Minneapolis: Fortress Press, 2003.

Frymer-Kensky, Tikva. "Israel." Pages 251–63 in *Security for Debt in Ancient Near Eastern Law*. Edited by Raymond Westbrook and Richard Jasnow. Culture and History of the Ancient Near East 9. Leiden: Brill, 2001.

Fuller, David J. "Debt-Slavery Passages in the Tanakh as a Lens for Reading Joseph's Enslavement of the Egyptians in Genesis 47:13–26: Explorations in Canonical Hermeneutics." *Biblical Theology Bulletin* 46, no. 4 (2016): 177–85.

Gabba, Emilio. "The Finances of King Herod." Pages 160–68 in *Greece and Rome in Eretz Israel: Collected Essays*. Edited by Aryeh Kasher, Uriel Rappaport, and Gideon Fuks. Jerusalem: Yad Ben-Zvi, 1990.

Gabrielsen, Vincent. "Banking and Credit Operations in Hellenistic Times." Pages 136–64 in *Making, Moving and Managing: The New World of Ancient Economies, 323–31 BC*. Edited by Zofia H. Archibald, John K. Davies, and Vincent Gabrielsen. Oxford: Oxbow Books, 2005.

Gager, John G. *Reinventing Paul*. Oxford; New York: Oxford University Press, 2000.

Gargola, Daniel J. *Lands, Laws, & Gods: Magistrates & Ceremony in the Regulation of Public Lands in Republican Rome*. Studies in the History of Greece & Rome. Chapel Hill; London: The University of North Carolina Press, 1995.

Garscha, Jörg. *Studien zum Ezechielbuch: eine redaktionskritische Untersuchung von Ez 1–39*. Bern: Herbert Lang, 1974.

Gauger, Jörg-Dieter. *Beiträge zur jüdischen Apologetik: Untersuchungen zur Authentizität von Urkunden bei Flavius Josephus und im I. Makkabäerbuch*. Bonner biblische Beiträge 49. Köln: P. Hanstein, 1977.

Gelb, I.J. "The Arua Institution." *Revue d'assyriologie et d'archéologie orientale* 66, no. 1 (1972): 1–32.

Geoghegan, Jeffrey C. "'Until This Day' and the Preexilic Redaction of the Deuteronomistic History." *JBL* 122, no. 2 (2003): 201–27.

Gerstenberger, Erhard S. *Leviticus: A Commentary*. The Old Testament Library. Louisville: Westminster John Knox Press, 1996.

Geva, Hillel. "A Chronological Reevalution of Yehud Stamp Impressions in Palaeo-Hebrew Script, Based on Finds from Excavations in the Jewish Quarter of the Old City of Jerusalem." *Tel Aviv* 34, no. 1 (2007): 92–103.

Geva, Hillel. "Jerusalem's Population in Antiquity: A Minimalist View." *Tel Aviv* 41, no. 2 (2014): 131–60.

Gibson, Shimon. "Agricultural Land-Management Methods and Implements in Ancient Ereẓ-Israel." Pages 471–83 in *Encyclopaedia Judaica, Second Edition, Vol. 1*. Edited by Fred Skolnik and Michael Berenbaum. Farmington Hills, MI: Thomson Gale, 2006.

Ginzberg, Louis. *An Unknown Jewish Sect*. Moreshet Series 1. New York: Jewish Theological Seminary of America, 1976.

Goetzmann, William N. *Money Changes Everything: How Finance Made Civilization Possible.* Princeton, NJ: Princeton University Press, 2016.
Goldstein, Jonathan A. *I Maccabees: A New Translation, with Introduction and Commentary.* The Anchor Bible. New Haven: Yale University Press, 1976.
Goodman, Martin. "The Pilgrimage Economy of Jerusalem in the Second Temple Period." Pages 69–76 in *Jerusalem: Its Sanctity and Centrality to Judaism, Christianity, and Islam.* Edited by Lee I. Levine. New York: Continuum, 1999.
Goodman, Martin. "The Purpose of Room F." Pages 71–72 in *Excavations at Ancient Meiron, Upper Galilee, Israel 1971–72, 1974–75, 1977.* Edited by Eric. M. Meyers, James. F. Strange, and Carol. L. Meyers. Meiron Excavation Project III. Cambridge, Mass: The American Schools of Oriental Research, 1981.
Gordon, Benjamin D. "The Misunderstood Redemption Fee in the Holiness Legislation on Dedications (Lev 27)." *Zeitschrift für die alttestamentliche Wissenschaft* 126, no. 2 (2014): 180–92.
Gordon, Benjamin D. "On the Sanctity of Mixtures and Branches: Two Halakhic Sayings in Romans 11:16." *JBL* 135, no. 2 (2016): 355–68.
Gordon, Benjamin D. "Debt Fraud, Herem Entrapment, and Other Crimes Involving Cultic Property in Late Hellenistic and Early Roman Judea." Pages 255–67 in *Expressions of Cult in the Southern Levant in the Greco-Roman Period. Manifestations in Text and Material Culture.* Edited by Zeev Weiss and Oren Tal. Turnhout: Brepols, 2017.
Grabbe, Lester L. *A History of the Jews and Judaism in the Second Temple Period. Volume 1, Yehud: A History of the Persian Province of Judah.* Library of Second Temple Studies 47. London: T&T Clark, 2004.
Graeber, David. *Debt: The First 5,000 Years.* Brooklyn, NY: Melville House, 2011.
Grätz, Sebastian. *Das Edikt des Artaxerxes: Eine Untersuchung zum religionspolitischen und historischen Umfeld von Esra 7, 12–26.* Beihefte zur Zeitschrift für die alttestamentliche Wissenschaft 337. Berlin; New York: De Gruyter, 2004.
Green, C. M. C. *Roman Religion and the Cult of Diana at Aricia.* Cambridge; New York: Cambridge University Press, 2007.
Greenberg, Moshe. "The Design and Themes of Ezekiel's Program of Restoration." *Interpretation* 38, no. 2 (1984): 181–208.
Greenberg, Moshe. "Ḥerem." Pages 10–13 in *Encyclopaedia Judaica, Second Edition, Vol. 9.* Edited by Fred Skolnik and Michael Berenbaum. Farmington Hills, MI: Thomson Gale, 2006.
Greengus, Samuel. *Laws in the Bible and in Early Rabbinic Collections. The Legacy of the Ancient Near East.* Eugene, OR: Cascade Books, 2011.
Greif, Avner. *Institutions and the Path to the Modern Economy: Lessons from Medieval Trade.* Political Economy of Institutions and Decisions. Cambridge: Cambridge University Press, 2006.
Grey, Matthew J. "Jewish Priests and the Social History of Post-70 Palestine." Ph.D. Dissertation, University of North Carolina at Chapel Hill, 2011.
Grindheim, Sigurd. *The Crux of Election: Paul's Critique of the Jewish Confidence in the Election of Israel.* Wissenschaftliche Untersuchungen zum Neuen Testament 2/202. Tübingen: Mohr Siebeck, 2005.
Gros, Pierre. "Le bois sacré du Palatin: une composante oubliée du sanctuaire augustéen d'Apollon." *Revue Archéologique*, no. 1 (2003): 51–66.

Gruen, Erich S. *Heritage and Hellenism: The Reinvention of Jewish Tradition.* Berkeley: University of California Press, 1998.
Gruen, Erich S. "The Origins and Objectives of Onias' Temple." Pages 47–70 in *Scripta Classica Israelica. Yearbook of the Israel Society for the Promotion of Classical Studies. Studies in Memory of Abraham Wasserstein II.* Vol. XVI. Edited by Hannah M. Cotton, Jonathan J. Price, and David J. Wasserstein. Jerusalem: The Israel Society for the Promotion of Classical Studies, 1997.
Gudme, Anne Katrine de Hemmer. *Before the God in This Place for Good Remembrance: A Comparative Analysis of the Aramaic Votive Inscriptions from Mount Gerizim.* Beihefte zur Zeitschrift für die alttestamentliche Wissenschaft 441. Berlin: De Gruyter, 2013.
Guggenheimer, Heinrich W. *The Jerusalem Talmud. First Order, Zeraïm. Tractates Ma'aser Šeni, Ḥallah, 'Orlah, and Bikkurim. Edition, Translation, and Commentary.* Studia Judaica 23. Berlin; New York: De Gruyter, 2003.
Guillaume, Philippe. *Land and Calendar: The Priestly Document from Genesis 1 to Joshua 18.* Library of Hebrew Bible/Old Testament Studies 391. New York: T&T Clark, 2009.
Guillaume, Philippe. *Land, Credit and Crisis: Agrarian Finance in the Hebrew Bible.* BibleWorld. Sheffield; Oakville, CT: Equinox, 2012.
Guillaume, Philippe. "פְּרוּ וּרְבוּ and the Seventh Year: Complementary Strategies for the Economic Recovery of Depopulated Yehud." Pages 123–49 in *The Economy of Ancient Judah in Its Historical Context.* Edited by Marvin Lloyd Miller, Ehud Ben Zvi, and Gary N. Knoppers. Winona Lake, IN: Eisenbrauns, 2015.
Haas, Peter J. *The Talmud of Babylonia, An American Translation. XXXII: Meilah and Tamid.* Brown Judaic Studies 109. Atlanta: Scholars Press, 1986.
Habel, Norman C. *The Land is Mine: Six Biblical Land Ideologies.* Overtures to Biblical Theology. Minneapolis: Fortress Press, 1995.
Hachlili, Rachel. *Ancient Synagogues—Archaeology and Art: New Discoveries and Current Research.* Handbook of Oriental Studies, Section 1: Ancient Near East 104. Boston: Brill, 2013.
Hachlili, Rachel. "The Inscriptions." Pages 142–58 in *Jericho: The Jewish Cemetery of the Second Temple Period.* Edited by Rachel Hachlili and Ann E. Killebrew. IAA Reports 7. Jerusalem: Israel Antiquities Authority; Civil Administration in Judea and Samaria, Staff Officer for Archaeology, 1999.
Halpern-Amaru, Betsy. "Land Theology in Philo and Josephus." Pages 65–93 in *The Land of Israel: Jewish Perspectives.* Edited by Lawrence A. Hoffman. Notre Dame, IN: University of Notre Dame Press, 1986.
Hanson, Richard S. "Paleography." Pages 15–23 in *The Paleo-Hebrew Leviticus Scroll (11QpaleoLev).* Edited by David Noel Freedman and K.A. Mathews. Winona Lake, IN: American Schools of Oriental Research, 1985.
Haran, Menahem. "'Ărākîm." Pages 391–94 in *Encyclopaedia Biblica.* Vol. 6. Jerusalem: Bialik Institute, 1971 [Hebrew].
Haran, Menahem. *Temples and Temple-Service in Ancient Israel: An Inquiry into the Character of Cult Phenomena and the Historical Setting of the Priestly School.* Oxford: Clarendon Press, 1977.
Haring, B. J. J. *Divine Households: Administrative and Economic Aspects of the New Kingdom Royal Memorial Temples in Western Thebes.* Leiden: Nederlands Instituut voor het Nabije Oosten, 1997.

Havemann, J. C. T. "Cultivated Olive—Wild Olive: The Olive Tree Metaphor in Romans 11:16–24." *Neotestamentica* 31, no. 1 (1997): 87–106.
Havrelock, Rachel. "The Two Maps of Israel's Land." *JBL* 126, no. 4 (2007): 649–67.
Hecht, Richard D. "Preliminary Issues in the Analysis of Philo's *De Specialibus Legibus*." *Studio Philonica* 5 (1978): 1–55.
Heger, Paul. *Cult as the Catalyst for Division: Cult Disputes as the Motive for Schism in the Pre-70 Pluralistic Environment*. Studies on the Texts of the Desert of Judah 65. Leiden; Boston: Brill, 2007.
Heltzer, Michael. "The Galgūla Family in South Judah and the Local Sanctuaries." Pages 127–31 in *Studien zu Ritual und Sozialgeschichte im Alten Orient: Tartuer Symposien, 1998–2004*. Edited by Thomas Richard Kämmerer. Beihefte zur Zeitschrift für die alttestamentliche Wissenschaft 374. Berlin; New York: De Gruyter, 2007.
Hempel, Charlotte. *The Laws of the Damascus Document: Sources, Tradition, and Redaction*. Studies on the Texts of the Desert of Judah 29. Leiden; Boston: Brill, 1998.
Hendin, David. *Ancient Scale Weights and Pre-Coinage Currency of the Near East*. New York: Amphora, 2007.
Henrey, K.H. "Land Tenure in the Old Testament." *Palestine Exploration Quarterly* 86, no. 1 (1954): 5–15.
Herzka, Eliezer. "Tractate Arachin Chapter 6." in *The Schottenstein Edition. Talmud Bavli. The Artscroll Series. Tractate Arakhin*. Edited by Yisroel Simcha Schorr and Chaim Malinowitz. New York: Menorah Publications, Ltd, 2004.
Herzog, Isaac. *The Main Institutions of Jewish Law. Volume I: The Law of Property*. London; New York: Soncino Press, 1965.
Hezser, Catherine. *The Social Structure of the Rabbinic Movement in Roman Palestine*. Texte und Studien zum antiken Judentum 66. Tübingen: Mohr Siebeck, 1997.
Hieke, Thomas. *Levitikus, Zweiter Teilband: 16–27*. Herders theologischer Kommentar zum Alten Testament. Freiburg: Herder, 2014.
Himmelfarb, Martha. *A Kingdom of Priests: Ancestry and Merit in Ancient Judaism*. Philadelphia: University of Pennsylvania Press, 2006.
Hirschfeld, Yizhar. *The Judean Desert Monasteries in the Byzantine Period*. New Haven: Yale University Press, 1992.
Hirschfeld, Yizhar and Donald T. Ariel. "A Coin Assemblage from the Reign of Alexander Jannaeus Found on the Shore of the Dead Sea." *IEJ* 55, no. 1 (2005): 66–89.
Holtz, Shalom E. *Neo-Babylonian Trial Records*. Writings from the Ancient World 35. Atlanta: Society of Biblical Literature, 2014.
Hopkins, David C. *The Highlands of Canaan: Agricultural Life in the Early Iron Age*. The Social World of Biblical Antiquity Series 3. Sheffield: Almond, 1985.
Hopkins, David C. "'All Sorts of Field Work': Agricultural Labor in Ancient Palestine." Pages 149–72 in *To Break Every Yoke: Essays in Honor of Marvin L. Chaney*. Edited by Robert B. Coote and Norman K. Gottwald. The Social World of Biblical Antiquity, Second Series 3. Sheffield: Sheffield Phoenix Press, 2007.
Horbury, William. "Extirpation and Excommunication." *VT* 35, no. 1 (1985): 13–38.
Horden, Peregrine and Nicholas Purcell. *The Corrupting Sea: A Study of Mediterranean History*. Oxford; Malden, MA: Blackwell, 2000.
Horowitz, Wayne. "A Combined Multiplication Table on a Prism Fragment from Hazor." *IEJ* 47, no. 3/4 (1997): 190–97.

Horowitz, Wayne, Takayoshi Oshima, and Seth Sanders. *Cuneiform in Canaan: Cuneiform Sources from the Land of Israel in Ancient Times.* Jerusalem: Israel Exploration Society and The Hebrew University of Jerusalem, 2006.

Horster, Marietta. *Landbesitz griechischer Heiligtümer in archaischer und klassischer Zeit.* Religionsgeschichtliche Versuche und Vorarbeiten 53. Berlin; New York: De Gruyter, 2004.

Houston, Walter. "Contrast in Tense and Exegesis. The Case of the Field Vowed and Sold, Lev. XXVII 20." *VT* 49, no. 3 (1999): 416–20.

Houston, Walter J. *Contending for Justice: Ideologies and Theologies of Social Justice in the Old Testament.* Library of Hebrew Bible/Old Testament Studies 428. London; New York: T&T Clark, 2006.

Houtman, Cornelius. *Exodus, Volume 3, Chapters 20–40.* Historical Commentary on the Old Testament. Leuven: Peeters, 2000.

Howe, Timothy. *Pastoral Politics: Animals, Agriculture, and Society in Ancient Greece.* Publications of the Association of Ancient Historians 9. Claremont, CA: Regina Books, 2008.

Hudson, Michael. "How Interest Rates Were Set, 2500 BC–1000 AD." *JESHO* 43, no. 2 (2000): 132–61.

Hudson, Michael. "Reconstructing the Origins of Interest-Bearing Debt and the Logic of Clean Slates." Pages 7–58 in *Debt and Economic Renewal in the Ancient Near East.* Edited by Michael Hudson and Marc Van de Mieroop. International Scholars Conference of Ancient Near Eastern Economies 3. Bethesda, MD: CDL Press, 2002.

Hurowitz, Victor Avigdor. "The Joseph Stories and Mesopotamian Writings: Enslaving the Egyptians (Gen 47:13–26)." *Beit Mikra*, no. 55/1 (2010): 94–106.

Hutton, Jeremy M. "The Levitical Diaspora (I): A Sociological Comparison with Morocco's Ahansal." Pages 223–34 in *Exploring the Longue Durée: Essays in Honor of Lawrence E. Stager.* Edited by J. David Schloen. Winona Lake, IN: Eisenbrauns, 2009.

Instone-Brewer, David. *Prayer and Agriculture.* Traditions of the Rabbis from the Era of the New Testament 1. Grand Rapids, MI; Cambridge, U.K.: William B. Eerdmans, 2004.

Instone-Brewer, David. *Techniques and Assumptions in Jewish Exegesis before 70 CE.* Texte und Studien zum antiken Judentum 30. Tübingen: J.C.B. Mohr (P. Siebeck), 1992.

Irshai, Oded. "The Priesthood in Jewish Society of Late Antiquity." Pages 67–106 in *Continuity and Renewal: Jews and Judaism in Byzantine-Christian Palestine.* Edited by Lee I. Levine. Jerusalem: Dinur Center, Yad Ben-Zvi, and Jewish Theological Seminary of America, 2004 [Hebrew].

Isager, Signe. "Kings and Gods in the Seleucid Empire: A Question of Landed Property in Asia Minor." Pages 79–90 in *Religion and Religious Practice in the Seleucid Kingdom.* Edited by Per Bilde, Troels Engberg-Pederson, Lise Hannestad, and Jan Zahle. Studies in Hellenistic Civilization 1. Aarhus: Aarhus University Press, 1990.

Isager, Signe. "Sacred Animals in Classical and Hellenistic Greece." Pages 15–19 in *Economics of Cult in the Ancient Greek World: Proceedings of the Uppsala Symposium 1990.* Edited by Tullia Linders and Brita Alroth. Boreas: Uppsala Studies in Ancient Mediterranean and Near Eastern Civilizations 21. Uppsala; Stockholm: S. Academiae Ubsaliensis; Almqvist & Wiksell, 1992.

Isager, Signe. "Sacred and Profane Ownership of Land." Pages 119–22 in *Agriculture in Ancient Greece. Proceedings of the 7th International Symposium at the Swedish Institute at Athens, 16–17 May 1990*. Edited by Berit Wells. Skrifter utgivna av Svenska institutet i Athen 42. Stockholm: Svenska Institutet, 1992.

Jacob, Edmond. "Les trois racines d'une théologie de la "terre" dans l'Ancient Testament." *Revue d'histoire et de philosophie religieuses* 55 (1975): 469–80.

Jacobson, Howard. *A Commentary on Pseudo-Philo's Liber Antiquitatum Biblicarum, with Latin text and English Translation, Volume One*. Arbeiten zur Geschichte des antiken Judentums und des Urchristentums 31. Leiden; New York: Brill, 1996.

Jaffee, Martin S. *Torah in the Mouth: Writing and Oral Tradition in Palestinian Judaism, 200 BCE–400 CE*. New York: Oxford University Press, 2001.

Jahn, P. Leopold Günther. *Der griechische Text des Buches Ezechiel: nach dem Kölner Teil des Papyrus 967*. Papyrologische Texte und Abhandlungen 15. Bonn: Rudolf Habelt, 1972.

Jameson, Michael H. "The Leasing of Land in Rhamnous." *Hesperia Supplements* 19 (1982): 66–74.

Janković, Bojana. "Uruk." Pages 418–37 in *Aspects of the Economic History of Babylonia in the First Millennium BC: Economic Geography, Economic Mentalities, Agriculture, the Use of Money and the Problem of Economic Growth*. Edited by Michael Jursa. Alter Orient und Altes Testament 377. Münster: Ugarit-Verlag, 2010.

Janssen, Jac J. "The Role of the Temple in the Egyptian Economy during the New Kingdom." Pages 505–15 in *State and Temple Economy in the Ancient Near East: Proceedings of the International Conference Organized by the Katholieke Universiteit Leuven from the 10th to the 14th of April 1978*. Vol. II. Edited by Edward Lipiński. Orientalia Lovaniensia Analecta 6. Leuven: Departement Oriëntalistiek, 1979.

Japhet, Sara. *From the Rivers of Babylon to the Highlands of Judah: Collected Studies in the Restoration Period*. Winona Lake, IN: Eisenbrauns, 2006.

Jastrow, Marcus. *A Dictionary of the Targumim, the Talmud Babli and Yerushalmi, and the Midrashic Literature*. New York: Pardes, 1950.

Jenson, Philip Peter. *Graded Holiness: A Key to the Priestly Conception of the World*. JSOT Supp. 106. Sheffield: Sheffield Academic Press, 1992.

Jewett, Robert. *Romans: A Commentary*. Hermeneia. Minneapolis: Fortress Press, 2007.

Johns, C.H.W. *Babylonian and Assyrian Laws, Contracts and Letters*. Library of Ancient Inscriptions 6. New York: Charles Scribner's Sons, 1904.

Johnson Hodge, Caroline. "Olive Trees and Ethnicity: Judeans and Gentiles in Rom. 11.17–24." Pages 77–89 in *Christians as a Religious Minority in a Multicultural City: Modes of Interaction and Identity Formation in Early Imperial Rome*. Edited by Jürgen Zangenberg and Michael Labahn. London; New York: T&T Clark International, 2004.

Jones, A. H. M. *The Later Roman Empire, 284–602: A Social Economic and Administrative Survey*. Norman: University of Oklahoma Press, 1964.

Jones, Gwilym H. *1 and 2 Kings, Based on the Revised Standard Version*. Grand Rapids, MI; London: W.B. Eerdmans; Marshall, Morgan & Scott, 1984.

Jonker, Louis. "Agrarian Economy through City-Elites' Eyes: Reflections of Late Persian Period Yehud Economy in the Genealogies of Chronicles." Pages 77–101 in *The Economy of Ancient Judah in Its Historical Context*. Edited by Marvin Lloyd Miller, Ehud Ben Zvi, and Gary N. Knoppers. Winona Lake, IN: Eisenbrauns, 2015.

Joosten, Jan. *People and Land in the Holiness Code: An Exegetical Study of the Ideational Framework of the Law in Leviticus 17–26*. Supplements to Vetus Testamentum 67. Leiden; New York: Brill, 1996.

Jordan, Borimir and John Perlin. "On the Protection of Sacred Groves." Pages 153–59 in *Studies Presented to Sterling Dow on His Eightieth Birthday*. Edited by Kent J. Rigsby. Greek, Roman, and Byzantine Monographs 10. Durham, NC: Duke University, 1984.

Joüon, Paul and T. Muraoka. *A Grammar of Biblical Hebrew, Vol. I*. Roma: Editrice Pontificio Istituto Biblio, 1991.

Joyce, Paul M. "Temple and Worship in Ezekiel 40–48." Pages 145–63 in *Temple and Worship in Biblical Israel*. Edited by John Day. Library of Hebrew Bible/Old Testament Studies 422. London; New York: T&T Clark, 2005.

Jursa, Michael. *Aspects of the Economic History of Babylonia in the First Millennium BC: Economic Geography, Economic Mentalities, Agriculture, the Use of Money and the Problem of Economic Growth*. Alter Orient und Altes Testament 377. Münster: Ugarit-Verlag, 2010.

Jursa, Michael. *Der Tempelzehnt in Babylonien: vom siebenten bis zum dritten Jahrhundert v. Chr*. Alter Orient und Altes Testament 254. Münster: Ugarit-Verlag, 1998.

Jursa, Michael. *Die Landwirtschaft in Sippar in neubabylonischer Zeit*. Archiv für Orientforschung, Beiheft 25. Wien: Institut für Orientalistik der Universität Wien, 1995.

Jursa, Michael. "The Remuneration of Institutional Labourers in an Urban Context in Babylonia in the First Millennium BC." Pages 387–427 in *L'archive des fortifications de Persépolis: état des questions et perspectives de recherches*. Edited by Pierre Briant, Wouter Henkelman, and Matthew Stolper. Paris: De Boccard, 2008.

Jursa, Michael. "Money-Based Exchange and Redistribution: The Transformation of the Institutional Economy in First Millennium Babylonia." Pages 171–86 in *Autour de Polanyi: Vocabulaires, théories et modalités des échanges : [actes de la rencontre] Nanterre, 12–14 juin 2004*. Edited by Ph. Clancier, F. Joannès, P. Rouillard, and A. Tenu. Paris: De Boccard, 2005.

Jursa, Michael. "Silver and Other Forms of Elite Wealth in Seventh Century BC Babylonia." Pages 61–71 in *Silver, Money and Credit: A Tribute to Robartus J. Van der Spek on the Occasion of His 65th birthday*. Edited by Kristin Kleber and Reinhard Pirngruber. PIHANS CXXVIII. Leiden: Nederlands Instituut voor het Nabije Oosten, 2016.

Kahane, Tuvia. "The Priestly Courses and Their Geographical Settlements." *Tarbiz* XLVIII, no. 1–2 (1978–1979): 9–30 [Hebrew].

Käppel, Lutz and Vassiliki Pothou, eds. *Human Development in Sacred Landscapes: Between Ritual Tradition, Creativity and Emotionality*. Göttingen: Vandenhoeck & Ruprecht, 2015.

Kasher, Aryeh. *Jews and Hellenistic Cities in Eretz-Israel: Relations of the Jews in Eretz-Israel with the Hellenistic Cities during the Second Temple Period (332 BCE–70 CE)*. Texte und Studien zum antiken Judentum 21. Tübingen: J.C.B. Mohr, 1990.

Kasher, Aryeh. *The Jews in Hellenistic and Roman Egypt: The Struggle for Equal Rights*. Texte und Studien zum antiken Judentum 7. Tübingen: J.C.B. Mohr (Paul Siebeck), 1985.

Kasher, Aryeh. *Jews, Idumaeans, and Ancient Arabs: Relations of the Jews in Eretz-Israel with the Nations of the Frontier and the Desert during the Hellenistic and Roman Era (332 BCE–70 CE)*. Texte und Studien zum antiken Judentum 18. Tübingen: J.C.B. Mohr, 1988.

Kasher, Rimmon. "Anthropomorphism, Holiness and Cult: A New Look at Ezekiel 40–48." *Zeitschrift für die alttestamentliche Wissenschaft* 110, no. 2 (1998): 192–208.

Kasher, Rimon. *Ezekiel: Introduction and Commentary. Volume 2: Chapters 25–48*. Mikra LeYisra'el: A Bible Commentary for Israel. Tel Aviv; Jerusalem: Am Oved Publishers; The Hebrew University Magnes Press, 2004 [Hebrew].

Kehati, Pinhas. *Seder Kodashim. Vol. 3: Temurah, Keretot, Me'ilah, Tamid, Middot, Kinnim. A New Translation with a Commentary by Rabbi Pinhas Kehati. Translated by Rabbi Nahum Wengrove*. Jerusalem: Eliner Library, 1995.

Kent, Eliza F. *Sacred Groves and Local Gods: Religion and Environmentalism in South India*. Oxford; New York: Oxford, 2013.

Kent, John Harvey. "The Temple Estates of Delos, Rheneia, and Mykonos." *Hesperia* 17, no. 4 (1948): 243–338.

Kisch, Guido. *Pseudo-Philo's Liber Antiquitatum Biblicarum*. Publications in Medieval Studies, the University of Notre Dame. Notre Dame, IN: University of Notre Dame, 1949.

Kitchen, Kenneth A. "The Patriarchal Age: Myth or History?" *Biblical Archaeology Review* 21 (1995): 48–57, 88–95.

Kitz, Anne M. "Undivided Inheritance and Lot Casting in the Book of Joshua." *JBL* 119, no. 4 (2000): 601–18.

Klawans, Jonathan. *Purity, Sacrifice, and the Temple: Symbolism and Supersessionism in the Study of Ancient Judaism*. Oxford; New York: Oxford University Press, 2006.

Kletter, R. and I. Beit-Arieh. "A Heavy Scale Weight from Tel Malhata and the Maneh (Mina) of Judah." Pages 245–61 in *Ugarit-Forschungen. Internationales Jahrbuch für die Altertumskunde Syrien-Palästinas, Band 33*. Edited by Manfried Dietrich and Oswald Loretz. Münster: Ugarit-Verlag, 2001.

Kletter, Raz. *Economic Keystones: The Weight System of the Kingdom of Judah*. JSOT Supp. 276. Sheffield: Sheffield Academic Press, 1998.

Kletter, Raz. "Weights and Measures." Pages 831–41 in *The New Interpreter's Dictionary of the Bible*. Vol. 5. Edited by Katharine Doob Sakenfeld. Nashville: Abingdon Press, 2009.

Kloppenborg, John. "The Growth and Impact of Agricultural Tenancy in Jewish Palestine (III BCE–I CE)." *JESHO* 51, no. 1 (2008): 31–66.

Kloppenborg, John S. *The Tenants in the Vineyard: Ideology, Economics, and Agrarian Conflict in Jewish Palestine*. Wissenschaftliche Untersuchungen zum Neuen Testament 195. Tübingen: Mohr Siebeck, 2006.

Knauf, Ernst Axel. "Bethel: The Israelite Impact on Judean Language and Literature." Pages 291–350 in *Judah and the Judeans in the Persian Period*. Edited by Oded Lipschitz and Manfred Oeming. Winona Lake, IN: Eisenbrauns, 2006.

Knohl, Israel. *The Sanctuary of Silence: The Priestly Torah and the Holiness School*. Minneapolis: Fortress Press, 1995.

Knowles, Melody D. *Centrality Practiced: Jerusalem in the Religious Practice of Yehud and the Diaspora in the Persian Period*. Society of Biblical Literature, Archaeology and Biblical Studies 16. Leiden; Boston: Brill, 2006.

Knowles, Melody D. "Pilgrimage to Jerusalem in the Persian Period." Pages 7–24 in *Approaching Yehud: New Approaches to the Study of the Persian Period*. Edited by Jon L. Berquist. Atlanta: Society of Biblical Literature, 2007.

Konkel, Michael. *Architektonik des Heiligen: Studien zur zweiten Tempelvision Ezechiels (Ez 40–48)*. Bonner biblische Beiträge 129. Berlin: Philo Verlagsgesellschaft, 2001.

Kozuh, Michael. *The Sacrificial Economy. Assessors, Contractors, and Thieves in the Management of Sacrificial Sheep at the Eanna Temple of Uruk (ca. 625–520 B.C.)*. Explorations in Ancient Near Eastern Civilizations 2. Winona Lake, IN: Eisenbrauns, 2014.

Kraemer, David. *Rabbinic Judaism: Space and Place*. Routledge Jewish Studies Series. London; New York: Routledge, 2016.

Kruse, Colin G. *Paul's Letter to the Romans*. The Pillar New Testament Commentary. Grand Rapids, MI: William B. Eerdmans, 2012.

Kwakkel, Gerg. "The Land in the Book of Hosea." Pages 165–81 in *The Land of Israel in Bible, History, and Theology. Studies in Honour of Ed Noort*. Edited by Jacques Van Ruiten and J. Cornelius de Vos. Supplements to Vetus Testamentum 124. Leiden; Boston: Brill, 2009.

Lambert, S.D. *Rationes Centesimarum: Sales of Public Land in Lykourgan Athens*. Archaia Hellas 3. Amsterdam: J.C. Gieben, 1997.

Lambton, Ann K. S. *Landlord and Peasant in Persia: A Study of Land Tenure and Land Revenue Administration*. London; New York: Oxford University Presss, 1953.

Landau, Y. H. "A Greek Inscription Found Near Hefzibah." *IEJ* 16, no. 1 (1966): 54–70.

Langdon, Merle. "Public Auctions in Ancient Athens." Pages 253–65 in *Ritual, Finance, Politics: Athenian Democratic Accounts Presented to David Lewis*. Edited by Robin Osborne and Simon Hornblower. Oxford: Clarendon Press, 1994.

Langgut, Dafna, Yuval Gadot, and Oded Lipschits. "'Fruit of Goodly Trees': The Beginning of Citron Cultivation in Israel and Its Penetration into Jewish Tradition and Culture." *Beit Mikra* 59, no. 1 (2014): 38–55 [Hebrew].

Lapin, Hayim. "Temple, Cult, and Consumption in Second Temple Jerusalem." Pages 241–53 in *Expressions of Cult in the Southern Levant in the Greco-Roman Period. Manifestations in Text and Material Culture*. Edited by Oren Tal and Zeev Weiss. Contextualizing the Sacred 6. Turnhout: Brepols, 2017.

Larson, Erik, Manfred R. Lehmann, and Lawrence H. Schiffman. "4QHalakha A." Pages 25–51 in *Qumran Cave 4, XXV: Halakhic Texts*. Discoveries in the Judaean Desert XXXV. Oxford: Clarendon Press, 1999.

Last, Richard. "Onias IV and the ἀδέσποτος ἱερός: Placing Antiquities 13.62–73 into the Context of Ptolemaic Land Tenure." *JSJ* 41, no. 4–5 (2010): 494–516.

Learmount, Brian. *A History of the Auction*. London: Barnard & Learmount, 1985.

Lefkovits, Judah K. *The Copper Scroll 3Q15: A Reevaluation. A New Reading, Translation, and Commentary*. Studies on the Texts of the Desert of Judah. Leiden: Brill, 2000.

Leibner, Uzi. *Settlement and History in Hellenistic, Roman, and Byzantine Galilee: An Archaeological Survey of the Eastern Galilee*. Texts and Studies in Ancient Judaism 127. Tübingen: Mohr Siebeck, 2009.

Lemaire, A. *Nouvelles inscriptions araméennes d'Idumée II: Collections Moussaieff, Jeselsohn, Welch et divers*. Supplément à Transeuphratène 9. Paris: Gabalda, 2002.

Lemaire, Andre. "Administration of Fourth-Century B.C.E. Judah in Light of Epigraphy and Numismatics." Pages 53–74 in *Judah and the Judeans in the Fourth Century B.C.E.* Edited by Oded Lipschits, Gary N. Knoppers, and Rainer Albertz. Winona Lake, IN: Eisenbrauns, 2007.

Lemaire, André. "Another Temple to the Israelite God. Aramaic Hoard Documents Life in Fourth Century B.C." *Biblical Archaeology Review* 30, no. 4 (2004): 38–44, 60.

Lemaire, André. "Nouveau Temple de Yahô (IVe S. AV. J.-C.)." Pages 265–73 in *"Basel und Bibel": Collected Communications to the XVIIth Congress of the International Organization for the Study of the Old Testament, Basel 2001*. Edited by Matthias Augustin and Hermann Michael Niemann. Beiträge zur Erforschung des Alten Testaments und des antiken Judentums 51. Frankfurt am Main: Peter Lang, 2004.

Lemaire, André. "New Aramaic Ostraca from Idumea and Their Historical Interpretation." Pages 413–56 in *Judah and the Judeans in the Persian Period*. Edited by Oded Lipschits and Manfred Oeming. Winona Lake, IN: Eisenbrauns, 2006.

Lemerle, Paul. *The Agrarian History of Byzantium: From the Origins to the Twelfth Century*. Galway: Officina Typographica, 1979.

Leuchter, Mark. *The Levites and the Boundaries of Israelite Identity*. Oxford: Oxford University Press, 2017.

Leuchter, Mark A. and Jeremy M. Hutton, eds. *Levites and Priests in Biblical History and Tradition*. Ancient Israel and Its Literature 9. Atlanta: Society of Biblical Literature, 2011.

Levine, Baruch A. *In the Presence of the Lord: A Study of Cult and Some Cultic Terms in Ancient Israel*. Studies in Judaism in Late Antiquity 5. Leiden: Brill, 1974.

Levine, Baruch A. *Leviticus: The Traditional Hebrew Text with the New JPS Translation*. The JPS Torah Commentary. Philadelphia: Jewish Publication Society, 1989.

Levine, Baruch A. "The Biblical 'Town' as Reality and Typology: Evaluating Biblical References to Towns and Their Functions." Pages 421–53 in *Urbanization and Land Ownership in the Ancient Near East*. Vol. II. Edited by Michael Hudson and Baruch A. Levine. Cambridge, MA: Peabody Museum of Archaeology and Ethnology, Harvard University, 1999.

Levine, Baruch A. "Farewell to the Ancient Near East: Evaluating Biblical References to Ownership of Land in Comparative Perspective." Pages 223–52 in *Privatization in the Ancient Near East and Classical World*. Vol. I. Edited by Michael Hudson and Baruch A. Levine. Peabody Museum Bulletin 5. Cambridge, MA: Peabody Museum of Archaeology and Ethnology, 1996.

Levine, Baruch A. "Tracing the Biblical Accounting Register: Terminology and the Significance of Quantity." Pages 420–43 in *Commerce and Monetary Systems in the Ancient World: Means of Transmission and Cultural Interaction*. Edited by Robert Roillinger and Christoph Ulf. Oriens et Occidens 6. Stuttgart: Franz Steiner, 2004.

Levine, Lee I. *The Ancient Synagogue: The First Thousand Years*. 2nd ed. New Haven; London: Yale University Press, 2005.

Levine, Lee I. *Jerusalem: Portrait of the City in the Second Temple Period (538 B.C.E.–70 C.E.)*. Philadelphia: The Jewish Publication Society, 2002.

Lilly, Ingrid E. *Two Books of Ezekiel: Papyrus 967 and the Masoretic Text as Variant Literary Editions*. Leiden; Boston: Brill, 2012.

Linders, Tullia. "Sacred Finances: Some Observations." Pages 9–12 in *Economics of Cult in the Ancient Greek World: Proceedings of the Uppsala Symposium 1990*. Edited by Tullia Linders and Brita Alroth. Boreas: Uppsala Studies in Ancient Mediterranean and Near Eastern Civilizations 21. Uppsala; Stockholm: S. Academiae Ubsaliensis; Almqvist & Wiksell, 1992.

Lipiński, Edward, ed. *State and Temple Economy in the Ancient Near East: Proceedings of the International Conference Organized by the Katholieke Universiteit Leuven from the 10th* to the 14th of April 1978. Vol. I of Orientalia Lovaniensia Analecta 5. Leuven: Departement Oriëntalistiek, 1979.

Lipschits, Oded. "Persian Period Finds from Jerusalem: Facts and Interpretations." *Journal of Hebrew Scriptures* 9 (2009): 2–30.

Lipschits, Oded. "On Cash-Boxes and Finding or Not Finding Books: Jehoash's and Josiah's Decisions to Repair the Temple." Pages 239–54 in *Essays on Ancient Israel in Its Near Eastern Context: A Tribute to Nadav Na'aman*. Edited by Yairah Amit, Ehud Ben Zvi, Israel Finkelstein, and Oded Lipschits. Winona Lake, IN: Eisenbrauns, 2006.

Lipschits, Oded. "The Rural Economy of Judah during the Persian Period and the Settlement History of the District System." Pages 237–64 in *The Economy of Ancient Judah in Its Historical Context*. Edited by Marvin Lloyd Miller, Ehud Ben Zvi, and Gary N. Knoppers. Winona Lake, IN: Eisenbrauns, 2015.

Lipschits, Oded, Yuval Gadot, Benjamin Arubas, and Manfred Oeming. "Palace and Village, Paradise and Oblivion: Unraveling the Riddles of Ramat Raḥel." *Near Eastern Archaeology* 74 (2011): 2–49.

Lipschits, Oded, Yuval Gadot, and Dafna Langgut. "The Riddle of Ramat Raḥel: The Archaeology of a Royal Persian Period Edifice." *Transeuphratène* 21 (2012): 57–79.

Lipschits, Oded and David S. Vanderhooft. *The Yehud Stamp Impressions: A Corpus of Inscribed Impressions from the Persian and Hellenistic Periods in Judah*. Winona Lake, IN: Eisenbrauns, 2011.

Lipschitz, Oded. *The Fall and Rise of Jerusalem: Judah under Babylonian Rule*. Winona Lake, IN: Eisenbrauns, 2005.

Lipschitz, Oded. "Achaemenid Imperial Policy, Settlement Processes in Palestine, and the Status of Jerusalem in the Middle of the Fifth Century B.C.E." Pages 19–53 in *Judah and the Judeans in the Persian Period*. Edited by Oded Lipschitz and Manfred Oeming. Winona Lake, IN: Eisenbrauns, 2006.

Liver, J. "The Half-Shekel Offering in Biblical and Post-Biblical Literature." *HTR* 56, no. 3 (1963): 173–98.

Liverani, Mario. *Israel's History and the History of Israel*. London; Oakville, CT: Equinox, 2005.

Lohfink, Norbert. "חָרַם ḥāram; חֵרֶם ḥērem." Pages 180–99 in *Theological Dictionary of the Old Testament*. Vol. V. Edited by G. Johannes Botterweck and Helmer Ringgren. Grand Rapids, MI: William B. Eerdmans, 1986.

Lohfink, Norbert. "Distribution of the Functions of Power: The Laws Concerning Public Offices in Deuteronomy 16:18–18:22." Pages 336–54 in *A Song of Power and the Power of Song: Essays on the Book of Deuteronomy*. Edited by Duane L. Christensen. Winona Lake, IN: Eisenbrauns, 1993.

Lundquist, John M. *The Temple of Jerusalem: Past, Present, and Future*. Westport, CT; London: Praeger, 2008.

Lupu, Eran. *Greek Sacred Law: A Collection of New Documents*. Religions in the Greco-Roman World 152. Leiden; Boston: Brill, 2005.

Luria, B.Z. "Priestly Cities in the Second Temple Period." *HUCA* 44 (1973): 1–18 [Hebrew].

Lyons, Michael A. *From Law to Prophecy: Ezekiel's Use of the Holiness Code*. Library of Hebrew Bible/Old Testament Studies 507. New York; London: T&T Clark, 2009.

Ma, John. "Seleukids and Speech-Acts: Performative Utterances, Legitimacy and Negotiation in the World of the Maccabees." Pages 71–112 in *Scripta Classica Israelica. Yearbook of the Israel Society for the Promotion of Classical Studies*. Vol. XIX. Edited by Hannah M.

Cotton, Jonathan J. Price, and David J. Wasserstein. Jerusalem: The Israel Society for the Promotion of Classical Studies, 2000.
Mackie, Timothy P. *Expanding Ezekiel: The Hermeneutics of Scribal Addition in the Ancient Text Witnesses of the Book of Ezekiel*. Forschungen zur Religion und Literatur des Alten und Neuen Testaments. Göttingen: Vandenhoeck & Ruprecht, 2015.
Magen, Yitzhak. *Mount Gerizim Excavations, Volume II: A Temple City*. Judea and Samaria Publications 8. Jerusalem: Staff Officer for Archaeology—Civil Administration of Judea and Samaria, 2008.
Magen, Yitzhak, Haggai Misgav, and Levana Tsfania. *Mount Gerizim Excavations Volume I: The Aramaic, Hebrew and Samaritan Inscriptions*. Judea & Samaria Publications 2. Jerusalem: Staff Officer of Archaeology—Civil Administration of Judea and Samaria, 2004.
Magness, Jodi. *The Archaeology of Qumran and the Dead Sea Scrolls*. Grand Rapids, MI; Cambridge, U.K.: William B. Eerdmans, 2002.
Magness, Jodi. *Stone and Dung, Oil and Spit: Jewish Daily Life in the Time of Jesus*. Grand Rapids, MI: William B. Eerdmans, 2011.
Mandelbaum, Irving J. *The Talmud of the Land of Israel: A Preliminary Translation and Explanation. Volume 4: Kilayim*. Chicago Studies in the History of Judaism. Chicago: University of Chicago Press, 1990.
Mann, Barbara E. *Space and Place in Jewish Studies*. Key Words in Jewish Studies. New Brunswick; London: Rutgers University Press, 2012.
Manning, J.G. *Land and Power in Ptolemaic Egypt: The Structure of Land Tenure*. Cambridge: Cambridge University Press, 2003.
Manning, J.G. *The Open Sea: The Economic Life of the Ancient Mediterranean World from the Iron Age to the Rise of Rome*. Princeton, NJ: Princeton, 2018.
Mason, Steve. "Of Audience and Meaning: Reading Josephus' *Bellum Judaicum* in the Context of a Flavian Audience." Pages 71–100 in *Josephus and Jewish History in Flavian Rome and Beyond*. Edited by Joseph Sievers and Gaia Lembi. Supplements to the Journal for the Study of Judaism 104. Leiden; Boston: Brill, 2005.
Master, Daniel M. "Economy and Exchange in the Iron Age Kingdoms of the Southern Levant." *Bulletin of the American Schools of Oriental Research*, no. 372 (2014): 81–97.
Maurer, C. "Rhíza." Pages 985–86 in *Theological Dictionary of the New Testament, Translated and Abridged*. Edited by Gerhard Kittel, Gerhard Friedrich, and Geoffrey Bromiley. Grand Rapids, MI: Eerdmans, 1985.
Mazar, Benjamin. "The Cities of the Priests and the Levites." *Supplements to Vetus Testamentum* 7 (1957): 193–204.
Mazar, Eilat. "The Wall that Nehemiah Built." *Biblical Archaeology Review* 35, no. 2 (2009): 24–33, 66.
McCarter, P. Kyle. "The Copper Scroll Treasure as an Accumulation of Religious Offerings." Pages 133–48 in *Methods of Investigation of the Dead Sea Scrolls and the Khirbet Qumran Site*. Edited by Michael O. Wise, Norman Golb, John J. Collins, and Dennis G. Pardee. Annals of the New York Academy of Sciences 722. New York, NY: The New York Academy of Sciences, 1994.
McInerney, Jeremy. "On the Border: Sacred Land and the Margins of the Community." Pages 32–59 in *City, Countryside, and the Spatial Organization of Value in Classical Antiquity*.

Edited by Ralph M. Rosen and Ineke Sluiter. Mnemosyne, Supplement 279. Leiden; Boston: Brill, 2006.

McKenzie, Judith S., Sheila Gibson, and A. T. Reyes. "Reconstructing the Serapeum in Alexandria from the Archaeological Evidence." *The Journal of Roman Studies* 94 (2004): 73–121.

Meir, Natan. "The Labor of Schnorring." *AJS Perspectives* (Fall 2013): 16–17.

Mendels, Doron. *The Land of Israel as a Political Concept in Hasmonean Literature: Recourse to History in Second Century B.C. Claims to the Holy Land*. Texte und Studien zum antiken Judentum 15. Tübingen: J.C.B. Mohr, 1987.

Mendels, Doron. "Was the Rejection of Gifts One of the Reasons for the Outbreak of the Maccabean Revolt? A Preliminary Note on the Role of Gifting in the Book of 1 Maccabees." *Journal for the Study of the Pseudepigrapha* 20, no. 4 (2011): 243–56.

Mendels, Doron. "Memory and Memories: The Attitude of 1–2 Macc toward Hellenization and Hellenism." Pages 41–54 in *Jewish Identities in Antiquity: Studies in Memory of Menahem Stern*. Edited by Lee I. Levine and Daniel R. Schwartz. Texte und Studien zum antiken Judentum 130. Tübingen: Mohr Siebeck, 2009.

Meyers, Carol L. and Eric M. Meyers. *Haggai, Zechariah 1–8: A New Translation with Introduction and Commentary*. The Anchor Bible. Garden City, NY: Doubleday, 1987.

Meyers, Eric M. "The Babylonian Exile Revisited: Demographics and the Emergence of the Canon of Scripture." Pages 61–74 in *Judaism and Crisis: Crisis as a Catalyst in Jewish Cultural History*. Edited by Armin Lange, Diethard Römheld, and Matthias Weigold. Schriften des Institutum Judaicum Delitzschianum 9. Göttingen; Oakville, CT: Vandenhoeck & Ruprecht, 2011.

Meyers, Eric M. and Sean Burt. "Exile and Return: From the Babylonian Destruction to the Beginnings of Hellenism." Pages 209–35 in *Ancient Israel: From Abraham to the Roman Destruction of the Temple*. Edited by Hershel Shanks. Washington, D.C.: Biblical Archaeology Society, 2010.

Meyers, Eric M. and Mark A. Chancey. *Alexander to Constantine: Archaeology of the Land of the Bible, Vol. 3*. The Anchor Yale Bible Reference Library. New Haven: Yale University Press, 2012.

Mildenberg, Leo. "On the Money Circulation in Palestine from Artaxerxes II till Ptolemy I. Preliminary Studies of the Local Coinage in the Fifth Persian Satrapy." *Transeuphratène*, no. 7 (1994): 63–71.

Milgrom, Jacob. "The Concept of Ma'al in the Bible and the Ancient Near East." *Journal of the American Oriental Society* 96, no. 2 (1976): 236–47.

Milgrom, Jacob. *Leviticus 17–22: A New Translation with Introduction and Commentary*. The Anchor Bible 3 A. New York: Doubleday, 2000.

Milgrom, Jacob. *Leviticus 23–27: A New Translation with Introduction and Commentary*. The Anchor Bible 3B. New York: Doubleday, 2001.

Milgrom, Jacob. "Profane Slaughter and a Formulaic Key to the Composition of Deuteronomy." *HUCA* 47 (1976): 1–17.

Milgrom, Jacob. *Studies in Cultic Theology and Terminology*. Studies in Judaism in Late Antiquity 36. Leiden: Brill, 1983.

Milgrom, Jacob and Daniel I. Block. *Ezekiel's Hope: A Commentary on Ezekiel 38–48*. Eugene, OR: Cascade Books, 2012.

Modrzejewski, Joseph. *The Jews of Egypt: From Rameses II to Emperor Hadrian.* Translated by Robert Cornman. Philadelphia: Jewish Publication Society, 1995.

Monson, Andrew. *From the Ptolemies to the Romans: Political and Economic Change in Egypt.* Cambridge; New York: Cambridge University Press, 2012.

Monson, Andrew. "The Jewish High Priesthood for Sale: Farming out Temples in the Hellenistic Near East." *JJS* 67, no. 1 (2016): 15–35.

Morris, Ian and J.G. Manning. "The Economic Sociology of the Ancient Mediterranean World." Pages 131–59 in *The Handbook of Economic Sociology.* Edited by Neil J. Smelser and Richard Swedberg. Princeton; New York: Princeton University Press; Russell Sage Foundation, 2005.

Mudge, Ken, Jules Janick, Steven Scofield, and Eliezer E. Goldschmidt. "A History of Grafting." *Horticultural Reviews* 35 (2009): 437–93.

Murphy-O'Connor, Jerome. "Demetrius I and the Teacher of Righteousness." *RB* 83, no. 3 (1976): 400–20.

Murphy, Catherine M. *Wealth in the Dead Sea Scrolls and in the Qumran Community.* Studies on the Texts of the Desert of Judah 40. Leiden; Boston: Brill, 2002.

Na'aman, Nadav and Ran Zadok. "Assyrian Deportations to the Province of Samerina in the Light of Two Cuneiform Tablets from Tel Hadid." *Tel Aviv* 27 (2000): 159–88.

Naaman, Nadav. *Borders and Districts in Biblical Historiography: Seven Studies in Biblical Geographic Lists.* Jerusalem Biblical Studies 4. Jerusalem: Simor, 1986.

Nanos, Mark D. "Romans 11 and Christian-Jewish Relations: Exegetical Options for Revisiting the Translation and Interpretation of This Central Text." *Criswell Theological Review* 9, no. 2 (2012): 3–21.

Nanos, Mark D. "Romans." Pages 253–86 in *The Jewish Annotated New Testament.* Edited by Amy-Jill Levine and Marc Zvi Brettler. Oxford; New York: Oxford University Press, 2011.

Nanos, Mark D. "'Broken Branches': A Pauline Metaphor Gone Awry? (Romans 11:11–24)." Pages 339–76 in *Between Gospel and Election: Explorations in the Interpretation of Romans 9–11.* Edited by Florian Wilk and J. Ross Wagner. Wissenschaftliche Untersuchungen zum Neuen Testament 257. Tübingen: Mohr Siebeck, 2010.

Nanos, Mark D. and Magnus Zetterholm, eds. *Paul within Judaism: Restoring the First-Century Context to the Apostle.* Minneapolis: Fortress Press, 2015.

Naveh, Joseph. *On Stone and Mosaic: The Aramaic and Hebrew Inscriptions from Ancient Synagogues.* Jerusalem: Israel Exploration Society, 1978 [Hebrew].

Naveh, Joseph and Yitzhak Magen. "Aramaic and Hebrew Inscriptions of the Second-Century BCE at Mount Gerizim." *'Atiqot* 32 (1997): 37–56 (Hebrew), 9*–17* (English).

Nelson, Richard D. *Raising Up a Faithful Priest: Community and Priesthood in Biblical Theology.* Louisville: Westminster/John Knox Press, 1993.

Nelson, Richard D. "Ḥerem and the Deuteronomic Social Conscience." Pages 39–54 in *Deuteronomy and Deuteronomic Literature: Festschrift C.H.W. Brekelmans.* Edited by Marc Vervenne and Johan Lust. Bibliotheca Ephemeridum Theologicarum Lovaniensium CXXXIII. Leuven: Leuven University Press; Uitgeverij Peeters, 1997.

Nemet-Nejat, Karen Rhea. *Cuneiform Mathematical Texts as a Reflection of Everyday Life in Mesopotamia.* American Oriental Series 75. New Haven: American Oriental Society, 1993.

Netzer, Ehud. *The Architecture of Herod, The Great Builder.* Texts and Studies in Ancient Judaism 117. Tübingen: Mohr Siebeck, 2006.

Neufeld, Edward. "The Prohibitions against Loans at Interest in Ancient Hebrew Laws." *HUCA* 26 (1955): 355–412.
Neusner, Jacob. *The Economics of the Mishnah.* South Florida Studies in the History of Judaism 185. Atlanta: Scholars Press, 1998.
Neusner, Jacob. *The Economics of the Mishnah.* Chicago Studies in the History of Judaism. Chicago: University of Chicago Press, 1990.
Neusner, Jacob. *A History of the Mishnaic Law of Holy Things. Part Five: Keritot, Meilah, Tamid, Middot, Qinnim. Translation and Explanation.* Studies in Judaism in Late Antiquity XXX. Leiden: Brill, 1980.
Neusner, Jacob. *A History of the Mishnaic Law of Holy Things. Part Four: Arakhin, Temurah. Translation and Explanation.* Studies in Judaism in Late Antiquity XXX. Leiden: Brill, 1979.
Neusner, Jacob. *A History of the Mishnaic Law of Holy Things. Part Six: The Mishnaic System of Sacrifice and Sanctuary.* Studies in Judaism in Late Antiquity 30. Leiden: Brill, 1980.
Neusner, Jacob. *Judaism: The Evidence of the Mishnah.* Chicago: University of Chicago Press, 1981.
Neusner, Jacob. "Map without Territory: Mishnah's System of Sacrifice and Sanctuary." *History of Religions* 19, no. 2 (1979): 103–27.
Neusner, Jacob. *Sifra: An Analytical Translation. Volume III: Aharê Mot, Qedoshim, Emor, Behar, and Behuqotai.* Brown Judaic Studies 140. Atlanta: Scholars Press, 1988.
Newman, Aryeh. "Sacrilege." Pages 649–50 in *Encyclopaedia Judaica, Second Edition, Vol. 17.* Edited by Fred Skolnik and Michael Berenbaum. Farmington Hills, MI: Thomson Gale, 2006.
Nickelsburg, George W. E. *1 Enoch 1: A Commentary on the Book of 1 Enoch, Chapters 1–36; 81–108.* Minneapolis: Fortress Press, 2001.
Niditch, Susan. "Ezekiel 40–48 in a Visionary Context." *Catholic Biblical Quarterly* 48 (1986): 208–24.
Niditch, Susan. *War in the Hebrew Bible: A Study in the Ethics of Violence.* New York: Oxford University Press, 1993.
Nihan, Christophe. *From Priestly Torah to Pentateuch: A Study in the Composition of the Book of Leviticus.* Forschungen zum Alten Testament 2. Reihe. Tübingen: Mohr Siebeck, 2007.
North, Douglass C., John Joseph Wallis, and Barry R. Weingast. *Violence and Social Orders: A Conceptual Framework for Interpreting Recorded Human History.* Cambridge: Cambridge University Press, 2009.
Noth, Martin. *Leviticus: A Commentary.* The Old Testament Library. Philadelphia: The Westminster Press, 1977.
O'Hare, Daniel M. *Have You Seen, Son of Man? A Study in the Translation and Vorlage of LXX Ezekiel 40–48.* Society of Biblical Literature Septuagint and Cognate Studies 57. Leiden; Boston: Brill, 2010.
Oakman, Douglas E. *Jesus and the Economic Questions of His Day.* Studies in the Bible and Early Christianity 8. Lewiston, NY: The Edwin Mellen Press, 1986.
Oelsner, Joachim. "Krisenerscheinungen im Achaimenidenreich im 5. und 4. Jahrhundert v.u.Z." Pages 1041–73 in *Hellenische Poleis II: Krise—Wandlung—Wirkung.* Edited by Elisabeth Charlotte Welskopf. Berlin: Akademie-Verlag, 1973.

Oelsner, Joachim. "The Neo-Babylonian Period." Pages 289–305 in *Security for Debt in Ancient Near Eastern Law*. Edited by Raymond Westbrook and Richard Jasnow. Culture and History of the Ancient Near East 9. Leiden: Brill, 2001.

Oppenheim, A. Leo. "A Fiscal Practice of the Ancient Near East." *JNES* 6, no. 2 (1947): 116–20.

Oppenheimer, Aharon. *The 'Am Ha-Aretz: A Study in the Social History of the Jewish People in the Hellenistic-Roman Period*. Translated by I.H. Levine. Arbeiten zur Literatur und Geschichte des hellenistischen Judentums 8. Leiden: Brill, 1977.

Otto, Eckart. "The Holiness Code in Diachrony and Synchrony in the Legal Hermeneutics of the Pentateuch." Pages 135–56 in *The Strata of the Priestly Writings: Contemporary Debate and Future Directions*. Edited by Sarah Schectman and Joel S. Baden. Abhandlungen zur Theologie des Alten und Neuen Testaments 95. Zürich: Theologischer Verlag Zürich, 2009.

Papazarkadas, Nikolaos. *Sacred and Public Land in Ancient Athens*. Oxford Classical Monographs. Oxford; New York: Oxford University Press, 2011.

Park, Hyung Dae. *Finding Herem?: A Study of Luke-Acts in the Light of Herem*. Library of New Testament Studies 357. London: T&T Clark, 2007.

Parker, Robert. *Greek Gods Abroad: Names, Natures, and Transformations*. Sather Classical Lectures 72. Oakland, CA: University of California Press, 2017.

Paschke, Boris. "The Land in the New Testament." Pages 277–304 in *The Earth and the Land: Studies about the Value of the Land of Israel in the Old Testament and Afterwards*. Edited by Hendrik J. Koorevaar and Mart-Jan Paul. EDIS: Edition Israelogie 11. Berlin: Peter Lang, 2018.

Pastor, Jack. *Land and Economy in Ancient Palestine*. London; New York: Routledge, 1997.

Patrick, Dale. *Old Testament Law*. Atlanta: John Knox Press, 1985.

Perluss, Preston Martin. "Monastic Landed Wealth in Late-Eighteenth-Century Paris. Principal Traits and Major Issues." Pages 51–74 in *The Economics of Providence: Management, Finances and Patrimony of Religious Orders and Congregations in Europe, 1773–c. 1930*. Edited by Maarten Van Dijck, Jan de Maeyer, Jeffrey Tyssens, and Jimmy Koppen. Leuven: Leuven University Press, 2012.

Piotrkowski, Meron M. "Josephus on Onias and the Oniad Temple." *Jewish Studies Quarterly* 25, no. 1–16 (2018).

Pirngruber, Reinhard. "Wages as Guides to the Standard of Living in First Millennium BC Babylonia." Pages 107–18 in *Silver, Money and Credit: A Tribute to Robartus J. Van der Spek on the Occasion of His 65th birthday*. Edited by Kristin Kleber and Reinhard Pirngruber. PIHANS CXXVIII. Leiden: Nederlands Instituut voor het Nabije Oosten, 2016.

Porten, Bezalel. *Archives from Elephantine: The Life of an Ancient Jewish Military Colony*. Berkeley: University of California Press, 1968.

Porten, Bezalel and Ada Yardeni. "Why the Unprovenanced Idumean Ostraca Should Be Published." Pages 73–98 in *New Seals and Inscriptions, Hebrew, Idumean, and Cuneiform*. Edited by Meir Lubetski. Hebrew Bible Monographs 8. Sheffield: Sheffield Phoenix Press, 2007.

Porter, J. R. "Lev XXVII 20: Some Further Considerations." *VT* 50, no. 4 (2000): 569–71.

Postgate, J. N. *Fifty Neo-Assyrian Legal Documents*. Warminster: Aris & Phillips, 1976.

Powell, Marvin A. "Late Babylonian Surface Mensuration." *Archiv für Orientforschung* 31 (1984): 32–66.

Premnath, D.N. "Loan Practices in the Hebrew Bible." Pages 173–85 in *To Break Every Yoke: Essays in Honor of Marvin L. Chaney*. Edited by Robert B. Coote and Norman K. Gottwald. The Social World of Biblical Antiquity, Second Series 3. Sheffield: Sheffield Phoenix Press, 2007.

Propp, William Henry. *Exodus 19–40: A New Translation with Introduction and Commentary*. The Anchor Bible. New York: Doubleday, 2006.

Qimron, Elisha. *The Temple Scroll: A Critical Edition with Extensive Reconstructions*. Judean Desert Studies. Beer Sheva; Jerusalem: Ben-Gurion University of the Negev; Israel Exploration Society, 1996.

Qimron, Elisha. "The Text of CDC." Pages 9–49 in *The Damascus Document Reconsidered*. Edited by Magen Broshi. Jerusalem: Israel Exploration Society, 1992.

Rabin, Chaim. *The Zadokite Documents. I. The Admonition. II. The Laws. Edited with a Translation and Notes*. Oxford: Clarendon Press, 1958.

Radner, Karen. "The Neo-Assyrian Period." Pages 265–88 in *Security for Debt in Ancient Near Eastern Law*. Edited by Raymond Westbrook and Richard Jasnow. Culture and History of the Ancient Near East 9. Leiden: Brill, 2001.

Rajak, Tessa. "Josephus in the Diaspora." Pages 79–97 in *Flavius Josephus and Flavian Rome*. Edited by Jonathan Edmondson, Steve Mason, and James Rives. Oxford; New York: Oxford University Press, 2005.

Rasor, Paul B. "Biblical Roots of Modern Consumer Credit Law." *Journal of Law and Religion* 10, no. 1 (1993): 157–92.

Rastoin, Marc. "Une bien étrange greffe (Rm 11, 17): Correspondances rabbiniques d'une expression paulinienne." *RB* 114, no. 1 (2007): 73–79.

Regev, Eyal. "Priestly Dynamic Holiness and Deuteronomic Static Holiness." *VT* 51, no. 2 (2001): 243–61.

Regev, Eyal. *The Sadducees and Their Halakhah: Religion and Society in the Second Temple Period*. Jerusalem: Yad Ben-Zvi Press, 2005 [Hebrew].

Regev, Eyal. "The Sadducees, the Pharisees, and the Sacred: Meaning and Ideology in the Halakhic Controversies between the Sadducees and the Pharisees." *Review of Rabbinic Judaism* 9 (2006): 126–40.

Regev, Eyal. *Sectarianism in Qumran: A Cross-Cultural Perspective*. Religion and Society 45. Berlin; New York: De Gruyter, 2007.

Regev, Eyal. "Reconstructing Qumranic and Rabbinic World-Views: Dynamic Holiness vs. Static Holiness." in *Rabbinic Perspectives: Rabbinic Literature and the Dead Sea Scrolls. Proceedings of the Eighth International Symposium of the Orion Center for the Study of the Dead Sea Scrolls and Associated Literature, 7–9 January, 2003*. Edited by Steven D. Fraade, Aharon Shemesh, and Ruth Clements. Leiden; Boston: Brill, 2006.

Reich, Ronny. "Stone Scale Weights of the Late Second Temple Period from the Jewish Quarter." Pages 329–89 in *Jewish Quarter Excavations in the Old City of Jerusalem*. Edited by Hillel Geva. Jerusalem: Israel Exploration Society, 2006.

Reich, Ronny and Zvi Greenhut. "Another 'Boundary of Gezer' Inscription Found Recently." *IEJ* 52, no. 1 (2002): 58–63.

Renger, Johannes. "Interaction of Temple, Palace, and 'Private Enterprise' in the Old Babylonian Economy." Pages 249–56 in *State and Temple Economy in the Ancient Near East: Proceedings of the International Conference Organized by the Katholieke*

Universiteit Leuven from the 10th to the 14th of April 1978. Vol. I. Edited by Edward Lipiński. Orientalia Lovaniensia Analecta 5. Leuven: Departement Oriëntalistiek, 1979.

Rengstorf, Karl Heinrich. *A Complete Concordance to Flavius Josephus.* Leiden: Brill, 1973.

Rhodes, P. J. and Robin Osborne. *Greek Historical Inscriptions, 404–323 BC.* Oxford: Oxford University Press, 2007.

Rigsby, Kent J. *Asylia: Territorial Inviolability in the Hellenistic World.* Hellenistic Culture and Society 22. Berkeley: University of California Press, 1996.

Ristau, Kenneth A. *Reconstructing Jerusalem: Persian-Period Prophetic Perspectives.* Winona Lake, IN: Eisenbrauns, 2016.

Rocca, Samuel. *Herod's Judaea: A Mediterranean State in the Classical World.* Texts and Studies in Ancient Judaism 122. Tübingen: Mohr Siebeck, 2008.

Rofé, Alexander. "The Laws of Warfare in the Book of Deuteronomy: Their Origins, Intent and Positivity." *JSOT* 32 (1985): 23–44.

Römer, Thomas. *The Invention of God.* Translated by Raymond Guess. Cambridge, MA: Harvard University Press, 2015.

Rooke, Deborah W. *Zadok's Heirs: The Role and Development of the High Priesthood in Ancient Israel.* Oxford Theological Monographs. Oxford; New York: Oxford University Press, 2000.

Rosenberg, Jacob and Avi Weiss. "Land Concentration, Efficiency, Slavery, and the Jubilee." Pages 74–87 in *The Oxford Handbook of Judaism and Economics.* Edited by Aaron Levine. Oxford; New York: Oxford, 2010.

Rosenfeld, Ben-Zion. "The 'Boundary of Gezer' Inscriptions and the History of Gezer at the End of the Second Temple Period." *IEJ* 38, no. 4 (1988): 235–45.

Rosenfeld, Ben Zion and Haim Perlmutter. "Landowners in Roman Palestine 100–300 C.E.: A Distinct Social Group." *Journal of Ancient Judaism* 2, no. 3 (2011): 327–52.

Rosivach, Vincent J. *The System of Public Sacrifice in Fourth-Century Athens.* American Classical Studies 34. Atlanta: Scholars Press, 1994.

Rostovtzeff, Michael I. *The Social and Economic History of the Hellenistic World.* Oxford: Clarendon Press, 1959.

Rousset, Denis. *Le territoire de Delphes et la terre d'Apollon.* Bibliothèque des écoles françaises d'Athènes et de Rome 310. Athènes: Ecole française d'Athènes, 2002.

Rubenstein, Richard L. *After Auschwitz: Radical Theology and Contemporary Judaism.* Indianapolis: The Bobbs-Merrill Company, 1966.

Russell, Stephen C. "Biblical Jubilee Laws in Light of Neo-Babylonian and Achaemenid Period Contracts." *Zeitschrift für die Alttestamentliche Wissenschaft* 130, no. 2 (2018): 189–203.

Safrai, Shemuel. *Pilgrimage to Jerusalem in the Second Temple Period.* Tel Aviv: Am Ha-Sefer, 1965 [Hebrew].

Safrai, Shemuel. "The Temple." Pages 865–907 in *The Jewish People in the First Century: Historical Geography, Political History, Social, Cultural and Religious Life and Institutions.* Vol. 2. Edited by Shemuel Safrai and Menahem Stern. Compendia Rerum Iudaicarum ad Novum Testamentum 2. Assen: Van Gorcum, 1976.

Safrai, Shemuel. "Religion in Everyday Life." Pages 793–833 in *The Jewish People in the First Century: Historical Geography, Political History, Social, Cultural and Religious Life and Institutions.* Vol. 2. Edited by Shemuel Safrai and Menahem Stern. Compendia Rerum Iudaicarum ad Novum Testamentum 2. Assen: Van Gorcum, 1976.

Safrai, Shmuel and Ze'ev Safrai. *Tractate Skalim (sic) (Moed E) with Historical and Sociological Commentary.* Mishnat Eretz Israel. Jerusalem: E.M. Liphshitz, 2009 [Hebrew].

Safrai, Ze'ev. *Seeking Out the Land: Land of Israel Traditions in Ancient Jewish, Christian and Samaritan Literature (200 BCE–400 CE).* Jewish and Christian Perspectives Series 32. Leiden; Boston: Brill, 2018.

Safrai, Zeev. "When Did the Priests Transfer to the Galilee? A Response to Dalia Trifon." *Tarbiz* 62 (1993): 287–92 [Hebrew].

Safrai, Zeev. "The Agrarian Structure in Palestine in the Time of the Second Temple, Mishnah and Talmud." Pages 105–26 in *The Rural Landscape of Ancient Israel.* Edited by Aren M. Maier, Shimon Dar, and Ze'ev Safrai. BAR International Series 1121. Oxford, England: British Archaeological Reports, 2003.

Sand, Shlomo. *The Invention of the Land of Israel: From Holy Land to Homeland.* London; New York: Verso, 2012.

Sanders, E. P. *Judaism: Practice and Belief, 63 BCE–66 CE.* London: SCM Press, 1992.

Sanders, E. P. *Jewish Law from Jesus to the Mishnah: Five Studies.* London; Philadelphia: SCM Press; Trinity Press International, 1990.

Sanders, E. P. *Paul, the Law, and the Jewish People.* Minneapolis: Fortress Press, 1983.

Sasson, Jack M. "Bovine Symbolism in the Exodus Narrative." *VT* 18, no. 3 (1968): 380–87.

Schaper, Joachim. "The Jerusalem Temple as an Instrument of the Achaemenid Fiscal Administration." *VT* 45, no. 4 (1995): 528–39.

Schaper, Joachim. *Priester und Leviten im achämenidischen Juda: Studien zur Kult- und Sozialgeschichte Israels in persischer Zeit.* FAT 31. Tübingen: Mohr Siebeck, 2000.

Schectman, Sarah. "The Social Status of Priestly and Levite Women." Pages 83–102 in *Levites and Priests in Biblical History and Tradition.* Edited by Mark A. Leuchter and Jeremy M. Hutton. Ancient Israel and Its Literature 9. Atlanta: Society of Biblical Literature, 2011.

Schiffman, Lawrence H. *The Courtyards of the House of the Lord. Studies on the Temple Scroll.* Studies on the Texts of the Desert of Judah 75. Leiden; Boston: Brill, 2008.

Schiffman, Lawrence H. *Reclaiming the Dead Sea Scrolls: The History of Judaism, the Background of Christianity, the Lost Library of Qumran.* Philadelphia: Jewish Publication Society, 1994.

Schiffman, Lawrence H. "The Dead Sea Scrolls and Rabbinic Halakhah." Pages 27–33 in *The Dead Sea Scrolls as Background to Postbiblical Judaism and Early Christianity: Papers from an International Conference at St. Andrews in 2001.* Edited by James R. Davila. Studies on the Texts of the Desert of Judah 46. Leiden; Boston: Brill, 2003.

Schloen, J. David. *The House of the Father as Fact and Symbol: Patrimonialism in Ugarit and the Ancient Near East.* Winona Lake, IN: Eisenbrauns, 2001.

Schmidt, Francis. *How the Temple Thinks: Identity and Social Cohesion in Ancient Judaism.* Translated by J. Edward Crowley. The Biblical Seminar 78. Sheffield: Sheffield Academic Press, 2001.

Schneider, Anna. *Die Anfänge der Kulturwirtschaft: Die sumerische Tempelstadt.* Baedeker: Essen, 1920.

Schürer, Emil, Geza Vermes, and Fergus Millar. *The History of the Jewish People in the Age of Jesus Christ (175 B.C.–A.D. 135), Volume I, Revised and Edited.* Edinburgh: T&T Clark, 1973.

Schürer, Emil, Geza Vermes, Fergus Millar, and Matthew Black. *The History of the Jewish People in the Age of Jesus Christ (175 B.C.–A.D. 135), Volume II, Revised and Edited.* Edinburgh: T&T Clark, 1979.

Schwartz, Baruch J. *The Holiness Legislation: Studies in the Priestly Code.* Jerusalem: Magnes Press, 1999 [Hebrew].

Schwartz, Baruch J. "Israel's Holiness: The Torah Traditions." Pages 47–59 in *Purity and Holiness: The Heritage of Leviticus.* Edited by Marcel Poorthuis and Joshua Schwartz. Jewish and Christian Perspectives Series 2. Leiden; Boston: Brill, 2000.

Schwartz, Daniel R. *2 Maccabees.* Commentaries on Early Jewish Literature. Berlin; New York: De Gruyter, 2008.

Schwartz, Daniel R. *Studies in the Jewish Background of Christianity.* Wissenschaftliche Untersuchungen zum Neuen Testament 60. Tübingen: J.C.B. Mohr, 1992.

Schwartz, Joshua. "On Priests and Jericho in the Second Temple Period." *The Jewish Quarterly Review* 79, no. 1 (1988): 23–48.

Schwartz, Joshua. "Bar Qatros and the Priestly Families of Jerusalem." Pages 308–19 in *Jewish Quarter Excavations in the Old City of Jerusalem Conducted by Nahman Avigad, 1969–1982. Volume IV: The Burnt House of Area B and Other Studies. Final Report.* Edited by Hillel Geva. Jerusalem: Israel Exploration Society, 2010.

Schwartz, Seth. *Were the Jews a Mediterranean Society? Reciprocity and Solidarity in Ancient Judaism.* Princeton; Oxford: Princeton University Press, 2010.

Seeligmann, Isac Leo. *Gesammelte Studien zur Hebräischen Bibel.* Edited by Erhard Blum. FAT 41. Tübingen: Mohr Siebeck, 2004.

Shanks, Hershel. *Freeing the Dead Sea Scrolls and Other Adventures of an Archaeology Outsider.* London; New York: Continuum, 2010.

Sharfman, Keith. "Valuation in Jewish Law." Pages 168–81 in *The Oxford Handbook of Judaism and Economics.* Edited by Aaron Levine. Oxford; New York: Oxford, 2010.

Sheldon, Jean. "Ancient Seed Mensuration and Leviticus 27:16." Pages 2434–36 in *Leviticus 23–27: A New Translation with Introduction and Commentary.* Edited by Jacob Milgrom. The Anchor Bible 3B. New York: Doubleday, 2001.

Shemesh, Aharon. "4Q251: Midrash Mishpatim." *DSD* 12, no. 3 (2005): 280–302.

Shemesh, Aharon. *Halakhah in the Making: The Development of Jewish Law from Qumran to the Rabbis.* The Taubman Lectures in Jewish Studies. Berkeley: University of California Press, 2009.

Shemesh, Aharon. "The Laws of First Fruits in the Dead Sea Scrolls." Pages 147–64 in *Meghillot: Studies in the Dead Sea Scrolls.* Vol. 1. Edited by Moshe Bar-Asher and Devorah Dimant. Jerusalem; Haifa: The Byalik Institute; University of Haifa, 2003 [Hebrew].

Sievers, Joseph. *Synopsis of the Greek Sources for the Hasmonean Period: 1–2 Maccabees and Josephus, War 1 and Antiquities 12–14.* Subsidia Biblica 20. Roma: Pontificio Istituto Biblico, 2001.

Silver, Morris. *Prophets and Markets: The Political Economy of Ancient Israel.* Social Dimensions of Economics. Boston: Kluwer-Nijhoff, 1983.

Simkins, Ronald A. "Patronage and the Political Economy of Monarchic Israel." Pages 123–44 in *The Social World of the Hebrew Bible: Twenty-Five Years of the Social Sciences in the Academy.* Edited by Athalya Brenner and Stephen L. Cook. Semeia 87. Atlanta: Society of Biblical Literature, 1999.

Simon, Bennett. "Ezekiel's Geometric Vision of the Restored Temple: From the Rod of His Wrath to the Reed of His Measuring." *HTR* 102, no. 4 (2009): 411–38.
Ska, Jean Louis. *Introduction to Reading the Pentateuch*. Winona Lake, IN: Eisenbrauns, 2006.
Smith, Jonathan Z. *Map is Not Territory: Studies in the History of Religion*. Studies in Judaism in Late Antiquity 23. Leiden: Brill, 1978.
Smith, Jonathan Z. *To Take Place: Toward Theory in Ritual*. Chicago Studies in the History of Judaism. Chicago: University of Chicago Press, 1987.
Smith, Mark S. *Where the Gods Are: Spatial Dimensions of Anthropomorphism in the Biblical World*. The Anchor Yale Bible Reference Library. New Haven; London: Yale University Press, 2016.
Sosin, Joshua D. "Two Attic Endowments." *Zeitschrift für Papyrologie und Epigraphik* 138 (2002): 123–28.
Speiser, Ephraim A. "Leviticus and the Critics." Pages 29–45 in *Yehezkel Kaufmann Jubilee Volume: Studies in Bible and Jewish Religion Dedicated to Yehezkel Kaufmann on the Occasion of His Seventieth Birthday*. Edited by Menahem Haran. Jerusalem: Magnes Press, 1960.
Stackert, Jeffrey. "Leviticus." Pages 573–81 in *The Oxford Encyclopedia of the Books of the Bible*. Vol. 1. Edited by Michael D. Coogan. Oxford; New York: Oxford University Press, 2011.
Stackert, Jeffrey. "The Holiness Legislation and Its Pentateuchal Sources: Revision, Supplementation, and Replacement." Pages 187–204 in *The Strata of the Priestly Writings: Contemporary Debate and Future Directions*. Edited by Sarah Schectman and Joel S. Baden. Abhandlungen zur Theologie des Alten und Neuen Testaments 95. Zürich: Theologischer Verlag Zürich, 2009.
Steinkeller, Piotr. "The Renting of Fields in Early Mesopotamia and the Development of the Concept of 'Interest' in Sumerian." *JESHO* 24, no. 2 (1981): 113–45.
Stemberger, Gunter. "Die Bedeutung des 'Landes Israel' in der rabbinischen Tradition." *Kairos* 25 (1983): 176–99.
Stern, Ian. "The Population of Persian-Period Idumea According to the Ostraca: A Study of Ethnic Boundaries and Ethnogenesis." Pages 205–38 in *A Time of Change: Judah and Its Neighbours in the Persian and Early Hellenistic Periods*. Edited by Yigal Levin. Library of Second Temple Studies 65. London; New York: T&T Clark, 2007.
Stern, Menahem. *The Documents on the History of the Hasmonean Revolt with a Commentary and Introductions*. Tel Aviv: Hakibbutz Hameuchad, 1965 [Hebrew].
Stern, Menahem. *Greek and Latin Authors on Jews and Judaism. Edited with Introductions, Translations and Commentary. Volume One: From Herodotus to Plutarch*. Jerusalem: Israel Academy of Sciences and Humanities, 1974.
Stern, Menahem. "Aspects of Jewish Society: The Priesthood and Other Classes." Pages 561–630 in *The Jewish People in the First Century: Historical Geography, Political History, Social, Cultural and Religious Life and Institutions*. Vol. 2. Edited by Shemuel Safrai and Menahem Stern. Compendia Rerum Iudaicarum ad Novum Testamentum 2. Assen: Van Gorcum, 1976.
Stern, Philip D. *The Biblical Herem: A Window on Israel's Religious Experience*. Brown Judaic Studies 211. Atlanta: Scholars Press, 1991.
Stevens, Marty E. *Temples, Tithes, and Taxes: The Temple and the Economic Life of Ancient Israel*. Peabody, MA: Hendrickson Publishers, 2006.

Stevenson, Kalinda Rose. *Vision of Transformation: The Territorial Rhetoric of Ezekiel 40–48*. Society of Biblical Literature Dissertation Series 154. Atlanta: Scholars Press, 1996.
Stol, Marten. "The Old Babylonian 'I Owe You'." Pages 23–37 in *Silver, Money and Credit: A Tribute to Robartus J. Van der Spek on the Occasion of His 65th birthday*. Edited by Kristin Kleber and Reinhard Pirngruber. PIHANS CXXVIII. Leiden: Nederlands Instituut voor het Nabije Oosten, 2016.
Stolper, Matthew W. *Entrepreneurs and Empire: The Murašû Archive, the Murašû Firm, and Persian Rule in Babylonia*. Uitgaven van het Nederlands Historisch-Archaeologisch Instituut te Istanbul 54. Istanbul: Nederlands Historisch-Archaeologisch Instituut te Istanbul, 1985.
Strack, Hermann L. and Paul Billerbeck. *Kommentar zum Neuen Testament aus Talmud und Midrasch, Vol. III*. München: Oskar Beck, 1922.
Stromberg, Jacob. "Observations on Inner-Scriptural Scribal Expansion in MT Ezekiel." *VT* 58, no. 1 (2008): 68–86.
Stroup, Christopher. "A Reexamination of the Sons of the Pit in CD 13:14." *DSD* 18, no. 1 (2011): 45–53.
Sweeney, Marvin A. "The Problem of Ezekiel in Talmudic Literature." Pages 11–23 in *After Ezekiel: Essays on the Reception of a Difficult Prophet*. Edited by Andrew Mein and Paul M. Joyce. Library of Hebrew Bible/Old Testament Studies 535. New York; London: T&T Clark, 2011.
Sweeney, Marvin A. *I & II Kings. A Commentary*. The Old Testament Library. Louisville; London: Westminster John Knox Press, 2007.
Taggar-Cohen, Ada. "Between Ḥerem, Ownership, and Ritual: Biblical and Hittite Perspectives." Pages 419–34 in *Current Issues in Priestly and Related Literature: The Legacy of Jacob Milgrom and Beyond*. Edited by Roy Gane and Ada Taggar-Cohen. Atlanta: SBL Press, 2015.
Taggar-Cohen, Ada. "Covenant Priesthood: Cross-cultural Legal and Religious Aspects of Biblical and Hittite Priesthood." Pages 11–24 in *Levites and Priests in Biblical History and Tradition*. Edited by Mark A. Leuchter and Jeremy M. Hutton. Ancient Israel and Its Literature 9. Atlanta: Society of Biblical Literature, 2011.
Tal, Oren. *The Archaeology of Hellenistic Palestine: Between Tradition and Renewal*. Jerusalem: The Bialik Institute, 2007 [Hebrew].
Tal, Oren. "'Hellenistic Foundations' in Palestine." Pages 242–54 in *Judah between East and West: The Transition from Persian to Greek Rule (ca. 400–200 BCE)*. Edited by Lester L. Grabbe and Oded Lipschits. Library of Second Temple Studies 75. London: T&T Clark, 2011.
Tal, Oren. "Hellenism in Transition from Empire to Kingdom: Changes in the Material Culture of Hellenistic Palestine." Pages 55–73 in *Jewish Identities in Antiquity: Studies in Memory of Menahem Stern*. Edited by Lee I. Levine and Daniel R. Schwartz. Texte und Studien zum antiken Judentum 130. Tübingen: Mohr Siebeck, 2009.
Taylor, Joan E. "A Second Temple in Egypt: the Evidence for the Zadokite Temple of Onias." *JSJ* 29 (1998): 297–321.
Tcherikover, V. "The Ideology of the Letter of Aristeas." *HTR* 51, no. 2 (1958): 59–85.
Tcherikover, Victor. *Hellenistic Civilization and the Jews*. Philadelphia: Jewish Publication Society of America, 1959.

Tcherikover, Victor A. and Alexander Fuks. *Corpus Papyrorum Judaicarum*. Cambridge, MA: The Magnes Press; Harvard University Press, 1957.
Tcherikover, Victor A. and Alexander Fuks. *Corpus Papyrorum Judaicarum*. Cambridge, MA: The Magnes Press; Harvard University Press, 1960.
Thompson, Dorothy J. *Memphis under the Ptolemies*. 2nd ed. Princeton, NJ: Princeton University Press, 2012.
Tilley, Christopher. *A Phenomenology of Landscape*. Explorations in Anthropology. Oxford; Providence, RI: Berg Publishers, 1994.
Todd, S. C. *A Commentary on Lysias, Speeches 1–11*. Oxford: Oxford University Press, 2007.
Tov, Emanuel. "Recensional Differences between the MT and LXX of Ezekiel." *Ephemerides Theologicae Lovanienses* 62, no. 1 (1986): 89–101.
Trifon, Dalia. "Did the Priestly Courses (Mishmarot) Transfer from Judaea to Galilee after the Bar Kokhba Revolt?" *Tarbiz* 59 (1989–1990): 77–93 [Hebrew].
Trigger, Bruce G. *Understanding Early Civilizations: A Comparative Study*. Cambridge: Cambridge University Press, 2003.
Truax, Jean. "Building the Desert: Property Management According to the Early Cistercians." *Cistercian Studies Quarterly* 51, no. 1 (2016): 77–99.
Tsafrir, Yoram, Leah Di Segni, and Judith Green. *Tabula Imperii Romani. Iudaea-Palaestina: Eretz Israel in the Hellenistic, Roman and Byzantine Periods. Maps and Gazetteer*. Jerusalem: The Israel Academy of Sciences and Humanities, 1994.
Tuell, Steven Shawn. *The Law of the Temple in Ezekiel 40–48*. Harvard Semitic Monographs 49. Atlanta: Scholars Press, 1992.
Udoh, Fabian E. *To Caesar What is Caesar's: Tribute, Taxes, and Imperial Administration in Early Roman Palestine (63 B.C.E.–70 C.E.)*. Brown Judaic Studies. Providence, RI: Brown University, 2005.
Ussishkin, David. "On Nehemiah's City Wall and the Size of Jerusalem during the Persian Period: An Archaeologist's View." Pages 101–30 in *New Perspectives on Ezra-Nehemiah: History and Historiography, Text, Literature, and Interpretation*. Edited by Isaac Kalimi. Winona Lake, IN: Eisenbrauns, 2012.
Van de Mieroop, Marc. *The Ancient Mesopotamian City*. Oxford; New York: Clarendon Press; Oxford University Press, 1997.
Van de Mieroop, Marc. "Silver as a Financial Tool in Ancient Egypt and Mesopotamia." Pages 17–29 in *Explaining Monetary and Financial Innovation: A Historical Analysis*. Edited by Peter Bernholz and Roland Vaubel. Financial and Monetary Policy Studies 39. Cham, Switzerland: Springer International Publishing, 2016.
Van der Spek, Robartus J. "Land Ownership in Babylonian Cuneiform Documents." Pages 173–245 in *Legal Documents of the Hellenistic World. Papers from a Seminar arranged by the Institute of Classical Studies, the Institute of Jewish Studies and the Warburg Institute, University of London, February to May 1986*. Edited by Markham J. Geller and Herwig Maehler. London: The Warburg Institute, University of London, 1995.
Vanderhooft, David S. "The Israelite *mišpāḥâ*, the Priestly Writings, and Changing Valences in Israel's Kinship Terminology." Pages 485–96 in *Exploring the Longue Durée: Essays in Honor of Lawrence E. Stager*. Edited by J. David Schloen. Winona Lake, IN: Eisenbrauns, 2009.
VanderKam, James C. *From Joshua to Caiaphas: High Priests after the Exile*. Minneapolis: Fortress Press, 2004.

Visotzky, Burton L. "Anti-Christian Polemic in Leviticus Rabbah." Pages 93–105 in *Fathers of the World: Essays in Rabbinic and Patristic Literatures*. Wissenschaftliche Untersuchungen zum Neuen Testament 80. Tübingen: J.C.B. Mohr, 1995.

Waerzeggers, Caroline. *The Ezida Temple of Borsippa: Priesthood, Cult, Archives*. Achaemenid History 15. Leiden: Nederlands Instituut voor het Nabije Oosten, 2010.

Waltke, Bruce K. and M. O'Connor. *An Introduction to Biblical Hebrew Syntax*. Winona Lake, IN: Eisenbrauns, 1990.

Wardle, Timothy. *The Jerusalem Temple and Early Christian Identity*. Wissenschaftliche Untersuchungen zum Neuen Testament 291. Tübingen: Mohr Siebeck, 2010.

Watson, Alan. *The State, Law and Religion: Pagan Rome*. Athens, GA; London: The University of Georgia Press, 1992.

Watts, James W. "The Torah as the Rhetoric of Priesthood." Pages 319–31 in *The Pentateuch as Torah: New Models for Understanding Its Promulgation and Acceptance*. Edited by Gary N. Knoppers and Bernard M. Levinson. Winona Lake, IN: Eisenbrauns, 2007.

Watts, James W. *Ritual and Rhetoric in Leviticus: From Sacrifice to Scripture*. Cambridge; New York: Cambridge University Press, 2007.

Wazana, Nili. *All the Boundaries of the Land: The Promised Land in Biblical Thought in Light of the Ancient Near East*. Winona Lake, IN: Eisenbrauns, 2013.

Weinberg, Joel. *The Citizen-Temple Community*. JSOT 151. Sheffield: JSOT Press, 1992.

Weinberg, Joel P. "Das bēit 'ābōt im 6.–4. Jh. v. u. Z." *VT* 23, no. 4 (1973): 400–14.

Weinfeld, Moshe. *Social Justice in Ancient Israel and in the Ancient Near East*. Minneapolis; Jerusalem: Fortress Press; Magnes, 1995.

Weinfeld, Moshe. "The Ban on the Canaanites in the Biblical Codes and Its Historical Development." Pages 142–60 in *History and Traditions of Early Israel: Studies Presented to Eduard Nielsen, May 8th 1993*. Edited by André Lemaire, Benedikt Otzen, and Eduard Nielsen. Leiden; New York: Brill, 1993.

Weiss, Zeev. "Were Priests Communal Leaders in Late Antique Palestine? The Archaeological Evidence." Pages 91–111 in *Was 70 CE a Watershed in Jewish History? On Jews and Judaism before and after the Destruction of the Second Temple*. Edited by Daniel R. Schwartz and Zeev Weiss. Ancient Judaism and Early Christianity 78. Leiden: Brill, 2012.

Wellhausen, Julius. *Die Composition des Hexateuchs und der historischen Bücher des Alten Testaments*. Berlin: Georg Reimer, 1889.

Wellhausen, Julius. *Prolegomena to the History of Israel*. Charleston, SC: Bibliobazaar, 2007.

Wells, Bruce. "The Quasi-Alien in Leviticus 25." Pages 135–55 in *The Foreigner and the Law: Perspectives from the Hebrew Bible and the Ancient Near East*. Edited by Reinhard Achenbach, Rainer Albertz, and Jakob Wöhrle. Beihefte zur Zeitschrift für Altorientalische und Biblische Rechtsgeschichte 16. Wiesbaden: Harrassowitz, 2011.

Wendel, Adolf. *Das israelitisch-jüdische Gelübde*. Berlin: Philo-Verlag, 1931.

Wenell, Karen J. *Jesus and Land: Sacred and Social Space in Second Temple Judaism*. Library of Historical Jesus Studies; Library of New Testament Studies 334. London: T&T Clark, 2007.

Wenham, Gordon J. *The Book of Leviticus*. The New International Commentary on the Old Testament. Grand Rapids, MI: William B. Eerdmans, 1979.

Westbrook, Raymond. *Property and the Family in Biblical law*. Sheffield: Sheffield Academic Press, 1991.

Westbrook, Raymond. "Redemption of Land." *Israel Law Review* 6 (1971): 367–75.

Westbrook, Raymond. "Jubilee Laws." Pages 36–57 in *Property and the Family in Biblical Law*. Edited by Raymond Westbrook. The Library of Hebrew Bible/Old Testament Studies 113. Sheffield: JSOT Press, 1991.

Westbrook, Raymond. "Conclusions." Pages 327–40 in *Security for Debt in Ancient Near Eastern Law*. Edited by Raymond Westbrook and Richard Jasnow. Culture and History of the Ancient Near East 9. Leiden: Brill, 2001.

Westbrook, Raymond. "Introduction." Pages 1–3 in *Security for Debt in Ancient Near Eastern Law*. Edited by Raymond Westbrook and Richard Jasnow. Culture and History of the Ancient Near East 9. Leiden: Brill, 2001.

Westbrook, Raymond and Bruce Wells. *Everyday Law in Biblical Israel: An Introduction*. Louisville: Westminster John Knox Press, 2009.

Wildfang, Robin Lorsch. *Rome's Vestal Virgins: A Study of Rome's Vestal Priestesses in the Late Republic and Early Empire*. London; New York: Routledge, 2006.

Wilk, Florian and J. Ross Wagner, eds. *Between Gospel and Election: Explorations in the Interpretation of Romans 9–11*. Wissenschaftliche Untersuchungen zum Neuen Testament 257. Tübingen: Mohr Siebeck, 2010.

Williams, David S. *The Structure of 1 Maccabees*. The Catholic Biblical Quarterly Monograph Series 31. Washington, DC: Catholic Biblical Association of America, 1999.

Williams, Michael J. "Taking Interest in Interest." Pages 113–32 in *Mishneh Todah: Studies in Deuteronomy and Its Cultural Environment in Honor of Jeffrey H. Tigay*. Edited by Nili Sacher Fox, David A. Glatt-Gilad, and Michael J. Williams. Eisenbrauns: Winona Lake, IN, 2009.

Williamson, H.G.M. "Ezra and Nehemiah in the Light of the Texts from Persepolis." *Bulletin for Biblical Research* 1 (1991): 41–61.

Willrich, Hugo. *Urkundenfälschung in der hellenistisch-jüdischen Literatur*. Forschungen zur Religion und Literatur des Alten und Neuen Testaments 21. Göttingen: Vandenhoeck & Ruprecht, 1924.

Wolters, Al. "Copper Scroll." Pages 144–48 in *Encyclopedia of the Dead Sea Scrolls*. Vol. 1. Edited by Lawrence H. Schiffman and James C. VanderKam. Oxford; New York: Oxford University Press, 2000.

Wright, Christopher J. H. *God's People in God's Land: Family, Land, and Property in the Old Testament*. Grand Rapids, MI; Exeter, England: W.B. Eerdmans; Paternoster Press, 1990.

Wright, Logan S. "MKR in 2 Kings XII 5–17 and Deuteronomy XVIII 8." *Vetus Testamentum* 39, no. 4 (1989): 438–48.

Wright, Nicholas L. *Divine Kings and Sacred Spaces: Power and Religion in Hellenistic Syria (301–64 BC)*. BAR International Series 2450. Oxford: Archaeopress, 2012.

Wunsch, Cornelia. *Das Egibi-Archiv I. Die Felder und Gärten*. 2 vols. Cuneiform Monographs 20 A–B. Groningen: Styx, 2000.

Wunsch, Cornelia. "The Egibi Family's Real Estate in Babylon (6th Century BC)." Pages 391–419 in *Urbanization and Land Ownership in the Ancient Near East*. Vol. II. Edited by Michael Hudson and Baruch A. Levine. Cambridge, MA: Peabody Museum of Archaeology and Ethnology, Harvard University, 1999.

Wunsch, Cornelia. "Debt, Interest, Pledge and Forfeiture in the Neo-Babylonian and Early Achaemenid Period: The Evidence from Private Archives." Pages 221–55 in *Debt and Economic Renewal in the Ancient Near East*. Edited by Michael Hudson and Marc Van de

Mieroop. International Scholars Conference of Ancient Near Eastern Economies 3. Bethesda, MD: CDL Press, 2002.
Yadin, Yigael. *The Scroll of the War of the Sons of Light against the Sons of Darkness. Edited with Commentary and Introduction.* London: Oxford University Press, 1962.
Yadin, Yigael. *The Temple Scroll. The Hidden Law of the Dead Sea Sect.* New York: Random House, 1985.
Yardeni, Ada. "A Draft of a Deed on an Ostracon from Khirbet Qumrân." *IEJ* 47, no. 3/4 (1997): 233–37.
Zevit, Ziony. *The Religions of Ancient Israel: A Synthesis of Parallactic Approaches.* London; New York: Continuum, 2001.
Zimmerli, Walther. *Ezekiel 2: A Commentary on the Book of the Prophet Ezekiel, Chapters 25–48.* Hermeneia. Philadelphia: Fortress Press, 1983.
Zorell, Franz. "Zur Vokalisation des Wortes ערכך in Lev 27 und anderwärts." *Biblica* 26 (1945): 112–14.
Zsengellér, József. "Maccabees and Temple Propaganda." Pages 181–95 in *The Books of the Maccabees: History, Theology, Ideology. Papers of the Second International Conference on the Deuteronomical Books, Pápa, Hungary, 9–11 June, 2005.* Edited by Géza G. Xeravits and József Zsengellér. Supplements to the Journal for the Study of Judaism 118. Leiden; Boston: Brill, 2007.

Index of Ancient Sources

Hebrew Bible

Genesis
23:3–20	42
23:9	33
23:15	42
38:18	63 n. 98
41:45	128
47:13–26	68–69
47:22	68, 102
47:26	68
49:6	77

Exodus
12:4	72 n. 125
20:33	104 n. 70
21:1–23:19	183–84, 203
21:13	92 n. 27
21:15–17	79 n. 149
22:17–19	79 n. 149
22:18	79
22:20–23	80
22:24	57 n. 81, 59
22:29	183–84, 190
23:16–19	36
23:19	103 n. 67
30:11–16	107, 133, 174 n. 81
30:13–16	46 n. 58, 163
32:29	77
34:26	103 n. 67

Leviticus
2:8–10	106
5:15–16	205
5:16	45, 49
5:21	154
5:24	45, 49, 154 n. 19, 159
6:7–9	106
6:19	106, 108 n. 84
7:6–7	106, 108 n. 84
7:8	106
7:9	106
7:10	106
7:14	106
7:28–31	106
7:30–33	106
17–26	29
19:9	40
19:19	222
19:20	61
19:23–25	189
22:11	191
22:11–13	190–93, 204
22:12	98
22:15	98
23:10–15	50 n. 67
23:17	208 n. 7
23:22	40
25:3–7	34
25:8–17	33, 87
25:15–17	34
25:23	30
25:23–24	34 n. 19
25:25	58
25:25–28	33, 45
25:25–46	66
25:28	92
25:31	92
25:32–33	92
25:34	91, 94, 187 n. 25
25:36	58
25:39–54	31 n. 10
25:55	31 n. 10
26	35
26:34	35
27	24–25, 27, 35–36, 84, 100, 114, 134, 149, 152, 159–60, 180, 183, 225–26, 228
27:2	60 n. 90
27:2–25	60
27:2–7	36, 40 n. 42
27:2–8	176, 178
27:3	56 n. 79
27:3–7	51, 53, 55–56, 81
27:3–8	53 n. 70
27:8	40, 53, 54 n. 76

27:9	60 n. 90, 61 n. 93	18:24	25, 98
27:9–12	36	21:1–3	75 n. 133, 181 n. 3
27:9–24	57	25:6–13	77
27:10	60 n. 92, 61 n. 93, 73 n. 130	35:1–8	91, 227
27:13	44, 45, 54–55	35:2	93
27:14	40	35:4	94
27:14–15	36	35:9–11	193
27:15	44, 46	35:9–29	92
27:16	11 n. 36, 38, 41–43, 49, 51, 63, 81, 152, 179, 226	35:12	92
27:16–18	36–43	*Deuteronomy*	
27:16–21	37, 69	4:41–43	92
27:16–24	147	7:1–5	80 n. 150
27:17–18	41, 50, 62	11:12	30 n. 6
27:18	37 n. 26, 41	13:16–18	80
27:19	44–57, 46	13:17	25, 25 n. 97
27:20	73 n. 130	14:24–26	41 n. 44
27:20–21	69–71, 82	16:18–19	78
27:21	25, 60, 73, 74 n. 131, 79, 82, 167, 190, 230	17:8–13	77
		18:1–2	25, 98, 195
27:22–24	71–72	18:1–5	109
27:25	41, 46, 54 n. 76	18:3–5	135 n. 55
27:26–27	58	18:4	103 n. 67
27:27	44, 48	18:8	76 n. 137, 108
27:28	25, 60, 73–78, 82, 188, 192–93	18.3–8	98
		19:1–10	92
27:29	78–81, 188	23:20–21	59
27:30	73 n. 130	23:22–24	106 n. 79
27:30–31	58	24:10	153 n. 17
27:31	44	24:11	59 n. 89
27:32	190 n. 29	25:4	158
		26:1–11	36
Numbers		32:9	114 n. 106
3:44–51	55		
3:47	46 n. 58	*Joshua*	
5:9	98	6:19	79, 194
5:9–10	106, 108	6:21	80 n. 150
5:10	107	7:1–26	194
5:12–31	175 n. 87	7:21–26	79
15:18–20	208	8:26	80 n. 150
15:21	208 n. 7	10:28	80 n. 150
18:8	98	10:35	80 n. 150
18:8–32	36	10:37	80 n. 150
18:14	25, 73, 79, 185, 188–89, 230	10:39	80 n. 150
18:16	46 n. 58	10:40	80 n. 150
18:19–20	109	11:11	80 n. 150
18:20	25, 74 n. 132, 195	11:21	80 n. 150

13–19	105	*Isaiah*	
14:4	93	5:10	38 n. 30
19:9	114 n. 106	14:25	9 n. 26
20:1–9	92	19:21	75 n. 134
21:1–40	91, 227		
21:2	93	*Jeremiah*	
22:19	8	2:7	9 n. 26
		11:16	210
Judges		25:9	22 n. 84
1:1	75 n. 133	32:6–15	43
2:10–23	194	32:6–7	43 n. 50
3:9–10	194	32:7	46
11:29–31	181 n. 3	32:15	43 n. 50
11:30–31	53 n. 73, 75 n. 133	34:6–10	43 n. 49
11:34–40	53 n. 73	37:12	43 n. 49
		50:21	22 n. 84
1 Samuel		51:3	22 n. 84
1:11	53 n. 72		
2:12–17	106 n. 77	*Ezekiel*	
15:7–11	79 n. 148	18:13	57 n. 81
22:11	3 n. 6	18:17	57 n. 81
22:19	92 n. 23	22:12	57 n. 81
		32:3	157 n. 31
2 Samuel		36:5	9 n. 26
9:2	114 n. 106	38:16	9 n. 26
15:7	75 n. 134	40–48	25, 115
20:19	8 n. 26	40:1	84
24:18–23	42	40:1–42:20	87
		40:2	89
1 Kings		40:3	38 n. 28
1:39	93 n. 28	40:5	38 n. 28
2:26	100	40:13	88 n. 11
8:36	9 n. 26	40:15	88 n. 11
18:19	143	40:21	88 n. 11
18:31–33	143	40:45	93 n. 28
18:32	38 n. 29	40:46	93 n. 28
		40:48–41:26	85
2 Kings		41:8	38 n. 28
6:25	50 n. 67	43:1–12	87
12	116	43:13–48:35	87
12:3	108	43:17	104 n. 70
12:4	53 n. 71	44:1–46:24	87
12:5	107	44:9	85
12:6	76 n. 137, 107	44:9–16	93, 99
12:17	108	44:20	75
23:21–23	111	44:28	74 n. 132, 98–99
		44:28–30	109

44:29	73, 79, 188, 230	*Jonah*	
45:1	25, 98, 103, 105	2:10	75 n. 134
45:1–6	87, 226		
45:2	90, 94 n. 35	*Micah*	
45:2–5	87	2:5	105
45:4	89, 94–95	3:11	78
45:5	93	4:13	79 n. 148
45:7–10	99	7:2	150, 157
45:8	96		
45:9–12	96	*Habakkuk*	
45:12	46 n. 58	1:15–17	157 n. 31
45:13–17	99	2:7	57 n. 81
45:17	99		
46:2–10	96	*Haggai*	
46:16–18	99	2:10	77 n. 143
46:18	96	2:10–13	218
47:1–12	87		
47:1–7	89	*Zechariah*	
47:13–48:35	88, 90 n. 19	3:1	85 n. 2
48:1–35	105	3:7	77 n. 143
48:8–14	87–89, 226	3:8	85 n. 2
48:9	98, 103		
48:11	93 n. 28	*Psalms*	
48:12	89, 98, 103–4, 116	15:5	57 n. 81
48:13	103	16:6	105
48:14	103–4, 116	85:2	9 n. 26
48:15	95 n. 40, 96	105:11	105
48:17	95 n. 40	133:1	105
48:18–19	88		
48:19	103	*Proverbs*	
48:21	88	28:8	57 n. 81
48:21–22	99		
48:35	96	*Ecclesiastes*	
		8:10	198 n. 49
Hosea			
2:18	72 n. 126	*Daniel*	
9:3	8	11:13	80 n. 151
14:6	210		
		Ezra	
Joel		1:4	80 n. 151, 161 n. 41
2:18	9 n. 26	1:6	80 n. 151
		1:7–11	99
Amos		2:36–42	1, 3 n. 6, 96
7:17	100	2:61	187 n. 24
8:3	72 n. 126	5:14	99
		6:5	99
		6:11	81

7:24	99, 101	12:10	101
8:21	80 n. 151	13:10–14	110
8:33	201		
10:8	21–22, 80–81, 230	*1 Chronicles*	
		6:39–66	91
Nehemiah		19:8	77 n. 143
3:3	201	21:25	42 n. 47
3:21	201	23:1–26:2	3 n. 6
4:6	114	23:1–26:32	106 n. 76
5:1–12	66	23:4	77 n. 143
5:4	66 n. 104	24:1–8	3
7:39–42	106 n. 76	24:7–10	187 n. 24
7:39–45	1, 3 n. 6, 96	26:20–28	108 n. 86
7:63	187 n. 24	26:28	148
10	116	27:31	80 n. 151
10:1–40	108, 227	28:1	80 n. 151
10:29	109	28:11–18	108 n. 86
10:33–34	133	35:7–9	111
10:35	106 n. 76		
10:36–37	109	*2 Chronicles*	
10:39	110	23:7	77 n. 143
11:1–2	129	23:12–15	77 n. 143
11:3	101 n. 56	31:3	80 n. 151
11:10–22	1, 3 n. 6, 96	31:4–19	111
11:20	101	32:29	80 n. 151
12:1–26	1, 3 n. 6, 96		

New Testament

Matthew		*Acts*	
15:3–6	158	1:18–19	177
15:5	151, 191 n. 32	4:34–37	170
21:12–13	174	5:1–11	170
27:3–10	177–78	22:3	218 n. 33
		23:12–14	183
Mark			
7:9–13	76 n. 141, 158, 228–29	*Romans*	
7:11	151, 191 n. 32	9:21	209 n. 12
11:15–17	174	11	27–28
12:1–9	165 n. 54	11:16	206–19, 224, 229
		11:17–24	207, 219–24, 224
Luke			
15:12	80 n. 151	*1 Corinthians*	
19:45–46	174	5:6	209 n. 12
		16:1–4	174 n. 81
John			
2:13–17	174		

Galatians
5:9   209 n. 12

1 Timothy
6:10   213 n. 23

Hebrews
12:15   213 n. 23

Dead Sea Scrolls

4QapocrJoshua^b (4Q379)
3:6   184

4QDamascus Document^a (4Q266)
5i:2   154
6iii–iv   161
8ii:1–3   150–60
8ii:4   154
8ii:8–9   182

4QDamascus Document^e (4Q270)
3:19   208 n. 7
4:3   154
2ii   53 n. 71, 176
2ii:6–10   161
2ii:9   176 n. 92
6iii:14   154

4QDamascus Document^f (4Q271)
2:1–6   161
4ii   152
4ii:15–16   150–60

4QEnoch^a (4Q201)
III:1–3   183

4QHalakhah A (4Q251)
                 27, 136, 183–95, 203–4
5:4   208 n. 7
9:3   209
10   186–90
10, 14, 15   230
14   185–86, 190
15   186, 191–93
16   190–91

4QHalakhic Letter^a (4Q396)
4:11   202

4QHodayot^f (4Q432)
13:1   191

4QMezuzah^e (4Q153)
17:3   176 n. 92

4QMMT (B) (4Q395)
62–63   189
63–64   190 n. 29

4QOrdinances^a (4Q159)
                 133
1ii:6   176 n. 92
1ii 9:7   174 n. 81

4QpaleoGen-Exod (4Q11)
57   202

11QpaleoLev (11Q1)
6   53–55

4QpapAccount (4Q358)
10ii:6   191

4QRule of the Community^d (4Q258)
1:12   78, 160 n. 39, 186, 197

4QWords of the Luminaries^a (4Q504)
1–2iv, 8–11   175

CD (Damascus Document, Cairo Geniza)
                 147 n. 1
6:15   78, 197
6:15–17   160, 162
6:16   154
9:1   182
9:1–8   150
9:11   154
10:10   150 n. 10

10:14	150 n. 10	*Rule of the Community (1QS)*	
11:19–12:2	161		161
13:14	162 n. 45	9:5	161 n. 41
14:12–13	161 n. 43	9:7–9	169
16:6–12	150	1:24	191
16:13–20	161		
16:14–17	134, 150–60, 228	*Temple Scroll (11Q19)*	
			134
Copper Scroll (3Q15)		39:8–9	174 n. 81
	186–87	57:19–21	197
9:14–16	187	60:1	195 n. 39
11:4	209 n. 11	60:3–4	189
11:5–7	187	60:3–5	135 n. 55
		60:5	184
Pesher to Habakkuk (1QpHab)			
8:6–13	198	*War Scroll (1QM)*	
12:8–9	161	9:7	182
12:9–10	198	18:1–5	182

Josephus

Against Apion		11.181–83	129
1.199	127	11.214	80 n. 151
1.225	95, 127	11.269	80 n. 151
1.249	205	11.312	129
1.31–36	202	11.312	196
1.318–19	205	12.120	130 n. 36
2.8	127 n. 31	12.138–44	135
2.14	95, 127	12.142–44	142
2.66	95, 127	12.145–46	177 n. 93
2.81	95, 127	12.271	136
2.86	95, 127	12.328	182
2.108	2	12.359	205
2.112–14	127 n. 31	13.48–57	138 n. 69
2.128	95	13.51	164
2.187	197	13.56	148, 164, 228
		13.62–73	121
Antiquities		13.66	123
3.201	80 n. 151	13.66–70	95, 122
4.240–43	178	13.66–71	125–130, 227
4.67–75	178	13.181–83	132 n. 45
4.71	208 n. 7	13.213–18	132 n. 45
4.72	80 n. 151	13.255–58	132
4.73	53 n. 70, 176, 178	13.287	123
7.367	165	13.318	132, 164 n. 51
7.393–94	172 n. 78	14.72	172
11.103	80 n. 151	14.105–9	172

14.110–13	173 n. 81	*War*	
14.113	172	1.31–33	121 n. 17
14.131–33	123	1.50	132 n. 45
15.310–15	175 n. 86	1.61	172 n. 78
15.328–30	175 n. 86	1.152–53	172
15.364	80 n. 151	1.179	172
15.380	174	1.190–91	123
15.380–402	174	1.357	175
15.387	174	1.401	174
15.402	174	1.402–28	175 n. 86
16.45	205	1.648–55	174
16.146–49	175 n. 86	1.654	205
16.157–59	175 n. 87	2.50	173
16.161–62	175	2.122	80 n. 151
16.164	205	2.175	172, 177 n. 95
16.166–73	173 n. 81	2.275	176 n. 90
16.168	205	2.293–94	173
16.171	172 n. 78	2.409–10	144, 228
16.310	164 n. 51	2.411–17	175
17.151–63	174	2.412–13	144
17.264	173	2.464	80 n. 151
18:19	162 n. 44	3.35–58	178
18.60	172, 176 n. 90	3.518	178
18.65	177 n. 95	4.451–74	178
18.194	80 n. 151	4.552	200 n. 56
20.51–53	175 n. 87	5.35–36	171, 216 n. 27
20.179–81	3, 199	5.139	132 n. 45
20.205	196	5.562	175, 205
20.205–6	3	6.113–17	196
20.206–7	196 n. 44	6.115	200
20.219–22	172	6.282	177 n. 94
20.220	177 n. 95	6.358	177 n. 94
20.237	121 n. 17, 122	6.425	1
		7.161–62	174 n. 83
Life		7.216–17	179
7	196	7.218	174
80	196, 199 n. 53	7.423–36	121–22
81	183	7.426–30	122–25
167	176 n. 90	7.430	130, 227
199	172 n. 79	7.431–32	123
370	183		
422	129, 196		

Philo of Alexandria

Decalogue
76–80	95, 127
133	205

The Special Laws
1.74–75	95, 127
1.76	27, 148, 162–63, 228
1.77–78	163
1.117	163
1.122	191
1.123	191
1.126	191
1.131	163
1.132	208 n. 7
1.154	3
1.204	153 n. 15
2.13	205
2.34	53 n. 70
2.37	45, 159
3.83	205
4.87	205

Deuterocanonical Writings

Aristeas
40	133 n. 48
83	120
105–20	120

Ben Sira
35:14	78
45:20–22	195

1 Enoch
6:4–6	183

1 Esdras
9:4	80 n. 151

Joseph and Aseneth
3:5	127–28
4:2	127–28

Jubilees
1:16	210

Judith
6:13	213 n. 23
16:19	79 n. 148

1 Maccabees
1:21–24	138
2:1	196 n. 42
2:28	136
2:46	145
3:36	145 n. 89
3:42	145 n. 89
5:3–5	181
5:9	145 n. 89
5:43	182 n. 5
5:43–44	145 n. 90
5:58	182 n. 5
8:1–32	142 n. 80
8:31–32	142
9:1–22	142
9:23	145
10:18–20	143
10:24	139
10:24–45	139–145, 121
10:31	145, 164
10:34	148
10:39	143, 227–28
10:39–43	139–146
10:43	114, 145, 164, 178, 180, 228
10:46	140, 179
10:47	140
10:48–50	142
10:83–84	182 n. 5
10:87–89	142
11:30–37	143
12:35–38	132 n. 45
12:44–53	143
13:36–40	143
14:37	132 n. 45
15:2–9	143

2 Maccabees
3:2–3	137

3:10	177 n. 94	26:1	204
3:35	137	26:1–2	194
5:16	137	29:3	175 n. 87
6:8	143 n. 83		
9:16	137	*Sibylline Oracles*	
10:15–17	181	3:656–60	120
12:43	177	3:772–80	121
13:25	143 n. 83	7:702–5	120

4 Maccabees
4:1–14   177 n. 94

Testament of Levi
2:12   195
14–17   198
17:9–10   198

Psalms of Solomon
1:8   198 n. 49
2:3–5   198 n. 49
8:11–12   198 n. 49
8:22   198 n. 49

Testament of Moses
5:5–6   160 n. 39

Tobit
1:6–8   109 n. 87, 133 n. 48

Pseudo-Philo, LAB
25:2–26:15   194 n. 36
25:2–26:2   193–95, 230
25:10   194

Wisdom of Solomon
15:18–16:1   127

Rabbinic Writings

m. Pe'ah
1:6   167

m. Ḥallah
1:9   208 n. 7
4:9   193

m. Demai
6:3–5   197

m. Bikkurim
3:1   168

m. Kil'ayim
1:7   222
7:6   154 n. 18

m. Pesaḥim
4:8   201, 221, 222 n. 47

m. Šebi'it
2:6   222

m. Šekalim
1:5   144
2:1   163
2:2   166 n. 56
4:1–2   172 n. 77
4:1–5   177
4:3   171
4:6–8   167
4:9   23 n. 92
5:2   167
5:4   23 n. 92
6:5–6   161 n. 41, 211 n. 15

m. Terumot
3:1–2   209 n. 10
5:1–9   209 n. 10
6:4   168

m. Ma'aser Šeni
4:10–11   176 n. 90
5:1   168
5:1–5   190

7:1	161 n. 41, 177
8:8	148 n. 5

m. Yoma
3:10	175 n. 87

m. Sukkah
4:5	216 n. 25
4:9	215 n. 25

m. Megillah
4:3	167

m. Nedarim
1:2–3	176 n. 90
2:4	188
2:4–5	183 n. 13
5:4	183

m. Gittin
5:6	179

m. Baba Meṣiʿa
7:2–8	157 n. 30

m. Baba Batra
7:2	38 n. 31

m. Sanhedrin
1:3	44 n. 53, 74, 155, 167

m. Makkot
3:2	166 n. 56

m. Šabuʿot
6:5	166 n. 56

m. Zebaḥim
5:8	190 n. 29

m. Menaḥot
8:1	171
8:6	171
13:10	126 n. 29

m. Ḥullin
10:2	166 n. 55

m. Bekorot
2:2–3	166 n. 55
8:8	166 n. 56

m. ʿArakin
5:1	53 n. 71
6–8	23
6:1	154–57
6:1–2	159
6:2	155
6:2–3	24
7:4	74, 167
8:1	11 n. 36, 24
8:1–3	44
8:2–3	24, 156
8:3	159 n. 37
8:4–7	183 n. 13, 193
8:5	187
8:6	188, 192
9:4	177 n. 94

m. Temurah
7:1–3	167, 210–11
7:3	168

m. Keritot
5:2–3	166 n. 56
6:8	165 n. 55

m. Meʿilah
3	23
3:5	213
3:6	158, 211–14, 224, 229
3:6–8	24, 27, 206, 210–19
3:7	215–16
3:8	171, 216
5:1	217
5:1–2	166 n. 56, 177 n. 93
6:2	166 n. 57

m. Ṭebul Yom
3:4	209 n. 10

t. Demai
7:1–15	197

t. Kil'ayim		*y. Ma'aser Šeni*	
1:10	222, 223	56d	199 n. 53
t. Pesaḥim		*y. Ḥallah*	
3:19	201, 221 n. 44	60b	198–99
t. Ketubot		*y. Pesaḥim*	
11:2	155	30d	171 n. 76
t. Baba Meṣi'a		*y. Ta'anit*	
8:30	165	69a	197, 198 n. 49, 200–1
t. 'Abodah Zarah		*y. Ḥagiga*	
6:1	217 n. 28	79c	171 n. 73
t. Menaḥot		*b. Berakot*	
9:5–13	171 n. 73	44a	200
13:21	199		
		b. Pesaḥim	
t. 'Arakin		49a	222
4:1	154–57, 229		
4:3	23, 24 n. 92	*b. Ḥagiga*	
4:22	159	25a	171 n. 73
4:23–25	183 n. 13		
4:29–34	183 n. 13	*b. Yebamot*	
4:31	192–93	63a	222
4:34	188		
		b. Nedarim	
t. Temurah		62a	197
1:5	187		
1:6	211	*b. Yoma*	
4:12–13	210	35b	197
t. Me'ilah		*b. Sota*	
1:20	212 n. 17	38b	200
1:21	158, 213 n. 20		
1:24	216	*b. Ta'anit*	
1:25	216 n. 26	27a	201
t. Ṭebul Yom		*b. Baba Meṣi'a*	
2:7	209 n. 10	21a	165 n. 53
		53b–54a	159 n. 37
y. Berakot			
9d	200	*b. Baba Batra*	
		107a	155
y. Kil'ayim		26b	215 n. 24
27b	223		

b. Menaḥot		*Leviticus Rabbah*	
65a	199 n. 52	6:6	223
b. ʿArakin		*Sifra, Beḥuqotai*	
21b	154–57	10:10	167
22a	156 n. 25	12:4–5	74, 188
29a	148 n. 5, 192–93		
		Genesis Rabbah	
b. Meʿilah		68	223 n. 50
12b	211 n. 16		
13a	158, 212 n. 17, 217	*Sifre Deuteronomy*	
14a	216 n. 27	312	223 n. 50
b. Niddah			
46b	209 n. 10		

Other Ancient Writings

Aristotle, Athenaion Politeia
47.4–5   15
60.1–3   220 n. 41

Cicero, Pro Flacco
28.66–69   173 n. 81

Diodorus, Bibliotheca Historica
34.2–4   127 n. 31
40.3   130

Eusebius, Praeparatio Evangelica
9.27.4   130

Herodotus, Histories
3.142   32

Lucian, De Dea Syria
           117 n. 1

Plato, Laws
6.745b–c   105

Strabo, Geography
16.40   172 n. 78

Tacitus, Histories
5.3–4   127 n. 31

Index of Subjects

Aaron and Aaronides, 7, 77, 91, 93, 195. *See also* priests, in Judea
Abiathar (high priest), 100
Acraba, 181–82
Agrippa II, 171–72, 177, 216
Akeldama, 177–78
Akiva, R., 1, 167, 171, 206, 212, 224
Akra, 139
Amaziah (high priest), 100
Ananias (high priest), 3
anathematization. *See* herem
animals, sacred; at Leontopolis, 125–27; in Babylonia, 110; in Greece, 16; in Judea, 35–36, 49, 54–55, 60–61, 73, 79, 93–95, 170, 185, 190; hekdesh status of, 165–66, 168; protecting the byproducts of, 210–19. *See also* firstborn; tithes
antichresis, 57, 59, 61
Antiochus III, 130, 135, 140–41, 168, 177
Antiochus IV, 121, 127, 137–38
Antiochus VII, 143
Apollo. *See* Delos; Delphi
Arauna, threshing floor of, 42
Arsinoe, 120, 130–31, 227
Artaxerxes I, 99, 101
Aseneth, 127–28
Asherah, 143
asylum, 31, 141, 145, 164, 228; cities of refuge, 92
Athena, 17, 156, 168, 215, 220–21

Baal, 142–43
Babylonia; sacred land in, 12–14, 30–31, 226; priests of, 101. *See also* Eanna; Ebabbar
Baetokaike, 117–18
Balas, Alexander, 121, 138–43, 227
Barnabas, 170
benefaction, religious; by Herod, 175; by Judean priests and Levites, 111–12; by Nehemiah, 101, 129–30; by the Persians, 99, 115; by the Ptolemies, 26, 118–21; by the Romans, 143–44, 146, 175, 228; by the Seleucids, 135, 139–46; by foreign regimes in Josephus, 128–29, 175; by foreign regimes, negative attitude of the Hasmoneans towards, 136–46, 228. *See also* consecration; hekdesh; herem; Levites; priests, in Judea
bet kor. *See* homer
Bethel, 29, 100

Canopus decree, 119
Capharabis, 200
Carmel, Mt., 38, 142–43
Cenaz, 194–95
church; land of, 5–6, 17–19; organizational structure of, 3–4
cities of refuge, 92. *See also* asylum
citizen-temple community, 22–23
Cleopatra I, 125–26, 145, 227
Cleopatra III, 123
cleruchic land, 123
consecration; of a field, 26–27, 36–72; of foodstuffs, 207–9; of plants, 27–28; of trees, 171, 210–24; to block access to a property by a claimant, 150–60, 179, 204, 228–29; to secure a loan, 24–25, 57–69, 225–26; to support a priest, 75–76; to support the temple, 156–57; in the Damascus Document, 26–27, 148–60; in rabbinic writings, 23–24, 148–50, 154–60, 165–68, 228–29; protections for derivatives and byproducts of, 210–19; spiritual dimensions of, 10–11, 225. *See also* hekdesh; herem
credit, agrarian, 24, 61–72, 81–82, 153–57, 225–26. *See also* antichresis; hypothecation

Darius I, 81, 99, 110
Darius III, 129
debt. *See* credit, agrarian
dedication. *See* consecration

Delos, 15–16, 67–68, 136, 226
Delphi, 16, 95
Demetrius I, 121, 138–46, 148, 164, 179–80, 227
Diana Tifatina, 16–17
Dikhrin (Kefar Zechariah), 200
dough offering, 75, 99, 207–9, 224

Eanna, 12–14, 67, 102, 109–10
Ebabbar, 12–13, 31, 39, 50, 102, 110, 226
ecclesiastical estates, 5–6
economic models, 4–5
Edfu, 118–19, 125, 174
Egibi clan, 102
Egypt; sacred land in, 12–13, 124–28, 146, 163, 227; priests of, 118–19, 127–28, 130. *See also* Leontopolis; Ptolemies
Eleazar (son of the high priest), 143–44
Eleazar ben Harsom, 197
Eleazar, R., 222
Elephantine, 19–20
ephah, 38–39
Essenes, 147, 228, 231; and the Jerusalem temple, 160–62. *See also* Qumran, sectarians of; Yahad
euergetism. *See* benefaction

farming, 10–11, 61–62. *See also* credit, agrarian; land
fields, sacred. *See* sacred land
first fruits, 99, 103–4, 109, 168, 195, 208–9
firstborn, 48–49, 55, 58–59, 73, 94, 133, 161, 166, 183–85, 193, 230
Fiscus Iudaicus. *See* shekel tax
Florus, 173
fourth-year fruits, 161, 168, 176, 183–84, 189–90

Galilee, 5–7, 26, 139–40, 149, 172, 178, 188, 196–97, 200, 202
gardens, sacred, 99, 101, 126–27, 130–31, 187, 227
gerah, 41–42, 46–48, 225–26
Gerizim, Mt., 1, 76, 91, 114, 129–30, 132, 135–36, 194, 196
Goliath family, 202
Gophna, 196, 200

grafting, 206, 219–24
Greece; sacred land in, 14–16, 156; sacred trees in, 220–21, 224; sacrilege in, 205–6
groves, sacred, 11, 17, 95, 102, 126–27, 146, 168, 206. *See also* trees, sacred

hadru, 111
Hanamel, field of, 43, 45–46
Har Ha-melekh, 197
Hasmoneans, 1–2, 26, 135, 147, 174, 182, 196, 227; and Jericho, 201; and sacred land, 133–34; and taxation policy, 132–33, 168; land grants of, 197; attitude towards religious benefaction of non-Judeans, 136–46, 228
Hauswaldt papyri, 125
heave-offering, 98–99, 103–4, 168, 185, 187, 207, 209, 224, 230
hefqēr, 148
Hefzibah inscription, 26
hekdesh, 23–24, 28, 177, 228–29; as rabbinic neologism, 148–49; as temple property, 165–68, 187–88; auction of, 44, 154–57; prohibition of business dealings with, 1, 171; protection of, 192, 210–19
Heliodorus, 137–38, 177
Heliopolis. *See* Leontopolis
Hellenistic rulers. *See* Ptolemies; Seleucids
herem, 21–22; in the Copper Scroll, 186–87; in Pseudo-Philo, 193–95, 204; in rabbinic writings, 187–88, 192–93, 198–99, 204; in warfare, 22, 181–83, 230; the monetization of, 192–93; sanctity protections for, 190–95, 204, 230; as a bribe, 77–78, 197–98; as entrapment, 27, 157–58; in the form of a field, 73–78, 184–95; as a voluntary dedication to a priest, 25, 27, 60, 73–78, 82–83, 183–90, 203–4, 225; as imposed involuntarily on persons by decree, 21–22, 78–83, 230
Herod, 173; and the Jerusalem temple, 1–2, 174–75; religious benefaction of, 175; wealth of, 168, 172, 175

high priest: of Jerusalem temple, 2–3, 23, 85, 108, 120, 133, 135–36, 139, 143
Holiness Code, 24–25, 29–37, 40, 45–47, 61, 82, 92, 225; and the charging of interest, 58; and the Temple Vision of Ezekiel, 84
Holiness School, 29–30, 35, 82, 84. *See also* Holiness Code
holy land. *See* sacred land
holy shekel. *See* shekel, common or holy
homer, 36–39
horia, 145, 164–65
hypothecation, 57–69, 81–82, 154–57, 225–26, 228
Hyrcanus, John, 132, 134, 136, 172, 199

Idumea, 132, 162, 181–82; land-survey ostracon from, 26, 86, 112–16, 227
ilku service, 111
interest, 56–59, 82, 226
Italy, sacred land in, 16–17

Janneaus, Alexander, 136
Jason (high priest), 135
Jason (of Cyrene), 137
Jehoash, fiscal reforms of, 53, 77, 107–8, 116
Jericho, 80, 174, 178, 187; as a center of priests, 200–2; herem valuables stolen at, 79, 194–95; consecrated sycamore trees at, 221–22
Jerusalem; Early Roman period, 1–2, 91, 230; Hellenistic period, 132–33; Iron Age, 96; Persian period, 23, 84–85, 95–98. *See also* temple, in Jerusalem; Ramat Rahel
Jesus and the Jesus movement, 6–7, 174, 176; and the holy land, 9–10; condemnation of Pharisees and scribes over consecrations, 76, 151, 158; land donations for, 169–70, 180. *See also* Paul
John of Gischala, 171–72, 175, 183
Jonathan Maccabee, 121, 136–46, 148, 164, 179, 182, 227–28
Joseph; and the Leontopolis temple, 127–28; and the nationalization of Egyptian territory, 68–69
Josephus; and herem, 182–83; and the land of the Leontopolis temple, 121–30, 146,

227; and the *horia* of the Jerusalem temple, 164–65, 180, 228; and religious benefaction by foreign regimes, 128–29, 175; and sacred wealth of Judea, 172, 178; and sacrilege, 204; land theology of, 9; personal landholding of, 129–30, 196
Jubilee, 32–34, 41–43, 62–63, 69, 87, 167, 225
Judah b. Beterah, R., 188, 203
Judah Maccabee, 138, 142, 177, 180–82
Judah, kingdom of, 29, 53, 96, 231; scale weights of, 46–48, 82; Jehoash, fiscal reforms of, 53, 77, 107–8, 116; Levitical settlements of, 91–95, 115, 226–27, 230–31
Judah, R., 156, 187, 212–13, 224, 229
Judea; in the Early Roman period, 1–2, 147, 170–79; in the Hellenistic period, 117, 120–21, 132–33, 147; in the Persian period, 29, 32, 227

Ketef Jericho, 20
Khirbet el-Kôm. *See* Maqqedah
Krokodilopolis. *See* Arsinoe

Labraunda, 118
land; auction of, 23–24, 44–45, 50, 124, 154–57, 159–60, 229; consecration of, 26–27, 36–72; cultivation of, 10–11, 61–62; seizure of, 69–71; redemption of, 44–57, 69–71, 226; valuation of, 34–43, 56. *See also* non-patrimonial land; patrimonial land; sacred land, in Judea; sacred land, outside Judea
leases, 5, 12, 15, 17, 19, 26, 156, 226; in Judea, 26, 33, 62, 165; by the Jerusalem temple, 165–68; similarity to sales in the Holiness Code, 33–34
Leontopolis, 1; land of, 26, 121–30, 163, 227; Josephus's view of, 121, 125–27; Ptolemaic benefaction of, 119, 121–25
Levi, R., 223–24
Levites, 3, 76–77; in rabbinic writings, 187, 197; in the Temple Vision of Ezekiel, 85–91, 93, 98, 103–4, 108, 227; private property of, 101, 111–12; as recipients of

Index of Subjects — 285

prebendary entitlements, 110, 129, 133, 168, 207–9; collectivization of entitlements by, 108, 110. *See also* Levitical settlements
Levitical settlements, 91–95, 115, 226–27, 230–31
liens. *See* hypothecation
loaf offering, 183–84. *See also* dough offering
loans. *See* credit, agrarian

Maccabees, 136. *See also* Hasmoneans; Jonathan Maccabee; Judah Maccabee; Simon Maccabee
Machpelah, 33, 42–43
Manasses (high priest), 129
Maqqedah, 112–15
Masoretic text, 53–55, 94–95, 103–4
Menelaus (high priest), 135
mina, 50, 80
Mishnah. *See* rabbis
Mizpah, 29
Modiin, 136, 196
moriai, 220–21, 224
Moses, 77, 127, 165; as benefactor of priests, 130
Murabaha financing, 58
Murašû clan, 102, 110
Myrrhinous, 68

Nabonidus, 13, 102, 109–10
Nea (territory of Athena), 156. *See also* Athena
Nehemiah; and impoverishment of farmers, 66; and the shekel tax, 133; fiscal reforms of, 25–26, 66, 86, 108–10, 114–16, 227; religious benefaction of, 101, 129–30. *See also* Persian imperial authorities
New Institutional Economics (NIE), 4–5
non-patrimonial land, 71–72

olive trees. *See* Paul; trees, sacred
omer, 38–39, 50
Onias IV, 121–30, 145–46, 227. *See also* Leontopolis

pastureland, 125; of the Levitical settlements, 93–95, 198, 226; in the Temple Vision of Ezekiel, 87, 89, 93, 227. *See also* sacred land, outside Judea
patrimonial land, 32–33; consecration of, 36–37; seizure of, 69–71; as hypothecary pledge, 57–69; redemption of, 44–57; valuation of, 38–43
Paul, 174, 183, 228; and proto-rabbinic tradition, 218–19, 222, 229; and sacred admixtures, 207–9; and protecting derivatives of agricultural consecrations, 210–19, 229; and the olive tree metaphor in Romans, 27–28, 219–24
Persian imperial authorities; and temple administration, 22–23, 95–98, 109–116, 129; and religious benefaction, 99, 115; and fiscal reforms of Nehemiah, 25–26, 66, 86, 108–10, 114–16, 227
Pharisees, 10, 151–52, 158, 175, 199, 218
Philo of Alexandria; and the land of the Jerusalem temple, 1, 27, 162–64, 180, 228; and the redemption fee, 45, 159; and priests, 3, 191; and sacred groves, 95, 127; land theology of, 9
place-making, sacred, 7–10, 85–86
pledges. *See* antichresis; credit, agrarian; hypothecation
poletai, 156
Pompey, 172
Pontius Pilate, 172, 176–77
priests, in Judea, 2–4, 83–86, 225, 230–31; after 70 CE, 2–3; benefactors of, 76, 106; clan-based organization and divisions of, 3–4, 27, 198, 200–2, 204; collectivization of wealth among, 106–9, 116, 198–200; as landholders, 25, 100–1, 111–12, 135–36, 195–204; as creditors, 57–72, 81–83, 225–26; as an empowered class, 24, 77–78, 197–98; as land appraisers, 38–41; as recipients of gifts and prebendary entitlements, 22, 73–78, 82–83, 98–104, 106–10, 115, 163, 167–68, 183–90, 207–9; fragmentation among, 199–200; rights of household members to entitlements of, 190–91; settlement pat-

terns of, 96–98, 111, 129, 200–3. *See also* herem; temple, in Jerusalem
priests, outside Judea; in Babylonia, 101; in Egypt, 118–19, 127–28, 130. *See also* sacred land, outside Judea
prophetic book, genre of, 85
proscriptio, 155
Ptolemais (Akko), 26, 121, 136–46, 179, 227–28
Ptolemies; and temple administration, 118–19, 227; and religious benefaction, 26, 118–25; cleruchic land, 123. *See also* Leontopolis; sacred land, outside Judea
Ptolemy VI Philometer, 119, 122–28, 130, 144–45, 227

qorban and the Qorban fund, 76, 153, 176–77
Qumran, sectarians of, 27, 133, 169–71, 189, 202, 218. *See also* Yahad

rabbis, 20; and the book of Ezekiel, 104; and the consecration of land, 23–24, 148–50, 154–60, 165–68, 228–29; and the grafting of branches onto sacred trees, 221–22; and the idea of sanctity, 217–18; and landholding by priests, 196–97; and the priests of Jericho, 201–2; and the protection of derivatives of agricultural consecrations, 206, 210–19; and the temple revenuer, 167. *See also* hekdesh; herem
Rainer papyrus, 120
Ramat Rahel, 23, 29, 86, 97–98, 115, 120
redemption; of living things, 53–55; of patrimonial land, 44–57, 69–71, 226; of seized property, 154–58, 179; by public auction, 44–45, 154–57; with a fee of one-fifth, 44–48, 60, 151, 158–60
revenuers, of the Jerusalem temple, 167
Rhamnous, 15, 68
Roman authorities; and religious benefaction, 143–44, 146, 175, 228; and Judean land, 129–30
Rosetta decree, 119

sabbatical, land, 34–35, 41
Sabinius, 172
sacralization. *See* consecration
sacred land, in Judea; of the Jerusalem temple, 21–24, 27, 133–34, 147–48, 160–80, 226–30; of priests, 73–78, 197–98; and Israelite ethnic territory, 8–9, 30–32; in the Temple Vision of Ezekiel, 88–91; in rabbinic writings, 23–24, 148–50, 154–60, 165–68, 228–29; special boundary markers for, 168, 229; taxation of, 168. *See also* consecration; hekdesh; herem
sacred land, outside Judea, 11–12; in Babylonia, 12–14, 30–31, 226; in Egypt, 12–13, 124–28, 146, 163, 227; in Greece, 14–16, 156; in Idumea, 112–15; in Italy, 16–17. *See also* church land; groves, sacred; place-making, sacred
Sacred Orgas, 16
sacrilege, 27–28, 153–54, 157–58, 204–7, 210–19
Sadducees, 10, 144, 199, 218
Samaria, 7, 32, 117, 129, 135–36, 139–40, 180–81. *See also* Gerizim, Mt.
Sanballat, 129–30
sanctity; of place, 7–10, 85–86; in early Jewish thought, 217–18. *See also* consecration; sacred land, in Judea; sacred land, outside Judea
scale weights, Judahite, 46–48
seah, 38–39
second tithes, 133, 167, 176. *See also* tithes
securities. *See* antichresis; credit, agrarian; hypothecation
Seleucids; and temple administration, 117–18, 137–38; and religious benefaction, 135, 139–46
Septuagint, 53–55, 87, 89–90, 93–95, 103–4
shekel tax, 19–20, 109, 133, 144, 163, 171–74, 177, 199, 205, 227, 229–30
shekel, common or holy, 36, 41–42, 46–48, 59, 63, 82, 159, 225–26
Shelomi, 6
silver, loans of, 61–69. *See also* shekel, common or holy

Simeon, R., 158, 187, 211–13, 224, 229
Simon Maccabee, 136, 143
Sinuri, 118
Sippar. *See* Ebabbar
sūtu, 39
synagogues; of priests, 200; and priestly settlement inscriptions, 202–3; landholdings of, 19, 130–31, 227
syntaxis, 118–19

Tannaitic teachings. *See* rabbis
Tarfon, R., 197
Tebtunis papyri, 119
Tell el-Yehoudieh. *See* Leontopolis
temple land. *See* sacred land, in Judea; sacred land, outside Judea
temple states, 117–18
Temple Vision of Ezekiel, 25–26, 84–87, 115, 226–27; collectivization of wealth in, 108–10; distribution of territory in, 105; sacred reserve of, 87–98, 227; scribal emendations to, 103–4
temple, in Jerusalem, 91, 116, 120, 123, 137; in the Copper Scroll, 186–87; in rabbinic writings, 159–50, 167, 210–19; in the Temple Scroll, 134–35; collectivization of wealth at, 3, 105–10, 129, 132, 164–65, 177; condemnations of, 6–7, 197–98; economy of, 1–2, 25–26, 96–112, 120, 139–46, 150–53, 170–80, 229–30; organizational dysfunction of, 3, 27, 199–200; consecrated timber for construction at, 216. *See also* Levites; priests, in Judea; sacred land, in Judea; shekel tax
těrûmâ. *See* heave-offering
tithes, 3, 12, 22, 73, 94, 98, 109–10, 129, 199; of animals, 161, 190; forcibly taken by priests, 196, 199; paid by Judeans to the Ebabbar, 31; pricing of, 49; redemption of, 58–59; remission by Demetrius, 145, 164; second tithes, 133, 167, 176
Titus, 129–30, 196
trees, sacred, 24, 168, 206, 224; as an allegory for the early church, 27, 219–24; at Jericho, 201; at Leontopolis, 125–27; in Greece, 220–21, 224; for timber for the temple, 171, 216; grafting branches onto, 219–24; protecting byproducts of, 210–19, 229. *See also* consecrations; groves, sacred

Uruk. *See* Eanna

valuation; of persons, 51–57, 107; of land; 34–43, 56; rabbinic conception of, 74
Varus, 172
Vestal Virgins, land of, 16
vows and votive procedures, 23, 36, 40–41, 51, 53, 57, 59–60, 75, 78, 106, 151, 153, 183–84, 186–88, 225–26. *See also* consecration; herem; *qorban* and the Qorban fund

Yahad, land donations to, 169–70, 180. *See also* Essenes; Qumran, sectarians of
Yahweh; animals of, 35–36, 49, 54–55, 60–61, 73, 79, 93–95, 170, 185, 190; territory of, 8–9, 30–32, 88–91. *See also* consecration; Gerizim, Mt.; priests, in Judea; sacred land, in Judea; temple, in Jerusalem
Yehud. *See* Judea

Zadokites, 89, 93, 169. *See also* priests, in Judea
Zenon papyri, 26, 120

www.ingramcontent.com/pod-product-compliance
Lightning Source LLC
Chambersburg PA
CBHW030526230426
43665CB00010B/787